Contents

- **004** TOURIST MAP OF KOREA
- **006** KOREA IN BRIEF
- **015** UNFORGETTABLE MEMORIES
  - LIVING HISTORY
    - 016 National Museum of Korea
    - 022 Museums
    - 028 UNESCO World Cultural Heritages
    - 032 Korean War Battlefield—DMZ Tour
  - THE CHANGING FACE OF KOREA
    - 034 Cheonggyecheon Stream
    - 040 Geumgangsan Diamond Mountains
    - 042 Hallyu—The Korean Wave
  - UNIQUE FLAVORS OF KOREA
    - 047 Templestay
    - 050 Taekwondo
    - 052 Bird-watching
    - 054 Festivals
    - 060 Food
    - 064 Shopping
    - 070 Entertainment
    - 076 Sports / Health
- **083** TOURIST ATTRACTIONS BY REGION
  - 084 Seoul
  - 134 Seoul Vicinity (Incheon, Gyeonggi-do)
  - 139 Eastern Area (Gangwon-do, Ulleungdo, Dokdo)
  - 144 Central Area (Daejeon, Chungcheongnam-do, Chungcheongbuk-do)
  - 149 Southeastern Area (Daegu, Gyeongju, Busan, Ulsan, Gyeongsangbuk-do, Gyeongsangnam-do)
  - 163 Southwestern Area (Gwangju, Jeollabuk-do, Jeollanam-do)
  - 169 Jeju-do
- **175** GENERAL INFORMATION
  - 176 Entry & Departure Procedures
  - 178 Transportation
  - 188 Accommodations
  - 206 Business Travel Tips
  - 208 Handy Facts
  - 217 Holidays
  - 218 Useful Korean Phrases
  - 220 Index
  - 222 KTO Offices

Cover Image: Pillow end embroidered with flowers and butterflies
Photograph by Suh Jae-sik

Tourist Map of Korea

SEOUL VICINITY — p.134
Incheon, Gyeonggi-do

SEOUL — p.84
Gyeongbokgung Palace,
Deoksugung Palace,
Insa-dong, Myeong-dong,
Mt. Namsan, Namdaemun Market,
Dongdaemun Market,
Hongik University Vicinity,
Itaewon, Yeouido, Gangnam Area,
Jamsil, Olympic Park, etc.

CENTRAL AREA — p.144
Daejeon, Chungcheongnam-do,
Chungcheongbuk-do

SOUTHWESTERN AREA — p.163
Gwangju, Jeollabuk-do, Jeollanam-do

JEJU-DO — p.169

YELLOW SEA

GYEONGGI-DO (경기도)
Yeoncheon (연천)
Dongducheon (동두천)
Yangju (양주)
Pocheon
Ganghwa (강화)
Goyang (고양)
Uijeongbu (의정부)
Gimpo (김포)
Bukhansan (북한산)
SEOUL (서울)
Guri (구리)
INCHEON (인천)
Bucheon (부천)
Anyang (안양)
Seongnam
Ansan (안산)
Gwangju
Hwaseong (화성)
Suwon (수원)
Yongin
Osan (오산)
Anseong (안성)
Pyeongtaek (평택)
Dangjin (당진)
Seosan (서산)
Asan (아산)
Cheonan
Taean (태안)
Yesan (예산)
Hongseong (홍성)
Gongju (공주)
CHUNGCHEONGNAM-DO (충청남도)
Boryeong (보령)
Gyeryongsan (계룡산)
Buyeo (부여)
Nonsan (논산)
Seocheon (서천)
Gunsan (군산)
Iksan (익산)
Gimje (김제)
JEOLLABUK
Jeonju (전주)
Buan (부안)
Jeongeup (정읍)
88 OLYMPIC
Gochang (고창)
Sunchang (순창)
Yeonggwang (영광)
GWANGJU (광주)
Naju (나주)
Muan (무안)
JEOLLANAM-DO (전라남도)
Mokpo (목포)
Wolchulsan (월출산)
Boseong (보성)
Yeongam (영암)
Suncheon
Jangheung (장흥)
Haenam (해남)
Gangjin (강진)
Jindo (진도)
Wando (완도)

Jeju (제주)
Hallasan (한라산)
JEJU-DO (제주도)
Seogwipo (서귀포)

07 Land
07 National Flag and Flower
08 Climate
08 Religion
08 Language
09 History
10 Arts
12 Customs

Korea in Brief

Land
KOREA IN BRIEF

The Korean Peninsula extends southward from the eastern end of the Asian continent. It is roughly 1,020 km (612 miles) long and 216km (105 miles) wide at its narrowest point. Mountains cover 70% of the land mass, making it one of the most mountainous regions in the world.

The lifting and folding of Korea's granite and limestone base has created breathtaking landscapes of scenic hills and valleys. The mountain range that traverses the length of the east coast plunges steeply into the East Sea, while along the southern and western coasts, the mountains descend gradually to the coastal plains that produce the bulk of Korea's agricultural crops, especially rice.

The peninsula is divided just slightly north of the 38th parallel. The democratic Republic of Korea in the south and communist North Korea are separated by the Demilitarized Zone. South Korea has a population of 48.2 million (2005). Administratively, the Republic of Korea consists of nine provinces (*do*); the capital Seoul; and the six metropolitan cities of Busan, Daegu, Incheon, Gwangju, Daejeon and Ulsan. In total, there are 77 cities (*si*) and 88 counties (*gun*).

National Flag
KOREA IN BRIEF

The Korean flag is called *taegeukgi*. The design symbolizes the principles of the yin and yang in Oriental philosophy. The circle in the center of the flag is divided into two equal parts. The red half represents the proactive cosmic forces of the yang. Conversely, the blue half represents the responsive cosmic forces of the yin. The two forces together embody the concepts of continual movement, balance and harmony that characterize the sphere of infinity. The circle is surrounded by a trigram in each corner. Each trigram symbolizes one of the four universal elements:
heaven (☰), earth (☷), fire (☲) and water (☵).

National Flower
KOREA IN BRIEF

The national flower of Korea is the *mugunghwa* (Rose of Sharon). Every year from July to October, a profusion of *mugunghwa* blossoms graces the entire country. Unlike most flowers, the *mugunghwa* is remarkably tenacious and able to withstand both blight and insects. The flower's symbolic significance stems from the Korean word *mugung* (immortality). This word accurately reflects the enduring nature of Korean culture and the determination and perseverance of the Korean people.

GEOGRAPHIC POSITION Between 33° and 43° north latitude and 124° and 131° east longitude (including North Korea)
HIGH MOUNTAINS IN S. KOREA Hallasan on Jejudo Island, 1,950 m (6,400 ft); Jirisan, 1,915 m (6,283 ft); and Seoraksan, 1,708 m (5,604 ft)
LONG RIVERS IN S. KOREA Nakdonggang, 522 km (313 miles); Hangang, 482 km (289 miles); Geumgang, 396 km (238 miles)
ECONOMIC STATUS (2004) GNI US$681 billion; GNI per capita US$14,162

KOREA IN BRIEF

Climate

Korea lies in the temperate zone and has four distinct seasons.
In late March or early April, the trees burst into leafy splendor to mark the beginning of spring. Mostly sunny days can be expected from March to May.
During the relatively hot and rainy summer season, the vegetation is lush. By June, the average temperature is over 20°C (68°F). Monsoon rains usually begin around the end of June and last until mid- to late-July. August is hot and humid.
The coming of autumn in late September brings continental winds and clear, dry weather, making the fall months perhaps the most pleasant time of year. October's vivid golds and vibrant reds create a colorful panorama.
December to February is cold and dry with occasional snow. During the winter months, three or four days of cold weather are often followed by a few warmer days.

Consonants					
ㄱ	g, k	ㅂ	b, p	ㅋ	k
ㄴ	n	ㅅ	s	ㅌ	t
ㄷ	d, t	ㅇ	silent, ng	ㅍ	p
ㄹ	r, l	ㅈ	j	ㅎ	h
ㅁ	m	ㅊ	ch		
Vowels					
ㅏ	a	ㅗ	o	ㅠ	yu
ㅑ	ya	ㅛ	yo	ㅡ	eu
ㅓ	eo	ㅜ	u	ㅣ	i
ㅕ	yeo				

KOREA IN BRIEF

Religion

Freedom of religion is fully guaranteed in the Republic of Korea. Korea's traditional religions—Shamanism, Buddhism and Confucianism—have all played an integral role in the country's sociocultural development. There are also minor religions based on various combinations of elements from these traditional religions. Christianity has developed a large following since its introduction to the peninsula in the late 18th century.

KOREA IN BRIEF

Language

The Korean language, like Hungarian, Turkish, Mongolian and Finnish, is classified into the Ural-Altaic language group. *Hangeul* (the Korean alphabet) is composed of 10 simple vowels and 14 consonants. A group of scholars under the patronage of King Sejong the Great developed this systematic rendition of spoken sound in 1443. It is widely acclaimed by linguists as an ingenious invention.
The chart on the above right presents the romanization of the 24 *hangeul* letters based on the new romanization system proclaimed by the

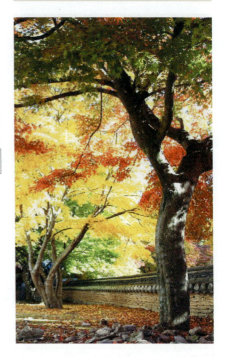

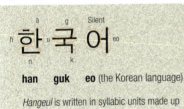

han guk eo (the Korean language)

Hangeul is written in syllabic units made up of two, three or four letters.

태평로, 포항 and 청주 become Taepyeongno, Pohang and Cheongju instead of T'aep'yŏngno, P'ohang and Ch'ŏngju.
4) 시 is written si instead of shi. Thus 신라 and 임실 become Silla and Imsil.

KOREA IN BRIEF

History

The habitation of early man in Korea appears to have started about half a million years ago. The first kingdom, named Gojoseon (Ancient Joseon), was formed in 2333 BC. By the 1st century BC, Korea's three ancient kingdoms of Goguryeo, Baekje and Silla ruled the entire Korean Peninsula and much of Manchuria; they were by far the most powerful and eminent kingdoms in the area. The period of their rule, 57 BC – 668 AD, is known as the Three Kingdoms period. Goguryeo and Baekje were ultimately vanquished by Silla in 668 and 660, respectively. In 676, Silla unified the peninsula for the first time. The Unified Silla period, 676 – 935, was a golden age for Korean culture and advancements in Buddhist art are especially noteworthy.
In the succeeding Goryeo Dynasty, 918 – 1392, an aristocratic government was instituted. Buddhism was established as the state religion

Korean government in 2000. For your understanding, major changes of the new system are listed below.
1) The previously used diacritical mark breve (˘) and apostrophe (') have disappeared in the new system. For example, the vowels 어, 으, 여, and 의 are romanized as eo, eu, yeo and ui instead of the erstwhile ŏ, ŭ, yŏ and ŭi. 인천, 영등포 and 여의도 become Incheon, Yeongdeungpo and Yeouido instead of Inch'ŏn, Yŏngdŭngp'o and Yŏŭido as written in the past.
2) When the sounds ㄱ, ㄷ, ㅂ, and ㅈ appear before a vowel, they are transcribed by g, d, b and j, but for the sake of phonetic consistency they are transcribed by k, t, p and t when followed by another consonant or forming the final sound of a word.
This means that 부산, 합덕 and 제주 have changed from Pusan, Haptŏk and Cheju to Busan, Hapdeok and Jeju.
Don't worry—when Koreans hear foreigners pronounce Pusan or Busan, both sound similar and there shouldn't be any confusion.
3) ㅋ, ㅌ, ㅍ, and ㅊ are romanized as k, t, p and ch instead of the old k', t', p' and ch'.

DANGUN AND THE FOUNDING MYTH OF KOREA
A long time ago, when Hwanung, a son of heaven, ruled the people, there lived a tiger and a bear. They wished wholeheartedly to become human and prayed every day to Hwanung to grant their wish. Upon hearing their fervent prayers, Hwanung called them to him and gave them 20 cloves of garlic and a bunch of mugwort and told them that if they could remain out of the sun for 100 days living on that food, he would grant them their wish.
The tiger gave up after a little while and left the cave, but the bear remained true and after 21 days, Hwanung transformed the bear into a beautiful woman. The bear-woman, Ungnyeo, was very grateful and made offerings to Hwanung, but she became lonely. Once again, she prayed to Hwanung beneath a sandalwood tree to be blessed with a child.
Hwanung, moved by her prayers, took her as his wife and soon she gave birth to a son. They named him Dangun Wanggeom, who later established Gojoseon (Ancient Joseon) in 2333 BC, which was the first kingdom on the Korean Peninsula.

and came to have great influence in the political and administrative spheres. The name "Korea" is a derivative of "Goryeo."

The Joseon Dynasty (1392 – 1910) was the peninsula's final dynasty. During this period, various political and economic reforms were enacted. The most prominent of these was the adoption of Confucianism as the state ideology. The surge of creative literary endeavors and the invention of *hangeul* (the Korean alphabet) in 1443 invest this period with special cultural significance. Hanyang, now known as Seoul, was established as the dynasty's capital city in 1394. Palaces and gates constructed during this period can still be seen in the city today.

The Japanese invasion of the peninsula in 1910 ended the Joseon Dynasty. Korea remained under Japanese colonial rule for 35 years until the end of World War II. On August 15, 1945, Japan surrendered to the Allies and withdrew from the Korean Peninsula, which was then divided into two: South Korea in the free world and North Korea in the communist bloc. The Republic of Korea in the south established an independent government three years later.

The Korean War began on June 25, 1950, when North Korea invaded the South. An armistice agreement was signed three years later in 1953. South Korea's tireless post-war reconstruction efforts were highly successful in the promotion of national prosperity and stability.

In 1988, Seoul, the capital of the South, hosted the Olympics. In September 1991, South and North Korea were simultaneously admitted to the United Nations, then in June 2000, historic summit talks between South and North Korea were held in Pyeongyang, the capital of the North. The 17th FIFA World Cup was held jointly in 2002 by Korea and Japan, during which the Korean national team achieved the legendary feat of being the first Asian national team to proceed to the semifinals in the history of the World Cup competition.

Arts

KOREA IN BRIEF

The artistic talents of the Korean people are expressed through music, dance and painting, which have evolved over Korea's 5,000-year history.

While in modern times many Western art forms have been introduced and embraced by Korea, her unique arts still flourish, both in their pure forms and in various harmonious combinations with modern genres.

TRADITIONAL KOREAN MUSIC

Gugak (traditional Korean music) shared a cultural background with China and Japan. But despite some superficial similarities, anyone who has heard *gugak* can tell that it is clearly different from other East Asian music.

Korean music has a triple rhythm (three beats per measure), while Chinese and Japanese music have

Gilt bronze contemplative bodhisattva, 7th century

two beats per measure.
Gugak can be divided into two types: *jeong-ak* (music of the upper classes) and *minsogak* (folk music). *Jeong-ak* has a slow, solemn, and complicated melody, while *minsogak*, such as *nong-ak* (farmers' music), *pansori* (epic solo song) and shamanistic music, is fast and vigorous.

TRADITIONAL DANCE
Korea's traditional dance, like its music, can also be classified into either court dances or folk dances. The slow, gracious movements of the court dances reflect the beauty of moderation and the subdued emotions formed as a result of the strong influence of Confucian philosophy. In contrast, the folk dances, mirroring the life, work and religion of the common people, are exciting and romantic, aptly portraying the free and spontaneous emotions of the Korean people. Some typical folk dances are farmers' dances, mask dances and shamanistic dances.

TRADITIONAL PAINTING
Traditional Korean painting is very different from Western painting. Its roots lie in the unique lines and colors of the Orient.
Evidence of early Korean paintings can be found in the royal tombs of the Three Kingdoms period (57 BC – 668 AD), which have helped us piece together details about the lifestyles of the time. During the later Goryeo Dynasty, Buddhism reached its peak, leaving many precious Buddhist paintings and images in temples around the country. Confucianism became the political ideology of the Joseon Dynasty (1392 – 1910) and the upper-class intellectuals who produced much of the art were profoundly influenced by Chinese works. Folk painting, which became popular among the lower classes, was not influenced by any particular school but used free, expressive techniques and bright colors to depict strength, humor and leisure.

POTTERY
Pottery-making techniques were transmitted from China to Korea over 1,000 years ago, when they flourished and produced an artistic tradition of which Koreans are justifiably proud.
The subtle beauty and unique bluish-green color of the celadon pottery of the Goryeo Dynasty (918 – 1392) have made it world famous and much sought after by antique dealers. The white porcelain of the Joseon Dynasty (1392 – 1910) is also renowned.
This pottery-making skill was transmitted to Japan at different periods in history, particularly during the Japanese invasions of the 1590s, greatly contributing to the development of the art form in Japan.

KOREA IN BRIEF

Customs

SENSE OF SENIORITY
Although the traditional Confucian social structure is changing, it is still prevalent in Korea. Age and seniority are all-important and juniors are expected to follow the wishes of their elders without question. Therefore, people often ask you your age and sometimes your marital status (interestingly, no matter how old you are, at least among family members, you cannot be regarded as an adult if you are not married) to find out their position relative to you. These questions are not meant to intrude on your privacy and Koreans will not be offended if you do not answer.

MARRIAGE
Today's typical wedding ceremony is somewhat different from what it was in old times: first a Western-style ceremony is usually held at a wedding hall or a church with the bride wearing a white dress and the groom wearing a tuxedo, and later in the day the bride and groom have a traditional ceremony in a different room of the venue in colorful traditional costumes.

JERYE (ANCESTRAL MEMORIAL RITE)
According to a traditional Korean belief, when people die, their spirits do not immediately depart; they stay with descendants for four generations. During this period, the deceased are still regarded as family members and Koreans reaffirm the relationship between ancestors and descendants through *jerye* on special days like *Seollal* (Lunar New Year's Day) and *Chuseok* (Korean Thanksgiving Day), as well as on the anniversary

Jongmyojerye (royal ancestral rite)

the ancestors passed away. Koreans also believe that people can live well and happily thanks to benefits their ancestors bestow upon them.

NAMES
The majority of Koreans have family names within one of a small set: Kim (about 21% of the population), Yi (or Lee or Rhee, 14%), Park (or Pak, 8%), Choi (or Choe), Jeong (or Chung or Jung), Jang (or Chang), Han, Lim, etc. A Korean name consists of a family name, in almost every case one syllable, plus a given name usually of two syllables. The family name comes first. A Korean woman does not take her husband's family name, but their children take their father's family name.

BODY LANGUAGE
When you beckon a person, do so with your palm down, then flutter your hand up and down with your fingers touching. It is not polite to beckon with your palm up, especially using only one finger, because that is how Koreans call dogs.

HANBOK
The *hanbok* has been the Korean people's unique traditional costume for thousands of years. The beauty and grace of Korean culture can be seen in photographs of women dressed in the *hanbok*. Before the arrival of Western-style

clothing 100 years ago, the *hanbok* was everyday attire. Men wore *jeogori* (Korean jackets) with *baji* (trousers) while women wore *jeogori* with *chima* (skirts).

Today, the *hanbok* is worn on special occasions such as weddings, *Seollal* (Lunar New Year's Day) and *Chuseok* (Korean Thanksgiving Day).

ONDOL

Traditional Korean rooms have multiple functions. Rooms are not labeled or reserved for a specific purpose; there is no definite bedroom or dining room for example. Rather, tables and mats are brought in as needed. Most people sit and sleep on the floor on thick mats.

Underneath the floors are stone or concrete flues.

For Koreans, a dinner table without kimchi is unthinkable.

ORIENTAL MEDICINE

Oriental medicine considers decreased vital energy and a weakened immune system to be the cause of disease — not a problem with a particular body part but rather an imbalance of the life forces in the whole body.

Therefore, Oriental medicine seeks to treat disease by strengthening the immune system and restoring harmony within the body, not by removing pathogenic factors.

Major fields of Oriental medicine include herbal medicine, acupuncture, moxa treatment and suction-cup therapy.

Traditionally, hot air was vented through the flues to provide heat. Clay or cement would be placed over the stones to protect the residents from noxious gasses.

This type of underfloor heating is called *ondol*. Nowadays, hot water is piped through cement floors covered with linoleum.

GIMJANG

Gimjang is the age-old Korean practice of preparing winter kimchi, which has been passed down from generation to generation.

Since very few vegetables are grown in the winter months, *gimjang* takes place in early winter and provides what has become a staple food for Koreans.

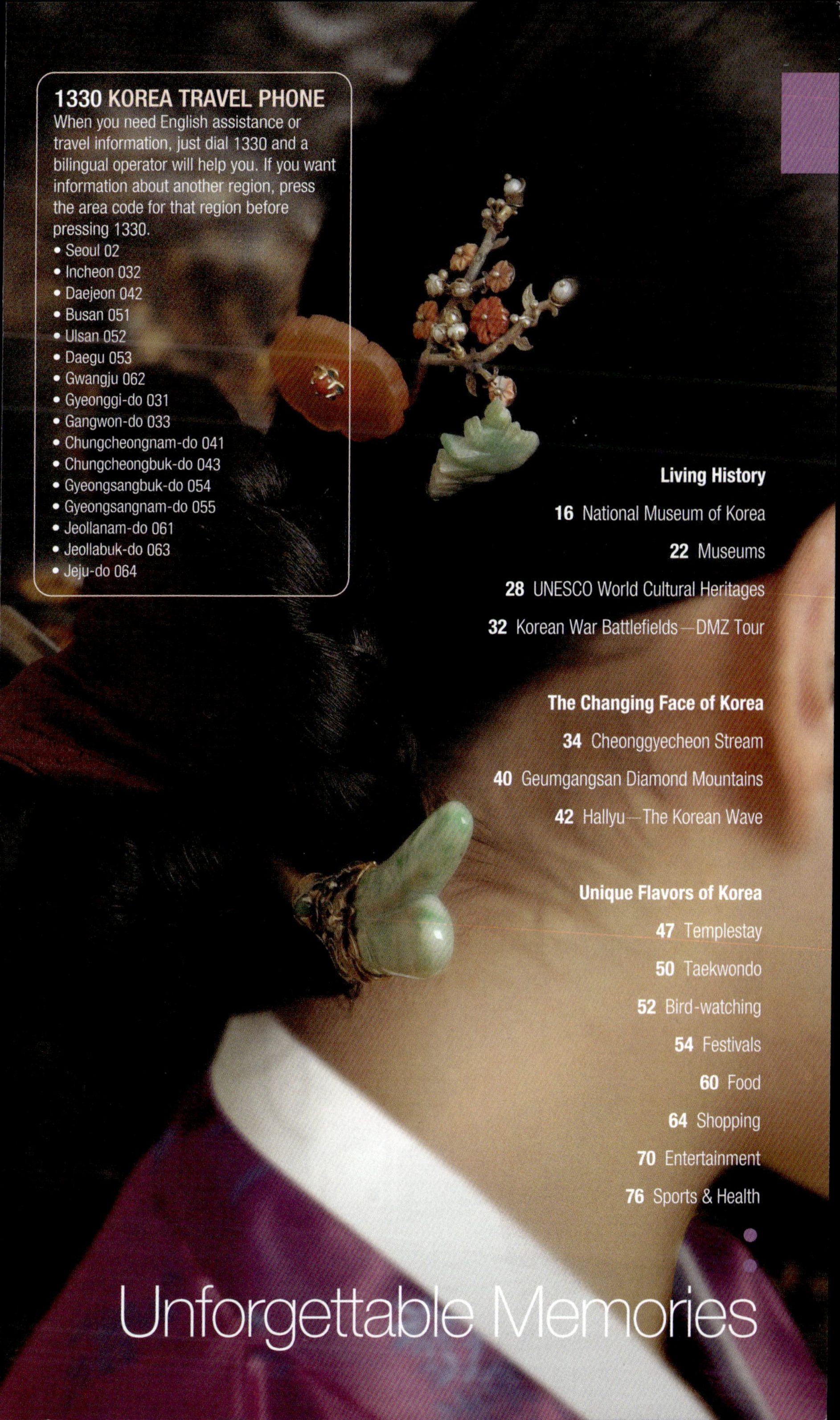

1330 KOREA TRAVEL PHONE

When you need English assistance or travel information, just dial 1330 and a bilingual operator will help you. If you want information about another region, press the area code for that region before pressing 1330.

- Seoul 02
- Incheon 032
- Daejeon 042
- Busan 051
- Ulsan 052
- Daegu 053
- Gwangju 062
- Gyeonggi-do 031
- Gangwon-do 033
- Chungcheongnam-do 041
- Chungcheongbuk-do 043
- Gyeongsangbuk-do 054
- Gyeongsangnam-do 055
- Jeollanam-do 061
- Jeollabuk-do 063
- Jeju-do 064

Living History
16 National Museum of Korea
22 Museums
28 UNESCO World Cultural Heritages
32 Korean War Battlefields—DMZ Tour

The Changing Face of Korea
34 Cheonggyecheon Stream
40 Geumgangsan Diamond Mountains
42 Hallyu—The Korean Wave

Unique Flavors of Korea
47 Templestay
50 Taekwondo
52 Bird-watching
54 Festivals
60 Food
64 Shopping
70 Entertainment
76 Sports & Health

Unforgettable Memories

National Museum of Korea

A window to the history of Korea and a treasure of cultural properties, the National Museum of Korea reopened at its new location in Yongsan-dong, Seoul, on October 28, 2005.
Spanning an area of approximately 76 acres, the new museum is roughly 400 m wide with exhibit spaces totaling about 6.6 acres. With a collection of about 11,000 works of art, the National Museum of Korea is the 6th largest museum in the world.

NATIONAL MUSEUM OF KOREA
A Look Around the Museum

OPEN PLAZA
The Open Plaza is the first place to stop as the ticket booth is located here. The plaza divides the museum into the East Wing, the West Wing and gift shops.
The plaza has a granite floor and open spaces at the front and back. The roof connecting the pavilions on each side provides shelter from the rain or sunlight, an idea modeled after the *daecheongmaru*, a typical architectural element of traditional Korean houses. The *daecheongmaru* is usually an elevated floor located at the center of a house, which serves as the main entry into the house and from one room to another. The Open Plaza has a view of the expansive front and back of the building as well as N Seoul Tower, the symbol of Seoul.

OUTDOOR EXHIBITION
The front of the museum is both a garden and an outdoor exhibition space. At the center is the Reflecting Pond with stone pagodas and sculptures. Some notable relics highlight the beautiful landscape. The curves of the oval pond balance the rigid geometrical feeling of the appearance of the main building, which was built in the shape of a traditional Korean fortress city.

EAST WING — EXHIBITION FLOORS
The East Wing is a three-story building housing six galleries (Archaeological, Historical, Fine Arts I, Fine Arts II, Asian Art and Donated) and 46 showrooms. On exhibit are major cultural properties from every part of the Korean Peninsula that span every age. The relics are exhibited so that they can be viewed from different angles. The colors and lines unique to Korean art are brought to life using special lighting. Here, visitors can

UNFORGETTABLE MEMORIES

experience the essence of Korean art from the finest handicrafts and ceramics known for their profound glazes and curves to statues of Buddha characterized by his mystical smile.

1st FLOOR
ARCHAEOLOGICAL GALLERY

This gallery displays various artifacts from ancient times. About 4,500 pieces are on display throughout the 10 exhibition rooms. Some date back to the Paleolithic era and others represent the Three Kingdoms and the Unified Silla periods. The gallery features ornamental art and everyday tools from ancient times. These include the Old Stone Age fist axe used for hunting large animals, Neolithic comb-pattern vessels with striking diagonal line patterns, and relics found in the tomb of King Muryeong of Baekje, who actively introduced Chinese culture to the peninsula. Representative pieces that shouldn't be missed are the Duck-shaped Vessel located in the Three Kingdoms showroom (ducks were believed to guide the dead to the afterlife); the gilt incense burner of the Baekje period in the Baekje room, whose design expresses the Taoist utopia, and the splendid Golden Crown exemplifying the advanced workmanship of the Silla period.

HISTORICAL GALLERY

In the Historical Gallery, visitors can see Korea's major cultural heritage *hangeul* (the Korean alphabet) and metal printing type as well as valuable epigraphs, documents and maps. Representative cultural properties of Korea depict the process through which *hangeul* was created, old documents written in *hangeul*, and the *Mugujeonggwangdae-daranigyeong*, which illustrates the woodblock printing technique of Korea. The *Mugujeonggwangdae-daranigyeong* was discovered in the Seokgatap Pagoda at

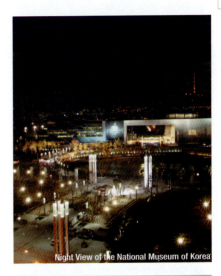
Night View of the National Museum of Korea

Reflecting Pond

Historical Gallery

Bulguksa Temple and is believed to have been produced in the mid-8th century, making it the oldest existing woodblock printed scripture in the world. Goryeo-period metal printing type and the production of metal printing type on about 30 different occasions during the Joseon Dynasty are also the proud cultural properties of Korea.

PATH OF HISTORY
The Path of History is the main hall that connects the galleries. At 155 m long and 25 m wide, it is like walking on a well-maintained avenue with the Archaeological and Historical Galleries on both sides. The Path of History is both a hall and an exhibit space. At the center stand stone works, including the Bukgwandaecheopbi Stone Monument, Godalsa Temple Lantern with Two Lions, and Gyeongcheonsa Temple Ten-story Stone Pagoda. These stone structures, which would normally be exhibited outside, create a feeling of grandeur inside the building.

2nd FLOOR
FINE ARTS GALLERY I
This gallery highlights the beauty of traditional Korean art, its unique sense of line and color and its religion. About 890 pieces are exhibited in four rooms. Representative works are categorized and displayed according to such themes as calligraphy, painting, Buddhist painting/art and woodworking.
The focal point of this gallery is the room of paintings from the Joseon Dynasty. One space is devoted to documents showing the types of materials used in old paintings and how pictures were drawn. There are also separate sections for landscape paintings, portraits, genre paintings, animal paintings, royal court documentary paintings and folk paintings.

DONATION GALLERY
This gallery exhibits about 1,000 pieces donated by Korean and Japanese art collectors and includes Korean art as well as numerous Chinese and Japanese cultural assets such as bronzeware, earthenware, ceramics, paintings, calligraphy and historic documents. Each exhibit room is named after its patron.

3rd FLOOR
FINE ARTS GALLERY II
On display here is the museum's collection of Korean arts and crafts such as Buddhist sculptures, metal crafts and ceramics.
A total of 630 pieces are exhibited in five rooms. Large Buddhist statues from the Unified Silla and Goryeo periods guard the Buddhist sculpture room, creating a majestic ambience.
Korean Buddhist statues are characterized by a life-like benevolent smile and a realistic sense of movement in the hands and feet. In the metal crafts room, visitors will find relics of the earliest metalwork, Buddhist sarira reliquaries and memorial caskets, and metal household tools. The last exhibit room is dedicated to ceramics. By viewing the celadon of Goryeo and the *buncheong* porcelain and *baekja* (white) porcelain of Joseon, visitors can see how Korean ceramics evolved over time.

ASIAN ART GALLERY
The gallery contains a wide collection of relics from China, Japan, and Central Asia featuring about 970 pieces in six exhibit rooms. In the Central Asia room, Buddhist statues,

Gyeongcheonsa Temple Ten-story Stone Pagoda

Children's Museum

earthenware, and clay dolls excavated in China offer insight into the cross-cultural and international characteristics of Central Asian art. The China room displays elegant ceramics and ornaments of that country, which occupied a major place in Asian art. The Japan room features 98 archaeological pieces on loan from the Tokyo National Museum as part of a two-year exchange exhibition.

WEST WING — COMPREHENSIVE CULTURAL SPACE
The National Museum of Korea is not just about arts and crafts. It is a comprehensive cultural space offering a wide range of facilities such as a theater, gift shops, restaurants and cafes.

THEATRE YONG
Theatre Yong is the first theater to be built inside a museum in Korea. The 805-seat multipurpose performing arts center will stage various performances such as classical music, dance and drama. For more information and reservations, visit the Web site of the Cultural Foundation of National Museum of Korea (www.cfnmk.or.kr). The theater is in the West Wing and can be reached via stairway from the Open Plaza.

CHILDREN'S MUSEUM
Another special feature of the National Museum of Korea is the Children's Museum. Here, children can touch models of the real works of art.

GIFT SHOPS
The gift shops sell 60 types of household goods and ornaments based on traditional Korean art and 300 additional gift items. The famous folk painting of Joseon artist Kim Hong-do is featured on umbrellas and the beloved *Chochungdo* (Grass and Insects) painting by Sinsaimdang beautifies handbags. Some items are adaptations of cultural properties such as the Silla-period gold earring patterns inscribed on rice cake knives. The shops are located on the 1st floor of the West Wing and the 1st and 3rd floors of the East Wing.

RESTAURANTS & CAFES
The museum offers a wide variety of dining options. The Korean restaurant Hancharim on the 1st floor of the West Wing serves home-style meals and the traditional teahouse Sayu specializes in tasty ginseng shakes and *omija* (schisandra berries) sorbet. On both sides of the East Wing, the cafeteria Mireumwe serves simple snacks such as *gimbap*, *udong*, and spaghetti, and the Arisu coffee shop is a great place to relax in a beautiful setting.

NATIONAL MUSEUM OF KOREA
Enjoying the National Museum of Korea

MOBILE AUDIO GUIDE SYSTEM
Digital guides (PDA) and audio guides (MP3) allow you to make the most of your museum visit

in a limited amount of time. Available in Korean, English, Chinese and Japanese, both systems are as good as a guided tour. There are 12 customized programs appropriate for children, students, adults, and experts. The following tours are highly recommended: 100 Must-see Masterpieces (2 hours, 20 minutes); Top 100 for Students (2 hours, 20 minutes), which covers relics found in history textbooks; the easy and fun Style of Joseon, Spirit of Joseon, which is designed for children; and Buddhist Art (40 minutes). Since PDA and MP3 sets are limited (300 and 400 sets, respectively), reservations must be made on the museum's Web site (www.museum.go.kr) at least one day prior to your visit. A picture ID is required for rental, and one person can rent up to five sets.
The rental fee is ₩3,000 for a PDA and ₩1,000 for an MP3 guide.

NATIONAL MUSEUM OF KOREA
Recommended Museum Tours

For visitors unfamiliar with Korean history and culture, it may be difficult to make the most out of their time. The following are recommendations for short and interesting museum tours.

Exploring 5,000 Years of Korean History (takes 2 hours)
This tour explores the Archaeological Gallery and Historical Gallery, where relics show how the history of Korea has evolved from the Old Stone Age to modern times.
Archaeological Gallery: Prehistory (Paleolithic Age, Neolithic Age, Bronze Age, early Iron Age) → The Three Kingdoms (Wonsamguk, Goguryeo, Baekje, Gaya, Silla) → Unified Silla → Balhae Historical Gallery: Hangeul → Historical Documents (printing, epigraphs, maps) → Society & Economy (kings, nation, traditional schools of thought)

Appreciating Korean Fine Arts (takes 2 hours)
This tour takes visitors to the Fine Arts Gallery I on the 2nd floor and the Fine Arts Gallery II on the 3rd floor, where calligraphy, paintings, Buddhist statues, and ceramics express the remarkable talent and artistic sensibility of the Korean people.
Fine Arts Gallery I: Calligraphy → Painting → Buddhist painting → Woodenlacquer ware
Fine Arts Gallery II: Buddhist statues → Metal crafts → Celadon porcelain → *Buncheong* porcelain → White porcelain

A Look at Asian Culture (takes 70 min.)
The China, Japan, Indonesia, and Central Asia rooms of the Asian Arts Gallery on the 3rd floor are the subjects of this tour.
By viewing these nations' unique works, visitors will gain insight into the similarities and differences of Asian cultures.
Indonesia → Central Asia → China → Nangnang-related relics → Underwater relics of Sinan → Japan

VISITOR INFORMATION
Transportation: Take Seoul Subway Line 1 or 4 to Ichon Station, Exit 2. It takes about 5 minutes on foot.
Open: 9:00 – 18:00 (on weekdays); 9:00 – 19:00 (on weekends and holidays); closed on New Year's Day and Mondays (the museum is closed on Tuesday if the holiday falls on Monday).
Admission: ₩2,000 for adults (19 – 64), ₩1,000 for students (7 – 18), free for senior citizens. Last admission is at 5 pm.
ⓘ: 📞 02-2077-9000 or www.museum.go.kr (English, Japanese, Chinese)

Gilt-bronze seated Buddha

Divine bell of King Seongdeok

TOP 10 WORKS AT THE NATIONAL MUSEUM OF KOREA

Gilt-bronze maitreya in meditation (National Treasure No. 83) | 금동미륵보살 반가 사유상
F3, Fine Arts Gallery II, Buddhist Sculpture Room, No. 13
This is the tallest gilt bronze contemplative bodhisattva statue in Korea. Measuring 93.5 cm, it is considered the masterpiece of Korean Buddhist statue art.

Mugujeonggwangdaedaranigyeong (National Treasure No. 126) | 무구정광대다라니경
F1, Historical Gallery, Old Documents Room, No. 16
The world's oldest scripture printed with wood type, it measures 650 cm in length and 6.5–6.7 cm in width. It is estimated to date back to 751, the 10th year of King Gyeongdeok's reign in the Silla Kingdom.

Gilt incense burner of the Baekje period (National Treasure No. 287) | 백제금동 대향로
F1, Archaeological Gallery, Baekje Room, No. 16
The essence of Baekje craftsmanship, this piece best represents the artistic talent and spiritual world of the period.

Silla Golden Crown (National Treasure No. 191) | 신라금관
F1, Archaeological Gallery, Silla Room, No. 1
While this crown is typical of gold crowns from the Silla period, it features more jade than the others and is more elegant.

Vessels in the shape of a warrior on horseback (National Treasure No. 91) | 도제기마 인물상
F1, Archaeological Gallery, Silla Room, No. 19
Both excavated in Gyeongju, the pieces are of warriors on horseback created in very similar styles. Realistic albeit unrefined, the vessels are thought to have been made specifically as burial items.

White porcelain jar with plum and bamboo designs in underglaze iron
(National Treasure No. 166) | 백자철화 매죽문대호
F3, Fine Arts Gallery II, Celadon Room, No. 39
Typical of early Joseon period white porcelain jars, the front and back of the jar are covered with decorations of bamboo and plum trees in iron brown. The brushwork is so outstanding that it seems more like a painting than ceramic surface design.

Celadon incense burner (National Treasure No. 95) | 청자 칠보 투각 향로
F3, Fine Arts Gallery II, Celadon Room, No. 5
This celadon porcelain incense burner from the Goryeo period includes many decorative details and demonstrates outstanding overall harmony and balance.

Sehando by Kim Jeonghui (National Treasure No. 180) | 김정희의 세한도
F2, Fine Arts Gallery I, Painting Room, No. 14
The painting is by Kim Jeonghui (pen name Wandang), a noble scholar-artist of the late Joseon Dynasty. The artist completed this painting in 1844 while living in exile on Jejudo Island. It was painted as a gift for one of his pupils who sent him rare books from Beijing on two different occasions.

Genre Painting Album by Kim Hong-do (Treasure No. 527) | 김홍도 풍속화, 단원 풍속 화첩
F2, Fine Arts Gallery I, Painting Room, No. 8
In his genre-painting album, Joseon artist Kim Hong-do (pen name Danwon) humorously depicts the lives of the common people. The album features a village school, boy dancers, a wrestling match, threshing field, and a blacksmith's workshop.

Gyeongcheonsa Temple Ten-story Stone Pagoda
(National Treasure No. 86) | 경천사지 10층 석탑
F1, At the end of the Path of History
This 13.5-m-high stone pagoda was built in the late Goryeo Dynasty for Gyeongcheonsa Temple in Gaepung-gun, Gyeonggi-do Province. The pagoda, which was smuggled out of Korea by a Japanese state minister, was returned in 1918.

UNFORGETTABLE MEMORIES

Museums

Korea boasts several national museums and numerous private museums dealing with specialized objects and themes. The national museums showcase a rich assortment of timeless properties that attest to 5,000 years of Korean history. An acquaintance with some of these museums will lead to a better understanding of Korean culture and history.

National Museums

NATIONAL FOLK MUSEUM OF KOREA
As the only national museum on folklore, it displays about 4,000 items on the traditional way of life.
There are three permanent exhibition halls, two special exhibition halls, a shop and a material room.
Ⓛ: Sejongno, Jongno-gu, Seoul (in Gyeongbokgung Palace) Ⓣ: 02-720-3137 02-3704-3114; www.nfm.go.kr
Ⓒ: Tuesdays, January 1

NATIONAL PALACE MUSEUM OF KOREA
Reopened in August 2005, the National Palace Museum has on exhibit 40,000 cultural properties that showcase the history and culture of the Joseon royalty.
Ⓛ: Sejongno, Jongno-gu, Seoul Ⓣ: a 5-min. walk from Exit 5 of Gyeongbokgung Station, Seoul Subway Line 3; or take any bus to Gwanghwamun, and it is a 5- to 10-min. walk from the bus stop. Ⓣ: 02-3701-7500 02-3701-7626; http://www.gogung.go.kr Ⓒ: Mondays

NATIONAL MUSEUM OF CONTEMPORARY ART, KOREA
Some 800 modern works by contemporary artists are on permanent display and special exhibits are presented throughout the year.
An outdoor sculpture park enhances its beauty.
Ⓛ: Makgye-dong, Gwacheon-si, Gyeonggi-do Ⓣ: A shuttle bus from Exit 4 of Seoul Grand Park Station, Line 4 Ⓣ: 02-2188-6000 02-2188-6123; www.moca.go.kr Ⓒ: Mondays, January 1

CHUNCHEON NATIONAL MUSEUM
It accommodates four permanent exhibition galleries, two special galleries, a 200-seat auditorium, an outdoor stage, an international seminar hall with simultaneous interpretation facilities, lecture rooms and a library.
The permanent exhibition galleries provide an overview of the ongoing search for relics in Gangwon-do Province and display newly discovered relics.
Ⓛ: San 27-1, Seoksa-dong, Chuncheon-si, Gangwon-do Ⓣ: From Chuncheon Intercity Bus Terminal, take a taxi to Aemakgol (20 min.).
Ⓣ: 033-260-1510/7 033-260-1519; http://chuncheon.museum.go.kr Ⓒ: Mondays, January 1

BUYEO NATIONAL MUSEUM
Around 7,000 articles from prehistoric times and Buddhist art, such as a gilt incense burner from the Baekje Kingdom, a very old-standing Buddha image, roof tiles and earthenware are on display.
Ⓛ: Dongnam-ri, Buyeo-eup, Buyeo-gun, Chungcheongnam-do Ⓣ: A 10-min. walk from Buyeo Bus Terminal Ⓣ: 041-833-8562/3 041-834-6321; www.buyeo.museum.go.kr
Ⓒ: Mondays, January 1

GONGJU NATIONAL MUSEUM
Displayed are 1,300 relics (from a total of 9,700) including those unearthed from the Tomb of King Muryeong of the Baekje Kingdom (stele, stone guardian animals, king and queen's crowns, earrings, necklaces), Buddhist statues, ancient roof tiles and pots.
Ⓛ: Ungjin-dong, Gongju-si, Chungcheongnam-do Ⓣ: No. 8 from Gongju Intercity Bus Terminal (Get off at the last stop) Ⓣ: 041-850-6360 041-856-8396; www.gongju.museum.go.kr
Ⓒ: Mondays, January 1

CHEONGJU NATIONAL MUSEUM
Houses 9,500 precious relics from prehistoric times, the Three Kingdoms period, and the Goryeo to Joseon Dynasties that were discovered in the central region.
Ⓛ: Myeongam-dong, Sangdang-gu, Cheongju-

National Museum of Contemporary Art

Gyeongju National Museum

Jinju National Museum

si, Chungcheongbuk-do ⓣ: 🚌 No. 230, 231, 232 or 233 from Bus Terminal ⓣ: ☎ 043-252-0710 📠 043-258-0711; www.cheongju.museum.go.kr ⓒ: Mondays, January 1

DAEGU NATIONAL MUSEUM

Full-sized and reduced models of buildings, including Byeongsanseowon Confucian School in Andong, genuine relics and and replicas of scholars' calligraphy are on display.

ⓛ: Hwanggeum-dong, Suseong-gu, Daegu ⓣ: 🚌 No. 242 or 514 from Dong Daegu Railroad Station ⓣ: ☎ 053-768-6051 📠 053-768-6053; http://daegu.museum.go.kr ⓒ: Mondays, January 1

GYEONGJU NATIONAL MUSEUM

One of finest museums in Korea, this institution houses over 200,000 items, including 17,000 artifacts from the Silla Kingdom.
On display are stone axes, statues of Buddha, a golden crown, the Bronze Bell of King Seongdeok the Great and pagodas.

ⓛ: Inwang-dong, Gyeongju-si, Gyeongsangbuk-do ⓣ: 🚌 No. 11, 600, 604 or 609 from Gyeongju Railroad Station ⓣ: ☎ 054-740-7518, 7538 📠 054-740-7522, 7545; http://gyeongju.museum.go.kr ⓒ: Mondays, January 1

GIMHAE NATIONAL MUSEUM

Contains 5,000 relics of the Gaya Kingdom (42 – 562) presenting the Neolithic and Bronze cultures of the southeastern region.

ⓛ: Gusan-dong, Gimhae-si, Gyeongsangnam-do ⓣ: 🚌 No. 1, 2, 4, 7, 9, 16 or 24 from Gimhae Bus Terminal ⓣ: ☎ 055-325-9332 📠 055-325-9334; www.gimhae.museum.go.kr ⓒ: Mondays, January 1

JINJU NATIONAL MUSEUM

The museum houses 6,000 items and features relics related to the Imjinwaeran (the Japanese invasion of Korea in 1592).

ⓛ: Namseong-dong, Jinju-si, Gyeongsangnam-do (in Jinjuseong Fortress) ⓣ: 🚌 No.15 or 25 from Express Bus Terminal ⓣ: ☎ 055-742-5951 📠 055-745-7020; www.jinju.museum.go.kr ⓒ: Mondays, January 1

JEONJU NATIONAL MUSEUM

Exhibits 2,000 items including old farming tools, food models, and replicas of the province's communal rites dedicated to tutelary gods and farmers' band performances. Korean mulberry paper and woodenware making are demonstrated.

ⓛ: Hyoja-dong 2 (i)-ga, Wansan-gu, Jeonju-si, Jeollabuk-do ⓣ: 🚌 No. 36, 51 or 118 from Jeonju

Railroad Station ①: ☎ 063-223-5651
🖷 063-223-5653; www.jeonju.museum.go.kr
ⓒ: Mondays, January 1

GWANGJU NATIONAL MUSEUM
Displayed relics are from the Paleolithic Age and Goryeo and Joseon periods, including Buddhist articles, paintings and handicrafts as well as relics of the Song and Yuan Dynasties of China that were recovered from offshore of Sinan.
ⓛ: Maegok-dong, Buk-gu, Gwangju
①: 🚌 No. 16, 19, 26, 35, 55 or 114 to the museum ①: ☎ 062-570-7000
🖷 062-570-7015 ⓒ: Mondays, January 1

JEJU NATIONAL MUSEUM
The museum preserves and displays historical and contemporary artifacts that document the culture and history of Jejudo Island.
ⓛ: Geonip-dong, Jeju-si, Jejudo
①: 🚌 A 20-min. taxi ride from Jeju Int'l Airport
①: ☎ 064-720-8000 🖷 064-720-8150;
www.jeju.museum.go.kr ⓒ: Mondays, January 1

MUSEUMS
Theme Museums in Seoul

KIMCHI FIELD MUSEUM
The Kimchi Field Museum is devoted to the world famous kimchi. A visit to the museum will teach you fascinating facts about kimchi that even many Koreans don't know about, its nutritional value, and the making and preservation of kimchi in a simple and easy-to-understand manner. The museum displays historic cooking utensils, various kinds of kimchi, kimchi storage jars and other kimchi-related items.
ⓛ: Samseong-dong, Gangnam-gu, Seoul

①: 🚇 Get off at Samseong Station, Line 2 (located in COEX Mall). COEX is connected through underground concourses from the station. ①: ☎ 02-6002-6456;
www.kimchimuseum.co.kr ⓒ: Mondays, January 1, Lunar New Year's Day, Chuseok and Christmas

MUSEUM OF KOREAN EMBROIDERY
The Museum of Korean Embroidery displays the painstaking, complex embroideries created by Korean women since 1976. The museum currently houses over 1,000 treasures of traditional embroidered works and costumes as well as embroidered folding screens, Buddhist paintings and decorative pieces collected by the museum's curator. Special exhibits as well as international exhibits are often presented.
ⓛ: Nonhyeon-dong, Gangnam-gu, Seoul
①: 🚇 A 2-min. walk from Exit 10 of Hakdong Station, Line 7
①: ☎ 02-515-5114/7
ⓒ: Saturdays and public holidays

MUSEUM OF KOREAN TRADITIONAL MUSIC
The Museum of Korean Traditional Music houses the traditional music history room (an area that explores Korean classical music from its roots), 53 traditional Korean instruments and 135 traditional instruments of other nations, a traditional music resource room (containing over 20,000 traditional music-related texts, sheet music, records, CDs and videotapes), audio visual room and lecture hall.

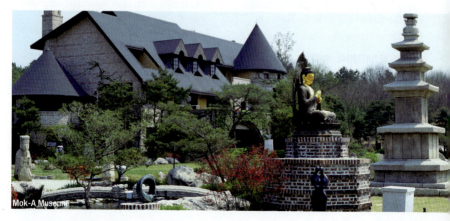

Mok-A Museum

Ⓛ: Seocho-dong, Seocho-gu, Seoul Ⓣ: 🚇 Exit 1 of Bangbae Station, Line 2 or Exit 5 of Nambu Terminal Station, Line 3 Ⓘ: ☎ 02-580-3130; www.ncktpa.go.kr
Ⓒ: Mondays, January 1

AGRICULTURAL MUSEUM
First opened in 1987, the Agricultural Museum reopened with a new look in June 2005. It is a place where visitors can learn the history and tradition of Korean agriculture with about 2,000 agricultural assets on display in three exhibition halls of Agricultural History, Agricultural Life and Nonghyup Promotion.
Ⓛ: Chungjeongno 1-ga, Jung-gu, Seoul
Ⓘ: ☎ 02-2080-5727/8; http://museum.nonghyup.com Ⓗ: 09:00 – 18:00 (closed on Sundays and holidays)
Ⓣ: 🚇 A 3-min. walk from Exit 5, Seodaemun Station, Seoul Subway Line 5

SEOUL MUSEUM OF HISTORY
On the grounds of Gyeonghuigung Palace, one of the five royal palaces in downtown Seoul, the museum features the history and culture of Seoul from the prehistoric era to modern times with an emphasis on the Joseon Dynasty (1392–1910).
Ⓛ: Sinmunno 2 (i)-ga, Jongno-gu, Seoul
Ⓣ: 🚇 Exit 4 of Seodaemun Station or Exit 7 of Gwanghwamun Station on Line 5 Ⓘ: ☎ 02-724-0114; www.museum.seoul.kr Ⓒ: Mondays, January 1

TTEOK • KITCHEN UTENSIL MUSEUMS
If you want to see a traditional Korean kitchen and cooking tools, visit the Tteok • Kitchen Utensil Museums. The Tteok Museum deals with traditional Korean rice cakes and the tools that were used to make them, introduces the varying tastes and colors of the textured morsels by era, and explains their close relationship to the lives of Koreans. The Kitchen Utensil Museum recreates kitchen life of the past with a traditional kitchen model fully equipped with all of the tools, tableware and containers such as the *jangdokdae* (large, covered earthenware pots used to store kimchi, red pepper paste, soy bean paste and other fermented foods).
Ⓛ: Waryong-dong, Jongno-gu, Seoul
Ⓣ: 🚇 From Exit 7 of Jongno 3 (sam)-ga Station, Lines 1, 3, or 5, walk 100 m in the direction of Changdeokgung Palace. Ⓘ: ☎ 02-741-5414; www.tkmuseum.or.kr Ⓒ: Chuseok and Seollal

MUSEUMS
Theme Museums in Other Areas

MOK-A MUSEUM
Inside are 6,000 Buddhist works including sutras, wooden, stone and bronze objects, paintings, and calligraphy works. In the open-air sculpture park are about 100 bronze and stone works including various Buddha images, a three-stone pagoda and a bell-shaped stupa.
Ⓛ: Iho-ri, Gangchon-myeon, Yeoju-si, Gyeonggi-do Ⓣ: 🚌 No. 10 or 10-1 at Yeoju Bus Terminal
Ⓘ: ☎ 031-885-9952 📠 031-885-9951; www.moka.or.kr

HO-AM ART MUSEUM
There are 15,000 precious items from prehistoric to modern times. The landscape around the museum including Heewon Garden (traditional Korean garden) and nearby Everland (a huge amusement park) make this museum all the

Museum of Korean Embroidery

Ho-Am Art Museum

O'sulloc Museum

more worth visiting.
ⓛ: 204 Yongin-si, Gyeonggi-do ⓣ: 🚌 No.1500 or 1500-1 from Yangjae Station, Line 3, and a shuttle bus from the main entrance of Everland ⓘ: 📞 031-320-1806 📠 031-320-1809; www.hoammuseum.org ⓒ: Mondays

CHAMSORI GRAMOPHONE & EDISON MUSEUM
A collection of 4,500 remarkable items, of which 1,500 are displayed at any time, documents the history of sound-producing machines.
ⓛ: Songjeong-dong, Gangneung-si, Gangwon-do ⓣ: 🚌 No. 19-1, 21 or 48 bound for Songjeong from Gangneung Bus Terminal to the museum (25 min.) ⓘ: 📞 033-652-2500 ⓒ: Open daily

CHEONGJU EARLY PRINTING MUSEUM
This museum opened in March 1992 in Cheongju, Chungcheongbuk-do Province, at the site of Heungdeoksa Temple. There are two exhibit halls, Printing Culture and Heungdeoksa Temple remains. In the former, visitors can take a look at the history of Korean printing using wooden printing blocks, moveable metal type, wooden Chinese character type and *hangeul* (the Korean alphabet) type.

ⓛ: Uncheon-dong, Heungdeok-gu, Cheongju-si, Chungcheongbuk-do ⓣ: 🚕 Take a taxi from Cheongju Railway Station (a 15-min. ride). ⓘ: 📞 043-269-0556; www.jikjiworld.net ⓒ: Mondays, January 1, Lunar New Year's Day and Chuseok

DAMYANG BAMBOO MUSEUM
The Damyang region in Jeollanam-do Province is where many bamboo items and crafts are created. Bamboo products are very practical but are works of art as well.
The museum has one underground floor and two above grounds.
The 1st floor exhibits 183 antique bamboo items and the tools used to create them, and the 2nd floor showcases 1,400 modern bamboo products. Over 200 foreign-made bamboo products are also on display.
ⓛ: Damyang-gun, Jeollanam-do ⓣ: 🚌 From Seoul Express Bus Terminal or Dong Seoul Bus Terminal, take the bus to Gwangju. Or from Gwangju Bus Terminal, take the bus to Damyang (35 min.), a 10 min.walk from Damyang Bus Terminal. ⓘ: 📞 061-380-3478 ⓒ: Open daily

O'SULLOC TEA MUSEUM
Exhibits on the history and production of tea, a vari-

Panasia Paper Museum

Teddy Bear Museum

ety of green tea products, an auditorium for seminars, and an observatory that has a commanding panoramic view of the largest tea farm in Korea.
ⓛ: Namjeju-gun, Jejudo ⓣ: 🚶 A 20- to 30-min. walk from Bunjae Artpia on Jejudo ⓘ: 📞 064-794-5312 ⓒ: January 1, Lunar New Year's Day and Chuseok

GOCHANG PANSORI MUSEUM
Exhibits related to every aspect of *pansori* (narrative solo song), including artifacts tracing its 200-year history and information on the backgrounds of well-known *pansori* singers, are displayed according to theme.
ⓛ: Gochang-gun, Jeollabuk-do ⓣ: 🚶 A 10-min. walk from Gochang Bus Terminal ⓘ: 📞 063-560-2761; www.pansori.museum.com
ⓒ: Mondays, January 1

PANASIA PAPER MUSEUM
It is the only museum in Korea devoted to the history, development, use and culture of paper. There are about 1,800 diverse arts and crafts related to paper. Visitors can also participate in the traditional papermaking process.
ⓛ: Palbok-dong Deukjin-gu Jeonju-si Jeollabuk-do ⓣ: 🚌 From Jeonju Bus Terminal, take a taxi (10 to 15 min.). ⓘ: 📞 063-210-8103; www.papermuseum.co.kr ⓒ: Mondays, January 1, Lunar New Year's Day and Chuseok

JEJU FOLKLORE AND NATURAL HISTORY MUSEUM
It features a significant collection of folk crafts, tools and equipment as well as plants, animals and minerals indigenious to Jejudo Island.
ⓛ: Ildo 2 (i)-dong, Jeju-si, Jejudo ⓣ: 🚌 From Jeju International Airport, take a taxi and get off next to the KAL hotel (10 min.). ⓘ: 📞 064-722-1588, http://museum.jeju.go.kr ⓒ: January 1, Lunar New Year's Day, Chuseok and May 24

TEDDY BEAR MUSEUM
The museum has 11 fascinating displays in which teddy bears are featured as the main characters of historical events of the 20th century.
Teddy bear fashion shows and teddy bear wedding ceremonies are also held.
ⓛ: Saekdal-dong, Seogwipo-si, Jejudo
ⓣ: 🚌 From Jeju International Airport, take a bus bound for Seogwipo and get off at Jungmun Resort (60 min.).
ⓘ: 📞 064-738-7600 📠 064-738-7800; www.teddybearmuseum.com ⓒ: Open daily

UNESCO World Cultural Heritages

Changdeokgung Palace

Recently, UNESCO has honored the Gangneung Danoje Festival as one of the UNESCO Masterpieces of Oral and Intangible Heritage of Humanity following *Jongmyojerye* and *Jeryeak* (royal ancestral ritual ceremony and music) and *pansori* (Korean narrative solo songs). Korea is now home to seven World Cultural Heritages, four World Documentary Heritages and three World Intangible Heritages, and hopes that even more will be acknowledged as valuable proof of human achievement and historical treasures that must be passed on to future generations.

THE BEAUTY OF TRADITIONAL LANDSCAPE ARCHITECTURE, CHANGDEOKGUNG PALACE | 창덕궁

Changdeokgung Palace was built in 1405 during the early Joseon Dynasty as the primary palace for royalty.
English tours are available at 11:30, 13:30 and 15:30. Admission is ₩3,000 for adults.
ⓘ: Changdeokgung Palace Maintenance Office ☎ 02-762-0648 ⓣ: Exit 3 of Anguk Station, Seoul-Subway Line 3 (a 5-min. walk) ⓒ: Mondays

JONGMYO SHRINE, JONGMYO JERYE AND JONGMYO JERYEAK | 종묘, 종묘제례, 종묘제례악

A Confucian shrine dedicated to the spirits of Joseon's kings and queens, Jongmyo Shrine's beautiful architecture and historical significance earned it a spot on the UNESCO World Cultural Heritage list in 2001.
Adding to the earnest historical importance of the occasion is *Jongmyojeryeak* (royal ancestral ritual music). It has been recognized and selected by UNESCO as a Masterpiece of Oral and Intangible Heritage of Humanity.

Jongmyo tours are available from 9 am to 6 pm from March to October, and is open for extended hours on Saturdays, Sundays and holidays from 9 am to 7 pm. During winter, the shrine is open until 5:30 pm. Admission is ₩1,000 for adults.
ⓘ: Jongmyo Maintenance Office ☎ 02-765-0195
ⓣ: Jongno 3 (sam)-ga Station on Seoul Subway Line 1, 3 or 5. (a 5-min. walk)

THE DREAM OF A KING, HWASEONG FORTRESS | 화성

Located in Suwon, Gyeonggi-do Province, Hwaseong Fortress was built by the 22nd Joseon king, Jeongjo, to honor his deceased father, Sado Seja. His father was heir to the kingdom but died before he took the throne.
In order to make the Hwaseong Fortress experience an even better one, Suwon City holds the Royal Guard Changing Ceremony every Sunday from April to October at 2 pm.
ⓘ: Tourist Information Center
☎ 031-228-4410 ⓣ: Suwon Station on Seoul Subway Line 1. Or 🚌 No. 2, 7, 8, or 13 and get off at the Jongno 4-way Intersection.

UNFORGETTABLE MEMORIES

Bulguksa Temple

Hwaseong Fortress

A 1000-YEAR-OLD TREASURE TROVE — GYEONGJU HISTORIC AREAS, SEOKGURAM GROTTO AND BULGUKSA TEMPLE |경주역사지구, 석굴암, 불국사

The capital of Silla (57 BC — 935 AD), the entire city of Gyeongju is a living history museum containing the remnants of the Silla Kingdom as well as relics pertaining to Buddhism, the national religion at the time. Gyeongju is divided into 5 separate regions: the Mt. Namsan Belt (a repository of Buddhist art), Wolseong Belt (the palace site of Silla), Hwangnyongsa Belt, Sanseong Belt and Tumuli Park Belt. Fifty-two historical sites and artifacts are located within the UNESCO-designated area. Especially worth visiting are Seokguram Grotto and Bulguksa Temple. Seokguram Grotto is open for tours from 6 am to 6 pm and from 7 am to 5 pm in winter. Admission is ₩4,000 for adults. (054-746-9933). Bulguksa Temple is open from 6:30 am to 5:30 pm (5 pm in winter). Admission is ₩3,000 for adults. (054-746-9913; see page 154).
ⓘ: • Terminal Tourist Information Center 054-772-9589 • Station Tourist Information Center 054-772-3843 ⓣ: From Seoul Station, take the bus to Gyeongju (4 hrs., 20 min.) or from Seoul Express Bus Terminal, take the Gyeongbuseon Line's bus to Gyeongju, which leaves every 30 min. (4 hrs., 30 min.). From Gyeongju Terminal, take the shuttle bus to the major tourist sites.

HAEINSA TEMPLE'S JANGGYEONG PANJEON (DEPOSITORIES OF TRIPITAKA KOREANA WOODBLOCKS) |해인사 장경판전

Haeinsa Temple's Janggyeong Panjeon (built in the 15th century) is the depository for the *Tripitaka Koreana Woodblocks*, the great collection of Buddhist scripture carved onto

Tripitaka Koreana Woodblocks

wooden plates that number about 80,000. It is the only building in the world constructed to serve such a purpose, and it is also designed in such a way that the temperature, ventilation and humidity can be controlled by taking advantage of the natural weather conditions.
The woodblocks are considered invaluable to the study of Buddhism today.

① Haeinsa Temple 055-934-3000
② From Seoul Express Bus Terminal, take the bus to Dong Daegu leaving every 15 min. (3 hrs., 40 min.). From Dong Daegu Bus Terminal, take the bus to Haeinsa Temple (1 hr., 10 min.).

THE LANGUAGE OF KOREA, HUNMINJEONGEUM
| 훈민정음

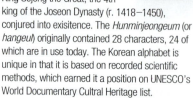

Meaning 'proper sounds to instruct the people,' *Hunminjeongeum* is the Korean alphabet in its original form as King Sejong the Great, the 4th king of the Joseon Dynasty (r. 1418–1450), conjured into exisitence. The *Hunminjeongeum* (or *hangeul*) originally contained 28 characters, 24 of which are in use today. The Korean alphabet is unique in that it is based on recorded scientific methods, which earned it a position on UNESCO's World Documentary Cultral Heritage list.

JOSEON WANGJO SILLOK (ANNALS OF THE JOSEON DYNASTY) AND SEUNGJEONGWON ILGI (THE DIARIES OF THE ROYAL SECRETARIAT) |
조선왕조실록, 승정원일기

The *Joseon Wangjo Sillok* is a historical record covering 472 years (1392 – 1863) of the Joseon Dynasty. Containing 1,393 chapters in 888 volumes, the *Joseon Wangjo Sillok* was published posthumously after each king's death and a temporary Sillokcheong (office for royal records) was set up under rigorous supervision of secrecy for the important undertaking.
The *Seungjeongwon Ilgi* is a written record of matters of national interest recorded by the Seungjeongwon (the royal secretariat's office to kings), which often dealt with matters of great secrecy.

JIKJI SIMCHE YOJEOL (ANTHOLOGY OF THE TEACHINGS OF ZEN BUDDHIST PRIESTS) | 직지심체요절

Written in 1372 by the monk Baegun Hwasang, it contains the teachings of Zen Buddhism. It was printed by metal typecast after his death, which is how the teachings of former monks have been handed down to the monks of today. Sadly, the original *Jikji Simche Yojeol* was removed from Korea and currently sits in the National Library of France. The oldest use of metal type in history, the book was designated as a UNESCO World Documentary Heritage.

THE SOUND OF KOREA, PANSORI | 판소리

Pansori (narrative solo songs) was registered as a UNESCO World Intangible Cultural Heritage in 2003 in a tribute long overdue.
One of the most Korean art forms in existence, *pansori* is a method of singing developed in the mid-Joseon Dynasty with the rise of commoner's culture. Its expressive singing style, theatrical

Pansori

Gangneung Danoje Festival

lyrics, and rich narratives are delivered by a single performer with song, expression and body language all playing a part. The vocalist is accompanied by a drum and some performances last over three or four hours. There were 12 *Madang* (repertoires), but only five have been passed down to the successors of former masters.
The National Center for Korean Traditional Performing Arts holds free performances at 5 pm every Saturday featuring *pansori* and more traditional Korean music, dance and theater.
ⓘ: National Center for Korean Traditional Performing Arts ☎ 02-580-3300; www.ncktpa.go.kr

GANGNEUNG DANOJE FESTIVAL |강릉단오제

The Gangneung Danoje Festival, a tradition that reaches back 1,000 years, is a major Korean festival held in honor of the *Daegwallyeong sansin* (the deity that protects the village).
It is also held to pray for an abundant harvest as well as peace in the home and community.
It encompasses all aspects of traditional festivals: life, games, annual events, memorial service, mountain, farm and fishing village culture and performances.
Included in UNESCO's Third Proclamation of Masterpieces of the Oral and Intangible Heritage of Humanity on November 25, 2005, the Gangneung Danoje Festival can be enjoyed by people from around the world.
ⓘ: Gangneung Danoje Committee ☎ 033-648-3014; http://www.danojefestival.or.kr

LIVING HISTORY, DOLMEN SITES |고인돌유적지

Dolmens, large burial monuments from ancient times, have been found across Northeast Asia but the highest concentration of this unique burial form has been found in Korea. Of the many dolmen sites in existence, the sites in Gochang, Hwasun and Ganghwa have been honored with designations as UNESCO World Cultural Heritage sites. The Gochang Dolmen Site is located in the center of Maesan Village in Gochang, Jeollabuk-do Province. On a land area of 1,764 m, there are about 442 individual dolmens. The dolmen site in Hwasun, Jeollanam-do Province, was discovered relatively recently and contains dolmens preserved in superior condition.
Located 1 hour, 30 min. from Seoul, the dolmens at the foot of Mt. Goryeosan in Ganghwa, Incheon, are some of the highest elevated dolmens ever discovered.
🚆: 🚌 From Gwangju Express Bus Terminal in Gyeonggi-do, take bus No. 217 toward Doam and get off at Dogok (40 min.).

Korean War Battlefields—DMZ TOUR

LIVING HISTORY

Panmunjeom

It has been over 50 years since the outbreak of the Korean War and the drawing of the 155-mile cease-fire line from the East Sea to the Yellow Sea, which created the Demilitarized Zone (DMZ). Symbolizing both war and peace, and division and unification, the DMZ is a place where time has come to a stop. Today, it is a haven for rare animals, birds and plants in one of the few places where nature remains undisturbed.

IMJINGAK | 임진각
Located in Munsan-eup, Paju-si, Gyeonggi-do Province, Imjingak is a park that was built to console the homesick refugees who left North Korea during the Korean War. Visitors to this tourist stop are reminded of the suffering of war and can say a prayer for unification. A train called "The Iron Horse Wants to Run" is at the park, symbolizing the railway connecting the North and the South that was cut off during the war. Also at the park are Mangbaedan, an altar that was set up for refugees so they could bow in the direction of their ancestral graveyards; Freedom Bridge, which recently became open to tourists after 50 years; Unification Pond, which is in the shape of the Korean Peninsula; and the Peace Bell.
ⓘ: Imjingak Main Office 031-952-2565; Tourist Information Center ☎ 031-953-4744 ⓣ: 🚇 From Imjingak Railroad Station, it is a 5-min. walk.

THE 3RD TUNNEL | 제3땅굴
Dug in 1978 by North Korea to infiltrate South Korean territory, this tunnel is 1,635 m long, 2 m wide and 2 m tall. It was built to allow the passage of 10,000 armed soldiers. At present, tourists can take walking tours through the tunnel, which is maintained as a circular cave with dimensions of 358 m in length and 3 m in width. It takes approximately 30–40 min. to complete the tour.
ⓘ: Mt. Dorasan Peace Park Management Office, ☎ 031-940-8342 ⓐ: ₩7,000 for adults and ₩6,000 for students ⓣ: 🚌 Use the shuttle tour bus for Paju Peace and Security Sites. (A bus departs every hour on the hour from Imjingak) ⓒ: Mondays and national holidays
* Cameras are not permitted in the tunnel.

DORA OBSERVATORY | 도라전망대
Built in 1986, the observatory is the only place in South Korea where visitors have a clear view of Gaeseong, the second largest city in North Korea. Through telephoto lenses, visitors can observe North Korean farmers going about their daily routines and sometimes even catch glimpses of elementary school children receiving military training.

UNIFICATION VILLAGE | 통일촌
Located some 10 km from Panmunjeom and approximately 50 km north of Seoul, this village is occupied by discharged soldiers and residents

UNFORGETTABLE MEMORIES

Imjingak

living near the border.
Other than the 450 residents of 90 families farming in the area, no one else is allowed to enter this district. As a result, the natural environment is well preserved.

FREEDOM VILLAGE (DAESEONG-DONG) |대성동 자유마을
The northernmost village in South Korea, Freedom Village is situated 400 m from the military demarcation line and 1 km from Panmunjeom.
The village residents are under strict control by the United Nations. At present, 250 people of 45 families reside in the area. They are not obligated to pay taxes or serve in the military.

PANMUNJEOM |판문점
Panmunjeom has received international attention as the place where the armistice agreement ending the Korean War was signed in 1953. Its original name was "Neolmulli" and is located approximately 50 km from Seoul and 8 km east of Gaeseong on the 38th parallel north. Panmunjeom is located in the Joint Security Area (JSA), where troops from both North and South Korea are present.

ODUSAN UNIFICATION OBSERVATORY |오두산 통일전망대
The Unification Observatory is on top of Mt. Odusan, which boasts a spectacular view above the Hangang and the Imjingang Rivers. Only 460 m from North Korean territory, this area is the narrowest part of the Demilitarized Zone along the 155-mile cease-fire line. From the circular observatory, built 140 m above sea level, visitors can watch North Korean residents farming across the border. They can also arrive at a better understanding of North Korean life by examining North Korean textbooks, clothing and household items on display.
ⓣ: ☎ 031-945-2390 ⓐ: Adults ₩2,000, teenagers and children ₩1,300 ⓣ: 🚇 No. 2 to Seongdong-ri at Geumchon Railroad Station (Gyeonguiseon Line)

DMZ TOUR GUIDELINES
1 Have your passport or foreign resident card on hand.
2 Entrance is prohibited to any person under the influence of alcohol or drugs.
3 All visitors to Panmunjeom must conform to the dress code; access may be denied to visitors wearing jeans, sandals, shorts, miniskirts, revealing clothing or military-style outfits.

DMZ PACKAGE TOURS
Individuals who do not wish to visit the DMZ independently or are short on time might want to consider a tour arranged by a travel agency. These tours are usually either half-day or full-day programs. Half-day programs are round-trip tours starting in Seoul and include visits to Imjingak, the 3rd Tunnel, Unification Village, etc. Prices range between ₩40,000–50,000. Full-day programs cost between ₩50,000–60,000 and include the half-day course, lunch and a tour of downtown Seoul.

INQUIRIES AND RESERVATIONS
DMZ Tour Office ☎ 031-954-0303 Korea Travel Bureau ☎ 02-777-6647; www.ktbonline.com International Cultural Service Club (ICSC) ☎ 02-399-2698–9; www.icsc.or.kr www.tourdmz.com Panmunjom Travel Center ☎ 02-771-5593; www.panmunjomtour.com Cosmojin Tour Consulting ☎ 02-318-0345; www.cosmojin.com Young Il Tours ☎ 02-730-1090; www.iloveseoultour.com Mercury Travel ☎ 02-774-3345; www.mct3300.com

Cheonggyecheon Stream

1960s and 70s

1970s and 80s

History of Cheonggyecheon

BEFORE THE 1960s
King Yeongjo (the 21st king of the Joseon Dynasty) launched large-scale operations to dredge Cheonggyecheon Stream. Around 200,000 workers cleared away earth from the stream to create a straight channel.
After the Korean War, the Cheonggyecheon Stream area became a shantytown. The polluted stream and its decimated surroundings were, nevertheless, an area where the less fortunate lived out their lives.

THE 1960s AND 70s
The stream was paved over from Gwanggyo Bridge to Ogansugyo Bridge in Dongdaemun as part of efforts to clear the slum and improve sanitary conditions. Burgeoning commercial enterprises and heavily congested streets sparked construction of elevated expressways, which were built on top of the cement-covered roads. As a result, more modern commercial facilities were constructed in the area.

THE 1970s AND 80s
With continued growth, the Cheonggyecheon Stream area gained a reputation as the center of Seoul. As time passed, dust and emissions from traffic on the roads and overpasses polluted the covered stream and corroded the roadway infrastructure, posing a threat to public safety.

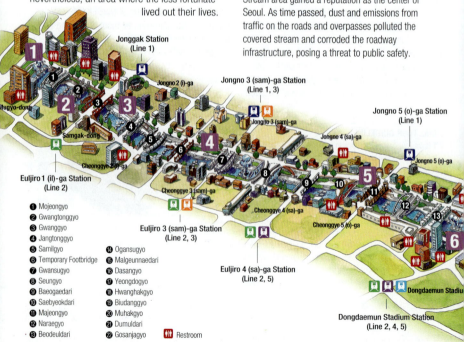

- ① Mojeongyo
- ② Gwangtonggyo
- ③ Gwanggyo
- ④ Jangtonggyo
- ⑤ Samilgyo
- ⑥ Temporary Footbridge
- ⑦ Gwansugyo
- ⑧ Seungyo
- ⑨ Baeogaedari
- ⑩ Saebyeokdari
- ⑪ Majeongyo
- ⑫ Naraegyo
- ⑬ Beodeuldari
- ⑭ Ogansugyo
- ⑮ Malgeunnaedari
- ⑯ Dasangyo
- ⑰ Yeongdogyo
- ⑱ Hwanghakgyo
- ⑲ Biudanggyo
- ⑳ Muhakgyo
- ㉑ Dumuldari
- ㉒ Gosanjagyo
- 🚻 Restroom

UNFORGETTABLE MEMORIES

Cheonggye Plaza

Gwangtonggyo Bridge

Banchado

2005

To make Seoul an environmentally viable city for residents in the 21st century, the project to restore Cheonggyecheon Stream began on July 1, 2003. On October 1, 2005, the clear blue waterway was revealed. The restoration of Cheonggyecheon Stream is a remarkable step toward making Seoul a city where nature, culture and history exist in harmony.

CHEONGGYECHEON STREAM
Places of Interest

A walk along Cheonggyecheon Stream features many interesting sights. You'll get to see nature in the city and experience the history and culture of Korea.

1 CHEONGGYE PLAZA
At the starting point of Cheonggyecheon Stream is a candle fountain illuminated by tri-color lighting, a circular firecracker fountain, and a two-tier fountain pumping 65,000 tons of water each day. The bottom of the stream glows with a soft light, creating a calm and serene atmosphere.

2 GWANGTONGGYO BRIDGE
Once the biggest bridge in the city, Gwangtonggyo Bridge was built in the 10th year of King Taejong (the 3rd king of Joseon) as a major thoroughfare for the royal family and ministers. As part of the Cheonggyecheon Stream project, the bridge was restored and relocated about 150 m upstream from its original location.

3 BANCHADO, PAINTING OF KING JEONGJO'S ROYAL PROCESSION
The largest ceramic wall painting in the world, *Banchado* decorates the left embankment of Cheonggyecheon Stream between Gwanggyo Bridge and Samilgyo Bridge. The original *Banchado* was an illustrated report of King Jeongjo's (the 22nd king of Joseon) eight-day

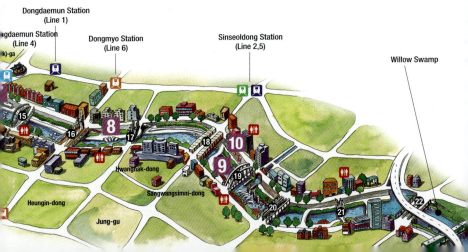

The Wall of Saekdong

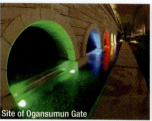
Site of Ogansumun Gate

Historic Laundry Site

visit to his parents' tomb. It has been reproduced as a 192-m-long wall painting showing the royal retinue of 1,700 figures and 800 horses. Viewers can see every detail of the formalities, costumes, and styles of the time, and the scale of the royal procession.

4 THE WALL OF CULTURE AND THE WALL OF SAEKDONG (RAINBOW-COLORED WALL)

The Wall of Culture, which is located upstream near Ogansumun Gate, approximately midway in the stream, shows the work of five contemporary artists under the theme "The Way to the Future." Together with the Wall of Saekdong, featuring the unique colors of Korea, it makes Cheonggyecheon Stream a space for enjoying culture and art.

5 SITE OF OGANSUMUN GATE

This is the site of the floodgates built between Heunginjimun (Dongdaemun) Gate and Gwanghwamun Gate during the construction of the capital city in the early Joseon Dynasty. Visitors can see photos of Ogansumun Gate's five floodgates through which water flowed out of the city and a symbolic reproduction of the gates. Next to the floodgates is Ogansugyo Bridge, and inscribed on the stones below it are King Yeongjo's *eopil* (royal autograph), which was presented to the royal court officials for their work to dredge the stream, *Juncheonga*, a paean in Chinese characters praising the king's achievements, and its translation in Korean.

6 HISTORIC LAUNDRY SITE

A recreation of the site where women once washed clothing is located between Dasangyo and Yeongdogyo Bridges. Seoul housewives preferred washing the family laundry here even in winter because it always had sunshine. To reproduce the effect, tilted stones slabs on which laundry was washed have been placed here but laundering is no longer permitted in the stream.

7 WALL OF HOPE

The Wall of Hope beautifies both sides of the stream between the Cheonggyecheon 8 (pal)-ga and 9 (gu)-ga Districts. Expressing the sorrow of Korea's South-North division, the wall is made of tiles created by 20,000 Seoul residents, North Koreans, and overseas Koreans in hopes of national unity and reunification. The wall is 50 m long on both sides and 2.2 m high, and is the world's largest ceramic tile wall.

8 RHYTHM WALL FOUNTAIN

Water flows down a marble wall 5 m high and 20 m wide. The surface of the wall is set with

---

HOW TO GET TO CHEONGGYECHEON STREAM

By subway From the subway stations highlighted on the map (page 34 – 35), it is a 2- to 5-min. walk.
By bus Take a bus that runs along Cheonggyecheon Stream
Yellow bus 01; Green bus 1011, 1017, 2016, 7101; Blue bus 100, 163, 202, 302

CHEONGGYECHEON STREAM WALKING TOUR

Course 1 2.9 km from Cheonggye Plaza to Ogansugyo Bridge, 3 hours
Cheonggye Plaza (nearby: Deoksugung Palace, Seoul Plaza) → Gwangtongggyo Bridge → Samilgyo (nearby: Jongno, Insa-dong, KTO Building) → Saebyeok Bridge (nearby: Gwangjang Market, Bangsan Market) → Ogansugyo Bridge (nearby: Dongdaemun Fashion Town)

Course 2 2.6 km from Cheonggyecheon Museum to Ogansugyo Bridge, 2.5 hours
Cheonggyecheon Museum → Muhakgyo → Hwanghakgyo (nearby: Hwanghak-dong Flee Market) → Yeongdogyo → Malgeunnae Bridge → Ogansugyo Bridge (nearby: Dongdaemun Fashion Town)

Contact Tourism Department, Seoul City 02-3707-9454, Seoul Metropolitan Facilities Management Corporation, or the Cheonggyecheon Management Center 02-2290-6849

Wall of Hope

Rhythm Wall Fountain

Jonchi Piers and Tunnel Fountain

black oval-shaped stones depicting fish swimming upstream. At night, the wall is illuminated, making it appear as if the water were falling to a rhythm.

⑨ TUNNEL FOUNTAIN
From 42 nozzles set on a wall 5 m high and 50 m wide, water sprays in a parabola over a promenade, creating a water tunnel. At night, multicolored lighting adds to the mystical ambience.

⑩ JONCHI PIERS
Between Biudanggyo and Muhakgyo Bridges stand three piers that once supported the Cheonggye Overpass. They were left standing as a visual reminder of the stream's confinement by the highways and to mark the significance of the Cheonggyecheon Stream restoration project.

CHEONGGYECHEON STREAM
Taste of Cheonggyecheon

Go on a culinary adventure along Cheonggyecheon Stream. The Cheonggyecheon Stream area has always bustled with restaurants catering to merchants and customers. While they may not boast the most up-to-date interior design, they are extremely popular for their warm ambience, hearty meals, and low prices.

THE LARGEST MARKET EATERY TOWN IN SEOUL — MEOKJAGOLMOK IN GWANGJANG MARKET
Gwangjang Market is famous for its *meokjagolmok*, an alley lined with 200 stalls selling a variety of food. The largest in Seoul, it offers a number of dishes at modest prices, including large, savory *nokdu bindaetteok* (Korean mung bean pancakes), a quick noodle meal, flavorful *bori bibimbap* (barley and rice and wild vegetables), and the popular snack *sundae* (Korean sausage). The prices are nearly the same everywhere: *nokdu bindaetteok* ₩4,000, *sundae* ₩5,000, *bori bibimbap* ₩3,000, noodles ₩2,000, so you don't have to worry about being overcharged. If you love the noisy, busy ambience of the market, you will have a great time.

DELICACIES ON EVERY CORNER— DONGDAEMUN MEOKJAGOLMOK
GRILLED FISH ALLEY
This *meokjagolmok* alley located near Jongno 5 (o)-ga is lined with grilled fish restaurants and you'll be able to smell the savory aromas before you get there. Many restaurants have been grilling fish at the same spot for over 30 years, and they have a credible reputation for good taste.
For 5,000 won, you can have your choice of Spanish mackerel, mackerel or saury served with rice and several side dishes. All of the fish are grilled over briquettes.

DAKHANMARI (WHOLE CHICKEN) ALLEY
The grilled fish alley leads into the *dakhanmari* (boiled whole chicken) alley. The chicken is eaten with seasonings or dipped in sauce and the remaining broth is enjoyed with noodles or rice. This is a great dish for people who prefer light and simple food to spicy dishes. In this alley, there are three or four popular restaurants known for their *dakhanmari*. The chicken is priced at ₩13,000 and a plate of noodles is ₩2,000.

GOPCHANG (INTESTINES) ALLEY
Deep in the alley is an area known as Dongdaemun *Gopchang Golmok*, literally "intestine alley." Most of the restaurants here have been in business for over 40 years. *Gopchang* are chopped into large chunks and grilled over a fire. One serving is ₩6,000, and the price is the same at every restaurant.

CENTRAL ASIAN EATERIES IN GWANGHUI-DONG
Homesick workers from Uzbekistan, Kazakhstan, and Mongolia come to Gwanghui-dong to enjoy

the food of their native land. Generous servings of skewered lamb kebab cost between ₩5,000 and ₩10,000. Visitors can get a feel of Central Asia while trying new and exotic dishes.

40 YEARS OF GOPCHANG — GOPCHANG ALLEY IN HWANGHAK-DONG

In addition to the Flea Market, Hwanghak-dong is also famous for its *gopchang* alley. The area, which started off with a small number of *gopchang* restaurants 40 years ago, has become a popular *meokjagolmok*. Young couples who came here for grilled *gopchang* come back with their children and the children, who are now adults, stop by once in a while with their friends. The price is around ₩7,000 for one serving.

Shopping around Cheonggyecheon Stream
CHEONGGYECHEON STREAM

The area between Cheonggye 2 (i)-ga and Cheonggye 8 (pal)-ga is home to a great number of markets and shopping arcades. From traditional markets to state-of-the-art malls, this is a true paradise for shoppers.

Dongpyeonghwa Market

> **RECOMMENDED RESTAURANTS AROUND CHEONGGYECHEON STREAM**
>
> **Guhwasan** An upscale Chinese restaurant near Cheonggyecheon Stream. Popular for savory dishes prepared by its head chef with 25 years of experience.
> Information 02-2279-5656/11:00 –22:00/ *Kkansosaeu* (Chinese-style fried shrimp) ₩37,000, *Samseon Nurungji Tang* (seafood and scorched rice with sauce) ₩45,000, set meal ₩18,000 –100.000 (per person) / B1, Blue Gate
>
> **Yujeong Restaurant** The merchants at Dongpyeonghwa Market in Cheonggye 7 (chil)-ga unanimously recommended this restaurant to those who want to taste the flavors of the traditional market in Seoul.
> Information 02-2232-5727/Open 24 hours / *Gejang baekban* (crabs marinated in soy sauce) ₩9,000, pork stew ₩10,000, stews ₩5,000/ Behind Dongpyeonghwa Market
>
> **Wonhalmoney Bossam**
> A traditional Korean dish, *bossam* is sliced boiled pork that is eaten with cabbage leaves. Wonhalmoney Bossam is a famous *bossam* restaurant in Seoul. The sweet-sour taste of kimchi complements the light flavor of the pork.
> Information 02-2232-3232/10:00 –23:00 / *Mat bossam* ₩23,000, *Bobae bossam* ₩39,000, *Modeum bossam* ₩38,000, *Bossam* set menu ₩7,000 / 100 m from Cheonggye 8 (pal)-ga toward the Hwanghak-dong intersection

100 YEARS OF FABRIC — GWANGJANG MARKET

Celebrating its centennial in 2005, Gwangjang Market is the oldest fabric market in Korea offering a wide variety of fabrics that meet the needs of all of its customers. Every day, it bustles with merchants from across the nation. The button shops on the 2nd and 3rd floors are a paradise for shoppers looking for vintage items. Over 80% of the vintage products in Korea are sold here and since everything is wholesale, items can be purchased at lower prices.

STACKS OF SECONDHAND BOOKS— THE STREET OF USED BOOKS

During its heyday 20 years ago, this was the center for all used bookstores where about 200 stores did business in the area but only 50 stores survive today. Out-of-print books can often be found here at affordable prices and since the restoration of Cheonggyecheon Stream, these stores have been tidied up to attract tourists.

DRIED SEAFOOD IN SEOUL— JUNGBU DRIED FISH WHOLESALE MARKET

Jungbu is a dried fish market located at the far end of the traditional market area stretching from Gwangjang Market to Bangsan Market (www.bangsanmarket.net). The area is well organized with each alley devoted to a specific item such as dried croaker, dried laver, and dried anchovies. With about 1,000 shops, the market is the largest of its kind in Seoul with about 15,000

people visiting every day.
The prices are 20 – 30% lower than at Namdaemun or Dongdaemun Market. This is a great place to buy gift boxes of dried laver, dried seaweed, or any type of dried fish.

ALL ABOUT COOKING UTENSILS — BANGSAN MARKET

From ingredients for making chocolate to bread machines, you can find everything you need for the kitchen at Bangsan Market. Housewives and professional cooks shop side by side in this treasure trove for people who love to cook. In addition to cooking utensils, plastic packaging materials are also sold here.

MUSEUM OF KOREAN WATCHES — WATCH ALLEY OF YEJI-DONG

Connected to the Seun Arcade, Watch Alley is the oldest watch and jewelry alley in Seoul.
The first merchants are said to have sold used watches from an apple crate "display counter." Here, you can buy a children's watch for 1,500 won or a luxury watch for millions of won. In any case, the prices are 30–40% lower than anywhere else. Some used items are as good as new and you can always negotiate for a better deal.

WHERE THE LATEST FASHION TRENDS BEGIN — DONGDAEMUN SHOPPING MALL TOWN

Dongdaemun Fashion Shopping Mall Town attracts all of the fashion-conscious Seoulites. Even though they are part of the traditional market, the malls are actually more like department stores. You can check out the fashion trends and get some great bargains. The malls are open late for post-midnight shopping, except on Sundays.
Check the shop's business hours in advance as each shopping mall may be closed on a different day (Doota, Migliore: closed on Mondays / apm, Blue Gate: closed on Tuesdays).

MUSEUM OF ELECTRONIC AND ELECTRIC GOODS — SEUN ARCADE

From electronic products to hardware, you'll find everything at Seun Arcade. Shopping is convenient as you can do one-stop shopping for any of the 4,000 types of electronic and electric goods, and the prices are more affordable than anywhere else.
In front of Seun Arcade, stalls line the street with merchants selling their wares.
It's great fun just to look around as items on sale range from medical equipment, whose efficacy is unproven, to other novel and unusual items.

LATE NIGHT FASHION MARKET — DONGPYEONGHWA MARKET IN CHEONGGYE 7 (CHIL)-GA

This is a wholesale fashion arcade that opens early in the morning. It may be inconvenient for tourists to shop in the day but for night shopping, this is the place to go. On weekends, merchants display all sorts of goods, creating the busy ambience of a traditional market.
More unique items can be found on the weekends and it is fun to try to get a deal. Prices are 20 – 30% lower than at the Dongdaemun shopping malls across the street.

RARE/UNUSUAL ITEMS — DONGDAEMUN STADIUM FLEA MARKET

Due to the Cheonggyecheon Stream restoration, the Hwanghak-dong Flea Markets moved to this area. It is the "Total Bazaar Fair" of Seoul, with everything from books to records to tools to shoes to clothes to musical instruments and antiques. You can handle the items and take pictures and the good-hearted merchants won't snub you. Prices vary, so try to negotiate as much as possible.
Even though a large number of merchants moved to Dongdaemun, the market there is still going strong. If you want the real flea market experience, go to Hwanghak-dong. You may find some precious antiques at a low price.

Geumgangsan Diamond Mountains

Geumgangsan Diamond Mountains

"The beauty of the Diamond Mountains is beyond comparison with any mountains in the world. The wonder of grand gorges enraptures us." - *Isabella Bird Bishop, British explorer, 1890 -*

No mountains in Korea have been more admired than the Geumgangsan Mountains. Poets, painters and artists have all applauded the magnificence of these 110 mountains. With 12,000 pinnacles and hundreds of valleys, odd-shaped rocks, crystal clear waters, endless saw-tooth ridges, diverse flora and fauna, these mountains have some of the most fantastic mountain scenery to be found anywhere on the globe. For most foreigners visiting Korea at the new millennium, the beautiful Geumgangsan in North Korea has been added as a tourist attraction since the first Geumgangsan tour on November 18, 1998. Travel to the North Korean Geumgangsan Diamond Mountains is a wonderful addition to the tour of South Korea's eastern coast and Seoraksan Mountains or Seoul.

GEUMGANGSAN DIAMOND MOUNTAINS ATTRACTIONS

All of the tour courses boast truly breathtaking scenery. Outer Geumgang is the zenith of masculine magnificence while Inner Geumgang displays feminine properties.

SAMILPO ESTUARY DISTRICT | 삼일포

The name Samilpo, literally "three-day estuary," originated from a historical fact involving the Elite Youth Corps of the Silla Kingdom who stayed here for three days lured by the scenic beauty.

To the west is a lake screened by 36 low hills with dense pine trees. Topped with pine and bamboo trees, four rocky islets, including Waudo, dot the glassy surface of the lake. The scenery of Samilpo Estuary viewed from Yeonhwadae Pavilion is absolutely stunning.

HAEGEUMGANG ROCKS | 해금강

About 4 km east of Samilpo Estuary are the Haegeumgang Rocks covering Namgang Estuary and its vicinity.
The fringe of Geumgangsan runs under the sea

UNFORGETTABLE MEMORIES

Manmulsang Rocks

MANMULSANG ROCKS | 만물상

Manmulsang is perhaps the most scenic site in the Geumgangsan Diamond Mountains. It features tens of thousands of rock images that resemble objects and living things. From every angle are displayed incredible images created by nature.

LAND ROUTE TOURS

The Hyundai-Asan Corporation offers land route tour packages to the Geumgangsan Diamond Mountains (1-day; 2-day, 1-night; and 3-day, 2-night trips).
You may select from among three tour courses and can enjoy *gyoye* (a North Korean acrobatic performance), hot springs bathing, hiking and shopping. Please note that you must book your trip at least 10 days in advance.

TOUR COURSES

1-DAY TOUR
Departure from Keumkangsan Condo → Unification Observatory (Customs Immigration and Quarantine of South Korea) → Guseonbong Peak (CIQ of North Korea) → Guryong Falls or Manmulsang Rocks → Lunch → Hot springs or shopping → Samilpo Estuary → CIQ of North Korea → CIQ of South Korea

2-DAY, 1-NIGHT TOUR
1st day Departure from Keumkangsan Condo → Unification Observatory (CIQ of South Korea) → Guseonbong Peak (CIQ of North Korea) → Guryong Falls → Hot springs or Samilpo Estuary → *Gyoye* Performance → Dinner → Free time
2nd day Breakfast → Manmulsang Rocks or Samilpo Estuary → Lunch → Free time → CIQ of North Korea → CIQ of South Korea

3-DAY, 2-NIGHT TOUR
1st day Departure from Keumkangsan Condo → Unification Observatory (CIQ of South Korea) → Free time (hot springs or shopping)
2nd day Breakfast → Guryong Falls → Hot springs bathing or Samilpo Estuary → *Gyoye* Performance → Dinner → Free time
3rd day Breakfast → Manmulsang Rocks and Samilpo Estuary or Haegeumgang Rocks → Lunch → CIQ of North Korea → CIQ of South Korea

For further information or a list of qualified agencies, contact Hyundai Asan at ☎ 02-3669-3000; www.mtkumgang.com.

and bursts up above the waves to produce this seaside wonder. Haemanmulsang, or "10,000 Images of Floating Rocks," stands alone among the Haegeumgang Rocks.
Transparent seawater mirrors schools of fish, emerald-blue waves tease the silver sand and break into a mist of creamy foam, and old green pine trees growing out of rock chasms add serendipitous moments to your visit.
On a clear day, the Unification Observatory of South Korea can be seen from the high spots in this area.

GURYONG FALLS | 구룡폭포

The 150-m-high Guryong (nine dragons) Falls is one of the most famous and exquisite falls in Korea. At the bottom of the falls are nine 10 m trenches caused by the crashing waters over hundreds of thousands of years.

GEUMGANGSAN HOT SPRINGS | 금강온천

About 300 m from the Geumgangsan Hotel are the famous healing hot springs where one can relax after hiking the mountain trails.

Hallyu — The Korean Wave

Hallyu (the Korean Wave) is the name for the phenomenon of Korean popular culture that is spreading across the world. In particular, Korean dramas and films have earned worldwide recognition for their artistic values. A few examples of their prominent success include the Grand Prix awarded to *Old Boy* at the 2004 Cannes Film Festival, three different awards to *Spring, Summer, Fall, Winter... and Spring* at the 2003 Locarno International Film Festival, and the Best Director prize for *Chihwaseon* at the 2002 Cannes Film Festival. A tour of Korea will be a wonderful chance to visit these filming locations and experience diverse aspects of Korean culture.

HALLYU
Daejanggeum

The TV drama *Daejanggeum* is the true story of a woman of the Joseon Dynasty 500 years ago. Originally from the lowest class, Janggeum became the best cook in the palace and eventually a royal physician, which earned her the title of the "Great Janggeum" (*Daejanggeum* in Korean). The show has became a huge hit at home and abroad, especially in Chinese-speaking countries, by integrating and entertaining aspects of Oriental medicine and royal cuisine.

FILMING LOCATIONS TOUR

OPTION A. SEOUL, GYEONGGI-DO AREA

Ancient palaces → Daejanggeum Theme Park in MBC's Yangju Culture Valley → Seoul Studio Complex in Namyangju

ANCIENT PALACES IN SEOUL
As the main set for period dramas, ancient palaces are the perfect place to appreciate traditional Korean architecture in modern downtown Seoul. You don't want to miss Changdeokgung Palace and Jongmyo Royal Shrine, both of which have been designated by UNESCO as World Cultural Heritage sites.

Transportation The Seoul City Tour Bus provides easy access to many places of interest. Buses start at the Donghwa Duty-Free Shop in Gwanghwamun Gate or Exit 6 of Gwanghwamun

Daejanggeum

UNFORGETTABLE MEMORIES

Subway Station (Line 5).

Information Seoul City Tour Bus ☎ 02-777-6090, www.seoulcitytourbus.com; 9:00 – 19:00 (except Mondays)

* Admission to Changdeokgung Palace is allowed at 15 and 45 min. past the hour. Last admission is at 15:45 or 17:15 (in summer). English, Chinese and Japanese guides are available as scheduled. For more information on Changdeokgung Palace, call 02-762-0648 or visit www.cdg.go.kr (Korean).

DAEJANGGEUM THEME PARK

The outdoor set used for *Daejanggeum* has been restored exactly to the way it was and renovated into a theme park that offers a wide array of sights, events and programs. There are numerous replicas representing a royal office from the 15th century Joseon Dynasty, ministerial chambers and commoners' inns. Each set features a collection of stage properties and costumes, which add authenticity because they were the ones used for the show. Visitors are shown highlights from the drama and can listen to stories about royal cuisine from the show's food consultant.

There are also many exciting events, including riding a *gama* (Korean palanquin), trying on *hanbok* (traditional Korean clothing) and archery.

Transportation Sangbong Terminal or Dong (East) Seoul Bus Terminal → Uijeongbu Bukbu Subway Station (Line 1) → MBC Yangju Culture Valley (bus No. 30)

Information ☎ 031-849-5150; 10:00 – 17:00 (18:00 from April to October); Admission: ₩5,000 for adults and ₩3,000 for children.

Hwaseong Fortress

Daejanggeum Theme Park

DAEJANGGEUM
1. Ancient Palaces / Seoul
2. Daejanggeum Theme Park / MBC's Yangju Culture Valley
3. Seoul Studio Complex / Namyangju
4. Hwaseong Fortress / Suwon
5. Korean Folk Village / Yongin
6. Naesosa Temple / Buan
7. Byeonsan Beach / Buan
8. Seonunsa Temple / Gochang
9. Hyeopjae Beach / Jeju
10. Jeju Folk Village Museum / Jeju
11. Seopjikoji / Jeju

CHIHWASEON
12. Ganghwa-do / Ganghwa
13. Seongmo-do / Incheon
14. Naganeupseong / Suncheon
15. Seonamsa Temple / Suncheon

WINTER SONATA
16. Namiseom Island / Chuncheon
17. Chuncheon Myeongdong / Chuncheon
18. Junsang's House / Chuncheon
19. Jungdo Resort / Chuncheon
20. Yongpyong Resort / Pyeongchang
21. Chuam Beach / Donghae
22. Oedo Maritime Park / Geojedo Island

OPTION B. GYEONGGI-DO, JEOLLA-DO AREA
Hwaseong Fortress → Korean Folk Village → Naesosa Temple in Jeollabuk-do → Byeonsan Beach → Seonunsa Temple (takes more than one day)

NAESOSA TEMPLE
This is where Janggeum looked after the queen's nanny, which was called Unmunsa Temple in the show. Constructed in 633 during the Baekje Kingdom, Naesosa Temple is especially famous for autumn leaves.

The maple trees lining the road to Iljumun Gate create a magnificent tunnel that makes for a scenic drive in autumn. Around the main entrance of the temple is a wonderful walking path filled with the fragrant scent of fir trees. In the vicinity are several other tourist attractions including Gaeamsa Temple, Jikso Waterfall, Byeonsan Beach and Nakjodae.

Transportation Seoul Gangnam Express Bus Terminal (3 hours, 30 min.) → Buan Bus Terminal → a bus bound for Naesosa Temple
* Buses operate every 30 min. (a 40-min. ride)

Information Byeonsanbando National Park Management Office ☎ 063-582-7808, www.npa.or.kr/pyonsan/main.asp

Chihwaseon
HALLYU

This movie is a story of a genius painter who lived a bohemian life, and also describes how the Joseon Dynasty tragically collapsed due to incursions by foreign nations. *Chihwaseon* features masterpieces by distinguished Joseon painters, along with traditional painting tools and priceless picture books.

Chihwaseon

FILMING LOCATIONS TOUR

OPTION A. INCHEON AREA (one-day tour)
Ganghwado → Seongmodo → Yeongjongdo

MINMEORU BEACH IN SEONGMODO AND YEONGJONGDO

Minmeoru Beach on Seongmodo Island is where Jang Seung-eop ran into his teacher, Kim Byeong-mun, on a cold winter day.
You can watch the picturesque sunset and dig for shellfish on Yeonjongdo Island, where Incheon International Airport is located. It is the place where Jang Seung-eop lived as a young man. Fields of red plants and black sea mud create a scene like an Oriental painting. Also a must-see is Ganghwado, which has earned the nickname "open-air history book" for its abundant historic sites and ancient temples.

Transportation Sinchon Bus Terminal in Seoul (1 hour, 40 min. ride, 15 min. intervals) → Ganghwa Bus Terminal → a bus bound for Oipo-ri (6:55 – 18:00) / 20-min. intervals → a ferry ride to Seongmodo (7:30 – 18:00) / 10-min. ride / 20-min. intervals) → buses leave at 10 min. past the hour.

Information Ganghwa-gun Culture and Tourism Department ☎ 032-930-3220, www.ganghwa.incheon.kr

OPTION B. JEOLLANAM-DO AREA (takes more than one day)
Naganeupseong Folk Village in Suncheon → Seonamsa Temple → Dolmen Park

NAGANEUPSEONG FOLK VILLAGE IN SUNCHEON

Naganeupseong Folk Village and Seonamsa Temple are where Jang Seung-eop's life in his late 20s was filmed. Built in 1626, Naganeupseong Folk Village is still home to 90-odd households: here, you may feel as if time has been turned back. The town wall, unusually constructed on a flat area with natural square rocks, remains well preserved in its original shape (4 m in height, 3–4 m in width and 1,410 m in length). Near Suncheon lies Dolmen Park, a historic site from the Old Stone Age that has been registered as a UNESCO World Cultural Heritage site.

Transportation Yongsan Railway Station in Seoul (5 hours) → Suncheon Railway Station → Bus No. 16, 63, or 68 to Naganeupseong Folk Village

Information Naganeupseong Management Office ☎ 061-749-3347, www.nagan.or.kr; 9:00-18:00; Admission: ₩2,000 adults, ₩1,000 children

Demonstration Programs straw crafts, blacksmith works and natural dyeing (9:00 – 17:00 from Tuesday through Sunday / reservations required for the dyeing program)

Naganeupseong Management Office ☎ 061-749-3347, www.nagan.or.kr

Winter Sonata
HALLYU

The TV drama *Winter Sonata* depicts nostalgia for a platonic love which seems to be missing in modern life, and has earned great sympathy from many female viewers. The two lovers reunite after a long separation and fall in love again despite the fact that one of them suffers from amnesia. This mellow story of sweet first love, friendship and family has served as a trigger to stir up Hallyu waves throughout Asia.

FILMING LOCATIONS TOUR

Namiseom Island → Chuncheon → Junsang's House → Jungdo Resort → Yongpyong Resort → Chuam Beach (takes more than one day)

Seongmodo

Naganeupseong Folk Village

NAMISEOM ISLAND

Namiseom Island, located in Chuncheon, Gangwon-do Province, is where the two main characters of *Winter Sonata* fell in love. You can feel the excitement of the show from the beautiful tree-lined paths, an exhibition hall featuring drama highlights, and filming locations. There are many places for a romantic date as well as a sledding slope that opens during the winter. A number of entertainment facilities will also usher you to worlds of joy.

Transportation Cheongnyangni Station → Gapyeong (a bus bound for Chuncheon) → city bus (10 buses a day / 15-min. ride) → Namiseom Island dock → a ferry ride (7:30 – 21:30 / 20- to 30-min. intervals)

Information ☎ 031-582-2181/4, www.chuncheon.go.kr; 7:30-21:30; Admission: ₩5,000 adults, ₩3,500 students, ₩2,500 children

Winter Sonata

☎ 033-242-4881, www.chuncheon.go.kr; Admission: ₩4,300 adults, ₩2,400 children (boat fare included)

JUNGDO RESORT

Jungdo Resort is the location where many scenes in *Winter Sonata* were shot.
Nestled in the middle of a huge lake and surrounded by mountain ridges, this unique resort area features a variety of recreational facilities and tree-lined walking paths. A bicycle ride may complete your perfect trip (bikes can be rented). Within the resort are several types of accommodations ranging from low-priced hostels to a condominium-style pensions. Other places of interest include a prehistoric dolmen site and ancient huts from the New Stone Age.

Transportation Chuncheon Bus Terminal → taxi → docks (in Samcheon-dong: 9:00 – 17:30; 30-min. intervals; in Geunhwa-dong: 7:00 – 20:40 / 40-min. intervals)

Information Jungdo Resort Management Office

CHUAM BEACH

This is where Yu-jin and Jun-sang took their first trip to the seaside and also where Jun-sang said goodbye to Yu-jin for the last time. Located in front of Chuam-ri village in Bukpyeong-dong of Donghae City, Chuam Beach features scenic bluffs, caves and sharp, pointed rocks. With calm and shallow water, it would make a nice place for a family outing. Another must-see is the sunrise over the East Sea as well as a visit to Cheongok Cave and Mureung Waterfall (4-hour tour). A few of the area's specialties are raw squid, *maeuntang* (spicy fish stew) and abalone porridge.

Transportation Donghae Bus Terminal → city bus or taxi (8.5 km, 15 min.)

Information Donghae City Tourism Development Department ☎ 033-530-2473, www.donghae.gangwon.kr

Namiseom

Jungdo Resort

UNFORGETTABLE MEMORIES
Templestay

The Korean Buddhist Jogye and Cheontae Orders offer an opportunity to lodge and witness the temple life of monks and nuns under a new templestay program. Rates are between ₩50,000 and ₩80,000, including three meals and translation fees. Reservations are required one week in advance. ℹ: ☏ 02-732-9926/7; www.templestaykorea.net; ts2002@buddhism.or.kr

PROGRAMS

EARLY MORNING CEREMONY Early in the morning, usually around 3 am, everyone in the temple gathers in the Main Buddha Hall and has a Dharma ceremony.
This magnificent ceremony clears all the dust and stray thoughts from one's mind.

SEON (Zen meditation) Participants will learn and practice some of the meditation positions that methods monks use to meditate to find their true selves.

DADO (tea ceremony) People in almost every Asian country habitually drink tea, but the tea ceremony established at Korean temples is unique for its refinement and etiquette.

ULLYEOK (community work) It is physical labor time, and depending on the season, people sweep the temple grounds, make food and repairs or other necessary labor.

BARUGONGYANG (Buddhist monastic meal with 4 bowls) *Barugongyang* is a unique and special Buddhist method of eating. *Baru* means bowls containing a moderate amount, and can also be referred to as monks' eating style, which is vegetarian. It follows Buddhist rules for all sentient being. This method of having a meal refreshes one's mind so that it is appreciative of one's environment physically, mentally and spiritually.

TEMPLE TOUR Participants will learn about the unique characteristics of Korean temples during their stay.

A DAY AT A TEMPLE

Day	Time	Schedule
Day 1	14:00	Uniform distribution and room assignment
	15:00	Opening ceremony
	16:00	Temple tour
	18:00	Dinner
	19:00	Evening Buddhist ceremonial service
	19:30	Tea ceremony & conversation with Buddhist monks and nuns
	20:30	Prepare for bed
Day 2	03:30	Pre-dawn Buddhist ceremonial service
	04:00	*Seon* meditation (sitting & walking meditation) & rest
	06:00	Breakfast
	07:00	Community work
	08:00	Hermitage tour
	11:00	Closing ceremony
	12:00	Lunch
	13:00	Departure

* The schedule varies from temple to temple. Please contact each temple for more detailed information.

TEMPLE INFORMATION

TEMPLES WITH TRANSLATION SERVICE

Name	Province	City	Availability	Reservations and Inquiries
Ganghwa Lotus Lantern International Meditation Center	Incheon	Ganghwa	Weekends	jajaesim@hotmail.com
Golgulsa	Gyeongsangbuk-do	Gyeongju	Daily	d-kumgang@hanmail.net
Magoksa	Chungcheongnam-do	Gongju	Daily	izen.art@gmail.com
Musangsa	Chungcheongnam-do	Gyeryong	Weekends (1-week programonly during retreat period)	info@musangsa.org
Jagwangsa	Daejeon	Yuseong	Daily	jakwangsa@kornet.org
Jogyesa	Seoul	Jongno	Last Saturday of month (Temple Life only)	http://www.ijogyesa.net (Internet Reservations)

TEMPLES WITHOUT TRANSLATION SERVICE

Name	Province	City	Availability	Reservations and Inquiries
Gapsa	Chungcheongnam-do	Gongju	Daily (From September)	gapsa52@yahoo.com
Daewonsa	Jeollanam-do	Boseong	Weekends	november111@korea.com
Mihwangsa	Jeollanam-do	Haenam	Daily	dalmaom@hanmail.net
Bongjeongsa	Gyeongsangbuk-do	Andong	Daily	id9000id9000@hanmail.net
Buseoksa	Chungcheongnam-do	Seosan	Daily	pksrhf3@hanmail.net
Silsangsa	Jeollabuk-do	Namwon	Daily	templestay@silsangsa.or.kr
Yeongpyeongsa	Chungcheongnam-do	Gongju	Daily	joyance7@hanmail.net
Hwaeomsa	Jeollanam-do	Gurye	Daily	kyung2574@hanmail.net

Musangsa Temple

Barugongyang Monastic Meal

TIPS FOR TEMPLESTAY PARTICIPANTS

▶ You must bring your own toiletries (razors, toothbrushes, soap, etc.)
▶ Quarters: > There are separate rooms for male and female guests. > Private quarters may be arranged for individuals and families upon request. > Lights go out at 21:30.
▶ Clothing: > Most temples provide comfortable uniforms, but it is a good idea to bring your own in case there is a shortage. > Comfortable clothes for children should be brought since there are no uniforms for them. > Refrain from wearing revealing clothing. Warm clothing may be necessary for early morning programs regardless of season. > Socks must be worn during Buddhist ceremonies.
▶ Program: Morning chanting is at 3:30 or 4:30 am, depending on the temple. Since this is the start of the day, all participants are urged to attend with an open heart. If this is impossible, kindly consult a program official ahead of time. > Taking pictures and recording are not permitted in a Buddha Hall.
▶ Environment: > Temples are Korean cultural properties and should be conserved and protected. > Smoking and drinking are not permitted.

Taekwondo

Taekwondo is a traditional Korean martial art. It is a method of self-defense that uses the hands and feet. The ultimate goal of taekwondo is to develop the character and personality of the practitioner through physical, mental and spiritual discipline. Taekwondo became a worldwide sport after it was designated an official Olympic sport.

WHAT MAKES IT SO ATTRACTIVE?
AS A SPORT The movements and techniques of taekwondo are made up so that the practitioner uses parts and regions of his/her body in a balanced manner, helping to evenly enhance the flexibility of the limbs. It also helps to eliminate stress as you shout while practicing kicking and punching.

AS A MEANS OF SELF-DEFENSE While it is similar to other martial arts in the use of hands and feet, taekwondo is markedly different in that it boasts a powerful level of attack that comes from the use of the feet. However, taekwondo is focused more on defense than attack and is a useful means of self-defense.

AS A MEANS OF SELF-DISCIPLINE Taekwondo is effective for self-discipline as it strengthens the body and mind and also teaches etiquette through matches with other opponents.

THREE BASIC COMPONENTS OF TAEKWONDO
PUMSAE A systematic framework of techniques that enable the individual to practice attack and defense moves as if he/she were faced with an opponent.

GYEOKPA (BREAKING OR DEFEATING)
Techniques used in examinations or demonstrations where the practitioner, one who has mastered the basic techniques and movements, uses great strength to break objects such as wooden boards, tiles and bricks.

GYEORUGI (CONTEST) This refers to both the process of mastering the techniques needed for attack and defense in one-on-one combat as well as the process of assessing the mastery of such techniques.

INTERNATIONAL TAEKWONDO EVENTS
WORLD TAEKWONDO HWARANG FESTIVAL
Held in Jincheon, the mecca of taekwondo, this festival serves as an opportunity for taekwondo lovers all over the world to admire *hwarang* relics and embrace the taekwondo spirit. (see page 55)
043-539-3930; www.lovetkd.com

KOREA OPEN CHUNCHEON INTERNATIONAL TAEKWONDO CHAMPIONSHIPS
Taekwondo practitioners worldwide gather in Chuncheon to compete in the three areas of *gyeorugi*, *pumsae* and color belts *gyeorugi*.
033-250-3648; www.koreaopentkd.org

UNFORGETTABLE MEMORIES

HANGANG TAEKWONDO CENTER
- ₩100,000 per month
- 14:00 – 20:00; Monday – Saturday
* Free admission to taekwondo contests
- Dongbuichon-dong, Yongsan-gu, Seoul
- 02-795-9333; hangang9333@hanmail.net

INTERNATIONAL TAEKWONDO ACADEMY AT CHUNG CHEONG UNIVERSITY
- $60 per day
- Cheongwon-gun, Chungcheongbuk-do
- 043-230-2450; www.ok.ac.kr

EXPERIENCE TAEKWONDO CULTURE
Experience taekwondo through a variety of programs including short introductory programs (5 hours / 3 hours), one-day programs (4 hours / 6 hours) and three-day tourist packages.

TAEKWONDO TOUR AGENCIES
Aju Incentive Tour 02-786-0028;
www.ajutours.co.kr
Cosmojin Tour Consulting 02-796-1134;
www.cosmojin.com
Darlin Tour System 02-3472-8410;
www.darlintour.com
Korea Travel Bureau 02-585-7072;
www.ktbonline.com
Plaza 21 Travel Service 02-752-4254;
www.koreatourplaza.com
Root Travel 02-549-8605;
www.roottravel.co.kr

TAEKWONDO ORGANIZATIONS

THE WORLD TAEKWONDO FEDERATION
Provides an explanation of taekwondo as well as news on related events and recent trends.
- 02-566-2505; www.wtf.org

KOREA TAEKWONDO ASSOCIATION
Contains an online encyclopedia of taekwondo news and schedules of international competitions, video clips and photos.
- 02-420-4271; www.koreataekwondo.org

WORLD TAEKWONDO HEADQUARTERS (KUKKIWON)
The history of taekwondo, taekwondo techniques and related video clips
- 02-567-1058; www.kukkiwon.or.kr

TAEKWONDO TRAINING INSTITUTES FOR FOREIGNERS

YONSEI INTERNATIONAL TAEKWONDO CENTER
- ₩10,000 per lesson; ₩80,000 per month
- 19:00 – 20:30 ; Mondays, Wednesdays and Fridays
- Yonsei University Campus, Sinchon-dong, Seodaemun-gu, Seoul
- 02-738-8397; ystae@chol.com

HAEDONG TAEKWONDO CENTER
- ₩53,000 per lesson; ₩90,000 per month
* Fees include uniform and *gyeokpa* lessons.
* Free admission to taekwondo contests
- Hannam-dong, Yongsan-gu, Seoul
- 02-794-1462; haedong57@yahoo.co.kr

Bird-watching

Korea is one of the greatest countries to visit in East Asia for both serious and casual bird-watchers with its varied landscape, good roads signposted in English, excellent but cheap public transportation and a rapidly-expanding network of local groups interested in promoting green tourism. The best bird-watching is generally in mid-winter, when many geese and ducks escape from the severe temperatures in the north or during the main migration seasons from April to May and September to November. With some of the world's widest and most extensive tidal-flats (totaling 280,000 ha — equivalent to 10 km in width along the entire west coast) together with one of the world's steepest tidal ranges (up to 10 m at Incheon), Korea offers fantastic shore bird-watching. Some 400 bird species have been spotted in Korea over the last decade. The detailed list, with Latin names and regions they are spotted, can be found at www.tour2korea.com (click on Sightseeing → Theme Tours → Birdwatching Tours).

HANGANG RIVER IN SEOUL, BIRD SANCTUARY ON BAMSEOM ISLET |한강, 밤섬

A wonderful place to watch some common species of ducks and raptors during the winter using high-powered binoculars set up for the public free of charge at Citizens' Park in Yeouido.
①: Hangang Citizen's Park in Yeouido, Seoul
Ⓣ: ⓜ Yeouinaru Station, Line 5. Walk 15 min. toward Seogang Bridge. ⓚ Or from Yoido Full Gospel Church, walk 3 min. toward the Hangang River.

GANGHWADO ISLAND, INCHEON |강화도

One of Korea's premier birding spots is located about 1 hour northwest of Seoul. Birding is great all year long, especially from August to May. According to experts, Ganghwado rivals or even exceeds the famous birders' destination of Beidaihe, China, for the ease of access and the

UNFORGETTABLE MEMORIES

opportunity to see East Asia's great birds.

Bird-watching Places
• Tidelands spread from Seondu-ri to Janghwa-ri (The southern point of the island) and the reed beds, rice fields and water courses surrounding them.
• Salt flats and the shore on Seongmodo Island
• Mt. Manisan, Bomunsa Temple, etc.

YEONGJONGDO ISLAND |영종도
A small bay in Unnam-ri on the south coast of Yeongjongdo Island is said to be the best shore bird high-tide roost in the northwest part of the country.
Ⓣ: 🚌 From Dongincheon Station, buses to Wolmido Island depart every 10 min.
📞 032-746-6321/2 ⛴ From Wolmido wharf, ferries to Yeongjongdo Island leave every 30 min. Yongju Ferry 📞 032-762-8880/2. ⓗ: 07:00 – 21:00

IRON TRIANGLE BATTLEFIELD IN CHEORWON, GANGWON-DO |철의삼각지
Located within the DMZ is a paradise for migratory birds because it has been uninhabited by humans for the past 50 years. It is visited by cranes, ash cranes and eagles.
Ⓣ: 🚌 From Sincheorwon or Dongsong, take a bus to Goseokjeong Pavilion (20 min).
📞 033-254-0101

SEOSAN RECLAMATION LAKES AND CHEONSUMAN BAY |서산호, 천수만
Situated about 3 hours from Seoul by Seohaean Expressway, this 17,000-ha area is the most important place for wildfowl nationwide. In the winter, raptors, Oriental White Storks and White Spoonbills are all present and relatively easy to see, peaking at 300,000 waterfowl in November on the two main lakes (simplistically referred to as Seosan Reclamation Lakes A and B).
Ⓣ: 🚌 From Nambu Bus Terminal in Seoul to Seosan (every 10 min., 1 hr., 40 min.).
Or 🚌 from Seosan Bus Terminal, buses to Cheonsuman Bay operate all day (40 min.).

EULSUKDO ISLAND (NAKDONGGANG RIVER) |을숙도
Although degraded and still threatened by reclamation, Eulsukdo Island or Nakdonggang Estuary, just west of Busan, is still one of the most impressive birding areas in Korea and is a must for birdwatchers.
Ⓣ: 🚇 From Hadan Station, Busan Subway Line 1, 🚌 No. 10 or 15.

GEUMGANG RIVER AND ESTUARY |금강하구
Towards the southwest, near the city of Gunsan, lies the best shore bird and estuarine birdwatching in South Korea at the Geumgang Estuary and the Mangyeonggang-Dongjingang Estuaries (the Saemangeum area). Bird-watching is at its peak here from August to May.
Ⓣ: 🚌 From Seocheon, take a bus to Geumgang River and Estuary (every 30 min., 25 min.); or 🚌 from Gunsan Bus Terminal, take a bus to Janghang or Seocheon. Get off at the Geumgang Estuary (15 min.).

Useful Web sites for bird-watching in Korea
www.tour2korea.com; www.wbkenglish.com;
www.koreabirding.com;
http://user.chollian.net/~viewbox

BIRD-WATCHING

Festivals

Many festivals are held annually in Korea, promoting everything from agricultural products and cuisine to crafts and arts.
Festivals introduced here are most significant in terms of scale and the number of participants. You will make wonderful discoveries and be enlightened and inspired when you visit these festivals.

APRIL

LOTUS LANTERN FESTIVAL
Ⓛ: Seoul Ⓘ: Buddha's Birthday Celebration Committee ☎ 02-2011-1747; www.llf.or.kr
This festival commemorates Buddha's birthday. Over 100,000 lotus lanterns parade the streets of Jongno in Seoul, creating a continuous wave of harmony and unity.

KOREAN TRADITIONAL DRINK AND CAKE FESTIVAL
Ⓛ: Gyeongju, Gyeongsangbuk-do Ⓘ: Tourism Promotion Division, Gyeongju City Hall ☎ 054-779-6396
The festival displays a variety of rice cakes and fermented drinks. Anyone interested can experience making and partaking in them.

SEOUL INTERNATIONAL FOOD EXPO (SIFE)
Ⓛ: Seoul Ⓘ: Korea Cooks Association ☎ 02-720-1815; www.sife.co.kr
It includes the Seoul International Food Festival and Culinary Competition. Visitors can enjoy traditional Korean cuisine from different parts of Korea.

JEONJU INTERNATIONAL FILM FESTIVAL
Ⓛ: Jeonju, Jeollanam-do Ⓘ: Jeonju International Film Festival Organizing Committee ☎ 063-288-5433, 02-2285-0562/3; 📠 063-288-5411; www.jiff.or.kr
The 3rd international film festival in Korea after Busan and Bucheon, this festival features mainly alternative films, digital films, and Asian independent films.

MAY

HI SEOUL FESTIVAL
Ⓛ: Seoul Ⓘ: Culture Department, Seoul City Hall ☎ 02-3707-9471; www.hiseoulfest.org
The Hi Seoul Festival is a major festival of Seoul that is held every May. For 10 days, Koreans and foreign residents in Seoul gather at Seoul Plaza in front of City Hall and Gwanghwamun Gate to take part in a cultural festival that showcases a variety of attractions to please every one in this dynamic city.

INSA-DONG TRADITIONAL CULTURAL FESTIVAL
Ⓛ: Seoul Ⓘ: Insa Traditional Culture Preservation Association ☎ 02-737-7890/1
Experience a traditional Korean festival in the most traditional area in Seoul with a masquerade, special performances and a Korean food contest.

MYSTIC SEA ROAD FESTIVAL
Ⓛ: Jindo and Modo Island, Jeollanam-do
Ⓘ: ☎ 061-544-0151 / 540-3125 📠 061-540-3577; http://tour.jindo.go.kr

Hi Seoul Festival

UNFORGETTABLE MEMORIES

The festival is held every year when the tide drops 6–7 m to part the sea between Jindo and Modo Islands. It is referred to as "Moses' Miracle."

HAMPYEONG BUTTERFLY FESTIVAL
ⓛ: Hampyeong, Jeollanam-do ⓘ: ☏ 061-320-3224 061-320-3466; www.inabi.or.kr
This festival is a celebration of the wonders of nature with live butterflies and insects. It features butterfly exhibits, a study of the magnificent flight of butterflies, and butterfly and insect specimens.

DAEGU YANGNYEONGSI HERB MEDICINE FESTIVAL
ⓛ: Daegu ⓘ: ☏ 053-253-4724 053-257-1950; www.herbmart.or.kr
This festival is designed to maintain the Oriental medicine market and promote herbal medicine. Highlights include an herb chopping contest, free medical checkups and an exhibition of Oriental medicinal materials.

CHUNCHEON INTERNATIONAL MIME FESTIVAL
ⓛ: Chuncheon, Gangwon-do ⓘ: ☏ 033-242-0585 033-242-0584; www.mimefestival.com
As a cultural and artistic festival combining pure dramatic arts in a festive atmosphere, the Chuncheon International Mime Festival offers something for everyone. A variety of performances are held by mime theatre groups from numerous countries and *Dokkaebi Nanjang* "goblin plays" are performed on weekends on Wido Island, also called Goseumdochi (hedgehog) Island because its shape resembles a hedgehog.

Visitors will surely remember the "goblin plays" in which natives and tourists join the performance onstage, which is actually 330,000 m² of green lawn.

HANSAN RAMIE FABRIC FESTIVAL
ⓛ: Seocheon-gun, Chungcheongnam-do ⓘ: ☏ 041-950-4224 041-950-4459
Pearly white and gracious in appearance, ramie fabric has been appreciated as the best fabric for summer wear. Highlights are the daybreak ramie market, ramie fashion show, ramie weaving demonstration and Hansan *mosi* (ramie) design contest.

HADONG MOUNTAIN DEW TEA FESTIVAL
ⓘ: Hadong-gun Office ☏ 055-880-2371; www.hadong.go.kr
Hadong tea undergoes nine painstaking repetitious cycles of meticulous hand picking, rubbing and drying. Join the leaf picking and tea sampling.

JUNE
WORLD TAEKWONDO HWARANG FESTIVAL
ⓛ: Jincheon, Chungcheongbuk-do ⓘ: ☏ 043-539-3930 043-539-3949; barru@jincheon.go.kr
A gathering of taekwondo enthusiasts will be held in an area known as the center of ancient history and the original site of the *hwarang* and *taekwon* spirit. Anyone who practices taekwondo is invited to join national athletes from around the world in this festival to strengthen unity and friendship and to appreciate the cultural value of taekwondo.

Chuncheon International Mime Festival

Hansan Ramie Fabric Festival

Boryeong Mud Festival

Muju Firefly Festival

JULY
BORYEONG MUD FESTIVAL
📞: Boryeong, Chungcheongnam-do ☎: 041-930-3541~2 📠 041-930-3757; www.mudfestival.or.kr

Daecheon Beach, boasting the longest coastline on Korea's west coast, holds an annual mud festival featuring varied and colorful programs. The black-colored mud is abundant along the clean and pure beach, and it is rich in minerals that contain germanium. This mud is well known for protecting skin and curing various skin diseases.
With its fun-filled programs, the Boryeong Mud Festival will add more enjoyment by offering visitors opportunities to receive facials and massages with pure, well-refined sea mud. The festival is sure to provide a fantastic opportunity with both for fun and relaxation for this summer's vacationers.

GANGJIN CELADON CULTURAL FESTIVAL
📞: Gangjin, Jeollanam-do ☎: 061-430-3223 📠 061-430-3577; www.gangjin.go.kr

Thanks to its favorable geographical location bordering the sea, mild climate, abundant clay and firewood,
Gangjin served as the home of Korea's celadon culture, which flourished for 500 years during the Goryeo Dynasty.
The Gangjin Celadon Cultural Festival began in 1996 with the goals of promoting celadon, an important traditional heritage of Korea, at home and abroad, thereby promoting the image of Gangjin as a celadon village as well as making celadon more familiar to the public.
The festival will offer visitors a great opportunity to enjoy, and learn about one of Korea's most glorious cultural heritages.

PUCHON* INTERNATIONAL FANTASTIC FILM FESTIVAL
📞: Bucheon, Kyeonggi-do ☎: PiFan Office 032-322-9225; www.pifan.com

PiFan is an independent film festival that offers an alternative to commercial movies. Films that are imaginative and future-oriented take center stage at this annual gala. PiFan has become a venue to introduce international fantasy films to Korean movie fans as well as a means to introduce Korean movies to foreign film critics. The festival also promotes the production of fantasy films in Korea and assists in their distribution.

*Puchon is the former spelling for Bucheon

AUGUST
MUJU FIREFLY FESTIVAL
📞: Muju, Jeollabuk-do ☎: 063-320-2128, 063-320-2133; www.firefly.or.kr

The Muju Firefly Festival is an environment-friendly festival that reminds us of the importance of nature and eco-system that are disappearing at a fast pace from our neighborhood due to rapid urbanization. Experiencing the fascinating sight of fireflies on scorching summer nights, visitors will become aware of the concept and spirit of "ecotopia," where human and nature coexist.

SEPTEMBER
SEOGWIPO CHILSIMNI FESTIVAL
📞: Seogwipo, Jejudo Island ☎: 064-735-3542 📠 064-735-3541; www.infojeju.com

Jejudo's comprehensive festival in which people can experience the beautiful island's unique lifestyle and culture. It features diverse art and cultural programs, most notably the Seogwipo Chilsimni parade, as well as a variety of hands-on activities.

Seoul Drum Festival

Puchon International Fantastic Film Festival

GEUMSAN INSAM FESTIVAL
ⓛ: Geumsan, Chungcheongnam-do
ⓘ: ☎ 041-750-2391 ☒ 041-750-2379; http://insamfestival.co.kr

This festival features a cornucopia of aromatic ginseng products and other medicinal herbs and health foods sold at good prices.

HYOSEOK CULTURAL FESTIVAL
ⓛ: Pyeongchang, Gangwon-do
ⓘ: ☎ 033-335-2323 ☒ 033-330-2592; www.happy700.or.kr, www.bongpyong.co.kr

The Bongpyeong region is known as a major producer of buckwheat as well as the backdrop of Lee Hyo-seok's famous novel *When the Buckwheat Blossoms*. Every September, the white buckwheat flower-filled region comes to life with a festival honoring the renowned author. Aside from the various performances and cultural events, delicious and healthy buckwheat dishes are offered to festival goers.

OCTOBER
SEOUL DRUM FESTIVAL
ⓛ: Seoul ⓘ: Festival Organizing Committee ☎ 02-399-1607; www.drumfestival.org

An international arts festival centered on percussion performances, the Seoul Drum Festival is an annual event held in early October in the Gwanghwamun area.

ANDONG INTERNATIONAL MASK DANCE FESTIVAL
ⓛ: Andong, Gyeongsangbuk-do
ⓘ: ☎ 054-851-6393/054-841-6398 ☒ 054-851-6399/852-9230; www.maskdance.com

The Andong Mask Dance Festival will be held in Andong, the home of Korea's Confucian culture. This year's festival will also feature refined domestic and international mask dance performances. At Hahoe Village, which has been designated as one of Korea's Cultural Heritages, visitors will not only be able to enjoy the spectacle of mask dance performances in the pine tree forests, but also the splendid *Hahoe Seonyujulbulnori*, the highlight of Korea's traditional fireworks, which will be featured across the night sky, leaving an unforgettable impression on the memories of visitors.

CHUNGJU WORLD MARTIAL ARTS FESTIVAL
ⓛ: Chungju, Chungcheongbuk-do ⓘ: ☎ 043-850-5171/4 ☒ 043-850-5178; www.martialarts.or.kr

With an aim to succeed and further develop Taekkyon, Korean ancient martial art designated as an Important Intangible Cultural Heritage No. 76, the Chungju Martial Arts Festival was conceived in 1998 when the martial arts contest, to which domestic martial groups were invited, was held. In 2000, the name was changed to Chungju World Martial Arts Festival. Since then, the festival has staged a variety of martial arts performances from around the world, which were a hit among tourists. With the participation of more than 30 international martial arts groups, a demonstration on the origin of martial arts as well as other martial arts demonstrations will be staged. It also features arms exhibitions, serving

Busan Jagalchi Festival

Jinju Namgang Lantern Festival

as an on-site learning place for students.

GIMJE HORIZON FESTIVAL
Ⓛ: Gimje, Jeollabuk-do Ⓘ: ☏ 063-540-3324
✉ 063-540-3454; www.egimje.net

The Gimje Horizon Festival is Korea's only agricultural culture festival. It serves as an excellent educational site where visitors can experience a variety of traditional rural Korean culture and customs. Through experiencing agrarian culture, the festival will offer both local people and foreigners a chance to truly appreciate nature. It will also provide foreigners with an opportunity to understand and experience Korea's family-oriented traditional culture and Koreans' respect for humanity, which has been deeply embedded in Korean customs.

YANGYANG PINE MUSHROOM FESTIVAL
Ⓛ: Yangyang, Gangwon-do Ⓘ: ☏ 033-673-0114/670-2723 ✉ 033-670-2733; www.yangyang-gun.gangwon.kr/festival

The Yangyang Pine Mushroom Festival will be held in Yangyang, Korea's representative pine mushroom production site. During the festival, visitors can pick *song-i* (pine mushrooms), accompanied by a pine mushroom expert. During the trip, they can take a stroll and enjoy the clean air of the fresh pine tree forests and the spectacular natural landscape. They can also take part in a homestay program at pine mushroom farms where people can experience Korea's countryside in autumn. There is also a half marathon in which participants run along roads full of pine mushrooms along the Namdaecheon Stream surrounded by thick forests.

Takjangsanori, one of Yangyang's traditional folk plays, is also featured during the festival.

JINJU NAMGANG LANTERN FESTIVAL
Ⓛ: Jinju, Gyeongsangnam-do Ⓘ: ☏ 055-749-5072 ✉ 055-749-2807

The tradition of floating lanterns on the Namgang River in Jinju dates back to the 1592 Japanese invasion of Korea. Visitors can enjoy events such as hanging wishing lanterns, the World Lantern Exhibition, and fireworks on the river every day during the festival.

BUSAN JAGALCHI FESTIVAL
Ⓛ: Busan Ⓘ: ☏ 051-243-9363 ✉ 051-254-6646

The Busan Jagalchi Festival is Korea's largest seafood festival held in October every year at Jagalchi Market, one of Busan's most famous places, and Nampo-dong, located in the center of Busan. The festival features many things to see, reenacting traditional fishing folk culture such as *Yongwangje* (sea king ritual) and *Manseonje* (a ritual praying for a good catch) as well as various seafood-related hands-on programs that visitors can participate in and enjoy. There are also free cruises around Taejongdae and Songdo Island as well as tours of Jagalchi Fish Market, where fresh raw fish and other seafood can be purchased at discounted prices.

NANGYE TRADITIONAL KOREAN MUSIC FESTIVAL
Ⓛ: Yeongdong, Chungcheongbuk-do
Ⓘ: ☏ 043-740-3223 ✉ 043-740-3209; http://nangye.yd21.go.kr

The Nangye Traditional Music Festival is aimed at commemorating Nangye (pen name) Park Yeon, one of the three greatest musicians in Korea who lived during the Joseon Dynasty. The festival

Pusan International Film Festival

Gwangju Kimchi Festival

promotes and futher develops traditional Korean classical music. By visiting the festival, you can see and enjoy a number of cultural properties that have been handed down over the generations.

ICHEON RICE CULTURAL FESTIVAL
Ⓛ: Icheon, Gyeonggi-do Ⓘ: ☏ 031-644-2606/7 🖨 031-644-2619; www.ricefestival.or.kr

Rice is the symbol of Icheon City and the autumn rice harvest is the highlight of Korea's agrarian culture. During the festival, farmers who work in the rice fields and urbanites who leave city life behind for a rest unite and celebrate the good harvest.

PUSAN INTERNATIONAL FILM FESTIVAL
Ⓛ: Busan Ⓘ: PIFF Organizing Committee ☏ 051-747-3010; www.piff.org

Despite its short history, the Pusan* International Film Festival (PIFF) has grown into one of the most influential film festivals in Asia, filling Busan with famous film makers, actors, critics, fans and huge audiences. PIFF is primarity focused on Asian films, but films are screened from all over the world, including North America and Europe. This enables movie fans to gain a comprehensive perspective of all the major trends. The films are screened at numerous theaters in the Nampo-dong Street area, at the Cinema Hall in Millak-dong, and on a giant outdoor screen in Suyeongman Bay.

* Pusan is the former spelling for Busan.

NAMDO FOOD FESTIVAL
Ⓛ: Seogwipo, Jejudo Island Ⓘ: Tourism Promotion Division, Jeollanam-do Provincial Government ☏ 061-286-5222

In the fortress town is held a huge food festival featuring hundreds of traditional delicacies of Jeollanam-do Province, the nation's epicurean home. A culinary contest, food exhibition and various events add to the festive mood.

GWANGJU KIMCHI FESTIVAL
Ⓛ: Gwangju Ⓘ: Tourism Department, Gwangju City Hall ☏ 062-613-3576/3578; www.kimchi.gwangju.kr

This festival celebrates everything about kimchi. Outstanding kimchi chefs and curious visitors attend to witness kimchi culture, and there are demonstrations for visitors on how to make kimchi and a kimchi culinary contest.

NOVEMBER
FOOD KOREA
Ⓛ: Seoul Ⓘ: Exhibition & Convention Team, Agricultural and Fishery Marketing Corporation ☏ 02-6300-1492/7; www.foodexkorea.com

Food Korea is a major international food show in Korea with well-known brands from around the world. A variety of events will introduce traditional but new Korean food and culture.

BUSAN INTERNATIONAL SEAFOOD & FISHERIES EXPOSITION (BUSAN SEAFOOD EXPO)
Ⓛ: Busan Ⓘ: ☏ 051-852-5470~3 www.busanseafoodexpo.com

It is a chance to discover new seafood-related technology, products, trends and information from all over the world. There are a variety of events, including a sliced-raw fish competition and sampling party, sales events, stuffed seafood exhibition, and folk performances from participating countries.

Food

Korean cuisine is made up of unique aromas and tastes. In addition to being highly nutritious, Korean food is also low in calories, being chiefly made of a wide variety of vegetables. Seasonings include garlic, red pepper, scallions, soy sauce, fermented bean paste, ginger and sesame oil. Visitors cannot really say they have been to Korea if they have not tasted kimchi, the internationally famous spicy fermented cabbage dish. Koreans eat it at almost every meal. There are actually dozens of varieties of kimchi, including some that are not spicy, but some are very pungent indeed.
Dishes more familiar to the Western palate are *galbi* and *bulgogi*.
These two meat dishes, either pork or beef, are always served at Korean dinner parties. *Galbi* is ribs; *bulgogi* is thin strips of marinated grilled meat. Neither is particularly spicy and, if cooked at your table over a charcoal fire, it resembles a barbecue. Other popular Korean dishes are *bibimbap* (a mixture of rice, vegetables, egg and chili sauce), *doenjangjjigae* (a thick soup made from fermented bean paste and vegetables, eaten with rice), *naengmyeon* (chewy noodles in a cold broth, popular in summer) and *samgyetang* (stewed whole chicken stuffed with rice and ginseng).

Table Setting and Manners | FOOD

Korean families usually eat rice, soup and three to four side dishes including the sine qua non, kimchi. From each person's left are arranged rice, soup, spoon and chopsticks, while stews and side dishes are placed in the center to be shared by all members.
Koreans use a spoon to eat rice, soup and stews and chopsticks for rather dry side dishes, but the spoon and chopsticks are not used simultaneously. Koreans also do not hold their bowls and plates while eating. When the meal is over, the spoon and chopsticks are placed on the table.
Koreans generally believe that sharing food from one bowl makes a relationship closer. Still, one who does not wish to share the one-for-all dish can ask the host for an individual bowl or plate. Today, many Korean restaurants automatically provide individual bowls and plates. In the old days, talking was not allowed at the dinner table but eating etiquette has become more liberal.

and gruel and the main courses include dishes mixed with seasonings either grilled, boiled, steamed, fried or salted.
Hot pots are also included and after the meal, traditional punches such as *sikhye* (sweet rice punch) or *sujeonggwa* (cinnamon-persimmon punch) and other desserts may be served.

Hanjeongsik

Kimchi

Hanjeongsik (Korean Set Meal) | 한정식 | FOOD

Hanjeongsik is a full-course Korean meal with many savory side dishes. The *hanjeongsik* tradition originated with the banquets served in the royal palaces or the homes of aristocrats. Usually, the course starts with a cold appetizer

UNFORGETTABLE MEMORIES

The dishes served in the *hanjeongsik* vary according to the season or region.

Kimchi | 김치 — FOOD

Kimchi is a fermented vegetable dish that can be stored for a long time. In the past, Koreans used to prepare it as a substitute for fresh vegetables during the winter months. Today, housewives still prepare a large amount of winter kimchi sometime from late November through early December. This nationwide annual event is called *gimjang*. The introduction of red pepper to Korea from Europe through Japan in the 17th century brought a major innovation to kimchi and the Korean diet in general.

There are now more than 160 kimchi varieties differentiated by region and ingredients, most of them quite spicy. Kimchi is the basic side dish at every Korean meal; it is also an ingredient in other popular dishes such as kimchi stew, kimchi pancakes, kimchi fried rice and kimchi *ramyeon* (ramen noodles). Kimchi is being widely used in various ways to create new tastes and flavors. These days, kimchi is gaining popularity worldwide for its nutritional value and disease-prevention effects.

Food for Special Occasions — FOOD

In the agricultural society of the past, Koreans were very attentive to the change of the seasons. For each month, the people developed unique folk customs to celebrate and commemorate the change of time and enjoyed special dishes made of seasonal products. Among numerous seasonal occasions, several are still widely observed by the general public.

SEOLLAL (LUNAR NEW YEAR'S DAY, JANUARY 29, 2006) | 설날

On the first day of the Lunar New Year, Koreans hold a memorial service for their ancestors and perform *sebae* (a formal bow of respect to their elders as a New Year's greeting). The most common food for this day is *tteokguk* (rice cake soup). It is said that one cannot become a year older without eating a bowl of *tteokguk* on Lunar New Year's Day.

JEONGWOL DAEBOREUM (1ST FULL MOON DAY, FEBRUARY 12, 2006) | 정월대보름

The 1st full moon day of the Lunar New Year is the time to perform rites to avert disasters and bad luck. The most typical dishes for this day are *ogokbap* (boiled rice with five grains: rice, red bean, kidney bean and two kinds of millet) and *mugeun namul* (9 to 12 dried vegetable dishes such as bracken fern, radish leaves, bellflower roots and mushrooms). At dawn on *Jeongwol Daeboreum*, people crack walnuts, chestnuts or peanuts and sip rice wine, praying for good health for the whole year.

SAMBOK (THREE DAYS TO MARK THE HOTTEST PERIOD OF SUMMER) | 삼복

The three days of *Chobok* (July 20, 2006), *Jungbok* (July 30, 2006), and *Malbok* (August 9,

Tteokguk

Namul assortment

2006) are called *sambok* and they mark the beginning, middle and end of the lunar calendar's traditional hottest periods of summer. Since the old days, people would eat hot meat dishes on these days to boost their stamina. A typical food for *sambok* is *samgyetang* (a whole chicken stuffed with sticky rice, ginseng, jujubes and garlic that is seasoned with salt and pepper).

CHUSEOK (KOREAN THANKSGIVING DAY, OCTOBER 6, 2006) | 추석

Chuseok and *Seollal* are the two biggest holidays in Korea. On *Chuseok*, people visit ancestral graves to thank their ancestors for a good harvest and the well-being of the family. Special foods for *Chuseok* are *songpyeon* (crescent-shaped rice cakes) and *torantang* (taro soup). *Songpyeon* is a rice cake that is filled with either red bean, chestnut, jujube or sweetened sesame seeds and steamed on a bed of pine needles. Along with newly picked fruits, these foods are presented at the altar for the ancestral memorial service.

DONGJI (WINTER SOLSTICE, DECEMBER 22, 2006) | 동지

Dongji is the shortest day of the year. On *Dongji*, Koreans eat *patjuk* (red bean porridge with rice balls). Since ancient times, it was believed that red beans drove away evil spirits and prevented bad luck.

Traditional Snacks   FOOD

Koreans have developed many traditional sweets and beverages that make nutritious snacks and delicious desserts.

HANGWA (TRADITIONAL SWEETS AND COOKIES) | 한과

Hangwa is appreciated for its artistic and decorative colors and patterns as well as for its pleasantly sweet taste. Often accompanied by traditional beverages, it is regarded as a health snack and classy dessert. Beautifully packaged baskets or boxes of *hangwa* also make excellent gifts that are especially appropriate for the elderly. They are available at shops specializing in traditional cakes and sweets and at special sections in department stores.

TTEOK (TRADITIONAL RICE CAKE) | 떡

Tteok is the traditional Korean cake made of rice powder. Koreans prepare it for festive occasions such as birthdays and weddings as well as for ancestral memorial services. They also have it on seasonal occasions such as *Seollal* (Lunar New Year's Day) and *Chuseok* (Korean Thanksgiving Day). It is a natural and healthy snack.

HWACHAE (TRADITIONAL COLD BEVERAGE) | 화채

Traditional cold beverages are called *hwachae*. They are usually made with fruits or grains and water sweetened by either sugar or honey or flavored and colored by *omija* (fruit of the "five-taste" tree, Schisandra chinensis).
There are also *hwachae* made from Oriental medicinal foods such as azalea or pine pollen.

Traditional Korean Tea   FOOD

Green tea was first introduced to Korea during the reign of Queen Seondeok (r. 632 – 647) of the

TEA CEREMONY FOR OVERSEAS VISITORS

	Yejiwon Cultural Institute	Panyaro Institute	Yemyeongwon	Samcheonggak
Program Tuition	1.5 hours (upon request) ₩50,000 (Group of 10 or more)	1.5 hours (upon request) ₩50,000 (Group of 2 or more)	1 hour (upon request) ₩40,000 (Group of 10 or more)	90 minutes ₩50,000
Inquiries	02-2253-2211/2 yejiwon@yejiwon.or.kr	02-763-8486 panyaro@naver.com	02-765-3767 iyemyung@hanmail.net	02-765-3756 www.samcheonggak.or.kr

* Institutes run various types of programs upon request.

Silla Kingdom (57 BC – 935 AD). Tea helps ward off drowsiness and invigorates the mind and body, so Buddhist monks used it as an aid to cultivate their minds. It was during the Goryeo Dynasty (918 – 1392) that Buddhism was at its peak on the peninsula and *dado* (tea ceremony) was developed, a protocol to guide the preparation, serving and drinking of tea. During the Joseon Dynasty (1392 – 1910), when Buddhism was suppressed under the influence of Confucianism, tea drinking declined. Today, it is perceived as a chic and healthy practice. Grains, fruits and medicinal foods are also used in making tea. Popular teas today are *insamcha* (ginseng tea), *nokcha* (green tea), *yujacha* (citron tea), *daechucha* (jujube tea), *saenggangcha* (ginger tea), *yulmucha* (job's tears tea), *omijacha* ("five-taste" tea from the fruit of Schisandra chinensis), and *gugijacha* (Chinese matrimony vine tea). At home, grain teas such as *boricha* (roast barley tea), *oksusucha* (roast corn tea) and *gyeolmyeongjacha* (tea from the fruit of C. obtusifolia) are often served cold in place of water.

Traditional Liquors and Wines

Traditional Korean drinks are made chiefly from rice, grains or sweet potatoes with kneaded wheat malt. They are classified according to purity, percentage of alcohol contained, whether or not they are distilled, and materials used. There are largely five types: *yakju* (refined pure liquor fermented from rice), *soju* (distilled liquor), *takju* (thick, unrefined liquor fermented from grains), fruit wines and medicinal wines from various seeds and roots. Each type has dozens of varieties. The famous *cheongju* is a *yakju* and popular *makgeolli* is a *takju*. Acacia, *maesil* plum, Chinese quince, cherry, pine fruits and pomegranate are some popular fruit wines. *Insamju* is a representative example of medicinal wine that is made from ginseng.

Street Food

Having a meal in a fancy restaurant is a great experience, but tasting all of the delicious and inexpensive food on the streets is also an opportunity for discovery.
Sausages, fish cakes, spicy rice cake dishes, tempura and ice cream are just a few of the many foods available at a very low cost.

POJANGMACHA (COVERED WAGON) | 포장마차
This is a place where you can soothe your hunger pangs for just ₩2,000 and get a variety of food including spicy rice cake dishes, fried foods and sausages. The streets around Jongno and universities are lined with these wagons.

TTEOKPPOKKI (SPICY RICE CAKES) | 떡볶이
Tteokppokki is a variation of a traditional dish called *japchae* (made with thinly sliced beef and various vegetables flavored with soy sauce). When red pepper paste arrived on the peninsula, the dish changed into the spicy version now known as *tteokppokki*.
One portion costs about ₩2,000 and is filling enough to substitute for a meal.

EOMUK (SKEWERED FISH CAKES) | 어묵
Fish cakes are made from pureed fish combined with minced vegetables and flour, which is then rolled onto long skewers and deep-fried.
Lines of eager patrons form at street stalls to see the fish cakes being made fresh.
Other than fish cakes, there are more snacks available on skewers. Skewered hot dogs and chicken basted with spicy-sweet sauce are popular and another much-loved steady seller is the Korean-style hotdog, which is a hotdog wrapped in a pastry and deep fried. A skewered delight costs about ₩1,000 to ₩2,000.

Shopping

COEX Mall

Seoul and other major Korean cities offer a wide variety of shopping opportunities such as arcades, department stores, and duty-free shops. However, if you really want to experience the vivid lifestyle of Koreans, why not visit the local markets around the country? They feature the local regions' specialty products. Major department stores are open from 10:30 to 19:30, including Sundays, while smaller shops tend to be open from mid-morning till late evening every day of the week. 24-hour convenience stores are dotted throughout the cities. At midnight, Namdaemun and Dongdaemun Markets in Seoul serve as all-night wholesale districts and you can find many great deals.

SHOPPING IN SEOUL
Shopping Malls

CENTRAL CITY | 센트럴시티
Conveniently connected to Seoul Express Bus Terminal, Central City is a multipurpose leisure complex.
It encompasses a wide range of the latest facilities including the JW Marriott Hotel, a convention center, fitness clubs, Cinus-central theaters, Central Automall, a bookstore and a variety of restaurants and fast food stalls.

①: 02-6282-0114; www.centralcityseoul.co.kr
①: Express Bus Terminal Station, Line 3 (Exit 2) or 7 (Exit 3)

SKY CITY | 스카이 시티
Gimpo Airport boasts Sky City, a new shopping center with entertainment facilities with something for everyone. It is rapidly gaining popularity as a complete collection of shopping facilities, restaurants and cinemas.
The multiplex M Park 9 boasts a runway-style main hall and nine screens with seating for 2,000.

UNFORGETTABLE MEMORIES

Techno Sky City is a large electronics retailer with 700 stores nationwide selling computers, home appliances and much more.
- ☎ 02-6343-3000; www.sky-city.co.kr
- 🚇 Gimpo Airport Station, Line 5

WORLD CUP MALL | 월드컵몰
The Sangam (Seoul) World Cup Stadium that was built for the 2002 FIFA World Cup has an another name, the World Cup Mall, and it is Seoul's representative shopping/entertainment space. The mall contains a large discount market, multi-screen movie theater and over 100 clothing and accessory stores. Shoppers can enjoy a relaxing excursion to the nearby theme parks along the banks of the Hangang River.
- ☎ 02-2128-2002; www.seoulworldcupst.or.kr
- 🚇 Exit 1, 2, 3 of World Cup Stadium Station, Line 6

COEX MALL | 코엑스몰
Under the World Trade Center Seoul, this huge mall (about 12 ha) stretches from Samseong Subway Station to ASEM Tower. Along the underground labyrinth are a variety of amenities and facilities, including Lake Food Court with ethnic restaurants; Event Court for concerts and dramas; Game Champ; Megabox Cineplex; COEX Aquarium, displaying more than 40,000 fish of 600 species and dozens of large sharks; and the Kimchi Field Museum (☎ 02-6002-6456; www.kimchimuseum.or.kr), which contains extensive kimchi displays such as recipes, techniques, etc.
- ☎ 02-6002-5312; www.coexmall.com
- 🚇 Exit 6 of Samseong Station, Line 2
- 🕙 10:00 ~ 20:00 ₳ ₩14,500
- * COEX Aquarium ☎ 02-6002-6200; www.coexaqua.co.kr

SHOPPING IN SEOUL
Department Stores

Aekyung www.aktown.co.kr
Guro 5 (o)-dong, Guro-gu ☎ 02-818-1000
Paldal-gu, Suwon-si ☎ 031-240-1000
Galleria www.galleria.co.kr
Apgujeong-dong, Gangnam-gu ☎ 02-3449-4114
At Seoul Station, Jung-gu ☎ 02-390-4114
Hyundai www.ehyundai.com
Changcheon-dong, Seodaemun-gu
☎ 02-3145-2233
Apgujeong-dong, Gangnam-gu ☎ 02-547-2233
Samseong-dong, Gangnam-gu ☎ 02-552-2233
Cheonho-dong, Gangdong-gu ☎ 02-488-2233
Gireum 3 (sam)-dong, Seongbuk-gu ☎ 02-985-2233
Mok 1 (il)-dong, Yangcheon-gu ☎ 02-2163-2233
Lotte http://dpt.lotteshopping.com
 Sogong-dong, Jung-gu ☎ 02-771-2500
  Yeongdeungpo-dong, Yeongdeungpo-gu
   ☎ 02-2632-2500
   Jeonnong-dong, Dongdaemun-gu
    ☎ 02-966-2500
    Jamsil-dong, Songpa-gu
     ☎ 02-411-2500
     Sanggye 2 (i)-dong, Nowon-gu
      ☎ 02-950-2500
      Bongcheon-dong, Gwanak-gu
       ☎ 02-833-2500
Daechi-dong, Gangnam-gu ☎ 02-531-2500
New Core www.newcore.co.kr
Jamwon-dong, Seocho-gu ☎ 02-530-5000
Shinsegae department.shinsegae.com
Chungmuro 1 (il)-ga, Jung-gu ☎ 02-310-1234
Gireum 3 (sam)-dong, Seongbuk-gu
☎ 02-944-1234
Yeongdeungpo 4 (sa)-ga, Yeongdeungpo-gu
☎ 02-2639-1234
Banpo 1 (il)-dong, Seocho-gu ☎ 02-3479-1234

SHOPPING IN SEOUL
Fashion Outlets

MOK-DONG RODEO STREET | 목동
Here are 150 stores carrying domestic and international brand name clothing. Items in stock are discounted up to 70%, and it is teeming every day of the week with people in their 20s and 30s.
- 🚇 Exit 2 of Mok-dong Station, Line 5

MUNJEONG-DONG FASHION STREET | 문정동
Already a popular haunt with tourists, Munjeong-

dong Fashion Street sells all kinds of clothes from formal wear to sportswear and accessories from over 200 brand name manufacturers along a 300-meter street.

ⓣ: 11:00 – 21:00 ⓣ: 🚶 5-min. walk from 🚇 Exit 1 of Munjeong-dong Station, Line 8

GURO FASHION VALLEY | 구로동

It is unique in that so many of the stores cater to male clientele. Mario Outlet contains some 200 brand name fashion stores for everyone from newborns to adults at large discounts.

ⓘ: Mario Outlet Information Center 📞 02-2109-7000 ⓣ: 🚶 8 min. from 🚇 Exits 1 or 3 of Garibong Station, Line 1 or 7
ⓣ: 10:30 – 20:30

Special Shopping Areas
SHOPPING IN SEOUL

JANGANPYEONG ANTIQUE MARKET | 장안평 고미술상가

In this market of about 100 antique shops, the graceful flavor of ancient arts and crafts is mixed with the faint smell of dust and mold of objects weathered over time. There are also replicas of old objects and new arts and crafts items at very good prices.

ⓣ: 🚶 10 min. from 🚇 Exit 3 of Dapsimni Station on Subway Line 5
ⓒ: The 1st and 3rd Sundays of each month

GYEONGDONG HERBAL MEDICINE MARKET | 경동약재시장

This is Korea's most famous traditional herbal medicine market with over 1,000 shops and stalls. Here you can find herbal clinics, pharmacies, dealers, and various health-related shops and they sell medicinal herbs at prices 25 – 40% lower than other areas by directly dealing with herb growers.

ⓣ: 🚇 Exit 2 of Jegi-dong Station, Line 1
ⓣ: 09:00 – 18:30 (Mon. – Sat.) ⓒ: Some stores are closed on Sundays and holidays.

ART FREE MARKET IN THE HONGIK UNIVERSITY VICINITY | 홍대프리마켓

Every Saturday at the playground area across from the front gate of Hongik University, enterprising young merchants, buyers and browsers blend together indistinguishably. Amateur designers and artists, some who have majored in art and some who have taken it up as a part-time hobby, peddle their one-of-a-kind, distinct creations like accessories, dolls, clothing and everyday items. Weekly art demonstrations featuring glass blowing and other crafts as well as art performances brimming with youthful energy take place along with the Art Free Market.

ⓣ: 🚶 5 min. from 🚇 Exit 6 of Hongik Univ. Station, Line 2
ⓣ: 13:00 – 18:00, every Saturday

YONGSAN ELECTRONICS MARKET | 용산전자상가
This large-scale electronics shopping district has about 3,000 shops selling everything from computer hardware and software to appliances, TVs and audio sets. Prices are 10–30% lower than at regular retail stores.
ⓣ: 🚇 5 min. toward Yongsan Bus Terminal from 🚇 Yongsan Station, Line 1

TECHNO MART | 테크노마트
This enormous mall contains hundreds of stores specializing in electronic and computer-related goods. It is housed in a highrise building with an 11-screen multiplex theater, clothing shops, game rooms, restaurants, Lotte Magnet discount store, and a hall for exhibition and events.
ⓣ: ☎ 02-3424-3000, 0114; www.tm21.co.kr
ⓣ: 🚇 It is connected to Gangbyeon Station on Subway Line 2. ⓗ: Weekdays (10:00 – 20:00), weekends (B1, 1F: 10:00 – 21:00, 2F – 8F: 10:00 – 20:00, 9F: 10:00 – 22:00) ⓒ: National holidays

Traditional Souvenir Shops
SHOPPING IN SEOUL

CULTURAL PROPERTY ARTISANS HALL
ⓣ: ☎ 02-753-4472 ⓣ: floor B1 of the KTO building from 🚇 Exit 5 of Jonggak Station, Line 1 🚶 3 min.

NATIONAL SOUVENIR CENTER IN INSA-DONG
ⓣ: ☎ 02-735-6529; www.souvenir.or.kr
ⓣ: 🚶 7 min. from 🚇 Exit 4 of Jongno 3 (sam)-ga Station, Line 1, 3, or 5 ⓗ: 10:30 – 21:00 except January 1, Lunar New Year's Day and Chuseok

KOREA HOUSE HANDICRAFT SHOP
ⓣ: ☎ 02-2271-1275 ⓣ: 🚶 3 min. from 🚇 Exit 3 of Chungmuro Station, Line 3 or 4
ⓗ: 10:30 – 22:00, 10:30 – 21:00 on Sundays

Popular Buys in Korea
SHOPPING IN SEOUL

CLOTHING
The Korean textile industry has become famous worldwide for a colorful variety of well-made and inexpensive clothing, especially women's and children's wear. Several international high-fashion brands are made in Korea and are available in department stores, but less expensive local brands rival them in quality.
📍 Itaewon, Myeong-dong, Namdaemun and Dongdaemun Markets, Ewha Womans University area, Apgujeong-dong Rodeo Street, Munjeong-dong Fashion Street, Guro-dong Fashion Valley (Digital Fashions)

SPORTSWEAR
Tennis, squash and badminton rackets, soccer and baseball equipment, golf equipment of all kinds, rock climbing gear, and specialized sports clothing are some of the most popular purchases. Sports shoes are also a top item in Korea.
📍 Itaewon, Namdaemun and Dongdaemun Markets, Gukje Market in Busan

---

SHOPPING TIPS
Foreign visitors may be refunded 70–80% of their paid VAT (value-added tax) and SET (special excise tax) at certain retail outlets. For purchases of more than ₩30,000 at outlets with "Tax Free Shopping" or "Tax Refund Shopping" signs, you may pick up your refund in cash at the airport, have it mailed to you or in some cases have it credited to a credit card. Participating retail shops will issue a "VAT Refund Check" or "Korea Refund Check" and you should get a certificate stamp on it at the customs desk when you leave Korea. (You may have to show your purchase to a customs officer, so if you want to pack the items in your checked luggage, get your refund check stamped by showing it to the customs clerk near the airline check-in counter.) The refund can be obtained at the counters named "Global Refund Korea" or "Korea Tax Refund" near the duty-free shops.
ⓣ: Global Refund Korea: ☎ 02-776-2170/1
📧 02-776-2172; www.globalrefund.com
Korea Tax Refund: ☎ 02-539-4178
📧 02-539-4178; korea@korearefund.co.kr

LEATHER AND FUR GOODS
Some of Korea's specialties that are very competitive in the world market are leather and fur. Coats and jackets of the finest leather and furs in the world are available in an array of styles. Except from October through February, they are always sold at highly discounted prices. Belts, attache cases, and wallets in various colors and grains are also a good bargain.
📍 Itaewon, department stores, Namdaemun and Dongdaemun Markets

ANTIQUES AND REPLICAS
Some of the most sought-after antiques are the wooden chests, furniture and white porcelain of the Joseon Dynasty and the internationally renowned blue-jade celadon of the Goryeo Dynasty.
Antique items over 50 years old, including chests, calligraphic works and pottery, are not allowed to be taken out of the country, so if in doubt, check with the Art and Antiques Assessment Office (📞 032-740-2921). High-quality replicas can be found at affordable prices.
📍 Insa-dong, Janganpyeong Antique Market

JEWELRY
Korea is the home of amethyst, which comes in an infinite range of violet from dainty pale to deep and richly captivating. There is also the ever-popular smoky topaz. In elaborate gold settings, these stones form stunning and not-too-expensive high-fashion rings, pendants, earrings and bracelets. The same is true of jade, especially the famous Korean white jade. Korean-made gems and jewelry with native stones, including rubies, are widely available so you can find some nice bargains.
📍 Jongno 3 (sam)-ga and Yeji-dong Jewelry Shopping Shops, Gangnam Jewelry Shopping Center, Namdaemun Market, Iksan Gems and Jewelry Center in Jeollabuk-do Province, Oksanga in Chuncheon

GINSENG
Korean ginseng is recognized worldwide as the best with the greatest efficacy as an ancient tonic elixir and stamina builder. It has been shown to remove toxic matter from blood, invigorate digestion, counteract cancer-causing free radicals and help the body maintain homeostasis. Fresh, dried and powdered roots as well as concentrated extract and granule tea forms are widely available.
📍 Gyeongdong Herbal Medicinal Market, Namdaemun Market, ginseng wholesale centers and markets in Geumsan, Ganghwa, Daegu and Punggi.

FOLK ARTS AND CRAFTS
Dolls in splendid traditional costumes, fans, wooden masks, delicate and colorful embroidery, painted wedding ducks, kites, intricate mother-of-pearl lacquerware, and graceful ceramic pieces reflecting traditional design depict the people's joy, anger, sorrow and humor in exquisite articles for everyday use.
📍 Traditional souvenir shops in Seoul, Itaewon, Namdaemun Market, Janganpyeong Antique Market, Gyeongju Folk Craft Village

TRADITIONAL LIQUORS AND TEAS
Traditional Korean alcoholic drinks are largely classified in five categories: *yakju* (refined pure liquor), *soju* (distilled liquor), *takju* (thick, unrefined liquor), fruit wines and medicinal wines.
Famous traditional liquors are *munbaeju* (crab apple wine), *dugyeonju* (azalea wine), Gyeongju *beopju* (sticky rice wine), ginseng wine and Andong *soju*.
Traditional teas include ginseng tea, green tea, *ssanghwa* tonic tea, ginger tea, jujube tea and citron tea. *Jakseolcha* (new tea leaves gathered in the spring) is a delicacy.
Sikhye (a sweet drink made with rice malt) and *sujeonggwa* (a cinnamon-flavored punch) are refreshing drinks. Korean teas are sold in dried leaf, tea bag and powdered forms.
📍 Duty-free shops, department stores, shopping arcades, Namdaemun Market

KIMCHI AND OTHER FOODS
Kimchi is a fermented vegetable dish that is a must at every meal.
Kimchi is rapidly gaining public favor overseas as a health food providing bacteria culture that aids digestion and helps prevent disease.
Food items often given as gifts include various types of kimchi, baked laver, seafood fermented in salt, packed *galbi* (ribs), *gochujang* (red pepper paste), and dried *songi* (pine mushrooms) and other mushrooms.
Beautifully packaged baskets or boxes of *hangwa* (traditional sweets and cookies) will also make excellent gifts for your family.
📍 Duty-free shops, department stores, souvenir shops

DUTY-FREE SHOPS

Seoul
Dong Wha DFS www.dutyfree24.com
211-1 Sejongno, Jongno-gu ☎ 02-399-3270
Shilla www.dfskorea.com
202 Jangchung-dong 2 (i)-ga, Jung-gu ☎ 02-2230-3662
Lotte Hotel
10th Fl., Lotte Department Store, 1 Sogong-dong, Jung-gu
☎ 02-759-7586/8
Lotte World
40-1 Jamsil-dong, Songpa-gu ☎ 02-419-7000
SKM
159 Samseong-dong, Gangnam-gu ☎ 02-3484-9600;
www.skm.co.kr
Sheraton Walker Hill Hotel
21 Gwangjang-dong, Gwangjin-gu ☎ 02-450-6370;
www.walkerhill.co.kr

Incheon
Duty Free Korea
Inside Incheon Int'l Airport, managed by the KTO
☎ 032-743-2000
Inside Incheon Int'l Passenger Terminal, managed by the KTO ☎ 032-891-2221
Lotte Duty Free
Inside Incheon Int'l Airport ☎ 032-743-7700
Ak Duty Free
Inside Incheon Int'l Airport ☎ 032-743-2400; www.ak-dfs.com
DFS Seoul Limited
Inside Incheon Int'l Airport ☎ 032-743-3401/2

Busan
Duty Free Korea
Inside Gimhae Int'l Airport, managed by the KTO

☎ 051-973-1101
Inside Busan Int'l Passenger Terminal, managed by the KTO ☎ 051-469-7301
Paradise Duty Free Shop
1128-78 Jung-dong, Haeundae-gu ☎ 051-743-0181
Lotte
503-15 Bujeon-dong, Busanjin-gu ☎ 051-810-3880

Cheongju
Duty Free Korea
Inside Cheongju Int'l Airport, managed by the KTO
☎ 043-218-5533

Jeju-do
Lotte
2812-4 Saekdal-dong, Seogwipo ☎ 064-731-4450
Shilla
252-20 Yeon-dong, Jeju ☎ 064-735-5577
JDC
Inside Jeju Int'l Airport ☎ 064-740-9999
Inside Jeju Int'l Passenger Terminal ☎ 064-740-9939
* Koreans and overseas visitors to Jejudo Island are allowed to shop at JDC Duty Free shops.

Other Areas
Duty Free Korea
Pyeongtaek: Inside Pyeongtaek Int'l Passenger Terminal, managed by the KTO ☎ 031-683-8367
Sokcho: Inside Sokcho Int'l Passenger Terminal, managed by the KTO ☎ 033-635-6180
Gunsan: Inside Gunsan Int'l Passenger Terminal, managed by the KTO ☎ 063-471-7130

Entertainment

Korea's lively entertainment scene successfully blends traditional culture with the ever-increasing influences of foreign countries.
There are many choices from night clubs to classical concerts to casinos. Popular places for an evening out are the Myeong-dong, Itaewon and Apgujeong-dong districts.

Nightlife Zones In Seoul | ENTERTAINMENT

ITAEWON | 이태원
Itaewon is one of the most popular shopping districts in Seoul, particularly among foreigners. The densely packed shops in the area sell leather clothes, T-shirts, suits, watches, bags, shoes and accessories. ⓣ: Ⓜ Itaewon Station, Line 6

GANGNAM STATION AREA | 강남역 주변
There are many pubs, cafes, nightclubs, restaurants, cinemas, fashion shops, department stores and bookstores offering lots to do in an area filled with entertainment.
ⓣ: Ⓜ Exit 6 or 7 of Gangnam Station, Line 2

APGUJEONG-DONG | 압구정동
Consisting of numerous American-style clothing stores, cafes, nightclubs and restaurants, Apgujeong-dong is known to be Seoul's most fashionable and most expensive area.
ⓣ: Ⓜ Exit 2 of Apgujeong Station, Line 3

HONGIK UNIVERSITY VICINITY (HONGDAE STREET) | 홍대거리
Also called "Picasso Street" for the many art-related shops, cafes and clubs, the street between Hongik University and the Far East (Geukdong) Broadcasting Corporation is the center of the action.
ⓣ: Ⓜ Exit 6 of Hongik Univ. Station, Line 2

SINCHON | 신촌
Packed with coffee shops, cafes, clubs, beer houses, restaurants and fashion shops, the area is an important shopping and entertainment district with young people.
ⓣ: Ⓜ Sinchon Station, Line 2. Exit toward Yonsei University.

UNFORGETTABLE MEMORIES

ENTERTAINMENT

Theaters with Regular Traditional Korean Performances

IN SEOUL

CHONGDONG THEATER

Time	20:00, April – September; 16:00, October – March (except Mondays)
Admission	₩20,000 for A seats, ₩30,000 for S seats
Inquiries	02-7511-500, 02-751-1545; www.chongdong.com
Transportation	Behind Deoksugung Palace, a 5-min. walk from City Hall Station, Exit 1 or 12

NAMSANGOL HANOK VILLAGE

Time	July – August: 17:00, Saturdays and Sundays
Admission	Free
Inquiries	02-2266-6923; http://fpcp.or.kr
Transportation	A 3-min. walk from Exit 3 Chungmuro Station, Line 3 or 4

NATIONAL CENTER FOR KOREAN TRADITIONAL PERFORMING ARTS

Time (subject to change)	- U-myeon Dang (small hall): 19:30 (Tuesdays and Thursdays), 19:00 in November and December - Ye-ak Dang (main hall): 17:00 (Saturdays) / 20:00, 3rd Sunday (July and August) / 15:00, 3rd Sunday (October and November) - Byeolmaji Teo: 15:00 and 19:30, 3rd Sunday of each month (From April to September)
Admission	₩8,000 – ₩10,000
Inquiries	02-580-3300, 02-580-3045; www.ncktpa.go.kr
Transportation	Next to the Seoul Arts Center, a 10-min. walk from Exit 5 of Nambu Bus Terminal Station, Line 3

SEOUL NORI MADANG (OUTDOOR AMPHITHEATER)

Time	Saturday and Sunday; April to October (sometime between 15:00 and 17:00 depending on the season, no performances in winter)
Admission	Free
Inquiries	02-410-3168/9
Transportation	Behind Lotte World, a 10-min. walk from Jamsil Station, Line 2 or 8

SMALL HALL OF THE NATIONAL THEATER

Time	15:00, last Saturday monthly (full-length *pansori*), March – November
Admission	₩20,000
Inquiries	02-2280-4114, 02-2274-0105; www.ntok.go.kr
Transportation	A 15-min. walk from Exit 6 or the shuttle bus from Exit 2 of Dongguk Univ. Station, Line 3

IN OTHER AREAS

BUSAN CULTURAL CENTER

Features	Traditional music and dance performances
Time	16:00, Saturdays
Admission	Free
Inquiries	051-625-8130, 051-625-8138

Transportation	From Busan Station, take bus No.134 to the center.

NORI MADANG OF KOREAN FOLK VILLAGE, GYEONGGI-DO

Features	Farmers' percussion music and dance, tightrope walking, traditional wedding ceremony (residence No. 22, March – November)
Time	11:00 and 15:00
Admission	₩11,000 for adults
Inquiries	031-286-2111/3, 031-286-4051; www.koreanfolk.co.kr
Transportation	Take bus No. 37 or a shuttle bus from Suwon Station to the Korean Folk Village in Yongin.

JEONGSEON CULTURE AND ART HALL, GANGWON-DO

Time	16:40, 2nd, 7th, 12th, 17th, 22nd and 27th of every month
Admission	Free
Inquiries	033-560-2225
Transportation	Cheongnyangni Station, Seoul → Jeongseon Station

BOMUN AMPHITHEATER IN GYEONGJU, GYEONGSANGBUK-DO

Features	Scholar dance, fan dance, spiritual-cleansing dance, gayageum ensemble, songs of wayfaring beggars
Time	- April, October: 14:30, every day excluding Wednesday
	- May to June: 20:30, Saturdays, Sundays and public holidays
	- July to September: 20:30, every day excluding Wednesday
	- November: 14:30, Saturdays, Sundays and public holidays
Inquiries	054-740-7330/2, 054-740-7334
Transportation	From Gyeongju city, take bus No. 10 and get off at Yukbuchon.

INHERITANCE HALL OF THE HAHOE BYEOLSINGUT TALLORI IN ANDONG, GYEONGSANGBUK-DO

Features	Hahoe Byeolsingut Tallori, mask-dance drama performed after the communal shaman rite
Time	15:00, Sundays, March, April, November (on Saturdays, Sunday from May to October.)
Inquiries	054-854-3664, 054-856-3664
Transportation	From Andong Station, take city bus No. 46 to Hahoe Village, Jeonsuhougwan

NAMWON, JEOLLABUK-DO

Venue	Gwanghallu Pavilion Namwon Sightseeing Complex (open-air stage)
Time	14:00, Saturdays ; 20:00, Tuesdays, Thursdays, Saturdays and Sundays; April – June, October
	July – September
Admission	₩1,300
Inquiries	063-620-6178, 063-620-6535
Transportation	Seoul Station → Namwon Station, and a 5-min. taxi ride

JINDO REGIONAL CULTURE CENTER ON JINDO ISLAND, JEOLLANAM-DO

Features	Ssitgimgut*, dasiraegi*, Jindo manga*, Namdo deullorae*
Time	14:00, Saturdays, April – November
Inquiries	061-540-3226, 061-540-3577
Transportation	Seoul Express Bus Terminal → Gwangju, take a Jindo-bound bus, a 5-min. walk to the center

*Ssitgimgut: the shamanistic rite for the spiritual cleansing of the dead
*Dasiraegi: the entertainment for mourners performed the night before a burial in order to alleviate the bereaved family's grief through humor
*Jindo manga: the pallbearers' dirge sung as they carry a coffin
*Namdo deullorae: the farming song sung in the rice paddies of the southwestern region

Dinner Theaters in Seoul

There are many restaurants where you can enjoy traditional Korean music and dance performances with Korean dishes.

KAYAGUM HALL | 가야금 홀
- Dinner and Performance: ₩85,000 – ₩99,000
- Performance Only: ₩60,000 (17:30 and 20:00, every day)
- Ⓛ: floor B1, Sheraton Walker Hill Hotel, Gwangjang-dong, Gwangjin-gu
- Ⓣ: 02-4555-000; www.walkerhill.co.kr
- Ⓣ: A 10-min. ride by shuttle bus from Exit 1 of Gwangnaru Station, Line 5

KOREA HOUSE | 한국의집
- Korean Set Meal: ₩41,000 – ₩65,000
- Korean Buffet: Lunch ₩26,000, Dinner ₩28,000
- Performance Only: ₩29,000 (19:00 and 20:50, Monday through Saturday; 20:00, Sunday)
- Ⓛ: Pil-dong, Jung-gu
- Ⓣ: 02-2266-9101; www.koreahouse.or.kr
- Ⓣ: A 5-min. walk from Exit 3 of Chungmuro Station, Line 3 or 4

SAMCHEONGGAK | 삼청각
- Korean Set Meal: ₩37,000 – ₩150,000
- Performance Only: ₩40,000, Mondays and Wednesdays; ₩40,000, Thursday through Sunday (20:00 on Monday through Friday; 16:00 on Saturdays and Sundays)
- Ⓛ: Seongbuk 2 (i)-dong, Seongbuk-gu
- Ⓣ: 02-765-3700; www.samcheonggak.or.kr
- Ⓣ: Shuttle bus service is available every 20 – 30 min. between the Kyobo Bldg. (Gwanghwamun Stn., Line 5) and Samcheonggak.

KORYO JEONG | 고려정
- Korean Set Meal: ₩35,000 – ₩70,000
- Performance only: ₩17,000 (19:30 and 20:30, every day)
- Ⓛ: Nonhyeon-dong, Gangnam-gu
- Ⓣ: 02-518-0161/6 Ⓣ: A 5-min. walk from Exit 10 of Hak-dong Station, Line 7

PULHYANGGI | 풀향기
- Lunch: ₩25,000
- Dinner: ₩39,000 – ₩99,000
- Performance: 19:30 – 21:30 (every day excluding the 1st and 3rd Sunday of each month)
- Ⓛ: 726-54 Hanam-dong Yongsan-gu
- Ⓣ: 02-796-3490 Ⓣ: A 5-min. walk from Exit 2, Hangangjin Station, Line 6

SANCHON | 산촌
- Buddhist Vegetarian Cuisine: Lunch ₩18,700, Dinner ₩31,900
- Performance: 20:15, every day
- Ⓛ: Gwanhun-dong, Jongno-gu (map p.28)
- Ⓣ: 02-735-0312; www.sanchon.com
- Ⓣ: A 10-min. walk from Exit 6 of Jongno 3 (sam)-ga Station, Line 1, 3 or 5 (near Tong In Store on Insa-dong Street)

CHUNGSACHOLONG | 청사초롱
- Korean Set Meal: ₩35,000 – ₩75,000
- Performance: 19:00, every day
- Ⓛ: Hannam 2 (i)-dong, Yongsan-gu
- Ⓣ: 02-794-1177 Ⓣ: A 10-min. walk from Exit 2 of Itaewon Station, Line 6 (near the Itaewon Hotel)

Samcheonggak

ENTERTAINMENT

Movie Theaters

Korea's movie industry is growing rapidly and some of its films have achieved international acclaim.

Foreign films, many from the United States, are very popular among Koreans. These films are subtitled in Korean, not dubbed, so the foreign visitor can enjoy an evening at the movies. Films are shown from about 11:00 daily.

IN SEOUL

Name	Location	Tel.
Central 6	B1 level, Central City, Banpo-dong, Seocho-gu	1544-0070
CGV Bulgwang	11th, Town Square Bldg., Bulgwang-dong, Eunpyeong-gu	1544-1122
CGV Gangbyeon 11	10th Fl., Techno Mart, Guui-dong, Gwangjin-gu	1544-1122
CGV Guro 10	5th Fl., Aekyong Department Store, Guro 5 (o)-dong, Guro-gu	1544-1122
CGV Myeondong 5	8th Fl., Avatar Mall, Myeong-dong, Jung-gu	1544-1122
CGV Sang-am 10	1st Fl., World Cup Mall, Seongsan-dong, Mapo-gu	1544-1122
Cine Core	5-10, Gwancheol-dong, Jongno-gu	02-2285-2090
Cine Cube	B2, Heungkuk Life Bldg., Sinmunno, Jongno-gu	02-2000-7770/1
City	816, Yeoksam-dong, Gangnam-gu	02-540-1637
Daehan Cinema	125, 4 (sa)-ga, Chungmuro, Jung-gu	02-3393-3500
Lotte World	40-1, Jamsil-dong, Songpa-gu	02-417-0213
Megabox Cineplex	COEX Mall, Samseong-dong, Gangnam-gu	1544-0600
MMC	10th Fl., Freya Town, Euljiro 6 (yuk)-ga, Jung-gu	02-2268-0264
Myungbo Plaza	18-5, Cho-dong, Jung-gu	02-2274-2121
Seoul Cinema	59-7, Gwansu-dong, Jongno-gu	02-2277-3011
Star Six	22, Jeong-dong, Jung-gu	02-2004-8000

IN BUSAN

Name	Location	Tel.
Busan Cinema	18 Nampo-dong 5 (o)-ga, Jung-gu	051-241-1201/3
CGV Nampo	6th Fl., Kukdo Town, Nampo 6 (yuk)-ga, Jung-gu	1544-1122
CGV Seomyeon12	6th Fl., GEO Place, Busanjin-gu	1544-1122
Lotte Cinema	10th Fl., Lotte Department Store, Bujeon-dong, Busanjin-gu	1544-8855
Megabox Haeundae	6th Fl., Spongy Mall, U-dong, Haeundae-gu	1544-0600
Megabox Seomyeon	6th Fl., Milgliore Mall, Jeonpo-dong, Busanjin-gu	1544-0600

ENTERTAINMENT

Casinos

Casinos offer entertainment and excitement to the hunters of lady luck. Except Kangwon Land, casinos are open exclusively to foreigners and include roulette, craps, blackjack, baccarat and scores of slot machines. Most tourist hotels also have a game room devoted to slot machines.

SEVEN LUCK CASINO

Seven Luck, a huge world-class casino for foreigners only, will open with two locations in Seoul and in one in Busan. Seven Luck Casino, a subsidiary of the state-run Korea Tourism Organization, will feature table games and a variety of events and shows.

Seven Luck Casino Gangnam (opens on January 27, 2006): Exit 5, 6 of Samseong Station, Seoul Subway Line 2

Seven Luck Casino Gangbuk (opens in June 2006): Exit 8 of Seoul Station, Seoul Subway Line 1 or Exit 4 of Hoehyeon Station, Seoul Subway Line 4

Seven Luck Casino Busan (opens in June 2006): Seomyeon Station, Busan Subway Line 1 and 2

OTHER CASINOS

Name	Location	Tel.
Paradise Walker Hill	Gwangjin-gu, Seoul	02-2204-3321
Paradise Hotel	Jung-gu, Incheon	032-762-5181
Paradise Grand	Jeju-si, Jeju-do	064-740-7000
Jeju Oriental	Jeju-si, Jeju-do	064-752-8222
Jeju KAL	Jeju-si, Jeju-do	064-757-8111/7

Crown Plaza	Jeju-si, Jeju-do	064-741-8000
Pacific Hotel	Jeju-si, Jeju-do	064-756-9999
Hyatt Regency	Seogwipo-si, Jeju-do	064-735-8755
Cheju Shilla	Seogwipo-si, Jeju-do	064-738-8822
Lotte Hotel	Seogwipo-si, Jeju-do	064-731-2121
Kangwon Land	Jeongseon-gun, Gangwon-do	033-590-7700
Paradise	Haeundae-gu, Busan	051-742-2110
Wellich Chosun Hotel	Bomun Lake Resort, Gyeongju, Gyeongsangbuk-do	054-740-8152

ENTERTAINMENT

Bars, Beer Halls and Jazz Clubs

You can enjoy Korean drinks such as *soju* (distilled liquor) and *makgeolli* (thick, unrefined liquor fermented from grain) with local residents at a *minsokjujeom* (a Korean-style bar) as well as at street pubs, called *pojangmacha*, which are often open all night. You can also find many quality beer halls decorated in a Western style. Customers are expected to order snacks or food with their drinks. Although often crowded and noisy, they are nice places to experience the local atmosphere. Recently, fancy jazz clubs are enticing people with their urbane charms. A cup of coffee over an enchanting jazz melody could create an unforgettable moment in Seoul.

FAMOUS BARS IN SEOUL

Name	Location	Tel.
Maekju Changgo	Exit 4 of Jonggak Stn., Line 1	02-732-0487
Mumba	Exit 5 of Gwanghwamun Stn., Line 5 (B2, Seoul Finance Center Bldg.)	02-3783-0005
Geopum I, II, III	Exit 3 of Sinchon Stn., Line 2	02-362-8798
Haeyeolje	Exit 8 of Sinchon Stn., Line 2	02-332-8955
Bless U	Exit 1 of Itaewon Stn., Line 6	02-792-2550
Cafe 74	Cheongdam-dong, Gangnam-gu (next to the Napoleon Bakery)	02-542-7412
Goshen	Cheongdam-dong, Gangnam-gu (next to the Hankook Chinaware Outlet)	02-515-1863
Hard Rock Cafe	Cheongdam-dong, Gangnam-gu (in front of Bangju Hosp. at Hak-dong Intersection)	02-547-5671
ZZYZX	Cheongdam-dong, Gangnam-gu (behind the Hankook Chinaware Outlet)	02-515-0815

HOTEL BARS

● **Seoul**
Hotel Amiga (www.amiga.co.kr)
- Maestro ☏ 02-3440-8180/2
Grand Hyatt Seoul (www.seoul.hyatt.com)
- Helicon ☏ 02-799-8440
- The Paris Bar ☏ 02-799-8361
Intercontinental (www.seoul.interconti.com)
- Hunter's Tavern ☏ 02-559-7619
Lotte Hotel (www.lottehotel.com)
- Bobby London ☏ 02-317-7091
- Schoenbrun Bar ☏ 02-317-7185
- Windsor Bar ☏ 02-411-7701/2

Sheraton Walker Hill
(www.walkerhill.co.kr)
- Starlight ☏ 02-450-4516
The Westin Chosun
(www.westinchosun.co.kr)
- Compass Rose ☏ 02-317-0365
- O'Kim's ☏ 02-317-0388
● **Busan**
Lotte Hotel (www.lottehotel.co.kr)
- Windsor Bar ☏ 051-810-6420/1
Paradise Beach (www.paradisehotel.co.kr)
- Charlie's ☏ 051-749-2236/7

The Westin Chosun Beach
(www.chosunbeach.co.kr)
- O'Kim's ☏ 051-749-7439
● **Gyeongju**
Hyundai (www.hyundaihotel.com)
- Club Havana ☏ 054-779-7384
● **Jejudo Island**
Jeju KAL (www.kalhotel.co.kr)
- Eunhasu Sky Lounge ☏ 064-720-6585
Cheju Shilla (www.chejushilla.com)
- Dalmoree Karaoke Bar ☏ 064-735-5332

FAMOUS JAZZ CLUBS IN SEOUL

Name / Tel.	Live performance	Location
Once in a Blue Moon ☏ 02-549-5490	19:00	150m towards Gangnam-gu Office from Galleria Dept. Store of Apgujeong-dong
Cheonnyeondongando ☏ 02-743-5555	18:50 – 02:00 on weekdays (17:30 – 02:00 on weekends)	Near Blue Bird Theater in the KFC alley on Daehangno Street
Janus ☏ 02-546-9774	20:30 – 23:30 on weekdays (20:30 – 23:00 on weekends)	50m towards Sinsa-dong from Hotel Prima on Cheongdam-dong
All That Jazz ☏ 02-795-5701	21:00 – 23:30	100m towards Samgakji from Hotel Hamilton in Itaewon
Club Evans ☏ 02-3141-0626	21:00 – 23:00	30m from the main entrance of Hongik University
Jazz Story ☏ 02-725-6237	20:30 – 24:00	In front of Chilbosa Temple in Samcheong-dong
Moonglow ☏ 02-324-5205	21:00 – 23:00 (Mon. through Sat.)	Around Yeongbin Wedding Hall near Hongik Univ.

Sports & Health

Sports

WATER SPORTS
Since Korea is a peninsula, visitors can enjoy water sports all year round. The Hangang River in Seoul, the south coast of Korea, and Jejudo Island are some of the most popular places for water sports. The best time for these water sports is from June to November, when both the water temperature and stunning underwater scenery are at their best.

WATER SKIING
The Hangang River in Seoul features some excellent places for water skiing, especially the Ttukseom, Seongsan and Mangwon zones. Cheongpyeong Lake Resort, Namiseom Resort, Paldang Resort and Daeseong-ri Resort in Gyeonggi-do Province also have wonderful surroundings and clean water.
ⓘ: Seoul Water Ski Association 02-498-9026; The Korea Water Ski Association 02-2203-0488/9

WINDSURFING
Enjoy speeds of up to 60 km/h and the thrill of sailing through the waves. While Chungjuho Lake or Asanman Bay is for beginners, the Hangang River is suitable for the intermediate. Advanced windsurfers may ride at beaches such as Haeundae Beach in Busan and Sinyang, Hamdeok or Jungmun Beaches on Jejudo Island. Average rental fee: ₩30,000 – ₩50,000
ⓘ: Korean Windsurfing Association 02-373-9200; www.kwsa.or.kr

RAFTING
Though it was first introduced to Korea in the early 1970s, rafting has become a popular leisure-sport activity for the summer season. For beginners, the 65 km of the Donggang River in Yeongwol, Gangwon-do Province, is a good place to be initiated.
Intermediates will enjoy the Hantangang River in Yeoncheon, Gyeonggi-do Province, while 70 km from the Naerincheon Stream in Inje, Gangwon-do Province, awaits those who are more advanced. Average fee: ₩20,000 – ₩50,000
ⓘ: Korea Leisure Association 02-701-1762; Soondam Leisure 033-452-5353

SKIING AND SNOWBOARDING
Korea has several world-class resorts and the ski season lasts from December to early March. Most ski resorts open at the end of November

UNFORGETTABLE MEMORIES

and during the season, travel agencies operate convenient buses (most of them from Seoul). Fees for ski or snowboard rental range from ₩15,000 to ₩46,000 (full day), and lift tickets from ₩38,000 to ₩51,000 (full day).

SKI RESORTS

YONGPYONG RESORT | 용평리조트
The host of the 1999 Winter Asian Games. A variety of winter events are always planned at this all-weather resort.
①: 033-335-5757, 1588-0009 (reservations), 02-3270-1234 (Seoul office); www.yongpyong.co.kr; klatty@yongpyong.co.kr; ⓣ: From Dong (East) Seoul Bus Terminal, take a bus to Hoenggye (3 hrs.). Then use the free shuttle bus. (Daewon Tours 02-575-7710)

ALPS RESORT | 알프스리조트
In the northernmost region of Korea, the Alps Resort is renowned for its abundant snowfall.
①: 033-681-5030, 02-574-7560 (Seoul office), 02-574-6888 (Seoul office); www.alpsresort.co.kr; helpdesk@hotmail.com; ⓣ: From Dong (East) Seoul Bus Terminal, take a bus to Ganseong. Get off at the top of Jinburyeong Pass.

PHOENIX PARK | 휘닉스파크
Phoenix Park slopes are set in high valleys and receive a large volume of snowfall every year. This European-style ski complex offers the latest in fashionable facilities.
①: 033-330-6000, 02-527-9511 (Seoul office), 02-508-3401 (Seoul office); www.phoenixpark.co.kr; jack@phoenixpark.co.kr; ⓣ: From Dong (East) Seoul Bus Terminal, take a bus to Jangpyeong (every 40 min., 2 hrs. 30 min.). Get off at Jangpyeong Bus Terminal and take a free shuttle bus to the resort.

HYUNDAI SUNGWOO RESORT | 현대성우리조트
Opened in December 1995, this massive year-round resort has many state-of-the-art facilities such as a computerized snow making system, wave course and mogul course.
①: 033-340-3000, 02-523-7111 (Seoul office); 033-340-3171; www.hdsungwoo.co.kr

ⓣ: From Cheongnyangni Station in Seoul, take the train to Wonju, then use the free shuttle bus to the resort.

DAEMYUNG VIVALDI PARK | 대명비발디파크
Daemyung Vivaldi Park is 600 m above sea level. It is often referred to as a beginners' paradise because of its 150-m-wide beginner's slope, but there are challenging runs, too.
①: 033-434-8311, 02-2222-7000 (Seoul office); 033-434-8020, 02-2222-7123 (Seoul office); www.daemyungcondo.com ⓣ: From Dong (East) Seoul Bus Terminal, take the bus to Hongcheon (1 hr., 30 min.).

LG GANGCHON RESORT | LG 강촌리조트
LG Gangchon Resort provides slopes of varying difficulty (from beginner to intermediate). All slopes have a length of 1 km or more, and even advanced skiers can enjoy the S-shaped slope that connects the peak to the rest area.
①: 033-260-2554, 02-2005-9285 (Seoul office); 033-262-9090, 02-2005-9289 (Seoul office); ⓣ: From Cheongnyangni Station in Seoul, take the train to Chuncheon and get off at Gangchon Station. From Gangchon Station, free shuttle buses are operated every 20 min.

MUJU RESORT | 무주리조트
Muju Resort was the venue of the 1997 Winter Universiade. Set against the magnificent scenery of Deogyusan National Park, Muju is the largest ski resort in Korea.
①: 063-322-9000, 02-756-5621 (Seoul office), 063-320-7050, 756-5035 (Seoul office); www.mujuresort.com; webmaster@mujuresort.com; ⓣ: From Seoul Station, take the train to Yeongdong (2 hrs.), then transfer to a Muju-bound bus (30 min.). Shuttle Bus route: Muju-eup ↔ resort, Gucheon-dong ↔ resort (063-320-7196)

SUANBO SAJO RESORT | 수안보사조리조트
This family resort is situated in a natural hot

springs region so visitors can enjoy skiing and soaking in the hot springs.

☎ 043-846-0750, 02-3446-6699 (Seoul office)
📠 02-3446-7144 (Seoul office);
www.sajoresort.co.kr 🚌 Dong (East) Seoul Bus Terminal → Chungju Bus Terminal → Suanbo (free shuttle buses are operated between Suanbo and the resort.); 🚆 Seoul Station → Chungju Station → Suanbo Bus Terminal 🚌 → Resort (free shuttle buses are operated between Suanbo and the resort.)

YANGJI PINE RESORT | 양지파인리조트
Yangji Pine Resort is only 40 min. south of Seoul. Various tourist attractions are nearby such as Everland, Korean Folk Village, Icheon Hot Springs and the ceramics village.

☎ 031-338-2001, 02-540-6800 (Seoul office)
📠 031-338-1733, 02-512-3675 (Seoul office);
www.pineresort.com 🚌 From Nambu Bus Terminal in Seoul, take the bus to Jincheon (every 20 min. from 06:15). Get off at Yong-in Bus Terminal and use the free shuttle bus to the resort.

BEARS TOWN RESORT | 베어스타운리조트
A four-season resort, Bears Town offers both skiing and golf.

☎ 031-540-5000, 02-594-8188 (Seoul office)
📠 031-533-8427, 02-412-5044 (Seoul office);
www.bearstown.com 🚌 From Sangbong Intercity Bus Terminal in Seoul, take the bus to Ildong and get off at Naechon Station. Then take a taxi to the resort (2 km).

JISAN FOREST RESORT | 지산포레스트리조트
Jisan Forest Resort offers European-style slopes and hot springs that blend in with the lush forest and natural wildlife.

☎ 031-644-1242/1246 📠 031-638-5941;
www.jisanresort.co.kr
🚌 From Dong (East) Seoul Bus Terminal, take a bus to Icheon. From Icheon Bus Terminal, take bus No. 12 or 10
* Free shuttle buses are operated by the Jisan Forest Resort (☎ 031-644-1242/1246).
* Online reservations are required.

STAR HILL RESORT | 스타힐리조트
Just one hour from Seoul, Star Hill Resort has established a reputation for night skiing. Its proximity to Seoul makes it ideal for visitors with a limited amount of time.

☎ 031-5594-1211, 02-2233-5311 (Seoul Office) 📠 031-595-6117; www.starhillresort.co.kr
🚌 No. 9201 or 9205 in front of Cheongnyangni Station in Seoul. Get off at Maseok Station and walk about 15 min.

SEOUL SKI RESORT | 서울리조트
Only 50 min. from Seoul, this multipurpose resort is often the location of family retreats.

☎ 031-592-9400, 02-959-0866 (Seoul office)
📠 031-592-6222 🚌 No. 9205 or 9201 in front of the Hyundai Core (in Cheongnyangni, Seoul). Get off at Seoul Resort Station.

Golf Courses
SPORTS & HEALTH

Golf has emerged as a popular sport in Korea with the increasing popularity of such golf stars as Tiger Woods and Koreans Park Seri, Kim Mi-hyun and Grace Park. Korea has excellent golf courses and most tourist hotels in resort areas either have their own courses or have access to one. On some courses, weekend play is reserved for members. Wherever you plan to play, it is advisable to make reservations, perhaps through your hotel.

* Average green fees: ₩100,000 (Mon. – Fri.), ₩130,000 (Sat. – Sun.)

Major Public Golf Courses

Name	Address	Tel.	Holes
Lakeside	Neungwon-ri, Mohyeon-myeon, Yongin, Gyeonggi-do	031-334-2111	*54 (36)
Park Valley	Suam-ri, Soho-myeon, Wonju, Gangwon-do	033-731-0017	18
Cheonan Sangnok	Jangsan-ri, Susin-myeon, Cheonan, Chungcheongnam-do	041-529-9075	27
Bomun	Mucheon-ri, Cheonbuk-myeon, Gyeongju, Gyeongsangbuk-do	054-745-1680	18
Jungmun	Saekdal-dong, Seogwipo, Jeju-do	064-738-1202	18

* total holes (public holes)

Health Tours

HOT SPRINGS

From ancient times, hot springs have been known to be effective against skin disease, arthritis, neuralgia and certain gastrointestinal ailments. It is especially nice on a cold snowy day to soak in a hot spring spa. Most of the hot springs in Korea are not only equipped with hot spring bathing facilities but are also developed as comprehensive resorts for families. Admission is usually between ₩5,000 to ₩10,000.

Destination	Hot Springs (Type) Accommodations	Telephone	Transportation
Gyeonggi-do	Icheon Hot Springs (alkaline)		Dong Seoul Bus Terminal → Icheon (1 hr.)
	Hotel Miranda Icheon	031-633-2001	
	Seolbong Tourist Hotel	031-635-5701	
Gangwon-do	Cheoksan Hot Springs (alkaline)		Seoul Express Bus Terminal → Sokcho (4 hrs., 10 min.), and a local bus
	Cheoksan Hotel	033-636-4000	
	Osaek Hot Springs (alkaline)		Sangbong Bus Terminal → Osaek, and a 10-min. walk
	Greenyard Hotel	033-672-8500	
Chungcheong-do	Onyang Hot Springs (radium)		Janghangseon train at Seoul Station → Onyang Oncheon Station (1 hr., 30 min.)
	Grand Tourist Hotel	041-543-9711	
	Onyang Plaza Hotel	041-544-6111	
	Onyang Tourist Hotel	041-545-2141	
	Dogo Hot Springs (sulfur)		Janghangseon train at Seoul Station → Dogo Oncheon Station (1 hr., 40 min.), and a local bus (10 min.)
	Paradise Dogo Hotel	041-542-6031	
	Glory Condominium	041-541-7100	
	Asan Hot Springs		Janghangseon train at Seoul Station → Onyang Oncheon Station (1hr., 30 min.) and local bus No. 100-1
	Asan Spavis	041-539-2000	
	Asan Hot Springs Hotel	041-541-5526	
	Yuseong Hot Springs (alkaline radium)		Seoul Express Bus Terminal → Yuseong (2 hrs.)
	Yuseong Hotel	042-822-0811	
	Suanbo Hot Springs (simple thermal spring)		Dong Seoul Bus Terminal → Suanbo (2 hrs., 30 min.)
	Suanbo Park Hotel	043-846-2331	
	Suanbo Sang Nok Hotel	043-845-3500	

Gyeongsang-do	Gyeongju Hot Springs (simple thermal spring)		
	Kolon Hotel	054-746-9001	Seoul Station → Gyeongju (4 hrs., 15 min.), and local bus No. 10 or 11 to Bomun Lake Resort
	Wellich Chosun	054-740-9600	
	Kyongju Hotel Concorde	054-745-7000	
	Hyundai Hotel	054-748-2233	
	Kyongju Hilton Hotel	054-745-7788	
	Bugok Hot Springs (sulfur)		
	Bugok Royal Hotel	055-536-6661	Seoul Nambu Bus Terminal → Bugok (5 hrs.)
	Bugok Hawaii Hotel	055-536-6331	
	Lake Hills Hotel Bugok	055-536-5181	
	Dongnae Hot Springs (sodium)		Seoul Station → Busan Station (4 hrs., 30 min.); get off at Oncheonjang Station from Subway Line 1
	Hur Shim Chung Spa	051-550-2100	
	Haeundae Hot Springs (alkaline)		
	Busan Marriott	051-743-1234	Seoul Station → Busan Station (4 hrs., 30 min.), and a local bus
	Paradise Beach Hotel	051-742-2121	
	Westin Chosun Beach Hotel	051-749-7488	
Jeolla-do Province	Jirisan Spa Land (simple thermal spring)	061-783-2900	Seoul Station → Gurye (4 – 5 hrs.), and a bus towards Jirisan Spa Land from Gurye Intercity Bus Terminal
	Wolchulsan Spa Resort (alkaline sodium chloride)	061-473-6322	Seoul Express Bus Terminal → Yeongam (4 hrs., 40 min.), and a shuttle bus

MAJOR WATER PARKS

ASAN SPAVIS
⌚: 8 am – 10 pm ☏: 041-539-2080, 2000; www.spavis.co.kr 🚌: Nambu Bus Terminal in Seoul → Asan (1 hr., 30 min.) → Asan Spavis (at the bus stop across the terminal, take bus No. 100-1 or a taxi, 30 min.)

ICHEON SPAPLUS
⌚: 6 am – 10 pm ☏: 031-633-2001 🚌: Seoul Express Bus Terminal or Dong (East) Seoul Bus Terminal → Icheon (1 hr.) → Icheon SpaPlus (5 min.)

SORAK WATERPIA
☏: 033-635-7711; www.hanwharesort.co.kr 🚌: Dong (East) Seoul Bus Terminal or Sangbong Intercity Bus Terminal → Sokcho (3 hrs., 30 min.) → Sorak Waterpia (15 min. by bus)

BUGOK HAWAII
☏: 055-521-7034; www.bugokhawaii.co.kr 🚌: Seoul Nambu Bus Terminal → Bugok (5 hrs.) → Bugok Hawaii (5 min.)

SORAK AQUAWORLD
⌚: 10:00 am – 09:00 pm (weekdays); 09:00 am –

Sorak Aquaworld

09:30 pm (weekends and holidays)
①: ☎ 033-639-3400; www.daemyungcondo.com
⊤: 🚌 Dong (East) Seoul Bus Terminal or Seoul Express Bus Terminal → Sokcho Intercity Bus Terminal (3 hrs., 30 min.) → Take a taxi and get off at the Sokcho Fire Station (15 to 20 min.). → Bus No. 3-1 on the other side of the road to Daemyung Condo

TRADITIONAL KOREAN MEDICINE

Oriental medicine restores the body's balance and helps it withstand the heat and cold of the changing seasons. Recognized as alternative medicine to Western science, Oriental therapy is recommended to people who want to check their overall physical health or discover the imbalances and needs of their bodies.

GYEONGJU CONMAEUL HERB CLINIC

The hospital, built in traditional Korean style, has a variety of programs ranging from one-day programs to three-day programs (₩70,000 to ₩150,000). The programs include an informational video on Oriental medicine, blood tests to analyze the condition or stage of illness, chuna therapy performed by traditional medicine doctors, nerve function tests and aromatherapy.
①: ☎ 054-775-6600; www.conmaul.co.kr
⊤: 🚌 Take the KTX from Seoul Station to Dong Daegu and transfer to the Saemaeulho Express Train to Gyeongju.

CHORAKDANG

Chorakdang is a health care clinic where you can receive different kinds of traditional Korean therapy in a nature-friendly environment and tour interesting sites nearby. The programs include a red mud heat treatment, physical therapy, bedding therapy and an herbal bath treatment. After the treatments, a dinner is prepared with organic ingredients followed by free time to enjoy your surroundings. Everything at Chorakdang is done in the traditional Korean way from the red mud clothing to the food and bedding. A 2-day, 1-night stay is ₩100,000 per person, while a 3-day, 2-night tour with herbal bath costs ₩200,000.
①: ☎ 052-264-8001; www.chorakdang.com
⊤: 🚌 Take the KTX from Seoul Station to Gyeongju Station departing at 10:30 am.
🚌 Then get on the shuttle bus.

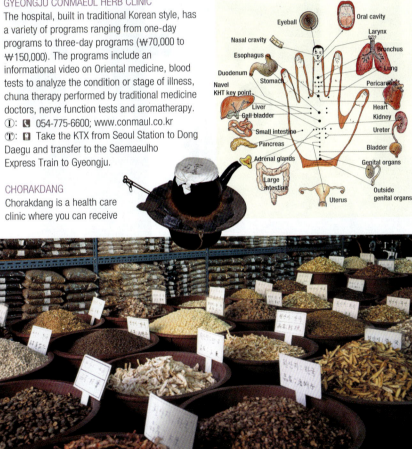

Herbal Medicine

084 Seoul

134 Seoul Vicinity

139 Eastern Area (Gangwon-do, Ulleungdo, Dokdo)

144 Central Area (Daejeon, Chungcheongnam-do, Chungcheongbuk-do)

149 Southeastern Area (Daegu, Gyeongju, Busan, Ulsan, Gyeongsangbuk-do, Gyeongsangnam-do)

163 Southwestern Area (Gwangju, Jeollabuk-do, Jeollanam-do)

169 Jeju-do

Tourist Attractions by Region

Seoul

Seoul has been the center of politics, economy, culture and transportation of Korea for six centuries since King Taejo, the founder of the Joseon Dynasty, moved the capital here in the 3rd year (1394) of his reign.

Today, a quarter of the population lives in Seoul, which serves as the core of all branches of knowledge. Seoul preserves numerous relics of the Joseon Dynasty: Dongdaemun and Namdaemun Gates; five extant palaces, namely Gyeongbokgung, Changdeokgung, Changgyeonggung, Deoksugung and Gyeonghuigung; royal tombs, including Hongneung and

TOURIST ATTRACTIONS BY REGION

Hi Seoul www.visitseoul.net

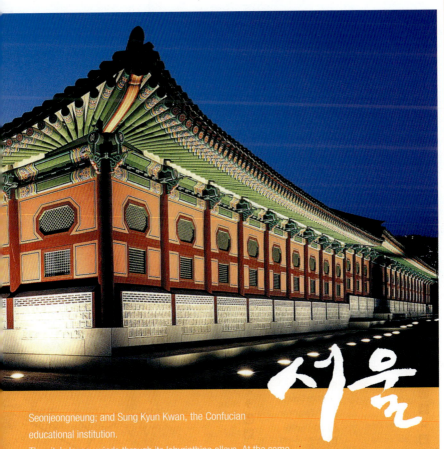

Seonjeongneung; and Sung Kyun Kwan, the Confucian educational institution.

The city's legacy winds through its labyrinthine alleys. At the same time, Seoul has risen as a global landmark of modernity with many must-see attractions: Lotte World, an amusement park; Seoul Tower, the symbol of Seoul; many parks and museums; department stores and other emporiums; jazz bars; cafes; casinos; etc. These make Seoul a favorite tourist destination where visitors find all the amenities and entertainment they could want.

www.visitseoul.net

Map of Seoul

LEGEND

- Road
- Subway Station
- Subway Transfer
- Railroad
- Boundary of District (gu)
- Tourist Information Center
- Airport
- Railroad Station
- Bus Terminal
- Seoul City Tour Bus Stop
- Recreational Boat Terminal
- On Foot
- By Subway
- By Train
- By Bus
- By Ferry
- Hotel
- Other Hotel
- Guesthouse
- Youth Hostel
- European, Western Restaurant
- Korean Restaurant
- Other Restaurant
- Coffee Shop
- Fast Food Restaurant
- Convenience Store
- Bank
- Money Exchange
- Shopping Center
- Duty Free Shop
- Museum, Gallery, Exhibition Hall
- Club
- Live Performance Hall
- Jazz Bar
- Casino
- Movie Theater
- Shooting Range
- Mountain
- Golf Course
- Ski Resort
- Beach
- World Cultural Heritage Site
- Fortress
- Royal Tomb
- Temple
- Church
- Cathedral
- Embassy
- Airline
- Hospital
- Pharmacy
- Police Station
- Post Office
- School
- University
- Parking Lot
- Others
- Telephone
- Fax
- Transportation
- Admission Fee
- Days Closed
- Open Hours
- Location

Signs such as A1 A2 ... after the tourist destinations in this book indicate their locations on the maps.

INFORMATION Tourism Department, Seoul City Hall, 02-3707-9453

SEOUL WALKING TOUR

Seoul City operates walking tours of Seoul that center around the major cultural artifacts and palaces. These tours are accompanied by "Seoul Cultural Artifact Translators," 50 of whom were designated by the Seoul Metropolitan Government to enlighten native and foreign tourists with valuable information and stories about each tourist location. To participate in one of the test tours, visit Seoul's cultural tourism Web site (www.visitseoul.net) to sign up.

DEOKSUGUNG PALACE, JEONGDONG ROUTE (STREETS OF MODERN HISTORY)

Route A: Deoksugung Palace (Royal Guard Changing Ceremony) → Jungmyeongjeon Hall → Former Russian Legation → Gyeonghuigung Palace → Seoul Museum of History
Route B: Deoksugung Palace (Royal Guard Changing Ceremony) → Seoul Museum of Art → Gyeonghuigung Palace → Seoul Museum of History

GYEONGBOKGUNG PALACE, INSA-DONG ROUTE (STREETS OF TRADITIONAL CULTURE I)

Route A: Gyeongbokgung Palace → Samcheongdonggil Street → Pass Cheong Wa Dae (the Blue House) → Hyoja-dong Sarangbang (where various gifts from foreign heads of state and other dignitaries are exhibited)
Route B: Gyeongbokgung Palace → Insa-dong
 * Insa-dong's Recommended Walking Routes: Gana Art Space → Seoul Souvenir Shop → Insa Art Center → Tong In Store → Kyung-in Art Gallery → Min's Club (Mingadaheon) → Dongyang Daye Shop

JONGMYO ROYAL SHRINE, CHANGGYEONGGUNG PALACE ROUTE (STREETS OF TRADITIONAL CULTURE II)

Route A: Jongmyo Royal Shrine (Jongmyo Ancestral Rite, Jongmyo Ritual Music) → Changgyeonggung Palace → Changgyeonggungno Street → Yulgongno Street → Changdeokgung Palace
Route B: Jongmyo Royal Shrine (Jongmyo Ancestral Rite, Jongmyo Ritual Music) → Changgyeonggung Palace → Changgyeonggungno Street → Seoul National Science Museum → Sung Kyun Kwan University → Munmyo Shrine

DAEHANGNO ROUTE (STREETS OF YOUTH) * A self-guided tour

Daehangno Street (Heungsadan → Parangsae Theater → Marronnier Park → Korean Culture & Arts Foundation) → Ihwajang → Naksan Park → Marronnier Park

NAMDAEMUN, MYEONG-DONG ROUTE (STREETS OF SHOPPING) * A self-guided tour

Namdaemun Market Shopping District → Shinsegae Department Store → Hoehyeon Underground Shopping Center → Postal Museum → Myeong-dong → Utoo Zone → Hyundai Investment Trust & Securities → Myeongdonggil Street → Catholic Center → Myeongdong Cathedral

INFORMATION 02-777-6090, www.seoulcitytourbus.com

SEOUL BUS TOUR

Making the rounds at all of Seoul's best-known spots with one ticket, the Seoul City Tour Bus is a favorite among foreign visitors to Seoul, native tourists, and couples on a date.
Visitors may get off anywhere during the tour, reboard and proceed. The 35-seat buses have headsets that play taped information in Korean, English, Japanese, Chinese and French. The Downtown Tour runs from 9 am to 9 pm and the Palace Tour from 9 am to 5 pm, every 30 min. (except Mondays). Tours start anywhere along the circuit and in front of Dongwha Duty Free at Gwanghwamun Station (Exit 6, Seoul Subway Line 5). A single-ride ticket is ₩5,000, and an all-day pass (Downtown and Palace Tour) is ₩10,000. Tour routes are listed below.

DOWNTOWN TOUR

Gwanghwamun Gate → Deoksugung Palace → Seoul Station → USO → Yongsan Station → National Museum of Korea → War Memorial of Korea → U.S. Army Post → Itaewon → Crown Hotel → Myeong-dong → Namsangol Hanok Village → Sofitel Ambassador Hotel → National Theater → N Seoul Tower → Grand Hyatt Seoul → Tower Hotel → Shilla Hotel → Dongdaemun Market → Daehangno Street → Changgyeonggung Palace → Changdeokgung Palace → Insa-dong → Cheong Wa Dae (the Blue House) → National Folk Museum of Korea → Gyeongbokgung Palace → Police Museum → Gwanghwamun Gate

PALACE TOUR

Gwanghwamun Gate → Deoksugung Palace → Cheonggye Plaza → Korea Tourism Organization → Samilgyo → Jogyesa Temple → Insa-dong → Changdeokgung Palace → Daehangno Street → Changgyeonggung Palace → Changdeokgung Palace → Insa-dong → Cheong Wa Dae (the Blue House) → National Folk Museum of Korea → Gyeongbokgung Palace → Gwanghwamun Gate

NIGHT TOUR

Gwanghwamun Gate → Deoksugung Palace → N Seoul Tower → Cheonggye Plaza

Around Gyeongbokgung Palace

At the north end of Sejongno Street appears the imposing Gyeongbokgung, the oldest palace of the Joseon Dynasty. On its grounds stands the National Folk Museum of Korea, where visitors can browse the unique cultural and historical traits of Korea and the lifestyle of olden days. Geunjeongjeon, the throne hall, Gyeonghoeru Pavilion in its lotus pond, Hyangwonjeong Pavilion, and many other buildings boast exquisite architecture in the grandest garden landscape. Geonchunmun, the east gate of Gyeongbokgung Palace, opens on Samcheongdonggil Street, which is lined with many art galleries. From the northern tip of the 1-km strip of Samcheongdonggil Street extends a tree-lined street in front of Cheong Wa Dae (the Blue House), adorned with manicured roadside patches. At its other end are the cozy Mugunghwa Dongsan (Rose of Sharon Garden) and Hyoja-dong Sarangbang (an exhibition hall that displays former presidents' gifts from overseas as well as memorabilia of Seoul history).

TOURIST ATTRACTIONS BY REGION

경복궁주변

Gyeongbokgung Palace

GYEONGBOKGUNG PALACE | 경복궁
Built in 1394 as the main palace of the Joseon Dynasty (1392–1910) by its founder King Taejo, it is the most comprehensive and grandest of the five palaces of the period. Daily guided tours of the palace are available at 9:30, 12:00, 14:00 and 15:00.
- ☎ 02-734-2458; http://gbg.cha.go.kr
- 🚇 Exit 5 of Gyeongbokgung Station, Line 3
- 🕐 9:00 – 18:00 (Nov.– Feb., 9:00 – 17:00)
- ⓒ Tue. ₩3,000

NATIONAL FOLK MUSEUM OF KOREA | 국립민속박물관
Located within Gyeongbokgung Palace, the museum is a showcase of the lifestyle of the Korean people from the prehistoric age to the Joseon Dynasty, displaying items of everyday use, funerary objects, major works of art and replicas.
- ☎ 02-3704-3114; www.nfm.go.kr
- 🕐 9:00 – 18:00 (Nov.– Feb., 9:00 – 17:00) ⓒ Tue. and Jan.1 ₩3,000

NATIONAL PALACE MUSEUM OF KOREA
| 국립고궁박물관 (see page 22)
- ☎ 02-3701-7500; http://www.gogung.go.kr;
- 🕐 9:00 – 18:00 on weekdays (9:00 – 19:00 on weekends, and closed on Mondays) ₩2,000 for adults and ₩1,000 for children and youth

CHEONG WA DAE (THE BLUE HOUSE) | 청와대
This is the presidential residence of the Republic of Korea. Tours of Cheong Wa Dae have been conducted since 1998. Individual and group tours are offered at 10:00 and 11:00 and 14:00 and 15:00 Tuesday–Saturday, except on public holidays. Reservations

National Folk Museum of Korea

must be made at least two weeks in advance by e-mail or post. Day-pass tours are held every Friday and Saturday except holidays in April, May, September and October. Admission tickets are distributed at the Cheong Wa Dae Tour Information Booth from 9:00 to 15:00.
- ☎ 02-730-5800; www.cwd.go.kr; e-mail tour@president.go.kr 🚇 Exit 5 of Gyeongbokgung Station, Line 3 🕐 10:00, 11:00, 14:00, 15:00 Tuesday-Friday (except public holidays)

SAMCHEONGDONGGIL STREET | 삼청동길
This street is lined with many famous art galleries such as Gallery Hyundai, Kumho Museum of Art, and the Artsonje Center. There are also Beomnyeonsa Temple, Korean Traditional Folk Dress Museum, Jeongdok Library, cafes, restaurants and craft shops. Shuttle bus service is offered on a circuit of art museums and well-known galleries around this area. It is available every hour on the hour from 13:00–17:00. The bus pass is ₩1,000 and available from the bus driver. Shuttle bus information can be found at www.tourholic.com.

Around Deoksugung Palace

Across from Seoul City Hall is Deoksugung Palace, one of the five royal palaces of the Joseon Dynasty (1392–1910). It was originally the residence of Prince Wolsan (1454–1488), the elder brother of King Seongjong, but was used as the main royal palace by later kings. King Gojong, the next-to-last king of the Joseon Dynasty, remained here even after being forced to abdicate the throne by the Japanese in 1907 until his death in 1919.

King Gojong's son, Sunjong, was the last king and he gave the palace the present name Deoksugung, which means "palace of virtuous longevity," in the hope that his father would live long here.

A detour onto the tree-lined street on the south side of the palace leads to the time-honored Chung Dong First Methodist Church. Just across the road is the Chongdong Theater, which presents performing arts all year round. Near the palace are such frequently visited spots as Gyeonghuigung Palace, the Chosun Ilbo Gallery, Munhwa Ilbo Hall, the old Anglican Cathedral, the Former Russian Legation, Nanta Theater and Tokebi Storm Theater.

Walking toward Sungnyemun Gate (which is also called Namdaemun or South Gate) from the main gate of Deoksugung takes you to Samsung Plaza, which contains the Rodin Gallery as well as a shopping mall. The other side of Sungnyemun Gate is Namdaemun Market, filled with hundreds of wholesale and retail shops, a favorite spot for visitors.

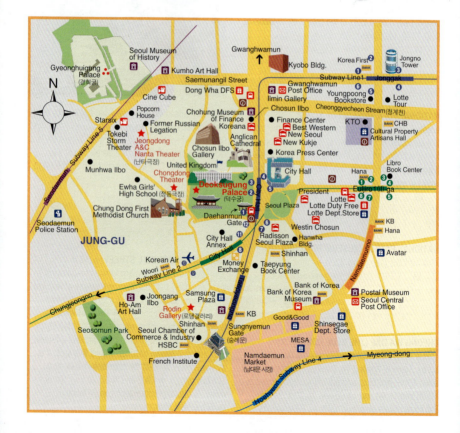

TOURIST ATTRACTIONS BY REGION

덕수궁주변

DEOKSUGUNG PALACE | 덕수궁
Deoksugung Palace is dotted with commanding structures: Daehanmun, the main gate; Junghwajeon, the throne hall and audience hall; and Seokjojeon, the only Western-style building in a Korean palace.
ⓘ: ☏ 02-771-9952; www.deoksugung.go.kr
ⓣ: ▣ Exit 2 or 3 of City Hall Station, Line 1; Exit 12 of City Hall Station, Line 2 ⓗ: 09:00–18:00 (Nov. to Feb., 09:00–17:30; Sat., Sun. and holidays, 09:00–19:00) ⓒ: Mon. ⓐ: ₩1,000

CHONGDONG THEATER | 정동극장
It was Korea's first repertory theater. It presents the "Korean Traditional Performing Arts Series" at 20:00 every day except Monday (16:00, Oct.–Mar.). Main programs include the drum dance, *pansori* (traditional narrative solo song), *sanjo hapju* (an ensemble of Korean instruments), *samullori* (percussion quartet), the sword dance and fan dance. Foreign tourists are given the chance to take pictures with performers wearing traditional Korean dress. English and Japanese subtitles are provided to help foreigners better understand the performances.
ⓘ: ☏ 02-7511-500; www. chongdong.com
ⓣ: ▣ Exit 1 of City Hall Station, Line 1; Exit 12 of City Hall Station, Line 2 ⓐ: ₩20,000–₩30,000

RODIN GALLERY | 로댕갤러리
The Rodin Gallery serves as the world's 8th and Asia's 2nd gallery dedicated solely to the display of Auguste Rodin's works. It is located on the ground floor of Samsung Plaza.
ⓘ: ☏ 02-2259-7781 www.rodingallery.org

ⓣ: ▣ Exit 9 of City Hall Station, Line 1 or 2
ⓗ: 10:00–18:00 ⓒ: Mondays

NANTA THEATER | 난타극장
The Nanta Theater is exclusively for the performance of *Cookin'*. This wild and funny percussion performance has won international awards and acclaim. *Cookin'* is performed using kitchen instruments and utensils, pots, pans, garbage cans, broomsticks, chopsticks, and some especially exciting vegetable chopping on blocks with sharp kitchen knives.
ⓘ: ☏ 02-739-8288; www.nanta.co.kr
ⓣ: ▣ Exit 5 of Seodaemun Station, Line 5 or Exit 12 of City Hall Station, Line 1
ⓐ: ₩40,000–₩60,000

ROYAL GUARD CHANGING CEREMONY
At Daehanmun of Deoksugung Palace, there is a re-enactment of the Royal Guard Changing Ceremony of the Joseon Dynasty. It takes place every day (weather permitting) except Mondays from 10:30–11:00, 14:00–14:30, 15:00–15:30.
ⓘ: ☏ 02-3707-9453

Cookin'

Rodin Gallery

Around Insa-dong

To experience the traditional culture of Korea while remaining in the heart of the city, visit Insa-dong. With art galleries, traditional craft stores, antique art dealers, traditional tea houses and restaurants, it is simply the place in Seoul for visitors wanting to experience traditional Korea.

The area is especially good for antiques — old paintings, ceramics, paper crafts and antique furniture can all be found in abundance at Insa-dong. The 70 or so art galleries in the area also make Insa-dong ideal as a cultural attraction. In 1999, Queen Elizabeth II visited the area and heaped praise upon the old artworks she saw. Insa-dong is designated as vehicle-free on weekends (Saturdays from 14:00 – 22:00, Sundays from 10:00 – 22:00), and a flea markets set up in the streets with people peddling their antiques, accessories and artwork. Travelers from abroad also gather here with wares from the world over, so the flea market items are not just limited to Korean goods.

Adjacent to Insa-dong are Nagwon Arcade (with its musical instrument market and rice cake and delicacy shops); Unhyeongung (the residence of the Regent Daewongun of the late Joseon Dynasty, who closed the doors of the kingdom to foreigners); and Jogyesa Temple (the head temple of Korea's largest Buddhist sect, Jogyejong). Visitors can experience a Buddhist worship service laden with the fragrance of incense performed in Jogyesa Temple. The street on which Jogyesa Temple lies is lined with shops packed with wooden clappers, gray robes, rosaries, incense, brassware and other Buddhist articles.

A bit further along towards Jonggak Station of Subway Line 1 is Jongno Tower, which commands a fine view of Seoul's nightscape. Across from Jongno Tower are Youngpoong Bookstore and the historical Bosingak Bell Pavilion.

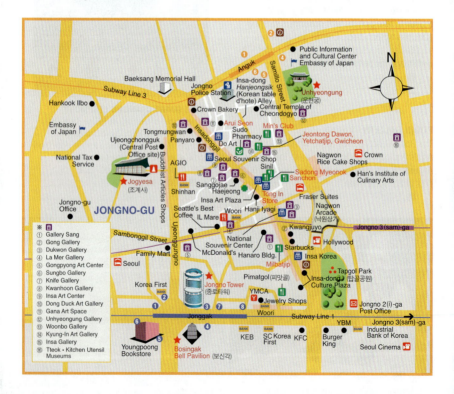

TOURIST ATTRACTIONS BY REGION

인사동주변

Traditional performances at Ssamziegil (Insa-dong)

GALLERIES | 갤러리

Art galleries began to settle in Insa-dong from the 1970s and presently account for more than 70 shops. Galleries in Insa-dong display and sell modern art pieces as well as antiques. Some galleries sell a variety of amateur and professional artists' art work. Kyung-In Art Gallery (02-733-4448) is an art house with three indoor exhibition halls, one outdoor exhibition hall, traditional tea house and garden. Tong In Store (02-735-9094) exhibits and sells traditional and modern crafts made with metals, ceramics, and dyed, woven rice paper. Insa Art Center (02-736-1020, www.ganaart.com) is an art complex with 4 exhibition halls and Gana Art Space (02-734-1333,www.ganaart.com) sells traditional items.

TRADITIONAL RESTAURANTS AND TEA HOUSES | 전통음식점과 찻집

There are enough traditional restaurants and tea houses in Insa-dong to fill every nook and cranny. Some are modern, but most have a distinctly traditional flavor. Sanchon (02-735-0312; www.sanchon.com) serves vegetarian temple food along with a traditional dance performance. Jirisan (02-723-7213) is famous for delicious dishes that taste of Korean homecooking. Min's Club (02-733-2966) provides traditional tea, wine and Korean and Western food in a reformed *hanok* (traditional Korean house). Sadong Myeonok (02-735-7393) is renowned for *manduguk* (dumpling soup), and Gaetmaeul Milbatjip (02-737-0229) is celebrated for *kalguksu* (noodle soup). Yetchatjip (02-722-5332), Gwicheon (02-734-2828) and Jeontong Dawon (02-730-6305), which are located inside Kyung-In Art Gallery, are popular traditional tea houses. Meditation Arui Seon (02-722-6653; www.arui.org) is a tea house introducing Korean-style meditation. It lets tourists drink tea under the guidance of meditation coaches. Another fun thing to try in Insa-dong is *hotteok* (Chinese stuffed pancake) and *kkultarae* (candy) from a street vendor.

ⓘ: Insa-dong Tourist Information Centers (There are tourist information centers at

Bosingak Bell Pavilion and Jongno Tower
Min's Club
Jogyesa Temple

both ends of Insa-dong Street. You can get free maps and guide booklets here or a complimentary tour guide.) 📞 02-731-1676, 02-731-1621 Ⓣ: 🚇 Jonggak Station, Line 1 🚶 3 min.; Jongno 3 (sam)-ga Station, Line 1, 3 or 5 🚶 3 min.; 🚇 Anguk Station, Line 3

UNHYEONGUNG | 운현궁
A private house of the royal family during the late Joseon period that consists of several elegant buildings. Here King Gojong (the next-to-last king of the Joseon Dynasty) lived until age 12, and his father, known as Daewongun, attended to state affairs as regent for 10 years (1863–1873). The wedding ceremony of King Gojong and Queen Myeongseong is re-enacted here on the 3rd or 4th Saturday in April and October annually.
Ⓘ: 📞 02-766-9190 Ⓣ: 🚇 Exit 4 of Anguk Station, Line 3 or Exit 4 of Jongno 5 (o)-ga Station, Line 5
Ⓗ: 09:00–19:00 (Mar.–May, Sep.–Oct.), 09:00–18:00 (Jun.–Aug.)
Ⓒ: Mondays Ⓐ: ₩700

BOSINGAK BELL PAVILION | 보신각
This is the belfry for a 3.18-m-tall bronze bell from the early Joseon period. Today, this bell tolls on New Year's Day, Independence Movement Day (March 1) and Liberation Day (August 15).
Ⓣ: 🚇 Exit 4 of Jonggak Station, Line 1

JONGNO TOWER | 종로타워
A distinct landmark in downtown Seoul with a unique design and a fantastic night view.
On the top floor is the Top Cloud & Grill Cafe, which is best known for its glass walls that provide stunning views of Seoul as well as for its savory fusion foods and live jazz performances. The underground is called Millenium Plaza and is occupied by a number of restaurants and shops.
Ⓣ: 🚇 Exit 3 of Jonggak Station, Line 1

JOGYESA TEMPLE | 조계사
Unlike most Buddhist temples in Korea that are nestled in the mountains, Jogyesa is located in the city center.
A grand lotus lantern parade takes place along Jongno Street from Dongdaemun Stadium to Jogyesa Temple on April 30, 2006 (Sunday evening) before Buddha's birthday, which falls on the 8th day of the 4th lunar month (May 5, 2006). Foreign tourists can be accompanied by an English-speaking guide free of charge upon request.
Ⓘ: 📞 02-725-6641; www.ijogyesa.net
Ⓣ: 🚇 Exit 2 of Jonggak Station, Line 1; Exit 6 of Anguk Station, Line 3 or Exit 2 of Gwanghwamun Station, Line 5

TOURIST ATTRACTIONS BY REGION

Around Myeong-dong

명동주변

Myeong-dong has long been the trendsetting center of Korean fashion. Lotte and Shinsegae Department Stores, Migliore, underground and aboveground shopping malls for apparel, shoes, accessories and cosmetics cater to every fad and mode. Every back alley has cafes and restaurants serving snacks and delicacies for breaks while shopping.

On the knoll at the far end of the main street of Myeong-dong stands Myeongdong Cathedral, the Korean Catholic headquarters. Within a stone's throw is the Young Women's Christian Association (YWCA), which works to promote women's rights.

MYEONGDONG CATHEDRAL | 명동성당

Completed in 1898, it is Korea's first Western-style brick building and was designed in a Neo-Renaissance style with a 45-meter steeple.

ⓘ : 02-774-3890; www.mdsd.or.kr
ⓣ : Exit 8 of Myeong-dong Station, Line 4 or Exit 5 of Euljiro 1 (il)-ga Station, Line 2 ⓗ : 06:30 – 20:00

Myeongdong Cathedral

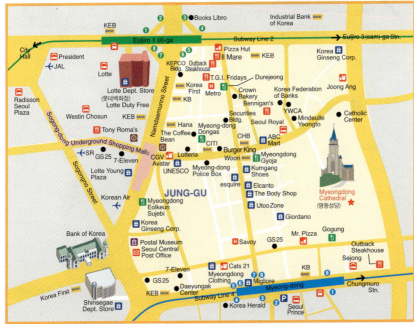

Around Namsan Park

Namsan Park climbs the slope of Mt. Namsan, on which N Seoul Tower, a city landmark, offers an unobstructed panoramic view of the city. Below it are the octagonal pavilion Palgakjeong, a botanical garden, Namsan Public Library, Patriot Ahn Choong Kun Memorial Hall and convenience facilities. Meandering paths and jogging courses through lush trees make this a perfect spot to unwind at the end of the day.

For an easy ascent of Mt. Namsan, visitors can take the cable car from the foot of the mountain or they may prefer taking the steps leading past Namsan Botanical Garden to Palgakjeong Pavilion all the way up to N Seoul Tower.

The tower accommodates the Global Village Folk Museum, a 3-D theater and Pulhyanggi Restaurant, which features mountain vegetable dishes accompanied by traditional arts performances. The tower also has a fine nightscape.

The northern end of Mt. Namsan is dotted with cultural facilities. Korea House offers traditional cuisine and traditional performing arts programs in an elegant ambiance. Namsangol Hanok Village has a cluster of traditional houses that were relocated and refurbished some years ago. The National Theater's opera and dance companies provide colorful repertoire all year round, and for those interested in learning about the traditional Korean tea ceremony, cookery, and etiquette, there is Yejiwon (02-2253-2211/2; yejiwon@yejiwon.or.kr).

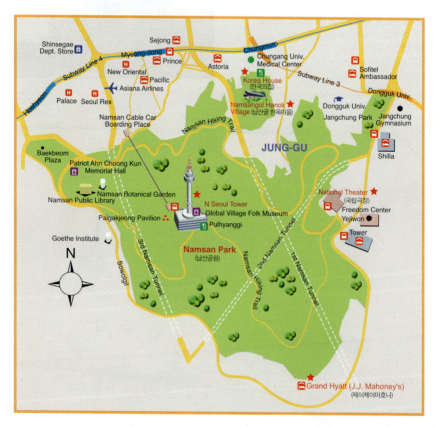

TOURIST ATTRACTIONS BY REGION

남산공원주변

N SEOUL TOWER | N서울타워

Commanding a fine view of Seoul, N Seoul Tower is equipped with observatories and a revolving restaurant for a full-circle view. There are also the Global Village Folk Museum, which maintains over 20,000 rare and precious relics from over 150 countries, a 3-D theater, etc.
CABLE CAR ☎ 02-753-2403; www.cablecar.co.kr
ⓣ: 🚇 Exit 3 of Myeong-dong Station, Line 4, then 🚶 15 min. ⓗ: 10:00 – 23:00 ⓐ: ₩4,800 for a one-way ticket, ₩6,300 for round trip
N SEOUL TOWER ☎ 02-3455-9277 / 9288; www.seoultower.co.kr ⓗ: 09:00 – 01:00 (for the observatory) ⓐ: ₩5,000 for observatory, and ₩11,500 for observatory, museum, Funny World and 3-D theater

NAMSANGOL HANOK VILLAGE | 남산골 한옥마을

This beautiful village, covering a site of 7,934 m², is composed of three parts: a traditional Korean garden, Time Capsule Plaza and the village itself, which includes *hanok* (traditional Korean houses) from the Joseon Dynasty. These houses were moved from their original locations around Seoul and restored completely.
ⓣ: ☎ 02-2266-6923 📠 02-2266-6936; www.hanokmaeul.org ⓣ: 🚇 Exit 3 of Chungmuro Station, Line 3 or 4, then 🚶 5 min.
ⓗ: 09:00 – 19:00 (Apr., May, Sep., Oct.)
09:00 – 19:00 (Apr., May, Sep., Oct.),
09:00 – 17:00 (Nov.– Feb.) ⓒ: Tue.

KOREA HOUSE | 한국의 집

Korea House is an excellent example of traditional architecture where visitors can enjoy authentic *hanjeongsik* (Korean table d'hôte) and traditional Korean music and dance

Namsangol Hanok Village

performances as well as purchase a variety of traditional handicrafts. Reservations are required.
ⓣ: ☎ 02-2266-9101/3 📠 02-2278-1776; www.koreahouse.or.kr ⓣ: 🚇 Exit 3 of Chungmuro Station, Line 3 or 4, then 🚶 5 min.

NATIONAL THEATER | 국립극장

Nestled on the slope of Mt. Namsan, it houses large and small performance halls and outdoor stages. It is the home of the National Drama Company, National Dance Company, National Changgeuk Company and National Orchestra Company.
ⓣ: ☎ 02-2280-4114; www.ntok.go.kr
ⓣ: 🚌 Shuttle bus from 🚇 Exit 2 of Dongguk Univ. Station, Line 3

J.J. MAHONEY'S | 제이제이마호니

J.J. Mahoney's is the Grand Hyatt Seoul's popular nightspot offering fun and excitement in nine themed settings.
ⓛ: B1, Grand Hyatt Seoul, Hannam-dong, Yongsan-gu ⓣ: ☎ 02-799-8601/798-0066
ⓗ: 18:00 – 02:00 (Sun.–Thur.); 18:00 – 03:00 (Fri. & Sat.)

National Theater

TOURIST ATTRACTIONS BY REGION

Namdaemun Market 남대문시장

Just a few minutes from Seoul's ancient Namdaemun Gate (Sungnyemun or South Gate) is an open-air market of the same name. It is close to the downtown area and deluxe hotels boasting the very best selection of merchandise in the nation.

The market's history traces back to the Joseon Dynasty and since then has become the main transactional place of daily products between urban and rural areas of Korea.

Namdaemun Market is also the nation's wholesale center and virtually anything you want can be found here: clothing, shoes, housewares, foodstuffs, flowers, tools, wigs, glasses, accessories of every kind, gift items, sporting goods, construction materials, electric appliances, furniture, etc. Having long been perceived as a traditional open-air market, it is changing its image with new, modern shopping centers such as Mesa.

ⓘ: Namdaemun Market Information Center

📞 02-752-1913 Ⓣ: Ⓜ Exit 5 of Hoehyeon Station, Line 4 Ⓒ: Sun

Namdaemun Fashion Town | 남대문 패션타운
Ⓣ: Ⓜ Exit 5 of Hoehyeon Station, Line 4
Mesa | 메사
Ⓣ: Ⓜ Exit 7 of Hoehyeon Station, Line 4
🕒 10:00 am–5:00 am (Closed on Sundays)
ⓘ: 📞 02-2128-5000 ext. 0

Namdaemun Market

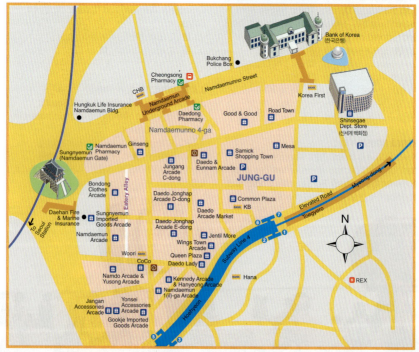

TOURIST ATTRACTIONS BY REGION
Dongdaemun Market 동대문시장

Some of the greatest bargains can be found at Dongdaemun Market, a large area packed with small shops and big malls.
Some 10 or so modern clothing malls have sprung up among the long-established older markets and these shops are open all night, brightly lit and play cheerful music.
The biggest items are fabrics, clothing, leather goods, women's and children's costumes, bedding, housewares, footwear, and sporting goods. The Dongdaemun Gate (Heunginjimun or East Gate) area has become famous for selling clothing similar to what can be found in department stores at reasonable prices.
Modern shopping malls such as Migliore, Doosan Tower, hello apM, Blue Gate and Designer Club attract many young people.
ⓘ: Dongdaemun Market Information Center 02-2236-9135 (interpretation and buying guide available) 📞 02-2236-9134 🚇: Dongdaemun Stadium Station, Line 2, 4 or 5

Doosan Tower

Dongdaemun Fashion Town | 동대문 패션타운
🚇: Dongdaemun Stadium Station, Line 2 or Dongdaemun Station, Line 1 or 4
Doosan Tower | 두산타워
🕐: 10:30 – 17:00 (Closed on Mondays)
ⓘ: 📞 02-3398-3114
Migliore | 밀리오레
🕐: 10:30 – 04:30 (Closed on Mondays)
ⓘ: 📞 02-3393-0001
Blue Gate | 청대문
🕐: 10:00 – 16:30 (Closed on Tuesdays)
ⓘ: 📞 02-2048-0445; www.cheongdaemun.com
Jeilpyeonghwa Market | 제일평화시장
🕐: 9:00 – 17:30 (Closed on Sundays)
ⓘ: 📞 02-2252-3633

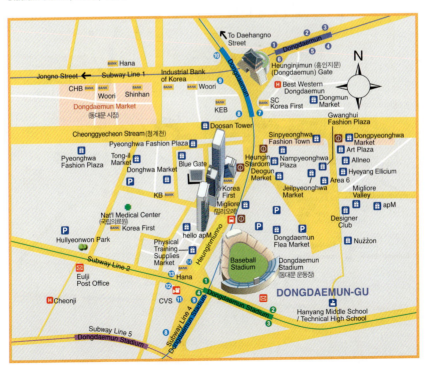

Around Daehangno Street

The literal meaning of Daehangno is "university street" because until the mid-1970s, the College of Liberal Arts and Sciences of the Seoul National University campus was located in the current Marronnier Park site. Daehangno is the cradle of Korean performing arts, the off-Broadway of Korea. Small theaters, galleries, cafes, folk taverns, and restaurants are sprawled across Marronnier Park. Various outdoor sculpture and painting exhibitions and performing arts are offered on makeshift stages on the street. About 40 theaters and several museums attract throngs of young people. Amid these heart-pounding streets is poised a serene compound called Ihwajang, which was once the manor of the first Korean president, Syngman Rhee, now renovated as a museum. Nearby are Jongmyo Royal Ancestral Shrine and Changgyeonggung Palace. A busy road cuts between Changgyeonggung Palace and Jongmyo Royal Ancestral Shrine but there is a pedestrian bridge connecting the two attractions. There is also Changdeokgung Palace with its beautiful rear garden, Huwon (or Biwon, "Secret Garden"). Jongmyo and Changdeokgung are registered on UNESCO's World Cultural Heritage list. Another nearby historical spot is Sung Kyun Kwan, the Confucian university that was founded in 1398 at the start of the Joseon Dynasty. Ⓣ: 🚇 Daehangno Station, Line 4

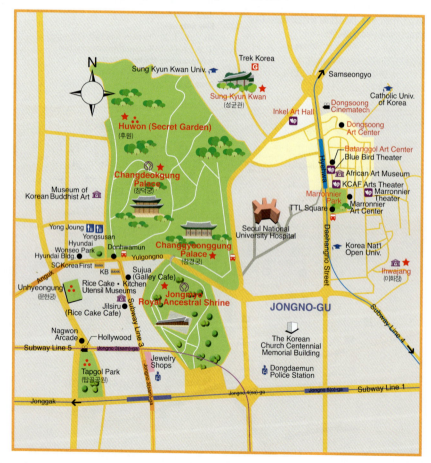

TOURIST ATTRACTIONS BY REGION

대학로주변

JONGMYO ROYAL ANCESTRAL SHRINE | 종묘
Jongmyo was one of three main state institutions of the Joseon Dynasty along with Gyeongbokgung (the main palace) and Sajikdan (the national altar for the gods of earth and crops), which is located in Sajik Park. Jongmyo enshrines the spirit tablets of Joseon kings and queens.
On the 1st Sunday of May each year, rituals are conducted according to strict procedures in an austere ambiance. Accompanying music and dance maintain the traditional form of the rites. Jongmyo is conveniently connected to Changgyeonggung Palace by a footbridge so that visitors can enjoy both for only ₩1,000.
①: 02-765-0195 ⓣ: Exit 11 of Jongno 3 (sam)-ga Station, Line 1, Exit 8
ⓗ: 09:00–18:00 (Sat., Sun. and national holidays, 09:00–19:00; Nov.–Feb., 09:00–17:30)
ⓒ: Tue. Ⓐ: ₩1,000

CHANGGYEONGGUNG PALACE | 창경궁
Suganggung Palace was first built by the 4th ruler of the Joseon Dynasty, King Sejong (r.1418–1450), for his retiring father, King Taejong, and was often used as residential quarters for queens and concubines. During the reign of King Seongjong (r.1469–1494), the palace was renovated and renamed Changgyeonggung Palace. This palace became a park with a zoo and a botanical garden during Japanese colonial rule.
The zoo was relocated and the palace regained its old grace in the 1980s after years of

---

BUKCHON HANOK VILLAGE, THE GUEST HOUSES
Bukchon, or North Village, is a traditional residential area located between Gyeongbokgung Palace, Changdeokgung Palace and Jongmyo Shrine. Its 600-year history spans the life of the city itself. At Bukchon Guesthouse, a *hanok* experience facility, visitors have the chance to enjoy the aesthetic charms of a traditional Korean house. The guesthouse's proximity to some of the popular tourist attractions of Seoul makes it another favorite destination for people seeking accommodations.
Bukchon Guest House 02-743-8530; www.bukchon72.com
Seoul Guest House 02-745-0057; www.seoul110.com
Urijip Guest House 02-744-0536
ⓣ: Exit 3 of Anguk Station, Line 3. The village is located at the street corner that leads to Jungang High School from the Gye-dong Hyundai Group building.

restoration. This palace is unique in that its front gate and the throne hall face east while those in all the other palaces face south.
①: ☎ 02-762-4868 ⓣ: 🚇 Exit 4 of Hyehwa Station, Line 4 ⓗ: 09:00 – 18:00 (Nov.–Feb., 09:00 – 17:30; Sat., Sun. and national holidays, 09:00 – 19:00) ⓒ: Tue. ⓐ: ₩1,000

CHANGDEOKGUNG PALACE | 창덕궁
HUWON | 후원

It was used as the main palace by many Joseon kings and the best preserved among the five royal Joseon palaces. It is best known for its beautiful garden for the royal family, Huwon (or Biwon, "Secret Garden") with its superb landscape with pavilions, ponds and wooded areas. It is only for group viewing and daily guided tours of the palace and garden are available in English at 11:30, 13:30 and 15:30.
①: ☎ 02-762-0648 ⓣ: 🚇 Exit 3 of Anguk Station, Line 3 ⓗ: 09:15 – 15:45 (09:15 – 15:45, Nov.–Feb.) ※ Entry is permitted every 15 and 45 minutes past the hour. ⓒ: Mon. ⓐ: ₩3,000

IHWAJANG, THE SYNGMAN RHEE MEMORIAL
| 이화장

Ihwajang is a typical Korean mansion that was built in the 1930s. Dr. Rhee lived here from 1947 until he moved to Gyeongmudae (the present Cheong Wa Dae) on August 15, 1948, as the first president of the Republic of Korea. It displays a

variety of personal and household items that he and his wife used. ①: ☎ 02-741-1945 ⓣ: 🚇 Exit 2 of Hyehwa Station, Line 4

SUNG KYUN KWAN | 성균관

This was the highest educational institution for Confucian teachings and studies during the Goryeo and Joseon Dynasties. It accommodated about 200 of the highest academic achieving students from across the country. The main facilities include a lecture hall, dormitories and a shrine to Confucius and distinguished Confucian scholars. Every spring and fall, a traditional Confucian memorial service is held at the shrine by Sung Kyun Kwan University students.
①: ☎ 02-765-0501 ⓣ: 🚇 Exit 4 of Hyehwa Station, Line 4 ⓗ: 09:00 – 17:00

Traditional Confucian rituals, Sung Kyun Kwan

THEATERS & CINEMAS

Black Box Theater | 블랙박스 씨어터 ⓛ: 1-60 Dongsung-dong, Jongno-gu ①: ☎ 02-744-8025
Dongsoong Art Center and Cinematech | 동숭아트센터 & 시네마텍 ⓛ: 185 Hyehwa-dong, Jongno-gu ①: ☎ 02-766-3390
Theater Hakchon | 학전소극장 ⓛ: 1-79 Dongsung-dong, Jongno-gu ①: ☎ 02-763-8233

HOT CAFES

Cheonnyeondongando ("Even for 1,000 Years") | 천년동안도 Famous for its live jazz performances
ⓛ: Behind the second carpark of Daehangno KFC alley ①: ☎ 02-741-5229 ⓗ: 12:00 – 02:00
Mindeulle Yeongto Annex Hall | 공간을 채우는 사람 Compound theme cafe with a fantastic exterior (consists of a family restaurant, theme cafe, outdoor terrace, seminar rooms, etc.) ⓣ: 🚇 From Exit 2 of Hyehwa Station, Line 4, 🚶 go toward Marronnier Park. ①: ☎ 02-745-5234/5 ⓗ: 10:00 – 24:00

TOURIST ATTRACTIONS BY REGION

Around Sinchon 신촌주변

Sinchon refers to the area where three major universities are located: Yonsei University, Ewha Womans University and Sogang University. Here you can find numerous coffee lounges, restaurants, snack bars, beauty salons, clothing and accessory shops, cinemas, theaters, jazz cafes, rock cafes nightclubs, department stores and shopping centers all catering to university students and the young at heart.
Ⓣ: Ⓜ Sinchon Station, Line 2

YONSEI UNIVERSITY STREET | 연세대학교 거리
This road takes you from Sinchon Subway Station right to Yonsei University. Like branching tree roots, the numerous side streets diverge off the main road in every direction. In 1999, Yonsei University Street was designated as "The Road One Wants to Walk." Since then, this famous street has been improved upon even more, placed on tourist maps and promoted by businesses. Visitors to this area have their choice of a plethora of restaurants, coffee shops and stores. In the afternoon, you can also enjoy the treats from small food stands that line the sidewalks. Every May, the Sinchon Cultural Festival comes to life on this street.
Ⓣ: Ⓜ Exit 3 of Sinchon Station, Line 2

FASHION STREET | 패션의 거리
"Fashion Street" starts at the main gate of Ewha Womans University and continues to Sinchon Rail Station and it is packed with copious amounts of clothing stores, hence the name "Fashion Street." It is lined with name brand retailers, secondhand shops, accessory shops and shoe stores. It is affordable and in tune with the current trends in Korea, making it very popular with the youth of Seoul.
Ⓣ: Ⓜ Ewha Womans University Station, Line 2

Sinchon

Around Hongik University

The area in front of Hongik University is commonly referred to as Hongdae, which is famous as a major art college in Korea. This area is one of the favorite hangouts for trendy youth in Seoul. Rock, techno, hip hop, and jazz enthusiasts gather in the restaurants, cafes and bars and uplift the atmosphere.
Ⓣ: Hongik Univ. Station, Line 2

ART FREE MARKET | 홍대 프리마켓
Every Saturday in the playground in front of the main gate of Hongik University, a colorful array of handcrafts, accessories, dolls, clothes, purses, and household items made of metal, fabric, and other materials can be bought here.
The market is held Saturday from 1:00 to 6:00 pm. Since it is an open-air market and the weather determines whether or not it will be held, it would be wise to check the weather forecast before starting out for the market.
Ⓣ: Exit 6 of Hongik University Station, Line 2. It is opposite the main entrance of Hongik University.

Fringe Festival and Street Art Festival

As part of efforts to keep the cultural assets of Hongdae free from commercial encroachments, the Seoul Fringe Festival and Street Art Festival are held every year. Intended to support the independent arts, the Seoul Fringe Festival is held throughout the area in theaters, clubs, art galleries and in the streets.
In addition to the plays, dance, mime, music, art, independent film and art exhibits, there are also academic events and various programs that contribute to the rich cultural display in the Hongdae district.
The streets of Hongdae also become an open gallery during the festival, utilizing the many interesting sights that characterize the area.
Ⓘ: 02-325-8150; www.seoulfringe.net

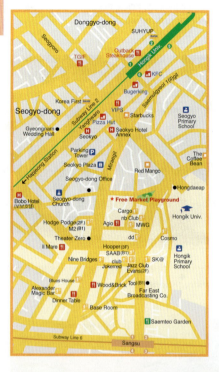

TOURIST ATTRACTIONS BY REGION

홍익대학교주변

Club Day
SEOUL

The area surrounding Hongik University is a nexus of Korea's youthful nightlife. Many of Seoul's idiosyncratic clubs that draw the younger set are clustered in the area, and on the last Friday of every month these clubs host a Club Day. Hongdae Club Day started in 2001 as a way to promote the club business and has since become a staple youth festival.
A ₩15,000 ticket gains partygoers admittance into about 15 clubs, with one drink on the house—ideal for people who find dancing and music irresistible. A wild gathering of young adults from all over the world is waiting. Participating clubs include: M.I, SK@, DD, MWG, NB, Hooper, SAAB, Hodge Podge, M2, Cargo, Cosmo, Joker Red, etc. (marked by a on the map to the left).
ⓘ: 02-333-3921 (Club Culture Promotion Committee) Ⓣ: Exit 6 of Hongik University Station, Line 2

Hongik Univ. Free Market

Nearby Attraction
SEOUL

INDEPENDENCE PARK |독립공원
Independence Park is comprised of Dongnimmun (Independence Gate) and Seodaemun Prison History Hall. Dongnimmun Gate was built in 1897 as a symbol of the nation's commitment to independence from foreign interference. Gyeongseong Prison was built in 1908 during Japanese colonial rule, and many Korean patriots were tortured and killed there.
The prison has been converted to the Seodaemun Prison History Hall, which chronicles the resistance with wall coffins, a solitary cell, interrogation chambers showing various torture scenes and many other informative exhibitions. Old jail cells and the dreadful execution house are open to tourists.
ⓘ: Seodaemun Prison History Hall 02-364-4686 Ⓣ: Exit 4 or 5 of Dongnimmun Station, Line 3 ⓗ: 09:30 – 18:00 Ⓐ: ₩1,500 Ⓒ: Mondays, January 1, Seollal and Chuseok

Fringe Festival

Club Day

Independence Park

Itaewon www.itaewon.go.kr

From the Itaewon Intersection, this special tourism zone stretches all the way past the Hamilton Hotel to Hannam-dong. It is honeycombed with about 2,000 shops as well as jazz bars, nightclubs and ethnic restaurants. This district is popular with both foreign residents and tourists.

In the core area around the Hamilton Hotel are clustered 1,000 shops selling leather goods, bags, clothes, shoes and tourist souvenirs. The sidewalk is fringed with about 400 roadside stalls attracting shoppers with accessories, hats, T-shirts, small gadgets and much more. Itaewon is the area most densely packed with diverse ethnic restaurants—Italian, Swiss, German, Mexican, Indian, Pakistani, Thai, etc.

Itaewon comes alive at night when the lights go out in the business districts. Roadside stalls shift to hundreds of carts serving drinks and snacks. With many karaoke and fancy disco clubs, Itaewon is ablaze with activity throughout the night.

ⓘ: Itaewon Information ☏ 02-792-9070, 02-794-2490, 02-3785-2514 (Tourist Information Center)
Ⓣ: 🚇 Itaewon Station, Line 6

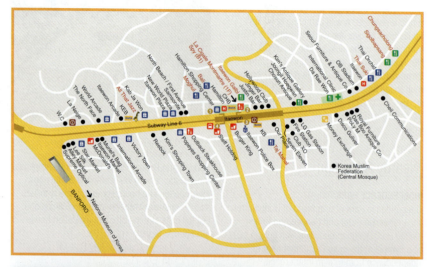

TOURIST ATTRACTIONS BY REGION

이 태 원

RESTAURANTS FROM AROUND THE WORLD

Chungsacholong Traditional Korean food
ⓘ: ☎ 02-794-1177 ⓗ: 6:00 – 22:00
Itaewon Galbi Korean food
ⓘ: ☎ 02-795-9716; www.kalbi.co.kr
ⓗ: 11:00 – 22:30
Sigolbapsang Traditional Korean food
ⓘ: ☎ 02-794-5072 ⓗ: 24 hours
Bali Indonesian food
ⓘ: ☎ 02-749-5271 ⓗ: 11:45 – 22:00
La Cigale Montmartre French food
ⓘ: ☎ 02-796-1244
ⓗ: 12:00 – 15:00, 17:30 – 02:00
Moghul Pakistani food
ⓘ: ☎ 02-796-5501 ⓗ: 12:00 – 22:30
Taj Mahal Indian food
ⓘ: ☎ 02-749-0316/7 ⓗ: 12:00 – 22:00
Thai Suki Thai food
ⓘ: ☎ 02-792-9740 ⓗ: 11:00 – 22:00

SIZZLING NIGHTCLUBS

Bobos9
ⓛ: Inside the Capital Hotel
ⓘ: ☎ 02-792-0161 ⓗ: 19:30 – 07:00
Interface
ⓛ: Inside the Itaewon Hotel
ⓘ: ☎ 02-790-8577 ⓗ: 19:30 – 07:00 Spy
ⓛ: Opposite side of the Itaewon Fire Station
ⓘ: ☎ 02-796-9993 ⓗ: 19:00 – 05:00

UNIQUE BARS AND CAFES

Our Place
Enjoy the view of Itaewon at night with steak, pasta, beer, wine, etc.
ⓣ: Exit 3 of Itaewon Station, Line 6
ⓘ: ☎ 02-792-7888 ⓗ: 16:00 – 03:00
All That Jazz
Live jazz bar since 1976
ⓘ: ☎ 02-795-5701 ⓗ: 17:00 – 01:00

Around Yeouido

Finance and business thrive here with the Korea Stock Exchange; surrounding headquarters of securities firms; the Federation of Korean Industries; the Korean Federation of Small and Medium Businesses; the Seoul Yeouido Exhibition Center, which sells top-notch products of small and medium entrepreneurs; and the studios of Korea's three major broadcasting stations KBS, MBC and SBS. The 63 City building, the golden landmark of Yeouido, is packed with fun facilities including a huge-screen IMAX Theater, a magnificent aquarium, rooftop observation deck, shopping mall and restaurants.

LG Science Hall in the LG Twin Towers shows children the scientific possibilities of tomorrow. Yeouido Park and Hangang Riverside Park are fine places for rest and outdoor sports and ferry boats ply the waterfront.

If you would like to take a pleasant stroll while enjoying the spring's blossoms, don't miss Yunjungno Street. It is a 7-km road lined with about 1,400 cherry trees ranging from 3 to 35 years old.

A cruise along the picturesque Hangang River will take you through the heart of Seoul.

Yeouido Park

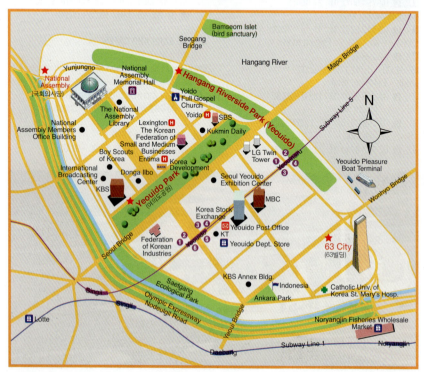

TOURIST ATTRACTIONS BY REGION

여의도주변

63 CITY | 63빌딩

With 3 underground and 60 aboveground floors, this golden tower offers much to see such as the rooftop observation deck, IMAX Theater, the Aquarium of 63 Sea World, etc. Sea World displays 20,000 marine creatures from 400 different species. A health club, shopping mall, classy restaurants, and snack bars offer visitors diverse options for spending a day by the river.
ⓘ: ☎ 02-789-5663/5; www.63city.co.kr
ⓣ: 🚇 From Exit 4 of Yeouinaru Station, Line 5 or Exit 5 of Yeouido Station, Line 5 🚌 take a free shuttle bus. ⓗ: 10:00 – 22:00 Ⓐ: ₩19,000 for use of all facilities

NATIONAL ASSEMBLY | 국회의사당

The site of the National Assembly covers 12.5% of Yeouido Island. This is the largest national assembly building in Asia. There are also the National Assembly Memorial Hall and the National Assembly Library. You may apply for a tour at the information desk at the rear gate. The road around the National Assembly is known for beautiful cherry blossoms in spring.
ⓘ: ☎ 02-788-2885, 2889; www.assembly.go.kr
ⓣ: 🚇 Take a shuttle bus from 🚇 Exit 3 of Yeouido Station, Line 5. ⓗ: 09:00 – 17:00 (Nov.– Feb., 09:00 – 16:00)

YEOUIDO PARK | 여의도공원

Yeouido Plaza, which was paved flat 27 years ago, was transformed into the enchanting Yeouido Park with groves, grass, pond and pavilions in 1999. A bike path and walking trails circle the park and are conveniently linked through an underground sidewalk to the waterfront of the Hangang River.

ⓘ: ☎ 02-761-4078/9; http://parks.seoul.go.kr/youido/english/main.htm ⓣ: 🚇 Exit 3 of Yeouido Station or Exit 1 of Yeouinaru Station, Line 5

Hangang River | 한강   SEOUL
http://hangang.seoul.go.kr

A symbol of Seoul, the Hangang River runs through Seoul east to west with an average depth of 2.5 m and a width of 175 m. The river is crossed by 23 bridges and there are excursion boats plying between Yeouido and Jamsil. At 12 different points along the 41.5-km-long riverbank are Hangang Riverside Parks, equipped with sports facilities such as soccer and baseball fields, volleyball and basketball courts and swimming pools. Facilities for water skiing, yachting, boating and fishing are also available.

PLEASURE BOAT CRUISE

The river cruise is a must for visitors to Seoul. There are various cruise courses that take about 1 hour. The fare is ₩9,000.
ⓘ: Han River Land www.hanriverland.co.kr
☎ 02-3271-6900

Round Trip	
Yeouido → Yanghwa → Yeouido	1hr.
Jamdubong → Yanghwa → (Yeouido) → Jamdubong	1hr.
Yanghwa → Hangang Bridge → Yanghwa	1hr.
Sangam → Yeouido → Sangam	1hr.
Jamsil → Ddukseom → Hangang Bridge → Jamsil	1hr.
Yeouido → Yeouido (Live concert cruise)	1hr., 30 min
Seoul Forest → Hannam Bridge → Jamsil → Ddukseom → Seoul Forest	1hr.
One-way	
Yeouido → Seoul Forest (or Ddukseom, Jamsil)	40 min –1hr.
Jamsil (or Ddukseom, Seoul Forest) → Yeouido	40 min –1hr.

National Assembly

Around the Gangnam Area

GANGNAM STATION VICINITY | 강남역
The Gangnam Station vicinity is always crowded with young people. There are many pubs, cafes, nightclubs, restaurants, theaters, clothing shops, department stores and bookstores offering a number of activities in an exciting atmosphere.
🚇 Exit 6 or 7 of Gangnam Station, Line 2

APGUJEONG-DONG AREA | 압구정동
About a 20-min. walk from Apgujeong Station is the flourishing area that surrounds the Galleria Department Store. This area is often referred to as Korea's Rodeo Street, with glittering businesses ranging from expensive designer stores to unique vintage clothing shops. The young and fashionable of Korea gather here, and much enjoyment can be derived from the simple pleasure of people-watching. Korean celebrities frequent Apgujeong-dong, and star sightings are not uncommon. One block away is Cheongdam-dong street, which is lined with boutiques, art galleries, trendy coffee lounges and bars.
🚇 Take a Galleria Department Store-bound bus from 🚇 Exit 2 of Apgujeong Station, Line 3

CHEONGDAM-DONG AREA | 청담동
Representative of luxury fashion trends, Cheongdam-dong is famous for shops selling brand name items from around the world as well as for sophisticated restaurants, bars, and cafes. The various Korean, Japanese, Chinese, Italian,

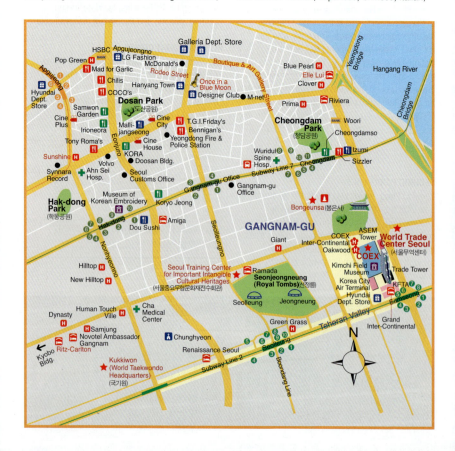

TOURIST ATTRACTIONS BY REGION

강남지역

Indian, Thai and fusion restaurants in the district are more than enough to satisfy the demanding tastes of their visitors.
Many people also meet here at night for the jazz bars, terrace cafes and tent bars.

SAMSEONG-DONG AREA | 삼성동
The Samseong-dong area is the showcase of Seoul's new quintessence. This area has been developed since the 1970s as a new business center. Including the World Trade Center Seoul, the area houses boutiques, world-class hotels, department stores, highrise apartment complexes, and the Teheran Valley, where many up-and-coming dotcom enterprises are located. Across the street from the Convention and Exhibition Center (COEX) lies the time-honored Bongeunsa Temple.

Near Seolleung Station of Subway Line 2 are Seonjeongneung, the Joseon Dynasty royal tombs. Another attraction is the Seoul Training Center for Important Intangible Cultural Heritages, showing and selling a variety of exquisite handicrafts made by nationally designated master artisans.

Ⓣ: 🚇 Apgujeong Station, Line 3 or Samseong Station, Line 2

WORLD TRADE CENTER SEOUL | 무역센터
The WTCS refers to a large area that includes COEX, a state-of-the-art convention and exhibition facility; 55-story Trade Tower, which houses trade-related organizations and export firms; ASEM Tower, a new office building; and the Korea City Air Terminal, which handles check-in and immigration procedures and

---

SIZZLING NIGHTCLUBS
NYLA
Ⓛ: Inside the Ellui Hotel; Cheongdam-dong, Gangnam-gu
Ⓘ: 📞 02-514-3509
BOSS
Ⓛ: Inside the Sunshine Hotel; Sinsa-dong, Gangnam-gu
Ⓘ: 📞 02-518-5966
SEDUCE
Ⓛ: Banpo-dong, Seocho-gu (in the Central City underground arcade) Ⓣ: Express Bus Terminal Station, Line 3 or 7
Ⓘ: 📞 02-535-4222

FAMOUS CAFES AND BARS
Cafe 74
Ⓛ: Cheongdam-dong, Gangnam-gu (next to the Napoleon Bakery) Ⓘ: 📞 02-542-7412 Ⓗ: 11:00 – 02:00
Gossen
Ⓛ: Apgujeong-dong, Gangnam-gu (next to Enprani Cosmetic, which is on the opposite side of the Galleria Department Store) Ⓘ: 📞 02-515-1864 Ⓗ: 10:00 – 06:00
Hard Rock Cafe
Ⓛ: Located on floor B1 of Donggung Wedding Hall at the Hak-dong Intersection Ⓘ: 📞 02-547-5671; www.hardrock.co.kr Ⓗ: Mon. to Thur., 17:00 – 02:00; Fri., 17:00 – 03:00; Sat., 12:00 – 03:00; Sun., 12:00 – 02:00
Jamusch
Ⓛ: Nonhyeon-dong, Gangnam-gu (near the Apgujeong Designer Club) Ⓘ: 📞 02-514-2986 Ⓗ: 17:30 – 07:00
Nyx & Nox
Ⓛ: Inside the Ritz-Carlton Hotel Ⓣ: Take a taxi from Gangnam Station or Yeoksam Station, Line 2.
Ⓘ: 📞 02-3451-8444 Ⓗ: 18:00 – 03:00 (Sun. 18:00 – 01:00)
Once in a Blue Moon
Ⓛ: Apgujeong-dong, Gangnam-gu (near the Apgujeong Designer Club) Ⓘ: 📞 02-549-5490 Ⓗ: 17:00 – 02:00
Tavern's Vil
Ⓛ: Cheongdam-dong, Gangnam-gu (behind the Hankook Chinaware Outlet) Ⓘ: 📞 02-540-0419 Ⓗ: 18:00 – 03:00
ZZYZX
Ⓛ: Cheongdam-dong, Gangnam-gu (behind the Hankook Chinaware Outlet) Ⓘ: 📞 02-515-0015; www.zzyzx.co.kr
Ⓗ: 17:00 – 02:00

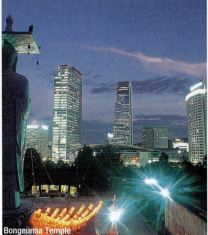
Bongeunsa Temple

Seoul Arts Center

provides nonstop airport limousine bus service. This is an ideal venue for any large-scale meeting or exhibition.
ⓘ: ☏ 02-6000-0114; www.coex.co.kr
ⓣ: ⓜ Exit 6 of Samseong Station, Line 2

COEX MALL | 코엑스몰
COEX Mall is an underground emporium that integrates shopping, dining, and a variety of entertainment, cultural activities and services in one place. Also here are the impressive aquarium (www.coexaqua.co.kr) and Kimchi Field Museum (www.kimchimuseum.org).
ⓘ: ☏ 02-6002-5312; www.coexmall.com
ⓣ: ⓜ Exit 6 of Samseong Station, Line 2

SEOUL ARTS CENTER | 예술의전당
The Seoul Arts Center is a worldwide art complex and it is comprised of the Opera House, Music House, Art Gallery, Art Library and Calligraphy Art Museum. You can enjoy various performances and exhibitions at this location. It is also famous for its relaxing outdoor environment. There is an outdoor theater, which has a half moon-shaped stage where many performances are held. From March to October, you can also enjoy watching the World Music Fountain, which features water dancing to music.
ⓘ: ☏ 02-580-1300; www.sac.or.kr ⓣ: ⓜ Take a shuttle bus from ⓜ Exit 5 of Nambu Bus Terminal Station, Line 3.

BONGEUNSA TEMPLE | 봉은사
The Venerable Yeonhoe built this temple in 794 during the reign of King Wonseong of the Silla Kingdom. Its Sutra Hall, in which hangs a commemorative wooden tablet inscribed by the nation's most celebrated calligrapher, Chusa (pen name) Kim Jeong-hui (1786-1856), preserves woodblocks for 15 Buddhist sutras, including the *Diamond Sutra*.
ⓘ: ☏ 02-511-6070 ⓣ: ⓜ Exit 6 of Samseong Station, Line 2 or Cheongdam Station, Line 7

SEOUL TRAINING CENTER FOR IMPORTANT INTANGIBLE CULTURAL HERITAGES | 서울중요무형문화재전수회관
This institution is designed to preserve and promote traditional Korean arts and the skills of artisans designated as "Important Intangible Cultural Heritages." The center has exhibition halls and a shop displaying and selling crafts, a traditional arts performing hall and workshops where artisans versed in different arts train aspiring successors and show their works to the public.
ⓘ: ☏ 02-566-7037 ⓜ 02-566-6314 ⓣ: ⓜ Exit 8 of Seolleung Station, Line 2

KUKKIWON (WORLD TAEKWONDO HEADQUARTERS) | 국기원
Established to promote taekwondo nationwide, it organizes national and international taekwondo competitions, judges ranking promotions and gives training courses to taekwondo coaches and international umpires.
ⓘ: ☏ 02-567-1058/9 ⓜ 02-552-3025; www.kukkiwon.or.kr ⓣ: ⓜ Exit 8 of Gangnam Station, Line 2 ⓗ: 09:00−18:00 (09:00−12:00 on Saturdays)

TOURIST ATTRACTIONS BY REGION

Around Jamsil
잠실주변

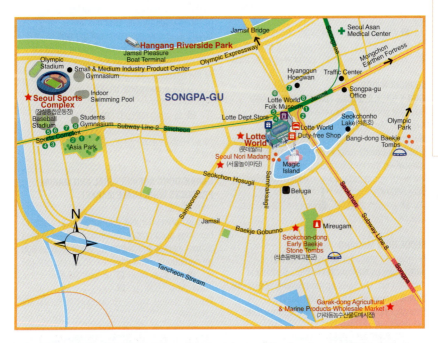

The area around Jamsil Station on Subway Line 2 or 8 is one of Seoul's subcenters. Here is Lotte World (Korea's largest indoor amusement park), which is the most frequently visited attraction by Korean youth. It is composed of Lotte World Adventure with Magic Island, a shopping mall, a folklore museum, movie theaters, an ice rink, a deluxe hotel and a sports center.
Seoul Nori Madang (an outdoor amphitheater) presents traditional performing arts and it is located on the banks of the lake behind Lotte World. A 10-min. stroll to the south brings visitors to the Seokchon-dong Early Baekje Stone Tombs, which preserve traces of the riverside dwellings of the Baekje Kingdom's capital, Hanseong, or, east to the Bangi-dong Baekje Tombs.
Nearby are Garak-dong Agricultural and Marine Products Wholesale Market and Munjeong-dong Rodeo Street, where you can buy Korean or foreign brand names at discounted prices. The Seoul Sports Complex was the global arena for the 1986 Asian Games and 1988 Seoul Olympic Games.

Seoul Sports Complex

LOTTE WORLD | 롯데월드

Cutting-edge roller coasters, fancy parades, variety shows, movies, and much more in the way of thrills are available here year round. The recommendable Folk Museum offers a pavilion course through Korean history, miniature villages, etc.

ⓘ: ☏ 02-411-2000; www.lotteworld.com
ⓣ: ▣ Exit 3 of Jamsil Station, Line 2 or 8
ⓗ: 09:30 – 23:00 ⓐ: ₩30,000 for an all-day pass

SEOKCHON-DONG EARLY BAEKJE STONE TOMBS | 석촌동 백제고분군

Here are six tombs from the early Baekje Kingdom. Among them, a representative stonepiled tomb of three stories was presumably built for a Baekje ruler in the Goguryeo-tomb style when the people of Goguryeo came from the north and estalished the Baekje Kingdom (18 BC – 660 AD).

ⓘ: ☏ 02-410-3662 ⓣ: ▣ Exit 6 of Seokchon Station, Line 8 ⓗ: 09:00 – 22:00

SEOUL NORI MADANG | 서울놀이마당

An open-air stage for traditional Korean performances such as the farmers dance and mask dance. On Saturday and Sunday afternoons, people crowd around the stage beside Seokchonho Lake for traditional performances.

ⓘ: ☏ 02-410-3168/9 ⓣ: ▣ Behind Lotte World, a 10-min. walk from Jamsil Station, Line 2 or 8

SEOUL SPORTS COMPLEX | 잠실종합운동장

This sports complex is comprised of the main stadium, swimming pool, gymnasium and baseball stadium. The spacious lawns, cozy pavilions, and walking paths of the well-manicured Asia Park make it a good place for cultural events as well as for relaxation.
At the baseball stadium, cheers rise to the sky during the professional baseball season from April to October.

ⓘ: ☏ 02-2240-8800 ⓣ: ▣ Exit 7 of Sports Complex Station, Line 2 ⓗ: 09:00 – 18:00 (Nov. – Feb., 09:00 – 17:00) ⓐ: ₩500 for the main stadium

GARAK-DONG AGRICULTURAL AND MARINE PRODUCTS WHOLESALE MARKET |
가락동 농수산물 시장

This is Korea's largest wholesale market with 17 buildings accommodating an agricultural market, fishery market and livestock market on a 54,000-m² compound. Products are sold at retail as well.

ⓘ: ☏ 02-3435-0400 ▣ 02-3435-0595; www.garak.co.kr ⓣ: ▣ Exit 3 or 4 of Garak Market Station, Line 8 ⓒ: January 1, Seollal and Chuseok

Seoul Nori Madang

Lotte World

TOURIST ATTRACTIONS BY REGION

Around Olympic Park
올림픽공원주변

Over a vast expanse of more then 1.5 million m², including the ancient site of the Mongchon Earthen Fortress dating back to the early Baekje Kingdom, Olympic Park houses six sports facilities where competitions were held during the 1988 Seoul Olympic Games, commemorative monuments and 200 original sculptures by world-renowned artists.
Nearby are Amsa-dong Prehistoric Settlement Site, boasting the largest number of ancient dwelling sites in Korea and suggesting something about the Neolithic lifestyle on the peninsula, the Bangi-dong Baekje Tombs and the Pungnap Earthen Fortress.

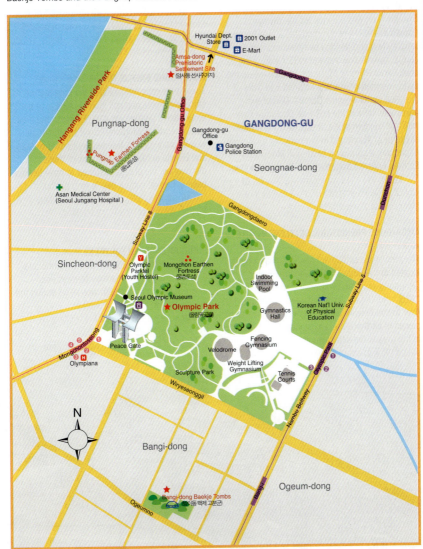

Olympic Park

OLYMPIC PARK | 올림픽공원

Olympic Park was a venue for the Olympic Games in 1988. It accommodates a velodrome, weightlifting and fencing gymnasiums, tennis courts, gymnastics hall and indoor swimming pool. Seoul Olympic Museum, located inside the park, commemorates the victories and glory of the 1988 Seoul Olympic Games. One of the attractions here is the open-air Sculpture Park with 200 modern stone, metal, wood and glass sculptures. Also found in the park are a lake with a fountain, a sprawling lawn, and Mongchon Earthen Fortress from the early Baekje Kingdom.
ⓘ: ☏ 02-410-1114; www.sosfo.or.kr ⓣ: 🚇 Exit 3 of Olympic Park Station, Line 5 or Exit 1 of Mongchontoseong Station, Line 8

AMSA-DONG PREHISTORIC SETTLEMENT SITE | 암사동 선사주거유적지

The prehistoric settlement site in Amsa-dong is located at the edge of the Hangang River in Gangdong-gu. The relics were discovered in 1925, when heavy rains that year caused the river to overflow its banks uncovering numerous pieces of earthenware and stoneware. Remaining in the area is the site of Neolithic habitation dating back to about 6,000 BC.
ⓘ: ☏ 02-3426-3867 ⓣ: 🚇 From Exit 1 of Amsa Station, Line 8, 🚌 take Maeul (village) bus No.2, 3 or 5. ⓗ: 09:30－18:00 (Nov.－Feb., 9:30－17:00), closed on Mondays ⓐ: ₩500

BANGI-DONG BAEKJE TOMBS | 방이동 백제 고분군

The eight tombs remaining in the park feature stone chambers and soil mounds typical of the early Baekje period (200-475). Found in the area was a hearth proving prehistoric habitation as well as stone tables, fragments of stone swords and Baekje earthenware. In view of these discoveries, the area is assumed to have been a base of Baekje culture over a long period.
ⓘ: ☏ 02-410-3661 ⓣ: 🚇 Exit 3 of Bangi Station, Line 5 ⓗ: 9:00－18:00 (Nov.－Feb., 9:00－17:00)

PUNGNAP EARTHEN FORTRESS | 풍납토성

Stretching to the southeast from Cheonho and Olympic Bridges, this earthen fortress was where Baekje's King Gaero was killed during the invasion of Goguryeo King Jangsu.
ⓘ: ☏ 02-410-3776 ⓣ: 🚇 From Cheonho Station, Line 5, 🚌 take Green bus No. 3312 and get off at Pungnap Earthen Fortress Stop.

Amsa-dong Prehistoric Settlement Site

TOURIST ATTRACTIONS BY REGION

Other Areas 기타지역

Bukhansan National Park

War Memorial of Korea

BUKHANSAN NATIONAL PARK | 북한산 국립공원
Easily accessible from anywhere in the Seoul metropolitan area, the Bukhansan Mountains are some of the most popular in Korea. They contain several imposing granite peaks, dozens of beautiful valleys, cultural relics such as Bukhansanseong Fortress, and hundreds of temples and hermitages. This park, within Seoul and embracing the Bukhansan (837 m) and Dobongsan Mountains, is a must-see for visitors who appreciate hiking or rock climbing.
In addition to famous temples such as Doseonsa and Hwagyesa, other historic relics include a stone stele erected by King Jinheung (r. 540–576) of the Silla Kingdom and ancient mountain fortress walls.
ⓘ: www.npa.or.kr/bukhan/index.asp
Ⓣ: 🚇 From Exit 4 of Suyu Station, Line 4 🚌 take Green bus No.1217 and get off at the last stop. Then hike about 30 min. to the Doseonsa Temple ticket booth.

KOREA MILITARY ACADEMY | 육군사관학교
Located in northeastern Seoul, the KMA was established to produce a select group of officers trained in literary and military arts. Founded in 1946, the KMA has opened its beautiful campus to tourists. The tour includes the Army Museum, KMA Tower, Field Weapons Exhibition site, etc. Every Saturday, a cadets' parade held on Hwarang Drill Field is added to the itinerary. Group tours of up to 40 require a two- or three-day prior reservation.
ⓘ: 📞 02-976-6454/5 📠 02-976-6453
Ⓣ: 🚇 From Hwarangdae Station, Line 6

🚶 walk 15 min. or take 🚌 No. 108, 1155, 1156, or 1225 and get off at the rear gate of Korea Military Academy Stop. Ⓗ: Individual Tour (10:00, 13:00, 15:00 / Sat., Sun. and public holidays), Group Tour (09:30–17:00 / Tue. through Sun.)
Ⓒ: Mon. Ⓐ: ₩2,000 (overseas visitors: ₩3,000)

WAR MEMORIAL OF KOREA | 전쟁기념관
Opened on June 10, 1994, it gives visitors a look at the many wars in which Korea has been involved. Many documents and war memorabilia are displayed as examples of Korea's 5,000-year history of resistance to numerous invasions, while maintaining national pride.
ⓘ: 📞 02-709-3139, 3114; www.warmemo.co.kr
Ⓣ: 🚇 Exit 12 of Samgakji Station, Line 4 or 6
🚶 5 min. Ⓗ: 09:30–18:00 Ⓒ: Mondays
Ⓐ: ₩3,000

NORYANGJIN FISHERIES WHOLESALE MARKET |
노량진수산시장
About 900 shops on the 69,000-m^2 compound sell everything from flopping live fish to dried and pickled fish products.
Every day, about 450 tons of fish caught from inshore and the deep seas are traded here.
The fishery auction starts at 1:30 am and retail sales operate afterwards, all day long year around.
Fresh fish prices usually go down on rainy days and on Wednesdays and Thursdays.
You can pick your fish from a tank and a cheerful fishmonger will prepare it for dining in or takeout.
ⓘ: 📞 02-814-2211/2 Ⓣ: 🚇 Noryangjin Station, Line 1

Subway Line 1, KNR Line

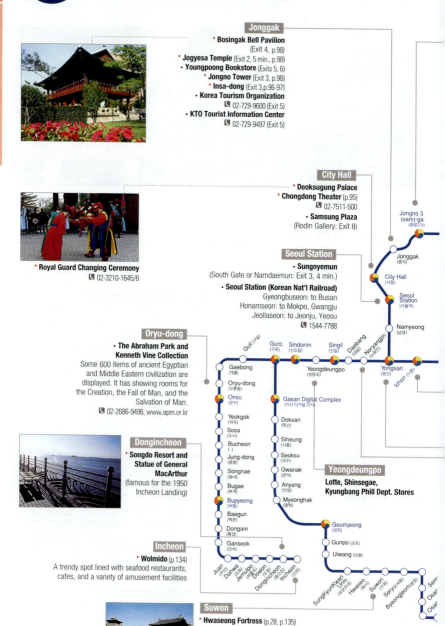

Jongno 3 (sam)-ga
- Jongmyo Royal Ancestral Shrine (Exit 11, 3 min., p.105)
- Yeji-dong Jewelry Shops (Exit 12)
- Tapgol Park (Exit 1, 7 min.)

Jongno 5 (o)-ga
- Dongdaemun Market (Exit 6, p.103)
- Gwangjang Market (Exits 7 or 8. p.37)

Dobongsan
- Mt. Dobongsan
  Hiking trails up Mt. Dobongsan start near the subway station. Part of Bukhansan National Park (Exit 1, 10 min.)

Jegi-dong
- Gyeongdong Herbal Medicine Market (Exit 2)

Dongdaemun
- Heunginjimun
  (East Gate or Dongdaemun / Exit 6, 2 min., p.103)

Ichon
- National Museum of Korea (Exit 2, 150m., p.16)

Cheongnyangni
- Hongneung Arboretum
  The arboretum boasts a total of 2,300 species of plants,
  (Exit 2, 7 min. by city bus No.1215)
  Open on Sunday only ☎ 02-961-2871/4
- King Sejong Memorial Hall
  ☎ 02-969-8851 (Exit 2, 5 min. by city bus No.1215)
- Cheongnyangni Station
  Jungangseon: to Andong, Busan
  Gyeongchunseon: to Chuncheon
  Yeongdongseon: to Gangneung

Yongsan
- Saenamteo Martyrs' Shrine
  Catholics were severely persecuted during the 19th century of the Joseon Dynasty. A large number of believers were executed here. (Exit 1, 15 min.) ☎ 02-716-1791
- Yongsan Electronics Market (Exit 2)

Noryangjin
- Sayuksin Park
  Commanding a fine view of the Hangang River, the shrine holds the tombs of six martyred high officials who resisted King Sejo when he disposed of his nephew King Danjong (the 6th king of the Joseon Dynasty) and usurped the throne. (Exit 1, 5 min.) ☎ 02-813-2130
- Noryangjin Fisheries Wholesale Market (p.121)
  ☎ 02-814-2211/2, 🕐: 04:00 - 20:00

★ indicates a feature described in another section of the travel guide.

Subway Line 2

Ewha Womans Univ.
* "Fashion street" and "youth town" in front of Ewha Womans Univ. (Exits 1, 2, p.107)

Sinchon
- **Bongwonsa Temple**
The home of Taegojong, a denomination of married monks. It is especially famous for traditional ceremonies, chanting, religious dancing and a special art called *yeongsanjae*. (Exits 3 or 4, 5 min. by taxi)
☎ 02-392-3007/8
- **Sinchon Bus Terminal** (to Ganghwado: Exit 7, 7 min.)
☎ 02-324-0611

Hongik Univ.
★ A "youth town" with rock cafes in front of Hongik Univ., Korea's major art college (Exit 6, p.108)

Hapjeong
- **Jeoldusan Martyrs' Shrine**
Jeoldusan was the main execution ground of Catholics in the late 19th century. There are a pilgrimage church, an underground sepulcher for 28 canonized martyrs, an exhibition hall, and a statue of Father Andrew Kim Dae-geon.
☎ 02-3142-4434/5 (Exit 7, 10 min.)

Dangsan
- **Seonyudo Park**
Centered on a former water purifying plant that was refurbished to create the Hangang River History Museum, the entire islet was turned into an ecology park. It is a popular venue for watching riverbank aquatic plants, trees, birds, and nighttime river views. (Exit 4, 15 min.)
☎ 02-3780-0590

Sillim
- **Sillim-dong Sundae Town**
Sundae (pork sausage) eateries are concentrated here. (Exit 3)

Nakseongdae
- **Nakseongdae Park**
This park has a fountain, shrine and walking paths, and is the birthplace of General Gang Gam-chan of the Goryeo Dynasty. Traditional wedding ceremonies are held at the open-air theater inside the park. (Exit 4, 10 min.)

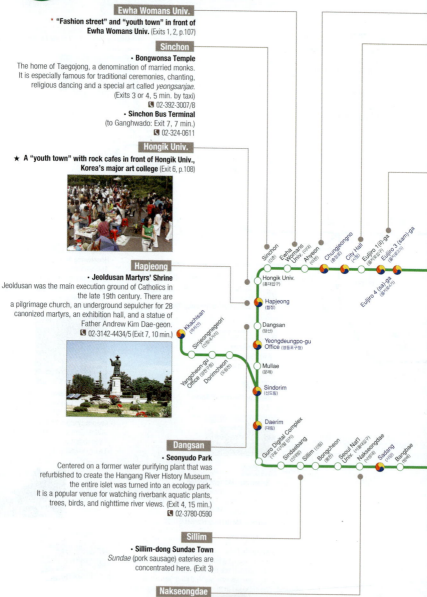

Ahyeon
- Ahyeon-dong Wedding Dress Street (Exit 2)

City Hall
- **Ho-Am Art Hall** (Exit 9, 10 min.)
- **Chongdong Theater** (Exit 11, 12, p.95)
- **Deoksugung Palace** (Exit 11, 12, p.95)
- **Samsung Plaza**
  Theater, restaurants, the Rodin Gallery, etc. (Exit 8)
- **Chung Dong First Methodist Church**
  Constructed in 1898, this is the oldest Protestant church in Seoul. (Exit 12)
- **Nanta Theater** (Exit 2, 5 min., p.95)
  ☎ 02-739-8288; www.nanta.co.kr

Euljiro 1 (il)-ga
- **Myeong-dong Street**
- **Myeongdong Cathedral** (Exits 5, 6, p.99)
- **Lotte Dept. Store** (Exit 7)
- **Shinsegae Dept. Store** (Exit 7)
- **Tourist Information Center**
  ☎ 02-757-0088

Dongdaemun Stadium
- **Dongdaemun Market** (Exits 1, 2, p.103)

Sindang
- **Sindang-dong Tteokppokki Alley**
  A large number of *tteokppokki* (rice cakes cooked in a spicy red pepper paste sauce with fish sausage and onions) stands line this alley.
  (Exit 4)

Gangbyeon
- **Dong Seoul Bus Terminal** (Exit 3, 3 min.) ☎ 02-446-8000
- **Techno Mart** Large electronics market (Exits 1, 2)

Jamsil
- **Seokchonho Lake** (Exit 2, 5 min.)
- **Seoul Nori Madang** (Exit 3, 5 min., p.118)
- **Lotte World** (Exit 3, p.118)
- **Lotte Dept. Store**
- **Seokchon-dong Early Baekje Stone Tombs**
  ☎ 02-410-3662 (Exit 3, p.118)

Sincheon
- **Hangang River Pleasure Boat Terminal** (Exits 6, 7)

Sports Complex
- **Seoul Sports Complex**
  (Exits 6, 7, 2 min., p.118)

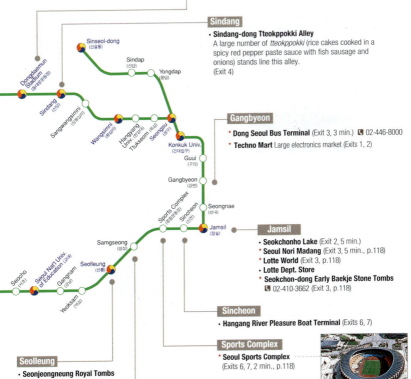

Seolleung
- **Seonjeongneung Royal Tombs**
  These tombs consist of the Seolleung Tomb built for King Seongjong and his second wife and the Jeongneung Tomb built for King Jungjong. Visitors can relax undisturbed within the graceful atmosphere of the royal tombs and the small wooded area. (Exit 8, 7 min.)
  ☎ 02-568-1291

Samseong
- **Bongeunsa Temple**
  The biggest temple in the Gangnam area (Exit 6, p.116)
- **World Trade Center Seoul** (Exit 6)
- **COEX** ☎ 02-6002-5312/3; www.coex.co.kr (p.115)
- **KCAT** (Korea City Air Terminal: Exits 5, 6, p.179)
- **Kimchi Field Museum** (Exits 5, 6, p.24)
  ☎ 02-6002-6456

Subway Line 3 | Bundangseon Line

━━━ Line 3
━━━ Bundangseon Line

Dongnimmun
* **Seodaemun Independence Park**
  ☎ 02-364-4686 (Exit 5, p.109)
* **Seodaemun Prison History Hall**
  Constructed on the site of the former prison complex in memory of patriotic martyrs, it has many relics showing the history of the bold resistance against the Japanese occupation (1910–1945).
  ☎ 02-363-9750/1 (Exit 5)

Yeonsinnae
* **Yeonsinnae Fashion Street**
  A variety of discount clothing stores are located here.

Jeongbalsan
* **Ilsan Lake Park**
  Known as the venue of the biennial world flower exhibition, Ilsan Lake Park has the largest man-made lake in Korea. The park attracts many weekend visitors, including roller bladers, bicyclists, and spectators of various performing arts held on the waterfront. (Exit 2, 10 min.)
  ☎ 031-906-4557, 031-905-1782

Jichuk (지축)
Samsong (삼송)
Wondang (원당)
Hwajeong (화정)
Daegok (대곡)
Baekseok (백석)
Madu (마두)
Jeongbalsan (정발산)
Juyeop (주엽)
Daehwa (대화)
Gupabal (구파발)
Yeonsinnae (연신내)
Bulgwang (불광)
Nokbeon (녹번)
Hongje (홍제)
Muakjae (무악재)
Dongnimmun (독립문)
Gyeongbokgung (경복궁)
Anguk (안국)
Jongno 3 (sam)-ga (종로3가)
Euljiro 3 (sam)-ga (을지로3가)

Jongno 3 (sam)-ga
* **Yeji-dong Jewelry shops**
  Located opposite the Gwangjang Market, this complex of wholesale and retail shops sell jewelry and watches at prices 20 to 50 percent lower than retail. (Exit 9)
* **Jongmyo Royal Shrine** (Exits 8, 11, 3 min., p.105)
  ☎ 02-765-0195

Chungmuro
* **Korea House** ☎ 02-2266-9101 (Exit 3, p.101)
* **Namsangol Hanok Village** (Exit 3, 3 min., p.101)
  ☎ 02-2266-6937/8
* **N Seoul Tower** (p.101)
  ☎ 02-772-1622

Dongguk Univ.
* **Jangchung Park**

* **Yejiwon** (Exit 6) ☎ 02-2253-2211
* **National Theater** (Exit 6, 15 min., p.101)
  ☎ 02-2280-4114; www.ntok.go.kr

Express Bus Terminal
* **Seoul Express Bus Terminal**
  Gyeongbuseon: to Daejeon and Busan
  Honamseon: to Jeolla-do
  Yeongdongseon: to Gangwon-do
  ☎ 02-535-4151
* **National Library of Korea**
  Korea's largest library (Exit 5)
  ☎ 02-590-0513/4
* **Gangnam Jewelry Market**
  Located near Honamseon Terminal of Seoul Express Bus Terminal, it sells wholesale and retail jewelry at a 20 percent discount.
* **Central City** (p.64)
  ☎ 02-6282-0114; www.centralcityseoul.co.kr

Gyeongbokgung

* **Gyeongbokgung Palace** (National Folk Museum, Exit 5, p.93)
  📞 02-734-2458
* **Cheong Wa Dae (the Blue House)** (Exit 5, p.93)
* **Samcheongdonggil 'Fine Arts' Street**
  Many art galleries line this street. (Exit 5, p.93)
* **National Folk Museum** (Exit 5, 10 min., p.93)

Anguk

* **Insa-dong** ("Mary's Alley:" Exit 6, 2 min., p.96)
* **Tourist Information Center**
  📞 02-731-1676, 731-1621
* **Changdeokgung Palace / Huwon** (Exit 3, 4 min., p.106)
* **Unhyeongung** (p.98)
  A re-enactment of the wedding of King Gojong and Queen Myeongseong is performed at 13:00 on the 3rd or 4th Saturday of Apr. and Oct. annually.
  📞 02-766-9090

Apgujeong

* **Apgujeong-dong** (Exit 2, p.114)
* **Galleria Dept. Store** (Exit 2)
* **Hyundai Dept. Store** (Exit 6)
* **Cheongdam-dong** (Exit 2)

Yangjae

* **Yangjae Flower Market**
  (Located near Yangjae Citizen's Forest: Exit 7, 5 min. by local bus for Seongnam)

Hangnyeoul

* **Seoul Trade Exhibition Center** (Exit 1)
  📞 02-2222-3811; www.setec.or.kr

Nambu Bus Terminal

* **Nambu Bus Terminal** (Exit 5, 2 min.) 📞 02-521-8550
* **Seoul Arts Center** (p.116)
  📞 02-580-1300; www.sac.or.kr
* **National Center for Korean Traditional Performing Arts**
  (Exit 5, 15 min.) 📞 02-580-3330 / 3; www.ncktpa.go.kr

Subway Line 4 Line 5

— Line 4
— Line 5

Gwanghwamun
- **Sejong Center** (Exits 1, 8, 4 min.)
  ☎ 02-3991-1111
- **Tourist Information Center** (Exits 1, 8, 4 min.)
  ☎ 02-753-5678
- **Samcheonggak** (Exit 3)
  ☎ 02-3676-3456; www.samcheonggak.or.kr

Seodaemun
- **Gyeonghuigung Palace**
  ☎ 02-731-0531
  (Exit 4, 10 min.)
- **Seoul Museum of History**
  ☎ 02-724-0114;
  www.museum.seoul.kr
  (Exit 4, p.25)
- **Nanta Theater**
  (Exit 5, 5 min., p.95)
  ☎ 02-739-8288;
  www.nanta.co.kr

Mok-dong
- **Rodeo Street** (Exit 2, 1 min.)
- **Mok-dong Sports Complex**
- **Paris Park**
  Built to memorialize the 100th anniversary of friendly relations with France (Exit 4, 1 km)

Yeouido
- **National Assembly**
  (Exit 3, 15 min., p.113)
  ☎ 02-788-2885, 2889
- **Yunjungno Cherryblossom Street**
  (Exit 1, 5 min.)

Yeouinaru
- **Hangang Riverside Park**
  (Pleasure Boat Terminal: Exit 2)
- **63 City** ☎ 02-789-5663/5 (Exits 1, 4, p.113)
- **Yunjungno Cherry Blossom Street**
  Yunjungno is a quiet four-lane street ideal for a drive or stroll. Every April, the Yunjungno Cherry Blossom Festival takes place here.
- **Yoido Full Gospel Church** (Exit 1)
  ☎ 02-782-4851 (day), 02-783-7485 (night/holiday);
  http://yfgc.fgtv.com

Seoul Grand Park
- **Seoul Land** (p.137)
  ☎ 02-504-0011; www.seoulland.co.kr
- **Seoul Grand Park** (p.137)
  ☎ 02-500-7114; http://grandpark.seoul.go.kr
  (Exits 1, 2, 7 min.)
- **National Museum of Contemporary Art** (p.22)
  ☎ 02-2188-6000; www.moca.go.kr (Exit 1, 7 min. by shuttle bus)

Seoul Racecourse Park
- **Seoul Racecourse Park**
  ☎ 1566-3333
  (Exits 1, 2, 5 min.)

Dongjak
- **National Cemetery**
  ☎ 02-813-9625 (Exit 4, 10 min.)

Hoehyeon
* **Namsan Park** (Exit 4, 15 min., p.100)
* **Namdaemun Market** (Exits 5, 6, 5 min., p.102)
* **Shinsegae Dept. Store** (Exit 7, 7 min.)
* **Sungnyemun** (South Gate or Namdaemun Gate: Exit 5)

Hyehwa
* **Daehangno Street** (Exit 2, p.104)
  Daehangno covers the broadway beginning at Hyehwa Rotary. It contains a number of small- and medium-sized theaters, including the Batanggol Art Center, the Dongsoong Art Center, etc.
* **Changgyeonggung Palace** (Exit 4, 10 min., p.105)
  ☎ 02-762-4868

Sungshin Women's Univ.
* **Donam-dong**
  The "youth town" in the northeastern area of Seoul. A variety of clothing and accessory shops and restaurants are concentrated here. (Exit 1)

Dapsimni
* **Janganpyeong Antique Market** (Exit 3)

Cheonho
* **Pungnap Earthern Fortress** (Exit 10, 5 min., p.120)
  ☎ 02-410-3776

Dongdaemun
* **Dongdaemun Market** (Exits 7, 8, p.103)
* **Heunginjimun** (East Gate or Dongdaemun: Exit 6, p.103)

Chungmuro
* **Namsangol Hanok Village** (Exit 3, 5 min., p.71, p.101) ☎ 02-2266-6937/8
* **Korea House** (Exit 3, 1 min., p.101)
  ☎ 02-2266-9101

Myeong-dong
* **Myeong-dong** (Exit 7, p..99)
* **N Seoul Tower** (Cable Car ☎ 02-753-2403, Exit 3, 15 min., p.101)
* **Myeongdong Cathedral** (Exit 8, 10 min., p.99)

Samgakji
* **War Memorial of Korea** (Exit 1, 7 min., p.121)
  ☎ 02-709-3139, 3114

Ichon
* **Yongsan Family Park** (Exit 2, 10 min.)
  Located near the Itaewon shopping district. A large expanse of picnic grounds, frisbee fields, and a jogging course ☎ 02-792-5661
* **National Museum of Korea** (Exit 2, 150m., p.16)

Bangi
* **Bangi-dong Baekje Tombs** (Exit 3, p.120)
  ☎ 02-410-3661

Olympic Park
* **Olympic Park** (Exit 3, 5 min., p.119)
  ☎ 02-410-1114

Subway Line 6

Itaewon

- **Itaewon** (p.70, p.110)
- **Itaewon Tourist Information Center**
  02-794-2490 (Exit 2)
- **Muslim Mosque** (Exit 3)

- **Seo-oreung Tombs** 02-359-0090 (Exit 1)

World Cup Stadium

- **Seoul World Cup Stadium** (Exits 1, 2 or 3)
  The opening ceremony and game of the 2002 FIFA World Cup Korea/Japan were held here.

- **World Cup Park**
  World Cup Park opened in celebration of the 2002 FIFA World Cup. It is comprised of the Peace, Sky, Sunset, Nanji Stream, and Nanji Hangang Parks. After years of landfill and restoration work, the previous garbage dumpsite was beautifully transformed into this eco-friendly park. The park's main street is vehicle-free on the weekend. (Exit 1, 10 min.)
  02-300-5500; http://worldcuppark.seoul.go.kr

Stations: Jeungsan, Susaek, World Cup Stadium, Mapo-gu Office, Mangwon, Sangsu, Hapjeong, Daeheung, Gwangheungchang, Gongdeok, Hyochang Park, Samgakji, Noksapyeong, Itaewon, Hangangjin, Beotigogae, Yaksu

Yeonsinnae, Gusan, Saejeol, Dokbawi, Bulgwang, Yeokchon, Eungam

Hapjeong

- **Seoul Foreigners' Cemetery** (Exit 7)
  About 480 foreigners from 13 countries who rendered service to missionary and social work in Korea are buried here. They include Bethell, Hulbert, Underwood and Appenjeller.
- **Jeoldusan Martyrs' Shrine** (Exit 7)
  02-3142-4434/5
- **Holt Children's Services** (Exit 8)
  1588-7501

Hyochang Park

- **Hyochang Park** (Exit 1)
  Here stand the tombs of patriots who fought for independence from Japanese colonial rule such as Kim Gu, Yoon Bong-gil and Lee Bong-chang.

Hwarangdae
- **Taereung Royal Tomb** (Exit 1)
  The tomb of Queen Munjeong of the Joseon Dynasty
- **Taereung Country Club**
- **Korea Military Academy** (Exit 4)
  ☎ 02-976-6454
- **Eastern Castle** (Exit 1, 5 min. by bus)
  This large resort complex surrounded by a forest has a shooting range of international standard, outdoor swimming pool, and hiking trails. ☎ 02-971-0741

Dongmyo
- **Dongmyo** (Exit 5)
  Completed in the year 1601, this is a shrine for Guan Wu, the great commander of Shu Han of China. Surrounded by earthen embankments, trees and benches, it serves as a nice place for relaxation. ☎ 02-731-0535

Korea Univ.
- **King Sejong Memorial Hall** (Exit 3)
  Documents related to *hangeul* (the Korean alphabet), printing type, meteorological tools, weights and measures, etc. ☎ 02-969-8851
- **Hongneung Arboretum** (Exit 3, 10 min.)
  ☎ 02-9612-871/4

Sindang
- **Sindang-dong** *Tteokppokki* **Alley** (Exit 8)
  Here you may try *tteokppokki* (rice cakes in sweet and spicy sauce) at many specialized shops.

Samgakji
- **War Memorial of Korea** (Exit 1, 11 or 12, p.121)
  A huge exhibition hall that calls to mind the lessons of war. It houses about 8,000 documents, pictures, weapons, and other war items from the Korean War.
  ☎ 02-709-3139/3114

Subway Line 7 / Line 8

— Line 7
— Line 8

Children's Grand Park
- **Children's Grand Park**
  A zoo, botanical garden, amusement park, outdoor concert stage and children's center
  ☎ 02-450-9334 (Exit 1, 2 min.)

Ttukseom Resort
- **Hangang Riverside Park**
  ☎ 02-3780-0522 (Exit 2)

Hak-dong
* **Museum of Korean Embroidery** (p.24)
  Korea's largest private collection of embroidery with over 3,000 pieces
  ☎ 02-515-5114/7; www.bojagii.com

Onsu (온수) – Cheonwang (천왕) – Gwangmyeong (광명) – Cheolsan (철산) – Garibong (가리봉) – Namguro (남구로) – Daerim (대림) – Sinpung (신풍) – Boramae (보라매) – Sindaebang-samgeori (신대방삼거리) – Jangseungbaegi (장승배기) – Sangdo (상도) – Soongsil Univ. (숭실대입구) – Namseong (남성) – Chongshin Univ. (총신대입구) – Nabang (내방)

Express Bus Terminal (고속터미널)

Express Bus Terminal
* **Central City** (p.144)
  It houses the JW Marriott Seoul, a department store, Marquis Thermal Spa & Fitness Club, a large bookstore, multiplex movie theater, world food court and Millenium Hall.
  ☎ 02-6282-0114; www.centralcityseoul.co.kr

Jamsil
* **Lotte World** (Exit 1, p.118)
  ☎ 02-411-2000; www.lotteworld.com
* **Seoul Nori Madang** (Exit 11, p.71, p.118)
  ☎ 02-410-3168/9

Seokchon
* **Seokchon-dong Early Baekje Stone Tombs**
  (Exit 6, 10 min., p.118)
  Assumed to be the tombs from the early Baekje Kingdom, they were built like pyramids with layers of mud, pebbles, and stones on a square base.
  ☎ 02-410-3662

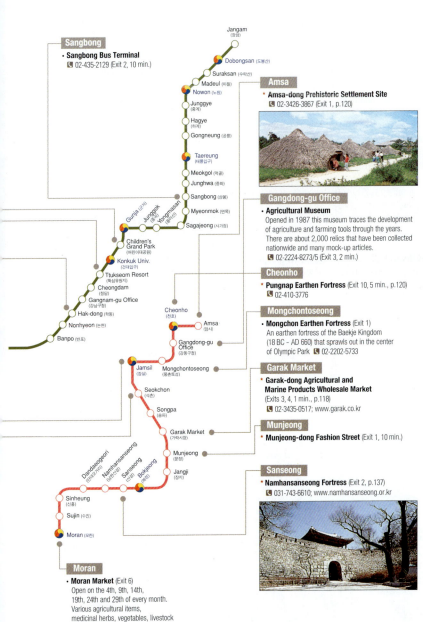

Sangbong
- **Sangbong Bus Terminal**
  ☎ 02-435-2129 (Exit 2, 10 min.)

Amsa
- **Amsa-dong Prehistoric Settlement Site**
  ☎ 02-3426-3867 (Exit 1, p.120)

Gangdong-gu Office
- **Agricultural Museum**
  Opened in 1987 this museum traces the development of agriculture and farming tools through the years. There are about 2,000 relics that have been collected nationwide and many mock-up articles.
  ☎ 02-2224-8273/5 (Exit 3, 2 min.)

Cheonho
- **Pungnap Earthen Fortress** (Exit 10, 5 min., p.120)
  ☎ 02-410-3776

Mongchontoseong
- **Mongchon Earthen Fortress** (Exit 1)
  An earthen fortress of the Baekje Kingdom (18 BC – AD 660) that sprawls out in the center of Olympic Park. ☎ 02-2202-5733

Garak Market
- **Garak-dong Agricultural and Marine Products Wholesale Market**
  (Exits 3, 4, 1 min., p.118)
  ☎ 02-3435-0517; www.garak.co.kr

Munjeong
- **Munjeong-dong Fashion Street** (Exit 1, 10 min.)

Sanseong
- **Namhansanseong Fortress** (Exit 2, p.137)
  ☎ 031-743-6610; www.namhansanseong.or.kr

Moran
- **Moran Market** (Exit 6)
  Open on the 4th, 9th, 14th, 19th, 24th and 29th of every month. Various agricultural items, medicinal herbs, vegetables, livestock and pets, etc.

Seoul Vicinity | Incheon, Gyeonggi-do

Many attractions lie just a short distance outside Seoul, and are easily accessible by bus, train or car. One hour away from Seoul, **INCHEON** (인천) (www.incheon.go.kr), the main gateway of Korea, has a newly opened international airport and an international seaport. On a small knoll overlooking the harbor is **JAYU PARK (FREEDOM PARK)** (자유공원) (032-761-4774), with a statue honoring General MacArthur's famous 1950 Incheon Landing. : From Dongincheon Station, Line 1, it is a 10-min. walk. Seafood enthusiasts will enjoy the **WOLMIDO** (월미도) area of Incheon. : From Incheon Station, Line 1, No. 2, 15, 23, 45 or 550. Get off at the last stop. The **SONGDO RESORT** (송도유원지) lies to the southwest. : From Dongincheon Station, No. 6, 8 or 64.

GANGHWADO ISLAND (강화도) (www.ganghwa.incheon.kr) lies northwest of downtown Incheon. The island holds 120 dolmens, including Korea's largest at 7.1m wide and 2.6m tall. Along with those of Gochang and Hwasun, Ganghwa's dolmen sites were registered on the UNESCO World Cultural Heritage list in December 2000. There is also Chamseongdan Altar on the summit of **MT. MANISAN** (마니산) (032-937-1624) , where ancient Koreans paid tribute to the heavens. The coastline of the island is dotted with numerous fort sites dating back to the Joseon Dynasty.
: From Sinchon Intercity Bus Terminal, take a direct bus to Mt. Manisan (16 times daily, 6:40 – 20:30).

JEONDEUNGSA TEMPLE (전등사) (032-937-0125; www.jeondeungsa.org) is another historic site on the island. The temple dates back to the ancient Three Kingdoms period about 1,600 years ago. The unique style of its architecture and iron bell are rarely seen elsewhere. In

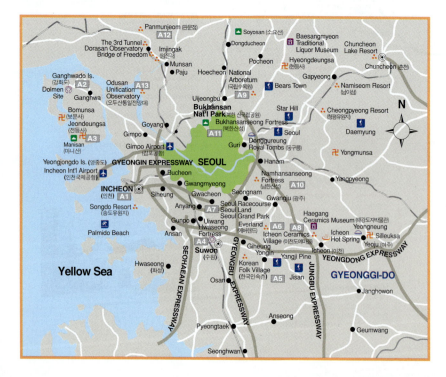

TOURIST ATTRACTIONS BY REGION

인천, 경기도

Jeondeungsa Temple

addition to exploring these historical sites, visitors can find local products such as ginseng and sedge mats. ①: Northwest of Incheon ⓣ: 🚌 From Sinchon Intercity Bus Terminal in Seoul, take a bus bound for Jeondeungsa Temple (1 hr., 40 min.) or from Yeongdeungpo Bus Terminal in Seoul, take a bus to Ganghwa (2 hrs.). Ⓐ: ₩2,000 (for Jeondeungsa Temple)

A subway train also connects Seoul with **SUWON** (수원) A4 (www.suwon.ne.kr), one of the principal cities of Gyeonggi-do Province. Included on UNESCO's list of World Cultural Heritages in 1997, **HWASEONG FORTRESS** (화성) A4 (📞 031-228-2763) embraces the downtown area of Suwon. It is a well-preserved structure of the Joseon Dynasty built of stone and oven-baked bricks over two years from 1794 during the reign of King Jeongjo. ①: Central Suwon ⓣ: 🚌 No. 11, 13, 36, 38 or 39 from Exit 4 of Suwon Station, Line 1

 INCHEON CITY TOUR
Downtown Tour
(11:00 – 15:00, Tuesday – Sunday, 1-hour intervals; 1 hr. , 35 min. ride; cost: ₩1,000 for a single ride)

Incheon Subway Station → Wolmisan Park → Wolmido Island → Incheon Port (Floodgate) → Yeonan Pier Passenger Terminal → Yeonan Fish Market → A-amdo Island → Songdo PR Hall → Songdo Resort → Neungheodae → Incheon Subway Station → Songdo Resort → The Memorial Hall for Incheon Landing Operation → Neunheodae → Incheon Subway Station

Incheon International Airport Tour
(09:45 – 17:15; 1 hr., 50-min. intervals; 2 hrs., 45 min. ride; cost: ₩6,000 for a round-trip ticket)

Incheon Subway Station → Wolmido Island → Yeongjongdo Island → Science Museum → Haesutang (Seawater Spa) → Airport Passenger Terminal 3rd Fl. (Gate 13) → Entrance of Hotels (Hyatt, Best Western) → Entrance of Geojampo (Muuido Island) → Masiran Beach → Fairy Rock → Eurwangri Beach → Wangsan Beach → North Dike (Floodgate) → Entrance of Sammok Port → Yeongjong Grand Bridge (North Incheon I.C) → Incheon Subway Station

ⓘ: Cheongsong Tours 📞 032-469-6060

Korean Folk Village

POTTERY MAKING PROGRAM

In the Icheon-Yeoju-Gwangju area of Gyeonggi-do Province are a wide variety of programs operated by private organizations, pottery associations, ceramics museums, and expo organizers allowing visitors to try their talents at making pottery. Visitors often choose simply to paint ready-made pottery, available to take home unglazed the very same day. Fees range anywhere from ₩10,000 to ₩50,000 depending on the type of program, region, and type of pottery (delivery costs paid extra).

- ⓘ: • World Ceramic Exposition Foundation:
   www.worldceramic.or.kr
  - Icheon World Ceramic Center
     ☏ 031-631-6507
  - Yeoju World Livingware Gallery
     ☏ 031-884-8644
  - Haegang Ceramics Museum
     ☏ 031-634-2266
  - Icheon Folk Ceramics Association
     (Reservations required for large groups)
     ☏ 031-633-6181
  - Yeoju Folk Ceramics Association
     ☏ 031-885-3937

The **KOREAN FOLK VILLAGE** (한국민속촌) A5 (☏ 031-286-2111; www.koreanfolk.co.kr) is a living museum that recreates the lifestyle of several centuries ago. There are potters, weavers, blacksmiths, and other artisans who practice their trades in a traditional fashion. There are also 260 traditional houses and a small amphitheater for folk music and dance performances.

ⓛ: East of Suwon ⓣ: 🚌 No. 37 or shuttle bus from Suwon Station to the Korean Folk Village in Yongin ⓗ: Apr. and Oct., 9:00 – 18:00; May to Sep., 9:00 – 18:30; Nov. to Mar., 9:00 – 17:30 Ⓐ: ₩11,000

EVERLAND (에버랜드) A6 (☏ 031-320-5000; www.everland.com) is three amusement parks in one. Festival World has thrilling rides, a jungle safari, a zoo and seasonal flower festivals. Caribbean Bay is a huge water park with wave pools and water slides. At Speedway, you can enjoy real car racing.

Everland is also the site of the Ho-Am Art Museum, displaying one of the finest private collections of Korean art in the world.

ⓛ: East of the Korean Folk Village ⓣ: 🚌 No. 1500 or 1500-1 from Exit 13 of Seoul Nat'l Univ. of Education Station, Line 2 or 3 ⓗ: 09:30 – 20:00 (Open till late from Mar. through Oct., usually until 22:00) Ⓐ: ₩24,000 for Festival World, ₩30,000 – ₩77,000 depending on the season for Caribbean Bay

SEOUL RACECOURSE PARK (서울경마공원) A7 (☏ 02-509-1273; www.kra.co.kr), with facilities for up to 1,400 horses, is in operation on weekends.

Everland

Wager tickets can be purchased starting from ₩100 up to ₩100,000. There are three kinds of bets: single entry, double entry, and multiple race.
ⓛ: Just north of Seoul Grand Park ⓣ: 🚇 Exit 1 or 2 of Seoul Racecourse Park Station, Line 4
ⓗ: 9:30 – 18:00 ⓐ: Free (weekends: ₩800)

SEOUL LAND (서울랜드) A7 (📞 02-504-0011; www.seoulland.co.kr) is an all-weather theme park located 30 min. from downtown Seoul. Fifty kinds of amusement facilities await visitors, and colorful events and seasonal fairs create a spectacle of fun.

SEOUL GRAND PARK (서울대공원) A7 (📞 02-500-7114; http://grandpark.seoul.go.kr) is right next to Seoul Land. It boasts a large zoo, botanical garden with 14,000 plants from 1,600 different species and a trained seal show.

The **NATIONAL MUSEUM OF CONTEMPORARY ART** (국립현대미술관) A7 (📞 02-2188-6016; www.moca.go.kr) is another attraction at the Seoul Grand Park complex.
ⓛ: Just south of Seoul ⓣ: 🚇 Take Line 4 (bound for Ansan or Oido), and get off at Seoul Grand Park Station. ⓗ: 9:00 – 19:00 (Oct.– Mar., 9:00 – 18:00) for Seoul Grand Park ⓐ: ₩1,500 (₩3,000 in Apr.– Jun., Sep.– Oct.) for Seoul Grand Park, ₩700 for National Museum of Contemporary Art, ₩12,000 for Seoul Land

ICHEON CERAMICS VILLAGE (이천도예마을) A8 is one of the largest ceramics villages in Korea where some 250 kilns are gathered.
Not only can you purchase ceramics but you can also make them yourself. The World Ceramic Biennale Korea is held mainly at the Icheon World Ceramic Center.
The HAEGANG CERAMICS MUSEUM (해강도자박물관) (📞 031-634-2266) is also here and it is devoted entirely to the ceramic arts. Within a 30-min. drive are **GWANGJU** (광주) and **YEOJU** (여주), which are both famous for ceramics.
ⓣ: 🚌 From Seoul Express Bus Terminal, take a bus to Icheon (every 30 min., 1 hr.). Or from Dong Seoul Bus Terminal, take a bus to Icheon (every 15 min., 1 hr.).

The **KOREA NATIONAL ARBORETUM** (국립수목원) A9 (📞 031-540-1030; www.koreaplants.go.kr) was originally part of the forest attached to **GWANGNEUNG** (광릉), where a Joseon king and queen are buried. Now the forest spans a vast area to the National Arboretum to make up 15 special arboretums and the Forest Museum.
ⓣ: 🚌 No. 21 (in front of former intercity bus terminal) from Uijeongbu Station, Line 1
ⓗ: 9:00 – 18:00, 9:00 – 17:00 from Nov – Feb (reservations required) ⓐ: ₩1,000 ⓒ: Sat., Sun. and national holidays

NAMHANSANSEONG FORTRESS (남한산성) A10 (📞 031-742-7856; http://namhansansung.or.kr) is located atop a mountain near the satellite city of Seongnam and served to protect the southern region from invasions.
ⓣ: 🚌 No. 9 (15 min.) 🚇 from Exit 2 of Namhansanseong Station, Line 8

BUKHANSANSEONG FORTRESS (북한산성) A11
(☎ 02-357-9698, 02-381-2775), encircling the impressive peaks of the Bukhansan Mountains, was once the stronghold that formed Seoul's northern boundary during the Joseon Dynasty.
🚇 🚌 From Gupabal, take a bus to Songchu or from Bulgwang-dong Terminal, take an intercity bus to Uijeongbu and get off at the entrance of Bukhansanseong Fortress.

PAJU (파주) (www.pajuro.net), with its untainted natural beauty, contains many Korean War-related tourist sites such as Panmunjeom, the 3rd Tunnel and Dora Observatory, Odusan Unification Observatory and Imjingak Pavilion. These sites bring home the lessons of war and the stark reality of a divided country.

PANMUNJEOM (판문점) A12, in the Demilitarized Zone, is where the armistice agreement was signed on July 27, 1953, and where South-North talks still take place. U.N. forces are stationed here to aid in diplomatic relations. THE 3RD TUNNEL (제3땅굴), about 73 m underground and 2 m wide and high, was constructed by North Koreans to infiltrate the South. It crosses 435 m under the North-South Demarcation Line and its total length is 1,635 m. At DORA OBSERVATORY (도라전망대), through a telescope, you can watch North Koreans go about their daily lives.
ODUSAN UNIFICATION OBSERVATORY (오두산 통일전망대) A13 (☎ 031-945-2390) is where you can see North Korea with high-powered binoculars. On display is a collection of items from North Korea including living necessities and clothes.
🕐 9:00–18:00, March–October; 9:00–17:30, November; 9:00–17:00, December–February
🚇 🚆 1 hr. and 10 min. from Seoul Station to Geumchon Station 🚌 No. 2 or 3 to the observatory (25 min.) ⓐ ₩2,000

Namhansanseong Fortress

FOODS TO TRY & PLACES TO SHOP OF GYEONGGI-DO PROVINCE

FOOD GALBI (marinated beef ribs) | 갈비 Suwon is famous for *galbi*. *Galbi* is marinated overnight and grilled over charcoal or a gas grill built into the center of the table and served with vegetables. *Dwaeji galbi* is pork ribs; *galbi* itself refers to beef ribs but this is sometimes referred to as *sogalbi*. Many *galbi* restaurants can be found in the market area near Paldalmun Gate.

SEOLLEONGTANG (ox-bone soup) | 설렁탕 This dish was prepared for rites held by the Joseon Dynasty kings in hopes of a fruitful harvest. Beef bones and water are placed in a stone pot and boiled for a very long time. Usually, the only seasoning used for this mineral-rich broth is salt, but some people choose to add red pepper powder.

JAPCHAE (potato noodles stir-fried with vegetables) | 잡채 *Japchae* is always served when there is a celebration in Korea. Vegetables, beef and mushrooms are mixed with chewy cellophane noodles. The colors are brilliant and invite people to have a taste.

SHOPPING GANGHWA MARKET Ganghwado Island is renowned for its *hwamunseok* (flower-patterned mats), which are woven with *wanggol* (sedge) dyed in seven colors: red, blue, aquamarine, scarlet, purple, black and white. *Hwamunseok* is designed and woven in colorful patterns such as phoenixes, orchids, pine trees and lotus blossoms. The cool texture of a *hwamunseok* mat provides a welcome relief during hot summer days. Ganghwado is also famous for its high-quality ginseng. The open-air market is open on the 2nd, 7th, 12th, 17th, 22nd and 27th of every month in the downtown area of Ganghwado, where *hwamunseok*, ginseng, orchids and many other items are sold. The imposing Local Specialties Center (☎ 032-934-3305) has about 40 outlets selling *hwamunseok* and ginseng.
🚇 🚌 **From Sinchon Intercity Bus Terminal in Seoul to Ganghwa (1 hr., 10 min.);** 🚌 5 min.

Eastern Area

TOURIST ATTRACTIONS BY REGION

Gangwon-do 강원도,
Ulleungdo 울릉도, Dokdo 독도

Seoul is connected to the scenic east coast by the Yeongdong Expressway, which ends at Gangneung. The trip takes about three hours by car. There are several hotels along the coast and the combination of mountains and beaches makes the eastern area an ideal vacation spot.
Historical sites and colorful daily scenes are seen in the small coastal towns as well as deep within the forested mountains of the region. The mountains also provide recreational opportunities with a number of ski resorts. ⓘ: Gangwon-do Tourist Information 📞 033-244-0088; www.gangwon.to

In the city of **GANGNEUNG** (강릉) B1 (www.gangneung.gangwon.kr) is the historical building OJUKHEON (오죽헌) (033-640-4457/9) B2, where Yi Yul-gok, the great Confucian scholar of the Joseon Dynasty, lived with his mother Sin Saimdang. Sin Saimdang was not only an ideal daughter, wife, and mother, but also a talented painter, calligrapher and poet; as such, she is the most widely acclaimed woman of the Joseon Dynasty.
Ⓣ: No. 200 - 205, 207, 300, 302 or 303 to Ojukheon from Gangneung City

GYEONGPODAE (경포대) B3 (033-640-4471), 6 km north of downtown Gangneung, is a beach where you can enjoy swimming and sea fishing. Many of the restaurants serve fresh fish prepared according to the diner's wishes.
Ⓣ: No. 202 to Gyeongpodae (every 20 min., 20 min.) from Gangneung City

There are several towns and excellent beaches north of Gangneung. NAKSAN BEACH (낙산해수욕장) B4 and the fishing port of Sokcho are especially noteworthy. Naksan Beach is famous for its clear water and the nearby Naksansa Temple.
Ⓣ: From Yangyang Bus Terminal, take a city bus to Naksan (every 10 min., 10 min.). Or from Sokcho Bus Terminal, take a city bus to Naksan (every 10 min., 25 min.).

SOKCHO (속초) B5 (www.sokchotour.com) is the gateway to Seoraksan National Park and it is a magnificent area with towering granite peaks, valleys, dense forests, Buddhist temples and hermitages, falls and clear streams.
Ⓣ: From Sangbong, Dong Seoul or Gangnam Bus Terminals, take a bus to Sokcho (takes about 4–5 hrs.)

SEORAKSAN NATIONAL PARK (설악산) B6 (033-636-7700, 7702, 7703; http://npa.or.kr/sorak/main.asp) is considered one of the Korea's most beautiful mountain areas, consisting of Oeseorak (Outer Seorak), Naeseorak (Inner Seorak) and Namseorak (Southern Seorak). It boasts numerous valleys well known for their spring blossoms and fall foliage. This 354-km^2 park is famous for lush green valleys, granite peaks, glorious falls, several temples and two hot springs.

The less-rugged outer area stretches east to SEORAK-DONG RESORT VILLAGE (설악동리조트단지) with inns, hotels, campsites, stores, parking lots and other public facilities. A 1,100-m-cable car connects the park entrance in SEORAK-DONG (설악동) with Gwongeumseong, an ancient mountaintop fortress of the Silla Kingdom. Other points of interest are BISEONDAE ROCK FLAT (비선대 적벽바위), named after the legend of an angel ascending to heaven from the rock flat, and OSAEK MINERAL SPRINGS (오색약수), which are thought to bring relief from digestive ailments. Visitors to the inner area entering from the west via the town of Inje can first visit BAEKDAMSA TEMPLE (백담사) (033-462-6969), the other gateway to Seoraksan.

Seoraksan Mountains

ⓛ: Just west of Sokcho ⓣ: 🚌 From Sokcho City, take bus No. 7 and get off at the last stop (every 10 min., 30 min.). ⓐ: ₩3,400

SORAK WATERPIA (설악워터피아) B7 (📞 033-635-7711; www.sorakwaterpia.com), located near Seoraksan National Park, is an all-season water theme park. It is famous for its outdoor hot spring (49°C) and it has a commanding view of Ulsan Rocks and the East Sea as well as a wave pool and water slides.
ⓣ: 🚌 A bus to Hanwha Resort from Sokcho Intercity Bus Terminal or Bus No. 3 from Sokcho City ⓗ: 6:00–20:30 (Sun.–Thu), 6:00–21:30 (Fri. and Sat.) ⓐ: ₩30,000

GOSEONG UNIFICATION OBSERVATORY (고성통일전망대) B8 is at the northernmost point of the east coast. Here, visitors can enjoy an excellent view of the beautiful mountains, lake and coast of North Korea. ⓣ: 🚌 A 1-hour bus ride to Unification Park from Sokcho Bus Terminal (every 15 min.). From Unification Park, take a shuttle bus to the Goseong Unification Observatory, which is 10 min. away (5 times daily).

THE IRON TRIANGLE BATTLEFIELD (철의삼각지) (📞 033-450-5558) is the triangular region connecting Cheorwon and Gimhwa with Pyeonggang at its apex in North Korea, a major frontline battlefield during the Korean War. It is worth visiting the ruins of the old (North) Korean Workers Party headquarters "HOUSE OF LABOR PARTY (노동당사지)" the 2ND TUNNEL (제2땅굴), and the

Sorak Waterpia

NEARBY ATTRACTIONS

ULLEUNGDO ISLAND (울릉도), B15 (📞 054-790-6396; www.ulleung.go.kr), along with the rocky islet Dokdo, comprises the easternmost part of Korea. It is a volcanic island like Jejudo Island but smaller, covering 73.15 km² and is surrounded by several islets such as Jukdo and Gwaneumdo. At the center of the island stands Seonginbong Peak. Boat tours around Ulleungdo are available for tourists to appreciate all of the charms of the island: steep cliffs, strange rock formations, and vegetation indigenous to the island. The island is famous among Koreans for its dried squid and pumpkin taffy.
ⓣ: 🚢 From Pohang Ferry Terminal (📞 054-242-5111), the high-speed boat 'Sun Flower' of Dae-A Express (02-514-6766) departs every day at 10 am (3 hrs.).
🚢 From Mukho Ferry Terminal (📞 033-531-5891), Hangyeoreho departs every day at 10 am (2 hrs., 20 min.). * Reservations are required.

DOKDO ISLET (독도) B15 Dokdo, a small islet located at the easternmost end of Korea, can be reached only by a 1.5-hour boat ride from Ulleungdo. Dokdo has an abundance of splendid rock formations and precipices. 30 or so species of birds, including the petrel, black-tailed gull, and kestrel, which inhabit the island, are also significant tourist attractions. In particular, about 2,000–3,000 black-tailed gulls live on the southwest side of island. In April and May, the birds' nests and eggs on the precipices and rocks and the wildflowers growing among them make a lovely scene.
The only ferries for Dokdo leave from Ulleungdo, which also must be accessed by ferry from Mukho Port in Donghae or Pohang Port in Gyeongsangbuk-do. The round-trip fare is 80,500 won from Mukho and 107,000 won from Pohang. It is wise to check with travel agencies, as some offer more convenient tour packages to Dokdo. (Dokdo Tour and Shipping Company 📞 054-791-8111/2; Daea Express Shipping Company 📞 054-791-0801/3)
ⓘ: Ulleung-gun County Office 📞 054-791-2191; http://www.ulleung.go.kr

Yongpyong Resort

rusted train hulk at Woljeong-ri Station. Nearby is the SAEMTONG MIGRATORY BIRD SANCTUARY (샘통철새도래지). Ⓣ: 🚌 Arrange private transportation or take a taxi in Sincheorwon.
🕐: 9:00 – 18:00 Mar.– Oct. / 9:00 – 17:00 Nov.– Feb. Ⓒ: Tuesday Ⓐ: ₩1,500

Haean-myeon, **YANGGU** (양구) (www.yanggu.gangwon.kr), is a low-lying area surrounded by mountains where many fierce battles took place during the Korean War.
PUNCH BOWL BATTLEGROUND (펀치볼) B9 in Yanggu, one of the most famous battlefields during the Korean War, includes NORTH KOREA HALL (북한관) (📞 033-481-9021), The 4TH TUNNEL (제4땅굴) and EULJI OBSERVATORY (을지전망대) There are only three buses a day, so you can either arrange private transportation or take a taxi in Yanggu.
Ⓣ: 🚌 From Dong (East) Seoul Bus Terminal, take a bus to Yanggu (4 hrs.). Then take a Haean-bound bus from Yanggu Bus Terminal (3 times daily, 1 hr.). Ⓗ: 9:00 – 17:00 (Nov.– Feb., 9:00 – 16:00) Ⓒ: Monday Ⓐ: ₩2,500

ODAESAN NATIONAL PARK (오대산) B10 (📞 033-332-6417; www.npa.or.kr/odae/main.asp), just south of Seoraksan, is the site of WOLJEONGSA (월정사) (📞 033-332-6664/5), one of the oldest temples of the Silla Kingdom, and SANGWONSA (상원사) (📞 033-332-6666), famous for its bronze bell cast in 725. This park consists largely of the Odaesan Mountains (1,563 m) and Sogeumgang Valley. The Odaesan Mountains have a smooth ridgeline connecting five peaks and the Sogeumgang Valley features beautiful rock formations, lush forests and many falls.
Ⓣ: 🚌 From Dong (East) Seoul Bus Terminal, take a bus bound for Jinbu (every 30 min.). Then from Jinbu-myeon in Pyeongchang-gun, Gangwon-do, take a city bus to Sangwonsa Temple (40 min.). Ⓐ: ₩1,600

Chiaksan Mountains

KOREA BOTANICAL GARDEN (한국자생식물원) B11 (☎ 033-332-7069), located at the entrance of Odaesan National Park, is home to over 1,000 types of wildflowers and plants native to Korea. The garden takes into consideration that many Korean flowers are best appreciated in large open areas, and seasonal gardens have been set up to display the flowers at their best.
Ⓣ: 🚌 20 min. from Odaesan National Park
Ⓗ: 9:00–18:00 (Open from Apr. 1 through Oct. 31, closed in winter) Ⓐ: ₩5,000

CHIAKSAN NATIONAL PARK (치악산) B12 (☎ 033-732-5231; www.npa.or.kr/chiak/main), stretching north to south, is located about 12 km northeast of Wonju. The Chiaksan Mountains (1,288 m) attract throngs of visitors throughout the year for their natural beauty and accessibility from Seoul. The Chiaksan valley, with its unusually shaped rocks and cliffs, is truly magnificent. There are several Buddhist temples inside the park, including **GURYONGSA TEMPLE** (구룡사) (☎ 033-732-4800), which was built during the Silla Kingdom.
Ⓣ: 🚌 From Sangbong Intercity Bus Terminal in Seoul, take a bus to Guryongsa Temple (4 times daily, 2 hrs., 40 min.). Or from Wonju Station, take bus No. 41 and get off at the Guryongsa Temple Stop (every 25 min., 45 min.). Ⓐ: ₩1,600

YONGPYONG RESORT (용평리조트) B13 (☎ 033-335-5757; www.yongpyong.co.kr) lies in the Daegwallyeong Pass south of Odaesan. Equipped with convenient facilities and excellent accommodations, the resort offers superb skiing as well as other all-season amenities.
Ⓣ: 🚌 From Dong Seoul Bus Terminal, take a bus to Hoenggye (3 hrs.). Then use the free shuttle bus to the resort.

Hwanseongul Cave

HWANSEONGUL CAVE (환선굴) B14 (☎ 033-541-9266), surrounded by scenic mountains, is one of the largest limestone caverns in Asia. It is 6.2 km long – only 1.6 km open to the public – yet that section alone will create unforgettable memories. It has 10 pools, six falls, a huge main chamber, and dozens of amazing sights loaded with fantastic formations.
Ⓣ: 🚌 From Dong (East) Seoul or Seoul Express Bus Terminal to Samcheok (3 hrs., 30 min.); 🚌 to Daei-ri (45 min.). It is about a 30-min. climb to the cave entrance. Ⓗ: 8:00–17:00 (Nov.–Feb., 8:30–16:00) Ⓐ: ₩4,000

SOBAEKSAN NATIONAL PARK (소백산) B15 Magnificent yet soft, the Sobaeksan Mountains (1,441 m) are famous for a unique beauty ushering in each season. The park also has several temples including Buseoksa, Huibangsa and Guinsa.

FOODS TO TRY & PLACES TO SHOP OF THE EASTERN AREA

FOOD GAMJA GYEONGDAN (potato dumplings) |감자경단 Gangwon-do Province is famous for potatoes and many of the province's recipes use potatoes as the main ingredient. Potato dumplings are one of these foods. Potato starch powder is kneaded into dough and steamed and dipped in cinnamon or soybean flour.
MEMIL MAKGUKSU (buckwheat noodles) |메밀막국수 This dish is especially enjoyed during the hot summer months. The chewy buckwheat noodles are mixed with red pepper powder, green onions, garlic, sesame oil and soy sauce. It is best when served with ice cold *dongchimi* (watery radish kimchi).

SHOPPING Mushrooms and honey from the Seoraksan Mountains and dried seafood from the east coast are famous local products that are highly recommended. Maps of Seoraksan's hiking trails are also a nice souvenir.

Central Area

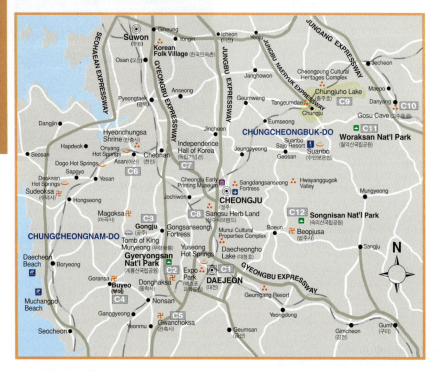

The central area of Korea encompasses Chungcheong-do Province. It is an area of broad stretches of rice paddy fields interspersed with rugged mountains.

DAEJEON(대전) (www.metro.daejeon.kr) is one of the area's principal cities, about two hours south of Seoul by car. It is a major junction for train lines and expressways and is rapidly becoming one of Korea's major centers for science. Yuseong Hot Springs Resort is located just northwest of the city.
①: From Seoul to Daejeon —1 hr., 30 min. by train (Saemaeulho); 1 hr., 50 min. by bus

EXPO SCIENCE PARK (엑스포과학공원) (042-866-5114/5; www.expopark.co.kr) is on an outdoor site of 627,000 m² (156.75 acres) in northwestern Daejeon. This is where the Daejeon EXPO 1993 was held. The area has since been renovated and turned into a public science park. Visitors can get an overview of state-of-the-art technology in a single visit to the park. Several major science facilities, such as the Daedeok Science Research Complex, are adjacent to the park.
①: No.103 near Daejeon Express Bus Terminal, or No.105, 180, 181, 513 or 814 near Daejeon Station to Expo Science Park ⓗ: 9:30 –18:00 (open until 19:00 during festivals) Ⓐ: ₩3,000 (admission fees for each pavilion are not included.) Ⓒ: Mondays

GYERYONGSAN NATIONAL PARK(계룡산) (042-825-3003, http://knps.or.kr/kyeryong/new/index.htm) is renowned for its magnificent natural beauty and the cultural relics of Buyeo and Gongju (capitals of the ancient Baekje Kingdom) are nearby. Gyeryongsan National Park is just west of Daejeon.
The hiking trails lead to two temples: **GAPSA TEMPLE** (갑사) (041-857-8981), which is famous

TOURIST ATTRACTIONS BY REGION

Daejeon 대전, Chungcheongnam-do 충청남도, Chungcheongbuk-do 충청북도

Donghaksa Temple

for the changing colors of leaves in autumn, and DONGHAKSA TEMPLE (동학사) (☎ 042-825-3002/3), located on the eastern slope of the mountain. A long-time center for shamanism, these mountains were named for their ridges, which resemble a dragon with a rooster's head.

ⓣ: 🚌 From Seoul Express Bus Terminal or Dong Seoul Bus Terminal, buses to Gongju or Daejeon depart all day. From Gongju, take a city bus to Gapsa Temple (30 min.) or from Daejeon, take a city bus to Donghaksa Temple (50 min.). Ⓐ: ₩3,200

GONGJU (공주) (www.gongju.go.kr) is northwest of Daejeon, and it was the capital of the ancient Baekje Kingdom from 475 to 539 before the kingdom moved its capital south to Buyeo. The kingdom fell when Silla unified the Korean Peninsula in the 7th century. Many remains of Baekje's former glory are well preserved in these two old capitals.

Gongju's main attraction is the GONGJU NATIONAL MUSEUM (공주국립박물관) (☎ 041-850-

---

DAEJEON CITY TOUR
(10:00–17:00, except Mondays, 7 hours, cost: ₩6,000 for the town tour and ₩10,000 for the out-of-town tour)

Departs from Dongbang Mart (10:00), Korea Express near Daejeon Station (10:05), Save Zone (10:25), Yuseong Hong-in Officetel (10:40)

Package Courses | Daedeok Research Complex (via Expo Science Park) → Main office of Dosolcheon Stream
(Tue., Thur., Sat.) (World Cup Stadium) → Ppuri (Root) Park → U-am Historical Park

(Wed., Fri.) ⎾ Daedeok Research Complex (via Expo Science Park) → National Cemetary →
⎿ Gongsanseong Fortress → Tomb of King Muryeong → Gongju National Museum (Donghaksa Temple)

Reservation-type Courses | A Course: Daecheong Dam, Cheongnamdae Villa, Munui Cultural Property Complex
B Course: Expo Science Park, Daejeon Zoo (shuttle buses operated)
C Course: Geumsan area, Baekje cultural area, etc.

Customized Courses | **Administration** National Government Complex, City Hall, Wolpyeong (Songcheon), Water
Filtration Plant, Daejeon Zooland
Science EXPO Park, Geological Museum, Currency Museum, National Science Museum, KAIST, Daejeon Observatory, Meteorology Administration, Korea Astronomy Observatory, Korea Research Institute of Standards and Science, Korea Aerospace Research Institute
Culture Punsan Prehistoric Site, Lookout, Dongchundang, Old House of Shin Chaeho
Experience Sangsin Ceramic Village

ⓘ: Tourism Department, Daejeon City Hall ☎ 042-600-3563; Baekje Tours ☎ 042-253-0005, 📱 02-222-5901

6360, http://gongju.museum.go.kr), which exhibits treasures from the 6th century tomb of King Muryeong. Although most Baekje tombs were pillaged over the centuries, the TOMB OF KING MURYEONG (무녕왕릉) (041-856-0331) was left undisturbed until its excavation in 1971.
①: 🚌 All buses (except No. 15) run to the Gongju National Museum. Get off at the Gukgogae and walk about 10 to 15 minutes. ⏲: 9:00 – 18:00
Ⓐ: ₩4,000

BUYEO (부여) C4 (www.buyeo.go.kr) is about 20 miles further southwest of Daejeon and it was the last capital of Baekje (539-660). It also has the distinctive BUYEO NATIONAL MUSEUM (부여국립박물관) (041-833-8562~3), which incorporates the unique architecture of the Baekje Kingdom. The bird's-eye view of the Baengmagang River from the top of BUSOSANSEONG FORTRESS (부소산성) (041-830-2512) is a splendid sight. NAKHWAAM ROCK (낙화암), on one side of the Baengmagang River, is the site of a tragic incident where some 3,000 women of the Baekje court leapt to their deaths to avoid dishonor at the hands of their enemies during the fall of the kingdom. The image of the women plummeting down in their colorful dresses gave the place its name, "Rock of Falling Flowers."
①: 🚌 Seoul → Nonsan → Buyeo 🚶 From Buyeo, they are all within a 10- to 20-min. walk.
Ⓐ: ₩2,000 for Busosanseong Fortress

GWANCHOKSA TEMPLE (관촉사) C5 (041-736-5700/2), to the southeast of Buyeo near Nonsan, has one of Korea's most interesting Buddhist statues, Eunjinmireuk.
This is "the Buddha of the future" and is more than 1,000 years old. With a height of 19 m (63

Gwanchoksa Temple

ft.), it is one of Korea's tallest Buddha statues.
①: 🚌 A city bus to Gwanchoksa Temple from Nonsan City (every 20 min., 10 min.). It is located at the foot of Mt. Banyasan, 3 km from downtown Nonsan. Ⓐ: ₩1,500

TAEAN SEASHORE NATIONAL PARK (태안반도) Located along the Yellow Sea, this park has many beaches, some 430 km of saw-toothed coastline, about 130 islands and picturesque rock formations.

ASAN (아산) C6 (www.asan.chungnam.kr) is about an hour's drive south of Seoul just off the Gyeongbu Expressway. Asan is famous for hot springs, including ASAN SPAVIS (아산스파비스) (041-539-2080) and the HYEONCHUNGSA SHRINE (현충사) (041-544-2161), which commemorates the historic feats of Admiral Yi Sun-sin, who defeated the Japanese navy in the late 16th century.
Asan Spavis ①: 🚌 From Nambu Bus Terminal in Seoul, take a bus to Asan (1 hr., 30 min.). Then at the bus stop across from Asan Bus Terminal, take

---

GONGJU CITY TOUR
(10:00, every Sunday from April to October, takes 7 hours, cost: free)

1st and 3rd Sundays |
Gongju Tourist Information Center → Gongju PR Center → Tomb of King Muryeong → Gom Shrine/Seonhwadang Shrine → Gongju National Museum → Ugeumchi Battle Site → Imlip Art Museum → Gongju Folk Drama Museum (traditional folk game experience) → Ungjin Education Museum → Gongsanseong Fortress → Ungjinseong Fortress Royal Guard Changing Ceremony → trying on ancient Baekje clothing

2nd and 4th Sundays |
Gongju Tourist Information Center → Gongju PR Center → Tomb of King Muryeong → Gongju National Museum → Forest Museum → Park Dong-jin Pansori Instruction Center (*pansori* lesson offered) → Ungjin Education Museum → Ungjinseong Fortress Royal Guard Changing Ceremony → trying on ancient Baekje clothing

*Reservations are required.
The tours are free of charge and include a guide book. A translator/guide will accompany the group.
①: Gongju Tourist Information 041-856-7700

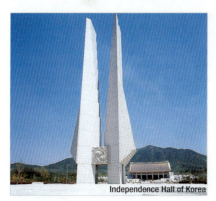
Independence Hall of Korea

bus No. 100-1 or a taxi (30 min.).
Hyeonchungsa Shrine ⓣ: 🚌 From Onyang Bus Terminal, take a bus to Hyeonchungsa Shrine (6:00–21:00, 15 min.).

The INDEPENDENCE HALL OF KOREA (독립기념관) C7 (📞 041-560-0114; www.i815.or.kr) is in the vicinity of Cheonan, about an hour and a half away from Seoul. The hall commemorates those who struggled for freedom against foreign invasions throughout Korea's long history. The hall collects, studies and exhibits historic artifacts and materials related to Korea's resistance to aggression, the fight for independence, the search for national identity, and a record of the nation's development and progress.
ⓣ: 🚌 From Cheonan Bus Terminal, take a bus bound for the Independence Hall of Korea (a 30-min. ride). ⓗ: 9:30–18:00 (Nov.–Feb., 9:30–17:00) Ⓐ: ₩2,000 Ⓒ: Mon.

SANGSU HERB LAND (상수허브랜드) C8 (📞 043-277-6633) is Asia's largest herb garden with over 500 herb varieties in its greenhouse allows even during the c restaurant on the dishes with her A favorite is kl traditional Ko assorted vege
ⓣ: 🚌 Take a city bus Bus Terminal and get off at the (40 min.). ⓗ: 9:00–19:00 (Dec.–Feb., 9:30– Ⓐ: ₩3,000

CHUNGJUHO LAKE (충주호) C9, 80 miles southeast of Seoul, offers a wide variety of water sports in the mountainous area of central Korea. Pleasure ferries ply the 32-mile-long waterway between Chungju and Danyang. Passengers can also enjoy the stunning view of Danyang Palgyeong, the "Eight Scenic Wonders" of the limestone region surrounding Danyang.
ⓣ: 🚌 From Chungju, buses to Chungjuho Lake depart every 1 hr., 20 min. (30 min.).

GOSU CAVE (고수동굴) C10 (📞 043-423-3071) is a famous cave that is located less than 1 mile from downtown Danyang. It contains glistening stalactites in all shapes and sizes and is called the "Underground Palace."
ⓣ: 🚌 From Danyang Station or Danyang Intercity Bus Terminal, take a bus to Gosu Cave (15 min.). ⓗ: 9:00–17:00 Ⓐ: ₩4,000

WORAKSAN NATIONAL PARK (월악산) C11 (📞 043-653-3250; www.npa.or.kr/worak/main.asp) is a great mountain range, 3,700 feet (1,093 m) high, 24 miles (40 km) southeast of Chungju. The summit of Mt. Woraksan reaches a modest

Chungjuho Lake

Beopjusa Temple

1,096 m, but it is a tough challenge for hikers because of its steep slopes.

DEOKJUSA TEMPLE (덕주사) (☏ 043-653-1773) was built by Deokju, the last princess of the Silla Kingdom, and it adds to the mountain's natural beauty and creates an atmosphere of mystery.
🚆: 🚌 From Chungju, take a city bus to Songgye. Ⓐ: ₩1,600

SONGNISAN NATIONAL PARK (속리산) G12 (☏ 043-542-3206, 3762; www.npa.or.kr/songni/main.asp) is northeast of Daejeon and is one of the most popular tourist spots in the central part of the Korean Peninsula. The Songnisan Mountains (1,058 m) have the time-honored Beopjusa Temple, a pine tree named Jeong-ipum-song that was once actually granted government ministership, Munjangdae Flat Rock Peak, and the Hwayang, Seonyudong and Ssanggok valleys.

The park's **BEOPJUSA TEMPLE** (법주사) (☏ 043-543-3615), established in 553, accommodated up to 3,000 monks in ancient times. A bronze statue of Maitreya Buddha stands 33 m tall on the temple grounds.
🚆: 🚌 From Boeun-gun, direct buses to Mt. Songnisan depart all day (20 min.). Ⓐ: ₩3,800

FOODS TO TRY & PLACES TO SHOP OF THE CENTRAL AREA

FOOD OLGAENGI-GUK (small freshwater snail soup) l 올갱이국 This soup is made by boiling small freshwater snails. The taste is slightly bitter yet savory and is good for breakfast.

SANCHAE BIBIMBAP (rice topped with vegetables, meat and optional red pepper paste) l 산채비빔밥 Wild herbs gathered from the mountains are mixed with red pepper paste and rice, and the aroma of these fresh herbs tantalizes the nose. Because this dish is low in calories, it is ideal for those who are on a diet.

GUL-BAP (steamed rice with oysters) l 굴밥 This dish comes from the West Sea area of Chungcheong-do Province. It is prepared by adding live oysters while the rice is boiling and mixing with soy sauce when they are cooked.

SHOPPING In Buyeo and Gongju, souvenirs of the Baekje Kingdom are available. The national museums in Buyeo and Gongju sell historical books and reproductions of Baekje relics. At Mt. Songnisan, items such as amethyst, dried mushrooms, dried wild greens and herbs and antique folkcrafts may be purchased. In Gyeryongsan National Park, there is a ceramics village where you can buy exquisite ceramic pieces.

HANSAN RAMIE MARKET
For its delicate, refined color and texture, Hansan-produced ramie fabric has long been valued as the best in Korea. The market is held in five-day intervals from the first day of each month, beginning before daybreak between 5:00 and 6:30 am like a "guerrilla market" to serve the big turnout of merchants. Hansan is also famous for *sogokju* (sticky rice liquor).
🚆: 🚌 Janghangseon Line from Seoul Station to Seocheon (3 hrs., 30 min.); 🚌 15 min. to Hansan Ramie Fabric Hall

Southeastern Area

TOURIST ATTRACTIONS BY REGION

Daegu 대구, Gyeongsangbuk-do 경상북도, Gyeongju 경주, Busan 부산, Gyeongsangnam-do 경상남도, Hallyeo Maritime National Park 한려해상국립공원

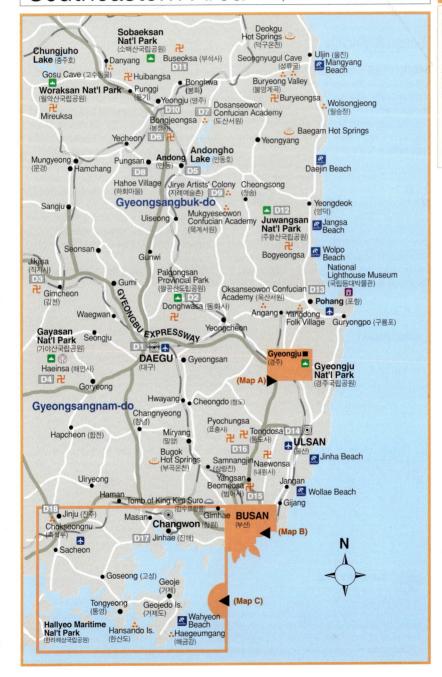

In terms of tourist attractions, the southeastern part of Korea is the richest in the country. The major cities of this area, the site of the remarkable ancient Silla Kingdom, are Daegu, Gyeongju and Busan.

Daegu & Vincinty SOUTHEASTERN AREA

DAEGU(대구) (www.daegu.go.kr) is the textile hub of Korea. In the central area is an Oriental medicinal herb market where as many as 300 Oriental medical clinics, herbal medicinal shops and herb processing facilities are located.
The 202 m Daegu Tower at Woobang Towerland commands a nice view of the city.

MT. PALGONGSAN(팔공산) towers over the city. From Seoul to Daegu – 50 min. by air; 3 hrs., 10 min. by train (Saemaeulho); 4 hrs., 30 min. by bus

JIKJISA TEMPLE(직지사) (054-436-6013) lies northwest of Daegu and can be reached by taking the Gimcheon exit off the Gyeongbu Expressway. The temple is famous for its blue-tiled roofs, the 1,000-year-old support pillars of the main gate and the 1,000 small statues of Buddha.
: Between Daejeon and Daegu : Take the train (Gyeongbuseon Line) to Gimcheon. In front of Gimcheon Station, take city bus No. 11 or 111 to Jikjisa Temple (every 10 min., 25 min.). : ₩2,500

GAYASAN NATIONAL PARK(가야산) (1,430 m) (055-932-7810; www.npa.or.kr/kaya/main.asp). is famous for historic sites and scenic landscapes, such as Haeinsa Temple, Yongmun Falls and the Hongnyudong Valley renowned for autumn colors.

HAEINSA TEMPLE(해인사) (055-934-3000; http://www.haeinsa.or.kr), in Gayasan National Park, is perhaps Korea's best known temple. Established in 802, it has a number of treasures in more than 90 buildings (shrines, hermitages and subtemples), but what really distinguishes this temple from the others is the collection of more than 80,000 wooden printing blocks, which compose the *Tripitaka Koreana*, the most complete collection of the Buddhist Canon found in East Asia.
Completed in 1251 as a plea to Buddha in an effort to ward off a Mongolian invasion, the

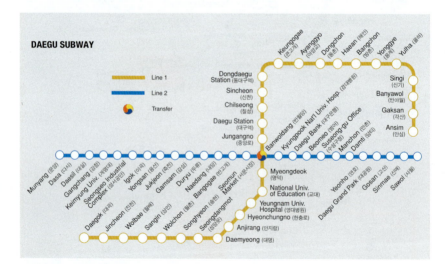

DAEGU CITY TOUR

The City Tour of Daegu offers eight courses leaving from downtown and seven that begin at Daegu International Airport. Tours leaving from the Daegu Tourist Information Center start every morning at 10 am. Destinations are determined by demand, so call ahead (or visit www.daegutour.or.kr) and check to make reservations. Tours also leave Daegu International Airport at 10 am, with a different course for every day of the week. Adult prices for all tours are ₩3,000.
: Daegu Tourist Information Center 053-627-8900

blocks remain in excellent condition and are the basis of the most authoritative editions of Buddhist scripture.
In 1995, Haeinsa Temple's Janggyeong Panjeon, the depositories for the *Tripitaka Koreana Woodblocks*, were placed on UNESCO's prestigious World Cultural Heritage list.
Ⓛ: West of Daegu Ⓣ: 🚌 Take a bus to Daegu. In front of Daegu Intercity Bus Terminal, take a bus to Haeinsa Temple and get off at the last stop (every 20 min., 1 hr.). Ⓐ: ₩3,500

ANDONG (안동) D5 (www.andong.go.kr) is a treasure trove of Confucian tradition and one of the last living vestiges of old Korea. Visitors are charmed by the old homes of the *yangban* (the noble class). Queen Elizabeth II visited Andong in April 1999 on the occasion of her 73rd birthday during her four-day state visit to Korea.
Ⓣ: 🚆 Seoul to Andong—4 hrs. by train (Saemaeulho); 🚌 3 hrs. by bus

BONGJEONGSA TEMPLE (봉정사) D6 (📞 054-853-4181) is famous for the oldest standing wooden building in the nation and the main hall reveals the construction methods of the early Joseon Dynasty.
Ⓣ: 🚌 No. 51 to Bongjeongsa Temple (7 times daily, 40 min.) Ⓗ: 7:00–18:00 Ⓐ: ₩1,500

DOSANSEOWON CONFUCIAN ACADEMY (도산서원) D7 (📞 054-856-1073) in Andong was founded by the scholar Toegye Yi Hwang in the 16th century.
Ⓣ: 🚌 No. 67 at Andong Bus Terminal (1 hr., 30 min.) Ⓗ: 15:00 (Mar., Apr., Nov., Sun.), 15:00 (May–Oct. Sat. & Sun.), No service (Dec.–Feb.), Ⓐ: Free

HAHOE VILLAGE (하회마을) D8 (📞 054-854-3669; www.hahoe.or.kr) is a small village with a delightful blend of thatched-roof peasant houses and tiled-roof *yangban* (the noble class) villas of the Joseon Dynasty. The village is known for a special form of mask drama called *Hahoe Byeolsingut Tallori*.
Ⓣ: 🚌 No. 46 across from Andong Bus Terminal (8 times daily, 1 hr., 20 min.) Ⓗ: 9:00–18:00

JIRYE ARTISTS' COLONY (지례예술촌) D9 (📞 054-822-2590; www.chirye.com) began in 1988 as a colony for artists and writers to ply their creative crafts in beautiful natural surroundings.
The colony now welcomes overseas visitors to experience the rich traditions of an aristocratic

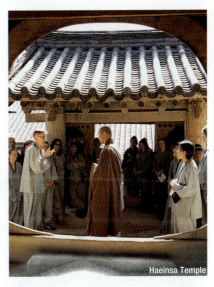
Haeinsa Temple

household in serene environs.
During *jesa* (a memorial service that takes place there 10 times a year), one can watch how Koreans pay respect to their ancestors. When reservations are made, a guide from the Jirye Artists' Colony will meet the party at Andong Railway Station.
Arrive at the station before 3:00 pm and you might catch a fantastic sunset.
The Colony has 17 *ondol* (heated floors with traditional mat-style bedding) rooms. It costs ₩32,000 per person and includes breakfast and dinner.
Ⓣ: 🚌 From Dong Seoul Bus Terminal, take a bus to Andong (every 30 min.). From Andong Intercity Bus Terminal, take a bus to Im-dong (20 min.) and then a taxi to the colony (20 min.).

YEONGJU (영주) D10 (www.yeongju.go.kr), about 20 miles north of Andong, can be reached by train from Seoul.

BUSEOKSA TEMPLE (부석사) D11 (📞 054-639-6498) is near Yeongju, and is noted for having one of the oldest wooden buildings in Korea.
Ⓣ: 🚌 From Punggi Intercity Bus Terminal, take a bus to Buseoksa Temple (every hour, 40 min.). Or from Yeongju City, take bus No. 27 (every hour, 1 hr.). Ⓗ: 6:30–18:00 (Nov.–Feb., 7:00–17:30) Ⓐ: ₩1,300

JUWANGSAN NATIONAL PARK (주왕산) D12 (📞 054-873-0014/5; www.npa.or.kr/chuwang/

main.asp) is at the southern end of the coastal highway and it is favored by those who want to get away from crowded areas.

The nearby coastal town of Yeongdeok is noted for giant crabs and other tasty seafood.

The Juwangsan Mountains (721 m) have spectacular rocky peaks forming a "stone folding screen," scenic valleys, several falls and mineral springs, temples and caves.

ⓘ: East of Andong ⓣ: 🚌 From Cheongsong-eup, Cheongsong-gun, buses to Juwangsan National Park operate all day.

On the southeastern coastal are many industrial cities, such as Pohang and Ulsan.

POHANG (포항) D13 (www.ipohang.org) is the site of the large POSCO (054-3457-0114; www.posco.co.kr) steel mill and the departure point for ferry boats to Ulleungdo Island.

ⓣ: ✈ From Seoul to Pohang– 50 min. by air; 🚌 5 hrs. by bus

ULSAN (울산) D14 (www.ulsan.go.kr) is the home of Hyundai Motor Company and Hyundai Heavy Industries. English-language tours provide insight into the development of one of Korea's major conglomerates.

ⓣ: ✈ From Seoul to Ulsan– 1 hr., by air; 🚌 5 hrs. by bus

 ULSAN CITY TOUR
(10:00 – 16:30, except Mondays, six tour courses for each day of the week, takes 6.5 hrs., cost: ₩5,000)

Tuesday   Taehwa Hotel → Hyundai Motors → Daewangam Songrim (Pine Forest) → Hyundai Heavy Industries → Onyang Pottery Complex → Taehwa Hotel

Wednesday Taehwa Hotel → SK Complex → Whale Museum → Cheonyongam → Gaeunposeong Site → Ganjeolgot → Seosaengpo Waeseong → Onyang Pottery Complex → Taehwa Hotel

Thursday Taehwa Hotel → Hyundai Motors → Hyundai Heavy Industries → Ulsan Dongheon and Naea → Hakseong Park → Choongee Temple → Taehwa Hotel

Friday   Taehwa Hotel → Seated Yeorae images carved on rock surface in Eomul-dong → Jujeon Beach → Daewangam Songrim (Pine Forest) → Jakgwaecheon → Standing Rock & Taehwa River Seepri → Taehwa Hotel

Saturday Taehwa Hotel → Eonyangeupseong → Gingko tree of Duseo-Myeon → Petroglyphs in Cheonjeon-RT, Ulju → Chiwisan Seowon Site → Eunpeon-ri dolmen → Standing Rock & Taehwa River Seepri → Taehwa Hotel

Sunday   Taehwa Hotel → Eunpeon-ri dolmen → Eonyang Traditional School → Jakgwaecheon → Eonyangeupseong → Petroglyphs in Cheonjeon-RT, Ulju → Standing Rock & Taehwa River Seepri → Taehwa Hotel

* The departure and arrival point for all tours is the Taehwa Hotel.
ⓘ: Taehwa World Tour 052-271-6633; http://www.ulsancitytour.com

Buseoksa Temple

Gyeongju

SOUTHEASTERN AREA

GYEONGJU (경주) (www.gyeongju.gyeongbuk.kr) was the capital of the Silla Kingdom for 1,000 years and the valley in which it is situated has a great concentration of historical buildings, temples and artifacts. After Silla unified the peninsula in 676, the city developed into one of the world's major cultural centers. The area is called a "museum without walls" because of the wealth of historical buildings and treasures.
ⓣ: 🚆 From Seoul to Gyeongju– 4 hrs., 30 min. by train (Saemaeulho); 🚌 4 hrs., 15 min. by bus

TUMULI PARK (대릉원) (☎ 054-772-6317),
a collection of royal Silla tombs from the Pre-unification era, is in the middle of Gyeongju. The park contains 23 of the more than 200 royal tombs that were found in Gyeongju. The Cheonmachong (Heavenly Horse Tomb) was excavated in 1974 and yielded more than 10,000 treasures. These treasures, including a golden crown and a girdle, are in the Gyeongju National Museum. The tomb itself is open for viewing, providing visitors with an opportunity to see how the huge tombs were constructed and how the various items were arranged in them.
ⓣ: 🚶 10 min. from Gyeongju Station 🚌 From Gyeongju Intercity Bus Terminal, take bus No. 10 or 11 and get off at Tumuli Park (Daereungwon). ⓗ: 8:00–20:00 ⓐ: ₩1,500

CHEOMSEONGDAE OBSERVATORY (첨성대)
(☎ 054-772-5134) is Asia's earliest known existing observatory. It is a 7th-century bottle-shaped stone structure admired by archeologists worldwide. The square window facing south in the middle of the structure is believed to have served as an entrance that was reached by a ladder.
ⓛ: South of Gyeongju Station ⓣ: 🚶 20 min. from Gyeongju Station ⓗ: 9:00–20:00
ⓐ: ₩500

ANAPJI POND (안압지) (☎ 054-772-4041), a 10-min. walk from Cheomseongdae, is the place where the Silla royal family relaxed and enjoyed themselves. The pond was temporarily drained in 1974 to reveal a veritable treasure trove of Silla artifacts that are now on display in the Gyeongju National Museum.
ⓣ: 🚶 20 min. from Gyeongju Station
ⓗ: 9:00–22:00 (Nov.–Feb., 9:00–18:00)
ⓐ: ₩1,000

GYEONGJU NATIONAL MUSEUM (경주국립박물관)
(☎ 054-740-7518, 7538; http://gyeongju.museum.go.kr) is a place of compelling interest that preserves much of the Silla heritage, including magnificent gold crowns, pottery, Buddhist artifacts and stone sculptures. The museum also houses the Divine Bell of King Seongdeok the Great, also referred to as the legendary Emille Bell, one of Asia's largest and

most resonant bells. It is 19 tons of bronze standing 11 feet high.

Ⓣ: 🚇 10 min. from Gyeongju Station
Ⓗ: 9:00–18:00 (Sundays and national holidays 9:00–19:00, Thursday, Friday and Saturday 9:00–21:00) Ⓐ: ₩400 Ⓒ: Mon. and Jan.1

BUNHWANGSAJI TEMPLE SITE (분황사지) E5

(📞 054-742-9922) is a 20-min. walk from the Gyeongju National Museum. Only three of the original nine levels of the stone brick pagoda are still standing.

Ⓣ: 🚇 5 min. from Gyeongju Station; 🚶 20 min. from Anapji Pond Ⓐ: ₩1,300

POSEOKJEONG PAVILION (포석정) E6

(📞 054-745-8484) is where Silla kings used to hold poetry-reciting and drinking parties. Kings would float wine cups to their statesmen seated around the watercourse made in the shape of an abalone shell.

Ⓣ: 🚇 20 min. from Gyeongju Station
Ⓗ: 8:30–18:00 (8:00–17:00, Dec.–Feb.)
Ⓐ: ₩500

BULGUKSA TEMPLE (불국사) E7

(📞 054-746-9913), one of Korea's best known temples, is a testimony to both the skill of Silla architects and the depth of Buddhist faith at the time. While most of the wooden buildings have been rebuilt over the centuries, all the stone bridges, stairways and pagodas are original. The temple, originally built in 535, was enlarged in 752.

Ⓛ: Western slope of Mt. Tohamsan Ⓣ: 🚇 No. 10 or 11 from Gyeongju Station (30 min.)
Ⓗ: 7:00–17:30 (Oct.–Mar., 7:00–17:00)
Ⓐ: ₩4,000

SEOKGURAM GROTTO (석굴암) E8

(📞 054-746-9933) is one of the world's finest shrines of Buddha, dating back to the same period as Bulguksa Temple.

Surrounded by bodhisattvas and guardian deities, the serene central statue of Buddha gazes out over the forested hills and across the East Sea to the horizon. The carving of the granite dome of Seokguram was a truly amazing architectural feat. In 1995, Bulguksa Temple and Seokguram Grotto were added to UNESCO's prestigious World Cultural Heritage list.

Ⓛ: Near the top of Mt. Tohamsan Ⓣ: 🚇 20 min. from Bulguksa Bus Stop Ⓗ: 6:30–17:30 (7:00–17:00 in winter) Ⓐ: ₩4,000

GYEONGJU FOLK CRAFT VILLAGE (경주민속공예촌)

E9 (📞 054-746-7270), along the way from Bomun Lake Resort to Bulguksa Temple and Seokguram Grotto, consists of 45 traditional houses where people produce filigree, earthen burial figures, wooden and stone pottery, handicraft items, jewelry, and embroidery. You can watch them at work in any of 17 workshops and there is an exhibition hall for viewing or

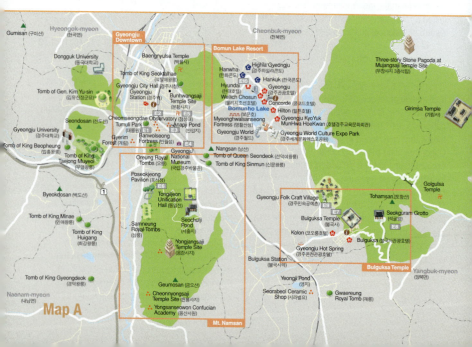

Map A

GYEONGJU CITY TOUR
(twice daily at 08:30 – 16:00 and 10:00 – 18:00, cost: Adults ₩12,000, Students ₩10,000)

Gyeongju Express Bus Terminal → Bomun Lake Resort → Bulguksa Temple → Gyeongju Folk Craft Village → Bunhwangsaji Temple Site → Tomb of General Kim Yu-sin → Poseokjeong Pavilion → Gyeongju National Museum → Anapji Pond → Cheomseongdae Observatory → Cheonmachong Tomb → Gyeongju Express Bus Terminal
ⓘ: Cheonma Tours ☏ 054-743-6001

Tumuli Park

Anapji Pond

purchasing handicrafts.
ⓣ: 🚌 No. 10 or 11 to the village (30 min.) from Gyeongju Station ⓗ: Jan. and Dec., 9:00 – 17:00; Feb. and Nov., 9:00 – 17:30; Mar.– Oct., 9:00 – 18:00; Apr.– Sep., 9:00 – 18:30 ⓐ: Free

BOMUN LAKE RESORT (보문단지) F10 (☏ 054-740-7330; www.ktd.co.kr) is east of downtown Gyeongju and has five super-deluxe hotels, a convention center, a casino, extensive shopping and dining facilities, golf courses, an amusement park, pleasure boats, a hot spring, and a contemporary art museum. Shuttle bus and taxi service connect downtown Gyeongju with the resort area.
ⓣ: 🚌 20 min. from Gyeongju Station

There are many more attractions are scattered around Gyeongju such as tombs of kings and generals, the holy Namsan Mountain, Yangdong Folk Village and Oksanseowon Confucian Academy.

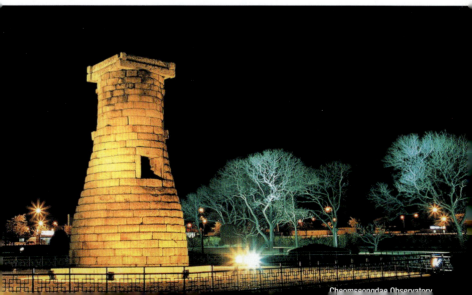
Cheomseongdae Observatory

Haeundae Beach

Jinjuseong Fortress

SOUTHEASTERN AREA
Busan & Vicinity

BUSAN (부산) (www.busan.go.kr) is Korea's principal port and second largest city. It is the primary port for ferry service to Japan and is the gateway to the Hallyeo Maritime National Park and its picturesque islands. As an international port city with a population of 3.8 million, Busan has first-class hotels and restaurants to match its excellent beaches and outstanding shopping and sightseeing areas. You can get from Seoul to Busan by expressway, rail or air.

T: From Seoul to Busan— ✈ 50 min. by air; 🚄 2hrs., 40 min. by KTX 🚄 4 hrs., 20 min. by train (Saemaeulho); 🚌 5 hrs., 20 min. by bus

Special places of interest in downtown Busan are Yongdusan Park (용두산공원) F1 (📞 051-246-8153) and the adjacent fashion and entertainment districts of Gwangbok-dong and Nampo-dong.
T: 🚌 No. 301 from Gimhae Airport. Get off Gumi Cultural Center in Daecheong-dong and walk about 10 min. 🚇 Take Line 1 and get off at Nampo-dong Station and walk about 10 min.
⏰: 8:30–22:00 (Mar.–Oct.) 9:00–22:00 (Nov.–Feb.) ©: No closed days

Busan's huge JAGALCHI FISH MARKET (자갈치시장) F2 (📞 051-245-2594/5) is a fantastic scene in the early morning as retailers haggle over fresh fish. The fishing fleet comes in before dawn and the catch is immediately unloaded onto the docks.
T: 🚇 From Jagalchi Station, Line 1, exit toward Sindonga Market and walk about 5 min. 🚌 From Gimhae Airport, take bus No. 310 or from Busan Express Bus Terminal, No. 35, and get off at the Nampo-dong Stop.

UNITED NATIONS MEMORIAL CEMETERY (유엔공원)
F3 (📞 051-624-2165; www.unmck.or.kr) is a somber yet beautiful place where many U.N. soldiers who sacrificed their lives during the Korean War almost five decades ago lay at rest.
T: 🚇 From Daeyeon Station, Line 2 (bound for Gwangalli), walk about 15 min. 🚌 From Busan Station, take bus No. 134 and get off at the U.N. Memorial Cemetery.

TAEJONGDAE PARK (태종대) F4 (📞 051-405-2004) is on the tip of Yeongdo Island, southwest of the downtown area. It is a very hilly and heavily forested area with rugged cliffs dropping straight down to the sea 150 m below.
T: 🚌 From Busan Station, take bus No. 88 or

BUSAN CITY TOUR
(twice daily at 9:00 and 13:30, except Mondays, two tour courses, takes 4 hrs., cost: ₩10,000)

Camellia Line (4 times a day, 9:00, 11:20, 12:50, 15:30 from Busan Train Station)
Busan Station → Hotel Lotte Busan → Bujun Station → UN Memorial Cemetery → Busan Museum → Gwangalli Beach → Haeundae Beach → Marriott Hotel → Paradise Hotel → Cruise Wharfs → Grand Hotel → The Western Hotel → Haeundae Beach → Haeundae Station → BEXCO/Metropolitan Art Museum →Gwangan Bridge (via) → Busan Station

Sea Gull Line (4 times a day, 9:30, 13:00, 15:10, 16:10 from Busan Train Station)
Busan Station → International Ferry Terminal → Commodore Hotel → Mt. Yongdu Park → 7.5 Square (Prospect Observation) → Taejongdae → Jagalchi Market → Coastal Ferry Terminal → Busan Station

Night Tour (once a day, 19:00 from Busan Train Station)
Busan Station → Democracy Park → Hwangryeongsan → Gwangan Bridge (via) → Dalmaji Hill → Haeundae Beach → Gwangan Bridge (via) → Busan Station
①: Arumtour inc. 📞 051-463-0084; http://www.busancitytour.com

101. Or in front of Jagalchi Market, No. 8, 13 or 30.

Other scenic attractions are HAEUNDAE BEACH (해운대해수욕장) F5 and GWANGALLI BEACH (광안리해수욕장) F6, both with many cafes, restaurants and hotels that produce a romantic neon-lit beach at night.
T: Haeundae Beach ▭ From Busan Staion, take bus No. 139, 140, 239, 240, 302, 2001 or 2003 (40 min.). From Gimhae Airport, No. 307 or KAL limousine bus (50 min.). From Gwangalli Beach ▭ Exit 3 or 5 of Gwangan Station, Line 2. ▭ From Busan Station, take bus No. 42, 139, 140, 239 or 240 and get off at the entrance of Gwangalli Beach or bus No.131 or 131-1 from Express Bus Terminal in Dongnae.

North of the downtown area is Geumgang Park (금강공원) F7 (☏ 051-555-1743) with its wooded slopes, sparkling streams, dramatic rock formations and several historical relics, including a fortress gate and tower that can be reached by cable car. The park is not far from the DONGNAE HOT SPRINGS (동래온천) F8. There are also temples and the ruins of an old fortress nearby. To the north is BEOMEOSA TEMPLE (범어사) D15 (☏ 051-508-3122; www.beomeosa.co.kr), which dates back to the late 7th century.
T: Geumgang Park ▭ From Oncheonjang Station, Line 1, walk about 15 min. It is located at Ujangchunno Road via the botanical garden. ▭ City bus No. 51, 51-2, 77, 80, 80-1, 100, 110, 110-1, 121, 130, 131-1, 189-1, 210, 37 or Jwaseok bus No. 51-1, 130-1, 183, 203, 301, 301, 347. Get off at the entrance of Geumgang Park and walk about 5 min.
Dongnae Hot Springs ▭ From Oncheonjang Station (Line 1), walk about 10 min. ▭ No. 21, 51, 80 or 100. Get off at the Oncheonjang Stop.
Beomeosa Temple ▭ Get off at Beomeosa Station, Line 1 and take circulation bus No. 90.

TONGDOSA TEMPLE (통도사) D16 (☏ 055-382-7182), one of the largest temples in Korea, is located between Gyeongju and Busan.
It does not appear especially expansive at first because many of the buildings are dispersed along the surrounding mountainside.
Besides the many fine statues housed in the shrines, there is an excellent collection of artwork on display in the temple museum.
L: 46 km (28 miles) north of Busan T: ▭ From Dong Seoul Bus Terminal, buses to Tongdosa Temple depart 5 times daily (5 hrs.). A: ₩2,000

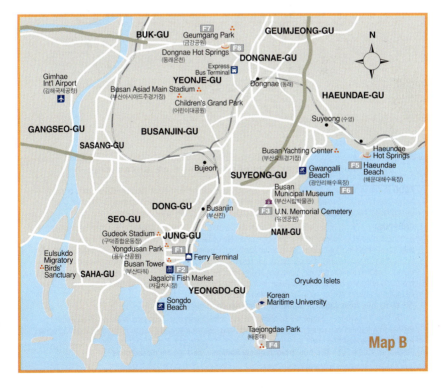

Map B

JINHAE (진해) `D17` (www.jinhae.go.kr), close to the industrial cities of Masan and Changwon, is a well-known port on the south coast that is famous for its cherry blossoms. Every street is lined with cherry trees and each year in early April, when the cherry trees are in full bloom, a naval port festival is held for 12 days. During the festival, people flock to this area to enjoy the arrival of spring.
Ⓛ: West of Busan Ⓣ: 🚌 1 hr. from Busan

JINJU (진주) `D18` (www.jinju.go.kr), a small city located on both sides of the Namgang River, makes a convenient base to explore the eastern part of Jirisan National Park. It is best known for the famous battles fought here during the Japanese invasions in the late 16th century.
Ⓛ: West of Busan Ⓣ: 🚌 1 hr., 30 min. from Busan

JINJUSEONG FORTRESS (진주성) (📞 055-749-2485), **CHOKSEONGNU PAVILION** (촉석루) and **NONGAE SHRINE** (논개사당) (📞 055-749-2114) are dedicated to a brave Korean woman who sacrificed her life to kill an enemy general.

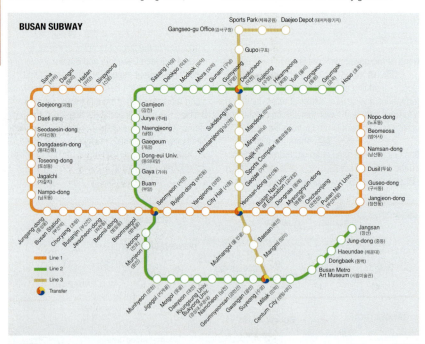

FOODS TO TRY & PLACES TO SHOP OF BUSAN CITY

FOOD Busan is famous for its seafood, and *hoe* (sashimi) can be enjoyed at Jagalchi Fish Market or many famous restaurants. Seafood restaurants also line the shores of Haeundae and Gwangalli Beaches. The Dongnae Hot Springs area is noted for its seafood and *pajeon* (green onion pancakes).

SHOPPING **BUSAN GUKJE MARKET AND GWANGBONGNO STREET** Gukje Market is the most representative traditional market in Busan, no less developed than Namdaemun Market in Seoul and even more crowded with foreign buyers. The market offers home appliances, clothing, bags, leather goods and furniture at better prices than anywhere else. It is closed on the 1st and 3rd Sundays of every month. Gwangbongno Street, Busan's leading fashion avenue, stretches 700 m from the old Busan City Hall site to Gukje Market. The area has many shopping and cultural facilities, including theaters, galleries, commercial banks, financial institutions, jewelry shops, souvenir shops and hotels.
Ⓣ: 🚇 10 min. from Jagalchi Station or Nampo-dong Station, Line 1

JAGALCHI FISH MARKET Jagalchi Fish Market is one of the top tourist attractions in Busan. It distributes to the nation a tremendous variety of marine products and creates a fantastic scene in the early morning when retailers haggle over fresh fish. For an interesting dose of Korean folk culture, visit the annual Jagalchi Festival in October. Ⓣ: 🚇 5 min. from Jagalchi Station, Line 1 Ⓒ: No closed days

SOUTHEASTERN AREA
Hallyeo Maritime National Park

HALLYEO MARITIME NATIONAL PARK is a unique maritime park that is better known as the Hallyeosudo Waterway. This maritime park stretches wide from east to west, covering both land and sea. Many like to go cruising around the archipelago at Tongyeong, Namhae, Geoje or Yeosu ferry terminals. It is a 93-mile-long waterway running from **GEOJEDO ISLAND** (거제도) G1, southwest of **BUSAN** (부산) (www.busan.go.kr), to **YEOSU** (여수) G2 (www.yeosu.go.kr) in the west.

- From Seoul to Yeosu—1 hr. by air;
- 5 hrs., 40 min. by train (Saemaeulho);
- 5 hrs., 50 min. by bus

This park is dotted with 400 mainly uninhabited islands and islets. The irregular coastline has created unusual rock formations and caves, providing for spectacular cruises. Apart from the natural scenery, much of the interest in the area is historical for it was here that Korea's famed Admiral Yi Sun-sin defeated the Japanese in several sea battles during the Japanese invasions of the late 16th century. He is noted for first using ironclad naval vessels in battle. Though greatly outnumbered, his *geobukseon* ("turtle ships") proved superior to the Japanese vessels.

Tongyeong

Oedo Paradise Island

TONGYEONG (통영) G3 (www.gnty.net) was the place of Admiral Yi's headquarters, and now is a charming port city with pleasant tourist hotels, fine seafood restaurants and plenty of watersports facilities. There are also several shrines dedicated to the admiral. It is a short boat ride to Hansando Island, where Yi won his most famous victory in July 1592.

This city is also famous for its 400-year tradition of making exquisite *najeonchilgi* (mother-of-pearl lacquerware). ⓣ : 🚌 5 hrs. from Seoul Express Bus Terminal (14 times daily)

GEOJEDO ISLAND (거제도) G1 (www.geoje.go.kr) is one of the major islands along the marine park.

On the south side of Geojedo are the spectacular rock formations known as the HAEGEUMGANG ROCKS (해금강) G4 . Their sheer cliffs rise magnificently out of the cobalt-blue waters and are topped with beautiful pine trees and camellias.

Geojedo Island ⓣ : 🚌 By car or taxi to the east of Tongyeong via Geoje Bridge.

Haegeumgang Rocks ⓣ : 🚌 Buses to Haegeumgang depart all day from Sinhyeon-eup or Jangseungpo on Geojedo Island (1 hr., 10 min.).

OEDO PARADISE ISLAND (외도해상공원) G5

(📞 031-717-2200; www.oedoisland.com) has become famous for its tropical botanical garden

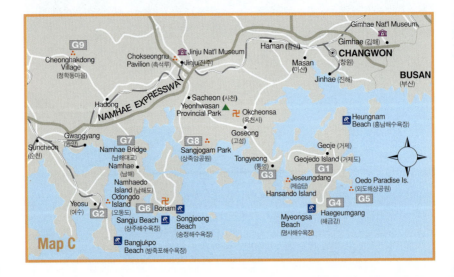

Sangjogam (Rock) Park

with about 3,000 species of plants including camellias and cacti as well as a sculpture park and observatory.

ⓣ: 🚌 From Nambu Bus Terminal in Seoul to Geojedo Island (5 hrs., 30 min.); 🚢 Then from Gujora, Wahyeon, Hakdong, Dojangpo, Jangseungpo or Haegeumgang Ferry Terminal on Geojedo Island, board a Oedo-bound ferry (15 min.). ⓗ: 7:00–18:00 (7:00–17:30, Nov.–Feb.) ⓐ: ₩ 5,000

ODONGDO ISLAND (오동도) G66 (📞 061-690-7301), covered with camellias, is linked to the port city of **YEOSU** (여수) (www.yeosu.go.kr) by a long breakwater. Growing on this island at the end of Hallyeo Maritime National Park is a very special type of bamboo tree.

ⓣ: 🚌 From Yeosu Station, take a city bus to Odongdo Island (every 5 min., 15 min.).

NAMHAEDO ISLAND (남해도) (www.namhae.go.kr) is connected to the mainland by the NAMHAE BRIDGE (남해대교) G67. This suspension bridge is 660 m long. Namhaedo is made up of a series of peaks linked by low-lying areas.
A road runs down from the bridge through Namhae-gun to the beautiful Sangju Beach further to the south.

ⓣ: 🚌 From Namhae Public Bus Terminal, take a city bus to the bridge.

ADMIRAL YI SUN-SIN

The historic Korean war hero Admiral Yi Sun-sin is to Korea what Admiral Nelson is to the United Kingdom.

There were two great wars at the end of the 16th century against the invading Japanese. Admiral Yi Sun-sin, through ingenious strategy and his development and usage of a unique battleship, the *geobukseon* "turtle ships," recorded legendary victories in all battles despite adverse conditions. Admiral Yi is one of the most respected figures in Korean history. There are many monuments built in his honor: a statue on Sejongno Street in downtown Seoul (at the far end of the broadway in front of Gwanghwamun Gate); Hyeonchungsa Shrine in Asan, Chungcheongnam-do Province and Jeseungdang in Tongyeong, Gyeongsangnam-do Province.

Geobukseon "turtle ship"

Cheonghakdong Village

More than 2,000 dinosaur footprints were found at SANGJOGAM (ROCK PARK) (상족암) C8 (055-670-2825) along the seashore at Deokmyeong-ri, Hai-myeon, **GOSEONG** (고성) (www.goseong.go.kr). Both carnivorous and herbivorous dinosaurs, including the tyrannosaurus rex, made these numerous prehistoric vestiges. Some fossil footprints are covered by water when the tide is high and can only be seen when the tide is out. This area, together with sites in Brazil and Canada, has one of the world's three largest concentrations of dinosaur footprints.

Sangjogam Park T: 6 hrs. from Nambu Bus Terminal in Seoul to Goseong Bus Terminal, and a Hai-myeon bound bus (5 times daily, 30 min.). H: 9:00 – 18:00 (Nov.– Feb., 9:00 –17:00) C: Monday A: ₩3,000

A visit to CHEONGHAKDONG VILLAGE (청학동) C9 (055-883-2609) is like taking a trip to the past. The people live in thatched houses and wear traditional Korean clothes. Visitors can observe everyday life in the village. T: Take a bus from Hadong Bus Terminal (055-883-2663) to Cheonghakdong (5 times daily, 50 min.).

FOODS TO TRY & PLACES TO SHOP OF THE SOUTHEASTERN AREA

FOOD BULGOGI (marinated barbecued beef or pork) | 불고기 Widely known as Korean barbecue, *bulgogi* is definitely a favorite of visitors. Thin strips of beef marinated in soy sauce, sesame oil, garlic, onion and chili are grilled over charcoal or on a special dripping pan. It is usually eaten in bundles with rice or vegetables wrapped in lettuce or other leaves.

ANDONG JJIMDAK (Andong braised chicken) | 안동찜닭 This dish is made by brushing soy sauce over the chicken before steaming it. The salty and spicy seasoning goes well with the tenderness of the chicken. After the chicken has been eaten, it is customary to mix rice with the seasonings that are left over.

DONGNAE PAJEON (green onion pancake with seafood) | 동래파전 This is a flat, fried pancake that originated in Busan City. Seafood such as squid and clams are mixed with green onions is very popular as a snack when accompanied by alcoholic beverages such as *dongdongju* (a traditional Korean liquor).

SHOPPING Gyeongju, where amethyst and topaz are mined, also has many stores selling beautifully embroidered items, antique paintings and traditional folk crafts. The stores can be found in the downtown area of Gyeongju and near Bulguksa Temple. Several duty-free shops are also located at the Bomun Lake Resort. Daegu, famous for its Yangnyeongsi Market that deals in raw materials for Korean herbal medicine, also has many specialty shops. Tongyeong is renowned for its high-quality *najeonchilgi* (lacquerware inlaid with mother-of-pearl).

Southwestern Area

TOURIST ATTRACTIONS BY REGION

Gwangju 광주, Jeollabuk-do 전라북도, Jeollanam-do 전라남도

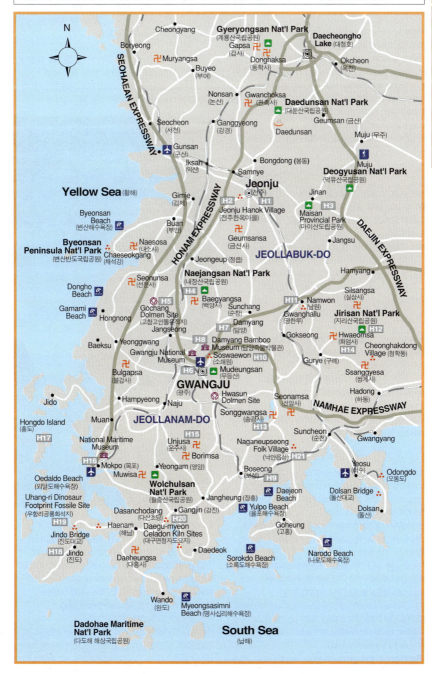

Often called the granary of Korea, the southwestern area is rich in fertile rice paddies. The farmland slopes gently down to the coast and the jagged coastline is indented with many small harbors.

Midway along the Honam Expressway is **JEONJU** (전주) (www.jeonju.go.kr). Here you can find shops specializing in *hanji* (traditional Korean mulberry paper). *Hanji* is used in calligraphy and in making umbrellas, fans and other items. Jeonju is also famous for its *bibimbap* (boiled rice mixed with vegetables and minced meat), so don't leave without tasting it.
ⓣ: From Seoul to Jeonju— 3 hrs. by train (Saemaeulho); 3 hrs. by bus

JEONJU HANOK VILLAGE (전주한옥마을) (hanok.jeonju.go.kr) overlaps Pungnam-dong and Gyo-dong with over 800 traditional Korean houses called *hanok*. While the rest of city has been industrialized, this village remained unchanged and retains its old traditions.
ⓣ: From Jeonju Bus Terminal, take a bus bound for Nambu Market and get off at Jeondong Catholic Church Stop. Or from Jeonju Station, take a bus bound for the Riviera Hotel, then walk about 20 min. to Hanok Village.

To experience traditional Korean culture, you should visit one of several places in and around Hanok Village. JEONJU TRADITIONAL CULTURE CENTER (전주전통문화센터; 063-280-7000; www.jt.or.kr) is composed of a traditional music theater, tea house, restaurant and wedding hall. Visitors can feel and taste Korean culture through various hands-on programs.

OMOKDAE CRAFT SHOP (오목대공예품점) (063-285-4403), located in a gracious *hanok* house, consists of eight galleries and shops selling exquisite crafts and Jeonju specialties such as handmade fans and *hanji*.
Something else of interest would be the *Hanok Life Experience Program* run by Jeonju City Hall. Tourists can stay at SAEHWAGWAN (세화관) *hanok* house (063-287-6300; www.saehwagwan.com) and experience the lifestyle of old Korea. You can enter either the *seonbibang* (gentleman's room) or the *gyusubang* (maiden's room) and sleep on a thick mat on the floor. Adding to the ambience is the wonderfully prepared traditional food.
One night in the *gyusubang* or *seonbibang* costs ₩100,000 for two people and regular rooms are ₩60,000 for two people. A traditional breakfast is included. THE KOREAN TRADITIONAL LIQUOR MUSEUM (한국전통술박물관) (063-287-6305), GYEONGGIJEON SHRINE (경기전), and JEONDONG CATHOLIC CHURCH (전동성당) are also walking distance from Hanok Village.

MAISAN PROVINCIAL PARK (마이산) (063-433-3313) "Horse Ears Mountain" lies east of Jeonju and is aptly named because of its two mountain peaks that resemble the ears of a

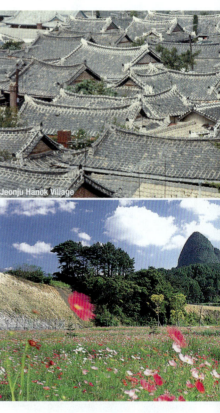
Jeonju Hanok Village

horse. Nestled at the foot of the mountain is TAPSA TEMPLE (탑사), with its 80 stone pagodas that rise up to 10 m tall. People say that about 100 years ago, a monk living in seclusion erected these pagodas as a prayer for peace. They still stand today, unaffected by the wind however strong it blows, creating an interesting monument to Buddhism.
ⓛ: 30 km east of Jeonju ⓣ: From Jeonju Bus Terminal, take a bus to Jinan (40 min.). And from Jinan Intercity Bus Terminal, take a bus to Mt.

Maisan or taxi (10 min., 12 km away). Ⓐ: ₩2,000

The lovely GEUMSANSA TEMPLE (금산사) (📞 063-548-4440/2), famous for its three-story wooden sanctuary, is about 20 miles southwest of Jeonju. South of the temple is NAEJANGSAN NATIONAL PARK (내장산) H4 (📞 063-538-7875; www.npa.or.kr/naejang/main.asp), which is comprised of the Naejangsan Mountains (763 m) centering on Naejangsa Temple, famous for red maples in autumn, and the Baegamsan Mountains (741m) with Baeyangsa Temple, which is loaded with

Geumsansa Temple

Mt. Maisan

cherry blossoms each spring.
Ⓛ: South of Jeonju Ⓣ: Geumsansa Temple 🚌 From Gimje City, take a bus to Geumsansa Temple (50 min.). Or from Jeonju City, take bus No. 2, 79-1, 776 or 887 (every 20 min., 40 min.). Naejangsan National Park & Baegyangsa Temple 🚌 From Jeongeup Bus Terminal, take a bus to Baegyangsa Temple (every 40 min., 20 min.).

BYEONSAN PENINSULA NATIONAL PARK (변산) 반도) The only peninsula park in Korea has a

number of beautiful sights, such as oddly shaped mountain peaks, historic temples, Jikso Falls, Bongnaegugok Valley, Chaeseokgang Seashore Cliff and four nice beaches.

GOCHANG DOLMEN SITE (고창고인돌유적지) H5 (📞 063-560-2793), registered on UNESCO's World Cultural Heritage list in December 2000, has more than 2,000 dolmens in 85 clusters. Maesan village in Jungnim-ri, Gochang-gun, has 447 dolmens lined up on hilly terrain stretching 1.76 km. The dolmens here vary considerably in size, weighing from under 10 tons up to 200 tons.
Ⓣ: 🚌 4 hrs. from Seoul Express Bus Terminal to Gochang-gun; to Jungnim or Asan (5 times daily, 20 min.)

GWANGJU (광주) H6 (www.metro.gwangju.kr) lies four hours south of Seoul by car or train. For centuries it has been the administrative, economic and educational center for the area including Jeollanam-do Province. It is famous for its Kimchi Festival in October and Gwangju Biennale. Ⓣ: From Seoul to Gwangju—45 min. by air; 🚆 3 hrs., 50 min. by train (Saemaeulho); 🚌 3 hrs., 55 min. by bus.

MT. MUDEUNGSAN (무등산) east of downtown Gwangju, hovers over the city like a guardian. It is famous for its watermelon and *chunseolcha* (green tea) made from soft buds that emerge from the snow in early spring.

DAMYANG (담양) H7 (www.damyang.jeonnam.kr), 22 km (13 miles) north of Gwangju, is the center of bamboo cultivation and craftsmanship. This area produces large quantities of quality bamboo furniture, household items, and artwork. Bamboo markets are held every 5th day in Damyang.
Ⓛ: North of Gwangju Ⓣ: 🚌 30 min. from Gwangju.

DAMYANG BAMBOO MUSEUM (담양죽물박물관) H8 (📞 061-380-3478), the only museum of its kind in the world, exhibits a total of 1,150 antique and modern works of bambooware from the Damyang area as well as from foreign countries. The museum also houses a gift shop that sells bamboo products.
Ⓣ: 🚌 10 min. from Damyang Bus Terminal
Ⓗ: 9:00 – 18:00 Ⓐ: ₩ 1,000 Ⓒ: No closed days

BOSEONG (보성) H9 (www.boseong.go.kr) is the birthplace of *Seopyeonje*, which is southwestern-

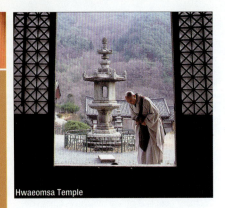
Hwaeomsa Temple

style *pansori* (narrative solo songs), and is also a home of some large green tea plantations that now supply 40% of the country's green tea. The Boseong Green Tea Festival *(Dahyangje)* is held around harvest season in the spring and includes a tea picking contest, a brewing contest and a tea ceremony demonstration. A green tea spa may be an interesting thing to try while you are there.
Ⓛ: South of Gwangju Ⓣ: 🚍 1 hr., 30 min. from Gwangju

SOSWAEWON (소쇄원) H10 is a mid-Joseon-style garden and at its entrance is a fantastic bamboo forest where clean water runs under a wall, over the rocks and into a pond. Standing beside a ravine are a few small summer houses. The best time to visit is from May to October.
Ⓣ: 🚍 In front of Gwangju Bus Terminal, take city bus No. 17. Get off at Gwangju Railway Station and take bus No. 125 (every 70 min.) and get off at the Soswaewon Stop (50 min.).

NAMWON (남원) H11 (www.namwon.jeonbuk.kr) is the gateway to Jirisan National Park. The town is famous as the home of Chunhyang, a legendary faithful maiden. The *pansori Chunhyangga*, a Korean traditional narrative song adapted from the original story, is often performed in Korea.
Ⓛ: Southeast of Jeonju Ⓣ: 🚍 3 hrs., 50 min. from Seoul; 🚍 1 hr., 20 min. from Jeonju

JIRISAN NATIONAL PARK (지리산) H12 (📞 061-783-9100; www.npa.or.kr/chiri/chiri.htm) is South Korea's second highest mountain after Mt. Hallasan on Jejudo Island. It is vast in area and its peaks, including the 1,915-m-high Cheonwangbong Peak, stretch across the three provinces of Jeollanam-do, Jeollabuk-do and Gyeongsangnam-do. The park contains some majestic mountains but it is advisable that only climbers with proper equipment and plenty of experience should attempt to climb the peaks in this area. With streams running through thick virgin forests and a sea of clouds covering the summits, Jirisan offers magnificent scenery. The foot of the mountain is dotted with many Buddhist temples including Hwaeomsa, Cheoneunsa, Ssanggyesa. You can enjoy the panorama of the largest, majestic mountains in Korea, trekking up and down peaks more than 1,500 m above sea level. (3 days, 2 nights)
Ⓛ: East of Namwon Ⓣ: 🚍 Baemsagol Valley is close to Namwon and Piagol Valley to Gurye. Take a Jeollaseon Line train from Seoul Station and get off at Namwon or Gurye Station (4 hrs., 30 min.); 🚍 1 hr., 30 min. from Gwangju Ⓐ: ₩1,600

SONGGWANGSA TEMPLE (송광사) H13 (📞 061-755-0108; www.songgwangsa.org) to the southwest, is one of the country's largest temples. Founded in Silla times, it became a center for Zen Buddhism in the 12th century.
Ⓛ: Southeast of Gwangju Ⓣ: 🚍 Take a bus from Seoul Express Bus Terminal to Suncheon (5 hrs., 20 min.). At Suncheon Bus Terminal, transfer to city bus No. 11 to Songgwangsa Temple (every 30 to 40 min., 1 hr., 20 min.). Ⓐ: ₩2,500

HWAEOMSA TEMPLE (화엄사) H14 (📞 061-782-7600), founded in 544, is the largest and most renowned among the seven major temples in Jirisan. The original structure was burned down and the current temple was reconstructed in 1606. A number of the treasures have been preserved, such as Gakhwangjeon, a representative Korean wooden building, and Daeungjeon, which is famous for its construction without the use of nails. The cherry blossoms and maple trees add to the outstanding scenery of this region. Ⓛ: East of Gwangju Ⓣ: 🚍 From Gurye, buses to Hwaeomsa Temple operate every 20 min. (20 min.) Ⓐ: ₩3,800

UNJUSA TEMPLE (운주사) H15 (📞 061-374-0660) is situated 26 km southwest of the town of Hwasun-eup. It was established by the great Buddhist monk Doseonguksa during the Unified Silla period (676–935). Eighteen pagodas and 80 statues of Buddha in and around the temple are all that remain of the 1,000 Buddhas and 1,000 pagodas that once belonged to this temple.
According to the traditional theory of geomancy, the Korean Peninsula was thought of as being

Jindo Island

unbalanced and in danger of capsizing because there were fewer mountains in Honam, the southwestern area, than in Yeongnam, the southeastern part. To prevent such a disaster, it is said that thousands of pagodas and statues of Buddha were erected at temples in the southwestern part of the peninsula.
①: 40 km (24 miles) southwest of Gwangju
⊤: 🚌 No. 318 from Gwangju Bus Terminal to Unjusa Temple (50 min.) Ⓐ: ₩2,000

WOLCHULSAN NATIONAL PARK Mt. Wolchulsan (809 m) is famous for its dramatic craggy rock formations and has old temples such as Muwisa and Dogapsa.

MOKPO (목포) H16 (www.mokpo.go.kr) is a port city on the southwestern corner of the peninsula that is noted for its fine seafood. Hydrofoils ply the waters between Mokpo and Hongdo Island.
①: Southwest of Gwangju ⊤: 🚌 4 hrs., 20 min. from Seoul Express Bus Terminal.

DADOHAE MARITIME NATIONAL PARK (다도해) Dotted with about 1,700 small and large beautiful islands such as Jindo, Hongdo, Heuksando and Bogildo, the emerald sky above the sea of cobalt blue, unusual rock formations and unending stretches of sandy beach present a world of untamed splendor.

HONGDO ISLAND (홍도) H17 (📞 061-246-3700) is an especially favored destination for photographers with its unusual rock formations.
⊤: 🚢 From Mokpo, high-speed ships such as the New Gold Star, New Gold, Namhae Queen, Namhae Star, and Namhae Prince are operated to Hongdo Island twice a day (7:50, 13:00, 2 hrs., 20 min.). ①: Sea World Express 📞 061-243-1927; Namhae Express 📞 061-244-9915 .

A rare natural phenomenon takes place on **JINDO** (진도) H18 (www.jindo.go.kr), an island south of Mokpo. Twice a year, an extremely low tide creates a land bridge, making it possible to walk from Jindo to a small neighboring island. This occasion is known to many as Korea's "Moses' Miracle."
①: 120 km (72 miles) south of Mokpo
⊤: 🚌 2 hrs., 30 min. from Gwangju; 1 hr., 10 min. from Mokpo

 JINDO SATURDAY FOLK TOUR

The *Jindo Arirang* is widely recognized as traditional folk song of Korea. The Jindo Saturday Folk Tour — not actually a tour but a series of performances such as the *ganggangsullae* and *ssitgimgut* — is operated by Human Cultural Property Assets, their students, and the area's residents.

Date	2 to 4 pm / every Saturday (April to November)
Place	Jindo Folk Cultural Hall
Performances	*ganggangsullae*, *ssitgimgut*, *dasiraegi*, Jindo drum dance, *Jindo Arirang*, *samullori* (a percussion quartet), etc.

①: 📞 061-540-3229, e-mail: ss55-park@hanmail.net ⊤: 🚌 Buses to Jindo leave 4 times daily from Nambu Bus Terminal in Seoul (6 hrs.), and 19 times daily from Mokpo (1hr.). ✈ Flights to Mokpo leave 12 times daily from Seoul (50 min.).

UHANG-RI DINOSAUR FOOTPRINTS FOSSIL SITE (우항리 공룡화석지) H19 (061-532-7225) includes about 1,000 of the world's oldest fossilized footprints of web-footed birds, about 300 footprints of huge flying dinosaurs, and about 500 other vivid footprints of dinosaurs from the same period. All discovered along the seashore of Uhang-ri, Hwangsan-myeon and Haenam-gun, the dinosaur group presumably inhabited this area about 83 million years ago during the Cretaceous period of the Mesozoic era. Some pterosaur footprints here are 30 cm long and are the largest in the world.

T: From Seoul Express Bus Terminal to Haenam (5 hrs. 30 min.); to Nam-ri (20 min.); ride a taxi to the site : 9:00 – 17:00 (Nov. – Feb., 9:00 – 16:00) ₩1,000

DAEGU-MYEON IN GANGJIN (강진) H20 (www.gangjin.go.kr) is a time-honored home of celadon art and currently the largest Goryeo celadon production site with over 180 kilns and about 5,000 pieces of celadon produced there each year. The Gangjin Celadon Cultural Festival is held every summer.

T: From Seoul Express Bus Terminal take a bus to Gangjin (5 hrs. 30 min.) or Maryang and get off at Celadon Village.

NAGANEUPSEONG FOLK VILLAGE (낙안읍성) H22 (061-749-3893; www.nagan.or.kr) is unique in that 108 households are actually leading their lives inside the ancient fortress walls. Every year in October, a huge food festival is held featuring hundreds of traditional Korean delicacies.

T: No. 63 or 68 from Suncheon Intercity Bus Terminal to Naganeupseong (every 40 min., 30 to 40 min.) : 9:00 – 18:00 ₩2,000

FOODS TO TRY & PLACES TO SHOP OF THE SOUTHWESTERN AREA

FOOD DAENAMU TONGBAP (rice steamed in bamboo) | 대나무 통밥 Instead of using a pot, a hollowed out bamboo canister is used to cook rice. Ginko nuts, dates and chestnuts are added to the rice, making this dish nutritious and healthy. The unique scent of bamboo permeates the rice and stimulates the nose.

BIBIMBAP (steamed rice with assorted beef and vegetables) | 비빔밥 Seasoned beef and various vegetables such as bean sprouts, spinach, crown daisy, bracken, roots of Chinese bellflower, watercress and shiitake mushrooms are nicely arranged over steamed rice and mixed with hot pepper soybean paste. The ingredients in *bibimbap* vary by region. It is a delicious and healthy dish that can be enjoyed a la carte.

YEONGGWANG-GULBI JEONGSIK | 영광굴비정식 This used to be served to Joseon Dynasty kings. *Gulbi* (dried yellow corvina) is an old time favorite, and is prepared by salting the corvina and drying it in the sun. This dish is served with 20 different kinds of side dishes centered around *gulbi*.

SHOPPING Jeonju is famous for its fans and *hanji* (Korean paper). *Hanji*, made from mulberry trees, is produced by an ancient process handed down over hundreds of years.
Gwangju has bamboo folk craft items made in nearby Damyang as well as *chunseolcha* (green tea from nearby Mt. Mudeungsan). For tea-lovers, Boseong, located between Mokpo and Yeosu, is an absolute must.

IRI GEMS AND JEWELRY CENTER
Since it opened in 1975, this center has exported precious stones and metals to 40 countries and has become world-famous for its truly beautiful jewelry and steeply dicounted prices. The Iksan Jewelry Festival is held in late October each year. : 063-835-8007 T: Jeollaseon or Honamseon Line from Seoul Station to Iksan (3 hrs.; 1hr., 40min. by KTX); 5 min. to the center

DAMYANG BAMBOO CRAFTS MARKET
Damyang is the land of bamboo, and this is Korea's only specialized bamboo market. There are about 20 wholesale shops and 50 factories dealing in various bamboo crafts: simple yet refined baskets, fans, scoops, furniture and tourist souvenirs. The market opens at five-day intervals beginning on the 2nd day of each month. It is also home to the Bamboo Museum (061-380-3478).
T: From Seoul Express Bus Terminal to Gwangju (4 hrs.); 30 min. to Damyang

Jeju-do

TOURIST ATTRACTIONS BY REGION

제 주 도

Jeju-do or Jejudo Island is one of the nine provinces of Korea and it is only 1 hour from Seoul by air. There are direct flights from Tokyo, Osaka, Nagoya, Fukuoka, Shanghai and Hong Kong. You can also reach Jeju-do by ferry from Busan, Wando, Incheon, Yeosu or Mokpo.

ⓘ: Jeju-do Tourist Information ☎ 064-742-8866; http://jeju.go.kr

As a result of its isolated location and romantic tropical image, Jeju-do has become a favorite retreat with honeymooners and tourists. The island has a mild marine climate with four distinct seasons and an average yearly temperature of 15°C (60°F). In summer, temperatures range from 22°C (72°F) to 26°C (80°F).

Jeju City & Eastern Jeju-do

JEJU CITY (제주시) (www.jejusi.go.kr) is located on the island's north shore and is the island's main tourist center. Western-style hotels and numerous Korean inns are located throughout the city.

ⓣ: From Seoul to Jeju—1 hr. by air; 5 hrs., 30 min. from Mokpo and 7 hrs. from Yeosu by ferry

YONGDUAM ROCK (용두암) is an unusual lava formation that lies on the coast just west of Jeju City. The basalt dragon's head with its open mouth is one of Jeju-do's most popular tourist sites.

ⓣ: Take a Jeju city bus and get off at Yongdam Rotary. 10 min.

TAMNA MOK SOK WON (목석원) (064-702-0203) is a special garden that displays artistically shaped natural stones and dried tree roots.

ⓣ: No. 500 or 502 at Jeju Int'l Airport (30 min.). ⓗ: Feb.–Apr., 8:00–17:30; May–Aug., 8:00–18:30; Sep.–Oct., 8:00–18:00; Nov.–Jan., 8:00–18:00 ⓐ: ₩2,000

RECOMMENDED TOUR COURSES

3-DAY, 2-NIGHT COURSES

Course A
1st day Jeju International Airport → Jeju City → Hallim Park → Geumneung Seongmurwon Park → Chagwido Islets
2nd day Mt. Songaksan → Yongmeori (Dragon Head) Coast → Jungmun Tourist Resort → Oedolgae Rock → Jeongbang Falls → Jeju Folk Village Museum → Seopjikoji → Seongsan Ilchulbong Peak → Mini World
3rd day Jeju City → Jeju International Airport

Course B
1st day Jeju International Airport → Jeju City → Manjanggul Cave → Hamdeok Beach → Sangumburi Crater → Seongsan Ilchulbong Peak → Seopjikoji
2nd day Hallim Park → Suwolbong Peak → Mt. Songaksan → Yongmeori Coast → Jungmun Tourist Resort → Cheonjiyeon Falls → Jeongbang Falls → Dokkaebidoro Road
3rd day Jeju City → Jeju International Airport

4-DAY, 3-NIGHT COURSES

Course A
1st day Jeju International Airport → Jeju City
2nd day Sincheonji Art Gallery → Jungmun Tourist Resort → Yeomiji Botanical Garden → Cheonjiyeon Falls → Dokkaebidoro Road
3rd day Myeongdoam Rock → Sangumburi Crater → Jeju Folk Village Museum → Seongsan Ilchulbong Peak → Jeju Natural History Museum → Yongdeam Rock
4th day Jeju International Airport

Course B
1st day Jeju International Airport → Jeju City
2nd day Bunjae Artpia → Jusangjeolli Cliffs → Cheonjiyeon Falls → Dokkaebidoro Road
3rd day Myeongdoam Rock → Sangumburi Crater → Jeju Folk Village Museum → Seongsan Ilchulbong Peak → Udo Islet → Jeju Natural History Museum → Yongdeam Rock
4th day Jeju International Airport

5-DAY, 4-NIGHT COURSES
1st day Yongduam Rock → Hallim Park → Chagwido Islets → Bunjae Artpia
2nd day Manjanggul Cave → Seongsan Ilchulbong Peak → Udo Islet → Seopjikoji
3rd day Mt. Songaksan → Yongmeori Coast → Jungmun Tourist Resort → Oedolgae Rock → Cheonjiyeon Falls → Jeongbang Falls → Dokkaebidoro Road
4th day Sangumburi Crater → Mini World → Horse riding → Seongeup Folk Village → Jeju Folk Village Museum
5th day Jeju City → Jeju International Airport

The JEJU FOLKLORE AND NATURAL HISTORY MUSEUM (제주민속자연사박물관) 14 (064-722-2465; http://museum.jeju.go.kr) features a significant collection of crafts, tools and equipment as well as plants, animals and minerals native to Jejudo Island.
①: 🚌 From Jeju International Airport, take a taxi and get off at the KAL hotel (a 10-min. ride).
②: 9:00 – 20:30 ③: ₩1,100 ④: 12 days, including Seollal and Chuseok.

On DOKKAEBIDORO ROAD (도깨비도로) 15 , a strange phenomenon happens on this gentle slope. Your car, in neutral with the brake off, seems to roll uphill.

The HALLA ARBORETUM (한라수목원) 16 (064-746-4423) has several greenhouses and a variety of gardens. The arboretum is relaxing and refreshing with many birds and flowers.
①: 🚌 Take a bus from Jeju International Airport and get off at Jeju Tour Industry High School (15 min.) ②: Mar. to Oct., 9:00 – 28:00; Nov. to Feb., 9:00 – 17:00 ③: Free

HALLASAN NATIONAL PARK (한라산) 17 (064-713-9950/3; www.npa.or.kr/halla) Mt. Hallasan, a long-extinct volcano, towers over the island and below it are fertile fields, forests, quaint villages and fine hotels near white sandy beaches. The snow-covered peak of the extinct volcano poking through brooding clouds is visible from nearly every point on the island. The mountain soars to 1,950 m above sea level, making it the nation's highest. Mt. Hallasan is home to many endangered plant species and has abundant subtropical and temperate vegetation. Some hiking trails will take you to Baengnokdam Crater Lake at the top.
①: 🚌 5.16 or 1100 Road ③: ₩1,600

SANGUMBURI CRATER (산굼부리) 18 (064-783-9900) is one of the three major craters on the island, the other two being Baengnokdam Lake at the summit of Mt. Hallasan and Sunrise Peak at Seongsanpo. Sangumburi Crater is about 2 km in circumference.
It is home to some 420 different species of subtropical, temperate and alpine flowering plants, so botanists call it a "floral treasure house." It is best viewed in summer or fall.
④: East of Mt. Hallasan ①: 🚌 From Jeju Intercity Bus Terminal, take a bus to Pyoseon (40 min.). ②: Mar. to June & Sep. to Oct.,

8:00–18:00; Jul. to Aug., 8:00–19:00; Nov. to Feb., 8:30–17:00 Ⓐ ₩3,000

SEONGEUP FOLK VILLAGE (성읍민속마을) 109 (☎ 064-787-1179) has been designated as a Folklore Preservation Zone. Here you can meet the friendly island people who still live behind stone courtyard walls in thatched-roof lava-wall homes.
Ⓛ: Southeast of Sangumburi Crater
Ⓣ: 🚌 Intercity buses depart Jeju City for Seongeup Folk Village (every 20 min., 50 min.).

MANJANGGUL CAVE (만장굴) 110 (☎ 064-783-4818) is situated on the northeastern coast. At 13.4 km (8.4 miles), it is the longest lava tube in the world.
Ⓣ: 🚌 In front of Jeju Intercity Bus Terminal, take a bus to Seogwipo via East Tourist Highway (40 min.). Ⓗ: 9:00–18:30 (Nov.–Feb., 9:00–18:00) Ⓐ ₩2,000

SEONGSANPO (성산포) 111 (☎ 064-783-0959), which means "fortress mountain port," is a small village on the island's eastern tip. The name describes the unusual volcanic cone that dominates the area. This cone, known as

---

JEJU-DO'S UNIQUE FEATURES
Two of the island's long-standing symbols are the *dolharubang* and the *haenyeo*. *Dolharubang* ("stone grandfather") can be seen everywhere. They are black lava statues of a kindly old man. In the old days they were considered guardian deities, but now they are objects for the tourists' cameras. Replicas are sold in souvenir shops and are available in various sizes, ranging from one inch to bigger than life size. *Haenyeo* are the island's women divers. During good weather they can still be seen bobbing just offshore, diving to the ocean floor for sea urchins, shellfish, octopus, etc.

SEONGSAN ILCHULBONG or SUNRISE PEAK (성산일출봉), is one of 360 parasitic volcanos that dot the island. Scaling up a steep slope, it winds a trail that takes you to the western edge of the crater. A climb up this narrow trail rewards the climber with a most spectacular view, especially at sunrise.
Ⓣ: 🚌 Take an intercity bus via East Tourist Highway (every 20 min.). Get off at Seongsan-ri and walk about 5 min. Ⓗ: 05:00–19:00 Ⓐ ₩2,000

Well known as a shooting location for TV dramas and movies, SEOPJIKOJI (섭지코지) 112

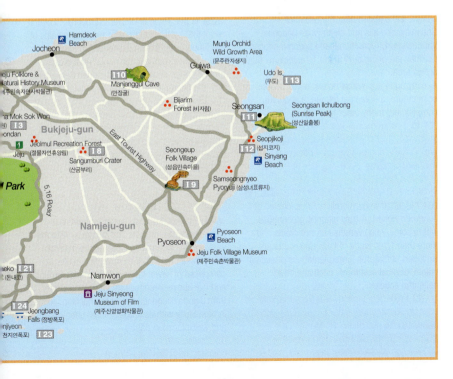

(064-730-1544) is a huge expanse of grassy field adjacent to the sea. The word *koji* means "small gulf" in the Jeju dialect. From the shore you can enjoy a beautiful rocky coastline. The strange stones that appear and disappear with the tide is a unique spectacle.
Ⓣ: 🚌 Take a direct bus via East Tourist Highway (every 15 min.). Get off at Sinyang-ri and take a taxi.

UDO ISLAND (우도) 113 has the only coral sand beach in Korea. The name came from its shape, which resembles a cow lying in the grass. The island is famous for Udopalgyeong (Eight Scenic Spots of Udo). Ⓣ: ⛴ 15 min. from Seongsanpo Port (064-782-5671) Ⓐ: ₩1,000

JEJU-DO
Seogwipo & Western Jeju-do

SEOGWIPO (서귀포) 114 (www.seogwipo.jeju.kr), the primary city of the south coast, is easily accessible from Jeju City by road. Seogwipo is a fishing port with lovely falls and fine hotels.

JUNGMUN RESORT (중문단지) 115 (064-735-7363) is a 20-min. drive west of downtown Seogwipo. An integrated tourism and recreation center, it is situated near the beautiful Cheonjeyeon Falls and clean white beaches. Various sport, recreational and accommodation facilities are being built in the 1.7-million-m^2 (420 acres) area.
Already open are deluxe hotels, a golf course, an oceanarium, a botanical garden, a shopping complex and many other facilities.
Ⓣ: 🚌 1 hr. from Jeju Int'l Airport; 20 min. from Seogwipo. Airport limousine buses link Jeju Int'l Airport with Jungmun Resort, operating every 15 min. and charging a one-way fare of ₩3,500.

YEOMIJI BOTANICAL GARDEN (여미지 식물원) 116 (064-738-3828; www.yeomiji.or.kr) is located at Jungmun Resort. A truly gigantic greenhouse where some 2,000 varieties of rare plants and more than 1,700 kinds of flowering plants are exhibited, it features large plantations of aquatic plants, tropical fruit trees, cacti and other delightful species.
Ⓣ: 🚌 From Jeju Intercity Bus Terminal, take an intercity bus to Seogwipo via Jungmun Resort (every 10 min., 50 min.). Ⓗ: Mar. to Oct., 8:30–18:30; Nov. to Feb., 9:00–18:00 Ⓐ: ₩6,000 Ⓒ: No closed days

Jungmun Resort

TEDDY BEAR MUSEUM (테디베어 박물관) 117 (064-738-7600; www.teddybearmuseum.org). Teddies are featured as the main characters of historical events of the 20th century as well as in teddy bear fashion shows, teddy bear wedding ceremonies, etc.
Ⓛ: Inside Jungmun Resort Ⓣ: 🚌 From Jeju Int'l Airport, take a bus bound for Seogwipo and get off at Jungmun Resort (60 min.). Ⓗ: 9:00–19:00 (July 16–August 25, 9:00–22:00) Ⓐ: ₩6,000

CHEONJEYEON FALLS (천제연 폭포) 118 (064-738-1529) is the "Pond of Heaven's Emperor." Legend has it that seven nymphs who were handmaids of the Emperor of Heaven descended in the middle of the night to bathe in the pool. There is an arched bridge above the pond named Seoningyo with the figures of seven maidens sculpted on it.
Ⓣ: 🚌 From Jeju Intercity Bus Terminal, take an intercity bus via Jungmun Resort (every 10 min., 50 min.). 🚌 Or take a limousine bus from Jeju Int'l Airport (every 15 min., 45 min.). Ⓗ: 8:00–19:00 (8:00–18:00 Nov.7 to Feb.) Ⓐ: ₩2,700

INTERNATIONAL CONVENTION CENTER JEJU (제주 국제컨벤션센터) 119 (064-735-1000; www.iccjeju.co.kr) hosts major international conventions, assemblies and concerts. With the vast Pacific Ocean at its fore and the majestic Mt. Hallasan behind, the convention center is comprised of seven levels with two underground and five above. Architectural inspiration came from Jejudo Island itself, and the building blends in beautifully with its surroundings, unobtrusive and well-placed in nature.
Ⓛ: Inside Jungmun Resort Ⓣ: Shuttle buses are operated from Jeju Int'l Airport.

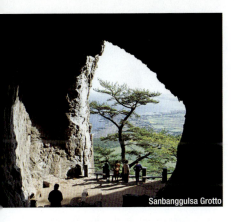
Sanbanggulsa Grotto

DAEYOO HUNTING GROUND (대유수렵장) 120
(064-738-0500) is just 2 km north of Jungmun Resort. The only private hunting area in Asia, it extends over 3 million m² and offers the newest sporting guns available.
Ⓣ: 🚌 40 min. from Seogwipo Ⓗ: 9:00 – 18:30 (Nov.– Feb., 9:00 – 17:30)

DONNAEKO RECREATIONAL AREA (돈내코) 121 (064-733-1584), located 400 m above sea level, is a valley with small but beautiful falls called *wonang*. The Halla orchid and winter strawberries, both indigenous to Jejudo Island, grow in this area.
Ⓣ: 🚌 From Seogwipo City, take a city bus to Donnaeko Tourist Resort. Ⓐ: Free

OEDOLGAE ROCK (외돌개) 122 (064-732-8027) is a high outcropping created by a volcanic eruption 1.5 million years ago. Legend has it that during the later Goryeo Dynasty, General Choe Yeong disguised the rock to appear like a giant military general to scare off Mongolian soldiers lurking on Beomseom Islet.
Ⓣ: 🚌 From Jungangno Street of Seogwipo City, take a bus to Oedolgae and get off at the last stop.

CHEONJIYEON FALLS (천지연폭포) 123 (064-733-1528) are located beyond a quiet path through the woods that leads to columns of water that rush over a cliff and splash into a pond below.
Ⓣ: 🚌 From Seogwipo Bus Terminal, 🚌 take a Seogwipo city bus or circulation bus and get off at the last stop (Cheonjiyeon Stop). Ⓐ: ₩2,000 Ⓒ: No closed days

JEONGBANG FALLS (정방폭포) 124 (064-733-1530) are the only falls in Asia that drop directly to the sea and one of the three most famous on Jejudo Island, along with Cheonjiyeon and Cheonjeyeon Falls. This place is famed with the legend of Seobul, an emissary of a Chinese emperor.
Ⓣ: 🚌 From Jungangno Street of Seogwipo City, take a city bus to Bomok and get off at the KAL hotel. Ⓗ: 7:30 – 17:10 Ⓐ: ₩2,000 Ⓒ: No closed days

SANBANGGULSA GROTTO (산방굴사) 125 (064-794-2940) is a natural grotto located halfway up the steep slopes of Mt. Sanbangsan on the southwestern coast. Reputed to be one of the 12 most famous sights on the island, the view from the grotto over the coastal fields and offshore waters is spectacular. The rocks on the Yongmeori coast below Sanbanggulsa also provide a fascinating view.
Ⓣ: 🚌 From Seogwipo City, take a bus to Jungmun and Sagye (40 min.). Ⓗ: 8:30 – 19:00 (Nov.– Feb., 8:30 – 18:00) Ⓐ: ₩2,500

HALLIM (한림) 126 is the west coast's major fishing center. HYEOPJAE BEACH (협재해수욕장) and HYEOPJAEGUL CAVE (협재굴) 127 (064-796-0001; www.hallimpark.co.kr) are two well-known tourist sites on the outskirts of Hallim.
The cave contains awesome light-colored stalactites and stalagmites that formed as winds blew calcium-rich sand over the ground and rainwater carried the calcium down into the black lava cave.
Ⓣ: 🚌 From Seogwipo or Jeju City, take a bus operating the West Tourist Highway and get off at the entrance of Hallim Park (40 to 50 min.).
Ⓗ: 8:30 – 18:00 (Nov.– Feb., 8:30 – 17:00)
Ⓐ: ₩5,000 (for the cave)

The BUNJAE ARTPIA (분재예술원) 128 (064-772-3701; www.bunjaeartpia.com) is the only park in Korea specializing in potted plant cultivation and garden plants and it is the largest of its kind in the world. Aside from small potted plants, the park contains more than 1,000 specimens and displays over 700 of them daily.
Chinese Chairman Jiang Zemin visited the park in November 1995.
Ⓛ: Between Hallim Park and Mt. Sanbangsan
Ⓣ: 🚌 1 hr., 30 min. from Jeju Intercity Bus Terminal to Sinchang; 🚌 25 min. to the park
Ⓗ: Mar.– Oct., 9:00 – 19:30; Nov.– Feb., 9:00 – 18:00; July 25 – Aug. 27, 8:30 – 21:00
Ⓐ: ₩7,000

O'SULLOC TEA MUSEUM (오설록 차박물관) 〔28〕

(☎ 064-794-5312; www.osulloc.co.kr). Near the Bunjae Artpia is the O'sulloc Tea Museum, featuring exhibits of the history and production of tea, a variety of green tea products, an auditorium for seminars, and an observatory that commands panoramic views of the largest tea farm in Korea.

- ⓣ: A 5-min. walk from Bunjae Artpia
- ⓗ: 10:00 – 18:00 (Oct.– Mar., 10:00 – 17:00)

MINIATURE THEME PARK (소인국 테마파크) 〔30〕

(☎ 064-794-5400; www.soingook.com) features 100 replicas of world famous architectural buildings such as Bulguksa Temple of Korea, the Forbidden City of China and the Leaning Tower of Pisa. It also offers visitors a wide range of things to see and experience including the stone culture of Jeju, a ceramic kiln site, an open-air theater, and a mini-car race field.

- ⓣ: 40 min. from Jeju Intercity Bus Terminal to Seogwangdong-ri; 5 min. to the park ⓗ: 8:30 – 19:30 (Oct.– Feb., 9:00 – 17:30) ⓐ: ₩6,000

CHOCOLATE CASTLE (초콜렛 박물관) 〔31〕 (☎ 064-711-3171) is Korea's first chocolate museum constructed with volcanic basalt stone from Jejudo Island. Chocolates in a plethora of shapes and sizes are collected from around the world. Ginseng, green tea, mango, and other new flavors are produced for chocolate lovers. You can watch the traditional hand-manufacturing process through large display windows.

- ⓣ: From Jeju Bus Terminal, take a bus bound for Moseulpo (1 hr.), and take a taxi (10-min.).

Chocolate Castle

JEJU-DO RENT-A-CAR CENTERS

When traveling around Jeju-do, renting a car enables you to enjoy more convenient sightseeing than by using public transportation.

Name	Jeju-si	Seogwipo-si
Arirang	☎ 064-724-2139	☎ 064-738-4567
Daesin	☎ 064-744-8123	☎ 064-738-8123
Dong-A	☎ 064-743-1515	☎ 064-763-1919
Geumho	☎ 064-747-8101	☎ 064-763-8000
Good Morning	☎ 064-742-8003	☎ 064-739-6005
Green	☎ 064-743-2000	☎ 064-733-1989
Seongsan	☎ 064-746-3230	☎ 064-732-5626
Asan	☎ 064-743-9991	
AVIS	☎ 064-726-3322	☎ 064-733-3313
e-Rent Car	☎ 064-713-6000	☎ 064-738-9008
Hanguk	☎ 064-748-5005	☎ 064-739-5505
Hanseong	☎ 064-747-2100	☎ 064-738-8880
Jeju	☎ 064-747-3301	☎ 064-739-5111
Uri	☎ 064-752-9600	

FOODS TO TRY & PLACES TO SHOP OF JEJU-DO PROVINCE

FOOD **OKDOM-GUI | 옥돔구이** *Okdom-gui* is a pink-colored fish that can only be found in the ocean around Jejudo Island. The fish is seasoned with salt, roasted over charcoal, and served with several side dishes. It is said that once you try *okdom*, other fish seem tasteless in comparison.

GALCHI-HOBAK-GUK (pumpkin soup with hairtail fish) | 갈치호박국 This is a traditional Jeju-do soup that is served when a particularly honorable guest visits. The pumpkin, combined with the fish, is seasoned with salt and boiled for a long time.

SHOPPING In Jeju-do, local products such as *dolharubang* ("stone grandfather"), *garot* (traditional worker's clothing), simple folk craft items, and marine products are the most popular souvenirs. There are several duty-free shops in Jeju City and one in Jungmun Resort. Almost every city and town on Jejudo Island has stores selling leather goods and clothing.

JEJU DONGMUN MARKET This market is an excellent place to experience the daily lifestyle of the Jejudo islanders. It trades in all the necessities of life, but the major goods here are fresh seafood and tropical and subtropical fruits, including the island's special products such as tangerines, abalone and *okdom* (sea bream).

- ⓣ: 15 min. from Jeju Int'l Airport to the market

176 Entry & Departure Procedures
178 Transportation
188 Accommodations
206 Business Travel Tips
208 Handy Facts
217 Holidays
218 Useful Korean Phrases
220 Index
222 KTO Offices

General Information

GENERAL INFORMATION

Entry & Departure Procedures

ENTRY & DEPARTURE PROCEDURES

Passport & Visa

Ministry of Justice: www.moj.go.kr

Foreign visitors to the Republic of Korea must have a valid passport and obtain a visa before arriving but citizens of 105 countries or regions who want to visit Korea temporarily are permitted to enter without a visa according to visa exemption agreements (Table 1) or in accordance with principles of reciprocity and national interest (Table 2).

Table 1. Countries Under Visa Exemption Agreements

Country	Period	Country	Period	Country	Period
Asia and Oceania		Jamaica	3 months	Iceland	3 months
Bangladesh	3 months	Mexico	3 months	Ireland	3 months
Israel	3 months	Nicaragua	3 months	Italy	60 days
Malaysia	3 months	Panama	3 months		(extendable up to 90 days)
New Zealand	3 months	Peru	3 months	Latvia	3 months
Pakistan	3 months	St. Lucia	3 months	Lithuania	3 months
Singapore	3 months	St. Kitts and Nevis	3 months	Luxembourg	3 months
Thailand	3 months	St. Vincent and	3 months	Malta	3 months
Turkey	3 months	the Grenadines		Netherlands	3 months
Americas		Surinam	3 months	Norway	3 months
Antigua - Barbuda	3 months	Trinidad and Tobago	3 months	Poland	3 months
Bahamas	3 months	**Europe**		Portugal	60 days
Barbados	3 months	Austria	3 months	Rumania (D.O.S)	3 months
Chile	90 days	Belgium	3 months	Slovak Republic	3 months
Colombia	3 months	Bulgaria	3 months	Spain	3 months
Commonwealth of Dominica	3 months	Czech Republic	3 months	Sweden	3 months
Costa Rica	3 months	Denmark	3 months	Switzerland	3 months
Dominican Republic	3 months	Finland	3 months	United Kingdom	3 months
Ecuador	3 months	France	3 months	**Africa**	
El Salvador	3 months	Germany	3 months	Morocco	3 months
Grenada	3 months	Greece	3 months	Tunisia	30 days
Haiti	3 months	Hungary	3 months		

Table 2. Countries or Regions Under Principles of Reciprocity and National Interest

Country	Period	Country	Period	Country	Period
Asia		Micronesia	30 days	**Europe**	
Brunei	30 days	Nauru	30 days	Albania	30 days
Hong Kong	90 days	New Caledonia	30 days	Andorra	30 days
Japan	30 days	Palau	30 days	Bosnia, Hercegovina	30 days
Kuwait	30 days	Samoa	30 days	Croatia	90 days
Macao	30 days	Solomon Islands	30 days	Cyprus	90 days
Oman	30 days	**North America**		Monaco	30 days
Qatar	30 days	Canada	180 days	San Marino	30 days
Saudi Arabia	30 days	United States	30 days	Servia & Montenegro	30 days
Taiwan	30 days	**South America**		Slovenia	90 days
United Arab Emirates	30 days	Argentina	30 days	Vatican	30 days
Yemen	30 days	Ecuador	30 days	**Africa**	
Oceania		Guatemala	30 days	Egypt	30 days
Australia	90 days	Guyana	30 days	Republic of South Africa	30 days
Fiji	30 days	Honduras	30 days	Swaziland	30 days
Guam	30 days	Paraguay	90 days	Mauritius	30 days
Kiribati	30 days	Venezuela	30 days	Seychelles	30 days
Marshall Islands	30 days				

ENTRY & DEPARTURE PROCEDURES
Alien Registration

A Korean embassy or consulate can issue two types of visas: a short-term visa for up to 90 days and a special long-term visa for periods longer than 90 days.
A visitor with a special long-term visa is required to apply for alien registration at a local immigration office within 90 days of arrival.

Immigration Offices
Seoul	02-2650-6212
Busan	051-461-3021
Incheon	032-889-9936
Gimhae Airport	051-972-1610/5
Incheon Int'l Airport	032-740-7015~9
Jeju-do	064-722-3494

ENTRY & DEPARTURE PROCEDURES
Customs

Korea Customs Service: www.customs.go.kr

Passengers who have no articles to declare should use the "nothing to declare" channel and those declaring non-duty free articles should use the "goods to declare" channel.
If a passenger declares non-duty free articles voluntarily, the declared amount will be accepted and the clearance procedure will be expedited.

DUTY FREE ARTICLES
- The non-resident visitor's goods that will be taken out of Korea upon departure (the total quantity of the goods should be declared for duty exemption)
- Goods that were declared upon departure from Korea and are being brought back
- Goods totaling US$400 or less that were purchased or acquired outside Korea
- 1 bottle (not over 1 liter) of alcoholic beverages
- 200 cigarettes (50 cigars or 250 g of tobacco)
- 2 ounces of perfume

For further information on goods subject to declaration and prohibited goods, please contact the Customs Information Office at Incheon International Airport.
032-740-3333, 080-742-7272, 080-545-7272

ENTRY & DEPARTURE PROCEDURES
Guidelines for Currency Regulation

Passengers entering Korea who are carrying foreign or Korean currency valuing over US$10,000 must declare it to customs officials. Departing non-residents of Korea who are carrying foreign or Korean currency (including traveler's or bank checks) valuing more than US$10,000 must obtain permission from the Bank of Korea or customs, not including any amount carried into Korea and declared on arrival, which may be carried out without declaration to customs. Residents of Korea must declare any currency or negotiable checks more than US$10,000 upon departure. Please be aware that violators of these regulations are liable to be fined and/or otherwise penalized under the Foreign Exchange Transactions Act.

ENTRY & DEPARTURE PROCEDURES
Quarantine

ANIMAL QUARANTINE
All live animals and animal products entering Korea must be accompanied by valid certificates issued by the exporting country's government. Declare all imported animals and animal products upon arrival to the National Veterinary Research and Quarantine Service, where they must be inspected. Cloven-hoofed animals and their products that are shipped from import-restricted areas will be sent back or destroyed.
For details, contact the National Veterinary Research and Quarantine Service.

031-467-1923; www.nvrqs.go.kr

Incheon Int'l Airport	032-740-2660
Gunsan Branch	063-445-7348
Seoul Branch	02-2650-0611
Jeju Branch	064-712-2762
Busan Branch	051-603-0610

PLANT QUARANTINE
Passengers who carry any plants, soil, fruit, vegetables, seeds, orchids, nursery stock or cut flowers, etc., must describe the items on the Customs Declaration Form and immediately declare them upon arrival.

- Import Restricted Items and Areas
- Fresh fruit, such as mangos, oranges, papayas, cherries, etc.: all countries
- Nursery stock of apples, grapes, etc.: most European countries
- Walnut fruits and kernels: most countries
- Soil or plants with soil: all countries

If you have any question about plant quarantine, contact the National Plant Quarantine Service.

031-449-0521, 0524, 0526; www.npqs.go.kr

Incheon Int'l Airport	032-740-2074
Gunsan Branch	063-467-3456
Incheon Branch	032-433-8632
Jeju Branch	064-747-6241
Busan Branch	051-467-0442

GENERAL INFORMATION

Transportation

ARRIVING IN KOREA

International Flights

There are six international airports in Korea: Incheon, Gimhae, Cheongju, Daegu, Yangyang and Jeju International Airports.
Incheon International Airport services flights to all parts of the world, but the others only service Asia. An airport tax of ₩17,000 for international flights and ₩4,000 or ₩5,000 for domestic flights is included in the ticket price.
For more details, visit www.airport.co.kr or call ☎ 1577-2600

Airline Offices with Regular Flights to and from Korea

Airline	Phone	Airline	Phone
Aeroflot Russian Int'l	02-551-0321	Korean Air	1588-2001
Air Canada	02-3788-0100	Krasair Airlines	02-777-6399
Air China	02-774-6886	Lufthansa Airlines	02-3420-0400
Air France	02-3483-1033	Malaysia Airlines	02-777-7761
Air Kazakstan	02-3788-0200	Mongolian Airlines	02-756-9761
Air Paradise	02-771-8300	Northwest Airlines	02-732-1700
Air Russia	02-725-8283	Orient Thai Airlines	02-3707-0114
All Nippon Airways	02-752-5500	Philippine Airlines	02-774-3581
American Airlines	02-319-3401	Pulkovo Airlines	02-3788-0230
Asiana Airlines	1588-8000	Qantas Airways	02-777-6871
Cathay Pacific Airways	02-3112-800	SAT Airlines	02-753-7131
Cebu Pacific Air	02-3708-8585	Singapore Airlines	02-755-1226
China Eastern Airlines	02-518-0330	Thai Airways	02-3707-0011
China Hainan Airlines	02-779-0600	Turkish Airlines	02-777-7055
Dalavia	02-3788-0222	United Airlines	02-757-1691
Delta Airlines	02-754-1921	Uzbekistan Airways	02-754-1041
Garuda Indonesia Airways	080-773-2092	Vietnam Airlines	02-757-8920
Japan Airlines	02-757-1711	Vladivostok Air	02-733-2920
KLM Royal Dutch Airlines	02-2011-5500		

KOREA CITY AIR TERMINALS
City air terminals can be found at the World Trade Center in Seoul and Gimpo Airport. They provide check-in service and passport inspection. A limousine bus operates between the city air terminals and Incheon International Airport. For further information, visit www.kcat.co.kr.
ⓣ: World Trade Center 🚇 10-min. walk from Samseong Station on Seoul Subway Line 2
ⓣ: Gimpo Airport 🚇 Get off at Gimpo Airport Station on Seoul Subway Line 5.

TRANSPORTATION
International Sea Routes

Busan is the country's largest port and second largest city. This international seaport is Korea's main maritime gateway (mostly to and from Japan). Another international port is Incheon, which operates service to China.
The following is a list of companies operating ferries between Korea and Japan, and China and Russia. Temporary entry is permitted for private cars with the proper documentation belonging to all visitors to Korea arriving by ferry. There are also high-speed hydrofoils plying the Busan-Fukuoka route.

Korea ↔ Japan

Routes	Inquiries
Busan ↔ Fukuoka	Korea Marine Express ☏ 02-730-8666, 051-442-6111; www.kmx.co.kr Korea Ferry ☏ 02-775-2323, 051-466-7799; www.koreaferry.co.kr Mire Jet ☏ 051-441-8200; www.mirejet.com
Busan ↔ Osaka	Panster Enterprise ☏ 051-462-5482
Busan ↔ Shimonoseki	Pukwan Ferry ☏ 02-738-0055, 051-464-2700; www.pukwan.co.kr
Busan ↔ Tsushima (Daemado)	Dae-a Ferry ☏ 054-242-5111; www.daea.com

Korea ↔ China

Routes	Inquiries
Incheon ↔ Dalian	Dae-in Ferry ☏ 02-3218-6550, 032-891-7100; www.dainferry.co.kr
Incheon ↔ Dandong	Dandong International Ferry ☏ 02-713-5522, 032-891-3322; www.dandongferry.co.kr
Incheon ↔ Shidao	Hwadong Ferry ☏ 02-318-1581, 032-891-8877; www.huadong.co.kr
Incheon ↔ Tianjin	Jincheon Ferry ☏ 02-515-6317, 032-777-8260; www.jinchon.co.kr
Incheon ↔ Weihai	Weidong Ferry ☏ 02-3271-6753, 032-777-0490/4;
Incheon ↔ Qingdao	www.weidong.com ☏ 032-777-0490
Incheon ↔ Yantai	C & K Ferry ☏ 02-360-6900, 032-891-8880; www.hanjoongferry.co.kr
Incheon ↔ Yingkou	Bumyeong Ferry ☏ 02-733-1300, 032-891-5555
Pyeongtaek ↔ Rizhao	Hwanghae Ferry ☏ 02-850-8800, 031-682-9120
Pyeongtaek ↔ Rongcheong	Dalong Ferry ☏ 02-511-9061, 031-683-0992; www.dalong.co.kr

Korea ↔ Russia

Routes	Inquiries
Sokcho ↔ Zarubino	Dongchun Ferry ☏ 02-720-0101, 033-683-2100; www.dongchunferry.co.kr

KOREA / CHINA THROUGH TICKET

This ticket provides travel between the two countries with discount rides on the Saemaeul train in Korea, a luxury train in China and a ferry operating between Incheon in Korea and Tianjin in China. The ticket is valid for 20 days from the first ride.

• Reservation Offices
Dae-a Travel Agency: Seoul 82-2-514-6226
📠 82-2-514-8053
Hwaun Travel Agency: Beijing 86-10-5189-2422

KOREA / JAPAN THROUGH TICKET

This ticket enables the holder to travel around Korea and Japan by train, transferring via the ferry crossing between Busan and Shimonoseki. This system is jointly developed by the KNR, JNR and a ferry company doing business between the two countries and offers significant travel savings.

• Discount
30% for KTX
9-30% for Japan railroads
30% for ferry

• Travel Agencies
Hongik Travel Agency (Seoul)
📞 82-2-717-1002
Nippon Travel Agency (Osaka)
📞 81-6-6312-1253
* Tickets are valid for one week from the first day of boarding.

GETTING AROUND IN KOREA

TRANSPORTATION

To and From Incheon International Airport

Built on an extensive reclaimed tidal land between two islands, Incheon International Airport is situated 52 km west of downtown Seoul and some 15 km off the coast of the port city of Incheon.

It operates 24 hours a day. The international airport code is ICN, and it is abbreviated "iia" or "IIA." Limousine buses may be the best way to travel at a minimal expense to and from various places around Korea.

Information and tickets are available at the Transportation Information Counters near exits No. 2, 4, 9 and 13 on the arrival floor of the passenger terminal. The major bus routes are listed on the next page.

📞 1577-2600; www.airport.or.kr

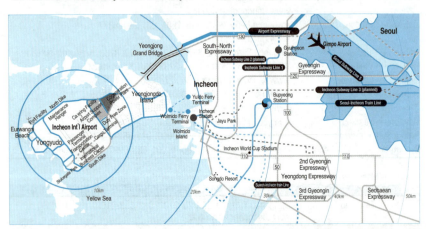

Destination (Bus No.)	Major Coach Bus Stops
Seoul (Gangbuk)	
* Nowon, Dobong	Incheon Airport – Taereung – Banghak Intersection
* Seoul Station, Yongsan Station	Incheon Airport – Yongsan Stn. – Seoul Stn.
Namsan	Incheon Airport – Via Hotels in Namsan Area
* City Hall	Incheon Airport – Via Hotels in City Hall Area – KAL Building
* Hannam-dong (Itaewon)	Incheon Airport – Yeouido Stn. – Via Hotels in Itaewon Area – Hannam-dong
Daehangno (602-1)	Incheon Airport – Seodaemun-gu Office – Gyeongbokgung Palace – Daehangno
Cheongnyangni (602)	Incheon Airport – Gwanghwamun Gate – Jongno – Cheongnyangni
Seoul Station (601)	Incheon Airport – Gimpo Airport – Yongsan Station – City Hall
Myeong-dong (605-1)	Incheon Airport – Chungjeongno – Jonggak – Myeongdong Stn. – Malli-dong
City Hall (605)	Incheon Airport – Mapo – City Hall – Chungjeongno Stn.
Seoul (Gangnam)	
* City Air Terminal (Trade Center)	Incheon Airport – City Air Terminal (Trade Center)
* Seoul Express Bus Terminal	Incheon Airport – Seoul Express Bus Terminal
* Gangnam	Incheon Airport – Via Hotels in Gangnam Area
* Jamsil	Incheon Airport – Sheraton Walker Hill Hotel – Lotte Hotel Seoul-Jamsil
Garak Market (609)	Incheon Airport – Seoul Express Bus Terminal – Daechi-dong – Suseo – Samsung Hospital
Cheonho-dong (606)	Incheon Airport – Apgujeong-dong – Samseong Stn. – Olympic Parktel
Jamsil (600)	Incheon Airport – Seoul Express Bus Terminal – Jamsil Stn.
Seoul (Gangseo)	
* Gimpo Airport	Incheon Airport – Gimpo Airport
Gwangmyeong (604-1)	Incheon Airport – Gwangmyeong Stn. – Gwangmyeong KTX Stn.
Seoul Nat'l Univ. (603)	Incheon Airport – Mok-dong Intersection – Seoul Nat'l Univ.
Geumcheon-gu Office (604)	Incheon Airport – Gaebong Stn. – Geumcheon-gu Office
Songjeong Stn. (607)	Incheon Airport – Songjeong Stn.
Yeongdeungpo Stn. (608)	Incheon Airport – Dangsan Stn. – Yeongdeungpo Stn.
Incheon	
Airport Town Square (223)	Passenger Terminal – Hyatt Hotel – Airport Town Square
Yeongdeungpo (301)	Eurwangni Beach – Passenger Terminal – Gimpo Airport – Yeongdeungpo Stn.
Yeongjong Ferry (203)	Passenger Terminal – Yeongjong Ferry – Airport Town Square
Dong Incheon (112)	Former Terminal – Gajeong Ogeori – Airport Town Square – Incheon Airport
Songdo Beach (111)	Incheon Airport – Bupyeong Stn. – Songdo Beach
Songnae Stn. (302)	Incheon Airport – Gyesan Stn. – Songnae Stn.
Incheon Stn. (306)	Incheon Airport – Dong Incheon Stn. – Incheon Stn.
Gejampo (222)	Incheon Airport – Jamjindo – Gejampo
Gyeonggi-do	
Ilsan (No. 3300)	Incheon Airport – Hwajeong – Daehwa Stn.
Yongin	Incheon Airport – Suji – Yongin Bus Terminal
* Ansan	Incheon Airport – Ansan Bus Terminal
* Suwon	Incheon Airport – Gwangmyeong Stn. Bldg. – Suwon
Anseong	Incheon Airport – Osan – Songtan – Anseong
Icheon	Incheon Airport – Dong Seoul Bus Terminal – Icheon
Jukjeon (Suji)	Incheon Airport – Gwacheon – Suji – Jukjeon
Yeoju	Incheon Airport – Dong Seoul Bus Terminal – Yeoju Intercity Bus Terminal
Namyangju (Maseok)	Incheon Airport – Geumgok (Namyangju)
* Uijeongbu	Incheon Airport – Uijeongbu Intercity Bus Terminal
* Seongnam	Incheon Airport – Yatap Stn. – Moran Stn. – Seongnam Save Zone
Anyang	Incheon Airport – Gunpo (Sanbon) – Anyang
Gupabal (602-2)	Incheon Airport – Gupabal
Gwangmyeong (604-1)	Incheon Airport – Haan Jct.
Ori / Bundang	Incheon Airport – Ori Station
Seongnam / Bundang	Incheon Airport – Seongnam Savezone
Other Provinces	
Chuncheon	Incheon Airport – Gapyeong – Chuncheon
Wonju	Incheon Airport – Munmak – Wonju
Gwangju	Incheon Airport – Gwangju Bus Terminal
* Jeonju	Incheon Airport – Iksan IC – Jeonju (Core Hotel)
Cheongju	Incheon Airport – 88 Olympic Expressway – Gyeongbu Expressway – Cheongju
Daejeon	Incheon Airport – Hotel Lotte Daedeok – Daejeon Government Administration Bldg. – Daejeon (Dongbu Intercity Bus Terminal)
* Gyeongsan (Daegu)	Incheon Airport – Gumi – Dong Daegu – Gyeongsan
Pohang / Gyeongju	Incheon Airport – Gyeongju – Pohang
Onyang	Incheon Airport – Cheonan – Onyang
Taean	Incheon Airport – Dangjin – Seosan – Taean
Mokpo	Incheon Airport – Mokpo Intercity Bus Terminal
Chungju	Incheon Airport – Chungju Intercity Bus Terminal
Shuttle Buses	
Long-term Parking Lot	Passenger Terminal – Long-term Parking Lot
Airport Town Square	Vehicle Maintenance Center – Passenger Terminal
For Cargo Terminal	Vehicle Maintenance Center – Airport Operations Center – Cargo Terminal B – Cargo Terminal C – Customs Building – Cargo Terminal A – Incheon Int'l Aitport Corp. – Passenger Terminal
Yeongjong (203)	Passenger Terminal – Airport ATM Bldg. – Daebo Ferry – Yeongjong Ferry

* Deluxe Limousine Coach

Domestic Flights

TRANSPORTATION

Korea has a well-developed domestic flight network served by Korean Air and Asiana Airlines linking 15 major cities. Reservations can be made by calling the airline offices listed below. Hanjin Travel Service (☎ 02-753-9870) also operates a ticket sales outlet at the KTO Tourist Information Center.
- Korean Air: ☎ **1588-2001**; www.koreanair.com
- Asiana Airlines: ☎ **1588-8000**; http://flyasiana.com

* All fares are given in KR₩.
* Fares vary depending on the airline, season and day. The above fares are based on Korean Air (*Asiana Airlines), Friday through Sunday, and include an airport tax of ₩4,000 (₩5,000 at Incheon Int'l Airport).

Domestic Ferry Boats

TRANSPORTATION

Boats are one of the most interesting ways to travel around Korea. Ferries ply the waterways between Busan and Jeju, Mokpo and Hongdo, Pohang and Ulleungdo, etc. For further information on sea routes, times or fares, please contact the Korea Shipping Association (☎ 02-6096-2000) or ferry terminals below.

Major Ferry Terminals

Busan	☎ 051-660-0256	Tongyeong	☎ 055-641-6181
Incheon	☎ 032-880-7530	Mokpo	☎ 061-240-6060
Pohang	☎ 054-245-1800	Yeosu	☎ 061-663-0117
Geoje	☎ 055-682-0116	Jeju	☎ 064-758-7181

Trains

TRANSPORTATION

Passenger trains operated by the Korean National Railroad are fast, reliable and very inexpensive by international standards.
There are the KTX, a super high-speed train operating at speeds of 300 km/h, super express Saemaeulho and express Mugunghwaho. Trains are usually full on weekends and holidays, so reservations and advance purchases are advisable at railroad stations or tour agencies such as Hanjin Travel Service (☎ 02-729-9680) at the KTO Tourist Information Center. Some of the major railroad stations have special ticket counters for overseas visitors. Timetables and fares are available at www.korail.go.kr.

<Saemaeulho & Mugunghwaho Express Line>

KTX http://ktx.korail.go.kr

The KTX (Korea Train Express), boasting super high speeds of 300 km/h, reduces the Seoul – Busan route from 4 hrs., 10 min. on the Saemaeul fleet to 2 hrs,, 40 min.

KTX Running Time & Rates for Major Train Stations (Departing from Seoul)

	Cheonan/ Asan	Daejeon	Dong Daegu
Duration	0:34	0:49	1:38
Fare (₩)	11,400	19,500	34,900
	Busan	Iksan	Gwangju	Mokpo
Duration	2:40	1:40	2:40	3:03
Fare (₩)	44,800	25,500	33,300	38,000

KR PASS FOR THE NATIONAL RAILROAD

The KR Pass is a rail pass for overseas visitors that is similar to the EURAIL Pass and JR Pass. You may purchase a KR Pass voucher at overseas travel agents or on the Web at www.korail.go.kr (credit card purchase only) and exchange the voucher for a KR Pass at a designated station (Seoul, Yeongdeungpo, Daejeon, Dong Daegu, Busan, Gyeongju, Gwangju) or an information desk at Incheon International Airport.

The pass allows free travel with reserved seating on Korean trains (excluding subways) for a set period of time with no restrictions on frequency or distance.

Inquiries
- Seoul 82-2-773-2535
- New York 1-212-643-0766
- LA 1-213-383-5511
- Tokyo 81-3-3255-6015

- For a list of ticket offices, visit www.korail.go.kr
- For more information, e-mail master@ustravel.co.kr

KR Pass Price List Unit: US$

Type	Normal		Youth Pass	Saver Pass
	Adult	Child		
3 days	76	38	61	68
5 days	114	57	91	103
7 days	144	72	115	130
10 days	166	83	133	149

TRANSPORTATION
Long Distance Express Buses

Three express bus terminals serve Seoul: Seoul Express Bus Terminal (Gangnam Gosok Terminal), Dong Seoul Bus Terminal and Sangbong Bus Terminal. Seoul Express Bus Terminal is the main bus depot for trips between Seoul and other major cities on Subway Line 3 or 7 at the station of the same name. Dong Seoul Bus Terminal operates similar routes but with less frequent service and fewer destinations, adjacent to Gangbyeon Station on Subway Line 2. The Sangbong Bus Terminal serves Cheongju, Daejeon, Jeonju or Gwangju and is near the station of the same name on Subway Line 7. Deluxe express buses are somewhat more expensive than regular buses, but they are popular for their spacious seats and facilities such as mobile phones and in-route movies.

REAL-TIME INFORMATION AND RESERVATIONS: www.kobus.co.kr/eng/index.jsp

EXPRESS BUS TERMINALS

Seoul
Seoul Express Bus Terminal
- Gyeongbuseon, Gumaseon and Yeongdongseon Lines — 02-535-4151/2
- Honamseon Line — 02-6282-0600/1,0808

Dong Seoul	02-455-3161	Sangbong	02-435-2129

Busan
051-508-9955

Daegu
053-743-1101, 053-755-1001

Incheon
032-430-7315

Gwangju
062-360-8114

Daejeon
Daejeon	042-623-8257	Yuseong	042-822-0386

Ulsan
052-268-1556

Gyeonggi-do
Anseong	031-677-6789	Goyang, Hwajeong	031-978-9881
Pyeongtaek	031-655-2453	Seongnam	031-781-8668
Suwon	031-267-7800	Uijeongbu	031-842-3018
Yeoju	031-882-9596	Yongin	031-339-3181

Gangwon-do
Chuncheon	033-256-6010	Donghae	033-531-3400
Gangneung	033-643-6092	Samcheok	033-572-7444
Sokcho	033-631-3181	Wonju	033-744-2290
Yangyang	033-672-4100	Yeongwol	033-374-2451

Chungcheongbuk-do
Cheongju	043-230-1600	Chungju	043-853-0114
Hwanggan	043-742-4015	Jecheon	043-648-3182

Chungcheongnam-do
Asan/Onyang	041-544-4880	Cheonan	041-551-4933
Geumsan	041-754-4854	Gongju	041-855-2319
Jochiwon	041-865-8066	Nonsan	041-735-3677
Yeonmudae	041-741-6670		

Gyeongsangbuk-do
Gimcheon	054-434-3093	Gumi	054-452-5755
Gyeongju	054-741-4000	Pohang	054-272-3194
Sangju	054-534-9002	Yeongcheon	054-334-2211
Yeongju	054-631-5844		

Gyeongsangnam-do
Changwon	055-288-0303	Gimhae	055-327-7880
Jinju	055-752-5167	Masan	055-255-2576
Tongyeong	055-644-0017		

Jeollabuk-do
Buan	063-584-2681	Gimje	063-547-0075
Gochang	063-563-3388	Gunsan	063-445-3824
Iksan	063-855-0345	Jeongeup	063-535-4240
Jeonju	063-277-1572	Jinan	063-433-2508
Namwon	063-625-5391	Sunchang	063-653-2186

Jeollanam-do
Beolgyo	061-857-6313	Dong Gwangyang	061-792-0512
Gangjin	061-432-9777	Goheung	061-835-3560
Gwangyang	061-761-3030	Haenam	061-534-0881
Hampyeong	061-322-0660	Jangheung	061-862-7091
Jido	061-275-0108	Jindo	061-543-5053
Mokpo	061-276-0221	Muan	061-453-0156
Naju	061-333-1323	Nokdong	061-842-2706
Suncheon	061-751-2863	Wando	061-554-2602
Yeongam	061-473-4183	Yeonggwang	061-353-3360
Yeongsanpo	061-334-3022	Yeosu	061-652-1877

Intercity Buses

TRANSPORTATION

Korea has an extensive intercity bus system connecting almost every city and town. These buses do not provide special facilities for the foreign traveler, there is no English timetable, and the seats are more cramped than express buses, but for adventurous visitors they are an interesting way to get closer to the spirit and lifestyle of the Korean people. Intercity bus terminals are usually housed within express bus terminals in major cities and near the downtown area in small cities.

City Buses

TRANSPORTATION

The bus system differs slightly from city to city in Korea. There are two types, regular local and seated coach buses, and both are numbered according to route. The bus system is so extensive that buses go virtually everywhere in every city. Since bus signs are written only in *hangeul* (the Korean alphabet), finding the right bus can be confusing for the first-time visitor. Hotel staff can assist in choosing the correct bus and stop for your destination. Fares can be paid as you board with cash (coins or ₩1,000 notes—change returned) or a transportation card.

To stop the bus at your destination, push one of the stop buttons located along the interior of the bus as you approach your stop. It may be better to let the driver know your destination. Ask someone to write it down for you to hand him as you board. City express coaches, called *jwaseok* buses, stop less frequently and travel more rapidly through congested areas. The fare for the city express coach is about ₩1,300.

SEOUL CITY BUS SYSTEM

FARE

Regardless of the type and number of transfers, an integrated fare scheme is applied to the total distance traveled.

Distance	Fare
For a basic distance of 10 km or less	₩900
For each additional 5 km	₩100

TYPES OF BUSES

All city buses are classified by one of four colors: Blue, Green, Red and Yellow. Using the bus number, it is possible to identify the departure point and destination of the bus.
- **Blue Bus:** Blue buses connect the city's outer areas with downtown Seoul.
- **Green Bus:** Green buses circulate within a district of Seoul, connecting branch line roads.
- **Red Bus:** Red buses, usually called *jwaseok* buses, connect downtown and newly emerging centers of Seoul with major suburban cities of the metropolitan area.
- **Yellow Bus:** Yellow buses circulate within a central area, connecting major business areas.

Transportation Card

Transportation cards are available for both buses and subways. They can be purchased at booths near bus stops or at subway stations. Cards can be charged in increments of ₩1,000 to ₩50,000.
The fare is automatically deducted from the card when it is passed over the card reader located next to the bus driver or at the subway turnstile.

T-Money Card

A T-Money card can be used for the bus and subway, and in the future, taxis will also accept the card. It can also be used to pay for public parking lots, tolls, and tours of cultural facilities such as royal palaces or museums.
The card, which is rechargeable, can be purchased for ₩11,500 at any GS25 convenience store in Seoul or at subway ticket counters.
ⓘ: Seoul City Tourist Information Center ☏ 02-735-8688

Subways

TRANSPORTATION

There are excellent subway train systems in Seoul, Incheon, Gyeonggi-do Province, Busan, Daegu and Gwangju. The subway is the most efficient and convenient way for travelers to get around the city. Station names, ticket windows and transfer signs are all clearly marked in English.

* See p. 88 – 89 for the Seoul, Gyeonggi-do and Incheon Subway Map, p. 150 for the Daegu Subway Map and p. 158 for the Busan Subway Map.

USING THE SUBWAY TICKET VENDING MACHINE

Other than at ticket counters, tickets can be bought from two types of vending machines:
one type only accepts coins (₩10, ₩50, ₩100 and ₩500), the other accepts both bills (₩1,000) and coins.

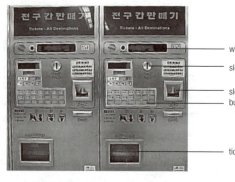

- window for indicating fare
- slot for coins
- slot for bills
- buttons for choosing destinations
- ticket drop

LOST & FOUND CENTERS (http://lost114.com)
Seoul
- Seoul Station (KTX, Saemaeulho/Mugunghwaho Trains) ☎ 02-755-7108
- Guro Station (Line 1, 2) ☎ 02-869-0089
- City Hall Station (Line 3, 4) ☎ 02-753-2408
- Chungmuro Station (Line 2, 5 and 8) ☎ 02-2271-1170
- Taereung Station (Line 6, 7) ☎ 02-949-6767
- Wangsimri Station (Line 2) ☎ 02-2298-6767
Incheon Bupyeong Station ☎ 032-451-3650
Busan Seomyeon Station ☎ 051-640-7339
Daegu Banwoldang Station ☎ 053-640-3333

Taxis

TRANSPORTATION

Taxis are plentiful, clean, safe and inexpensive in Korea. There are taxi stands in most busy city areas and taxis can also be hailed on the streets. Certain taxis can also be requested by phone though the fare for these special call taxis is somewhat higher than regular taxis.

REGULAR TAXIS

The fare is based on both distance and time. It is ₩1,900 for the first 2 km and ₩100 for each additional 144 m. If the taxi is going less than 15 km/h, a charge of ₩100 for each additional 35 seconds is added to the fare.
The fare between Incheon International Airport and downtown Seoul is usually around ₩42,000

(including the toll) though it could be higher in heavy traffic. Fares increase 20% between midnight and 4 am.

BRAND TAXIS

The Brand Taxis "Kind Call Taxi" and "KT Powertel" are equipped with a simultaneous interpretation machine, a receipt issuance machine and wireless data terminal with automatic vehicle location system (a 24-hour call center checks real-time taxi availability and dispatches the closest one). The fare is the same as that of regular taxi and there is a ₩1,000 surcharge for the call.
Kind Call Taxi ☎ 1588-3382;
KT Powertel ☎ 1588-0082

DELUXE TAXIS

Deluxe taxis, called *mobeom* taxi in Korean, are black with a yellow sign on top and the words "Deluxe Taxi" written on the sides. They offer more passenger space and a high standard of service. The fare is ₩4,500 for the first 3 km and ₩200 for each additional 164 m or 39 seconds if the speed drops below 15 km/h. The typical fare between Incheon Int'l Airport and downtown is about ₩70,000 (including toll). Receipts are given and there is no late-night surcharge. Deluxe taxis can be boarded at stands located at hotels, train stations, bus terminals and on major city streets. They also can be called at ☎ 02-558-8000.

TAXI VANS

Eight-passenger van taxis are installed with simultaneous foreign language interpretation by phone, receipt-issuing equipment and a credit card processing terminal. Fares are the same as for deluxe taxis. Passengers carrying large amounts of baggage may find them convenient. They can be called at ☎ 02-888-2000.

TRANSPORTATION
Car Rental

Rental cars are available for visitors and charges range from ₩62,000 to ₩460,000 per day. Driving safely in Korea takes some practice.

Visitors must meet the following requirements to rent a car:
- Have more than 1 year of driving experience.
- Have an international driver's license.
- Be over 21 years of age.
- Possess a valid passport.
- Pay by credit card.

Due to the different traffic laws and an unfamiliarity with the roads, it is advisable to hire a driver along with the car.
Visitors who wish to hire a chauffeur-driven car should be prepared to pay for the driver's meals and hotel expenses. The cost of hiring a driver in Seoul ranges from ₩142,000 to ₩510,000 for 10 hours a day, including the car rental.
For further details, call the Korea Rent-a-Car Association ☎ 02-525-4962 or Seoul Car Rental Association ☎ 02-525-9076/8.

Hertz (Kumho)
☎ 02-797-8000; www.kumhorent.com
VIP (Avis)
☎ 1544-1600; www.avis.co.kr

"FREE INTERPRETATION BY PHONE" TAXIS
Regular taxis with a "Free Interpretation by Phone" sign on the back door (passenger side) provide interpretation services in 7 languages (English, Japanese, Chinese, German, French, Russian, and Spanish) for foreign tourists (Operating hours 07:00 – 22:00).
The driver calls an interpreter through a phone installed in the car and three-way communication begins.

GENERAL INFORMATION

Accommodations

ACCOMMODATIONS

Hotels

There are many modern hotels in Korea's major cities and tourist destinations.
Tourist hotels are classified into five groups: super deluxe (SDL), deluxe (DLX), 1st, 2nd and 3rd classes. These ratings do not correspond with hotel ratings in Western countries. Facilities in most tourist hotels include one or more bars and cocktail lounges, restaurants, on-site recreational facilities such as tennis courts and swimming pools, souvenir shops, arcades, barber shops and beauty salons, laundry rooms and saunas. The hotels on pages 188 – 202 are all registered as tourist hotels.
The prices listed below are for a room with a double bed and do not include a 10% service charge and 10% V.A.T.

SEOUL www.seoul.go.kr

SUPER DELUXE

COEX Inter-Continental
02-3452-2500, 02-3430-8000
http://seoul.intercontinental.com
159, Samseong-dong, Gangnam-gu
₩350,000

Grand Hilton Seoul
02-3216-5656, 02-3216-7799
www.grandhiltonseoul.com
201-1, Hongeun-dong,
Seodaemun-gu
₩390,000

Grand Hyatt Seoul
02-797-1234, 02-798-6953
www. grandhyattseoul.co.kr
747-7, Hannam-dong, Yongsan-gu
₩390,000

Grand Inter-Continental
02-555-5656, 02-559-7990
http://seoul.intercontinental.com
159-8, Samseong-dong,
Gangnam-gu
₩390,000

Imperial Palace Hotel
02-3440-8000, 02-3440-8200
www.amiga.co.kr
248-7, Nonhyeon-dong, Gangnam-gu
₩356,000

JW Marriott
02-6282-6262, 02-6282-6263
www.jw-marriott.co.kr
19-3, Banpo-dong, Seocho-gu
₩264,000

Lotte Hotel
02-771-1000, 02-752-3758
www.lottehotel.co.kr
1, Sogong-dong, Jung-gu
₩390,000 – ₩430,000

Lotte Hotel Seoul-Jamsil
02-419-7000, 02-417-3655
www.hotellotte.co.kr
40-1, Jamsil, Songpa-gu
₩360,000

Mayfield
02-6090-9000, 02-6090-5555
www.mayfield.co.kr
426, Oebalsan-dong, Gangseo-gu
₩320,000

Millennium Seoul Hilton
02-753-7788, 02-754-2510
www.hilton.co.kr
395, Namdaemunno 5 (o)-ga, Jung-gu
₩410,000

Park Hyatt Seoul
02-2016-1234, 02-2016-1200
www.parkhyattseoul.co.kr
995-14, Daechi 3 (sam)-dong, Gangnam-gu
₩330,000

Radisson Seoul Plaza
02-771-2200, 02-755-8897
www.seoulplaza.co.kr
23, Taepyeongno 2 (i)-ga, Jung-gu
₩380,000

Renaissance Seoul
02-555-0501, 02-553-8118
www.renaissance-seoul.com
676, Yeoksam-dong, Gangnam-gu
₩390,000

Sheraton Grand Walkerhill
02-455-5000, 02-452-6867
www.sheratonwalkerhill.co.kr
21, Gwangjang-dong,
Gwangjin-gu
₩350,000

The Ritz-Carlton Seoul
02-3451-8135, 02-345-8155
www.ritz.co.kr
602, Yeoksam-dong, Gangnam-gu
₩390,000

The Shilla
02-2233-3131, 02-2233-5073
www.shilla.net
202, Jangchung-dong 2 (i)-ga, Jung-gu
₩430,000

The Westin Chosun, Seoul
02-771-0500, 02-752-1443
www.echosunhotel.com
87-1, Sogong-dong, Jung-gu
₩470,000

DELUXE

**Best Western Premier
Gang Nam Hotel**
02-6474-2000, 02-6474-2002
www.bestwesterngangnam.com
205-9, Nonhyeon-dong, Gangnam-gu
₩140,000

Holiday Inn Seongbuk Seoul
02-929-2000, 02-929-0204
www.holiday.co.kr
3-1343, Jongam-dong, Seongbuk-gu
₩230,000

Holiday Inn Seoul
02-717-9441, 02-715-9441
www.holiday-inn.co.kr
169-1, Dohwa-dong, Mapo-gu
₩240,000

Hotel Beluga
02-420-0100, 02-412-1932
www.hotelbeluga.com.
24, Seokchon-dong, Songpa-gu
₩185,000

Hotel Capital
02-792-1122, 02-796-0918
www.hotelcapital.co.kr
22-76, Itaewon-dong, Yongsan-gu
₩230,000

Hotel Ellui
02-514-3535, 02-548-2500
www.ellui.com
129, Cheongdam-dong, Gangnam-gu
₩220,000

Hotel Olympia
02-2287-6000, 02-2287-6103
www.olympia.co.kr
108-2, Pyeongchang-dong, Jongno-gu
₩231,000

Hotel President
02-753-3131, 02-752-7417
www.hotelpresident.co.kr
188-3, Euljiro 1 (il)-ga, Jung-gu
₩220,000

Hotel Prima
02-6006-9114, 02-544-8523
www.prima.co.kr
52-3, Cheongdam-dong, Gangnam-gu
₩133,636

Hotel Riviera
02-541-3111, 02-546-6111
www.hotelriviera.co.kr
53-7, Cheongdam-dong, Gangnam-gu
₩220,000

Koreana Hotel
02-2171-7000, 02-734-0665
www.koreanahotel.co.kr
61-1, Taepyeongno 1 (il)-ga, Jung-gu
₩215,000

Novotel Ambassador Doksan, Seoul
02-838-1101, 02-854-4799
www.ambatel.com/doksan
1030-1, Doksan 4 (sa)-dong,
Geumcheon-gu
₩286,000

Novotel Ambassador Gangnam, Seoul
02-567-1101, 02-564-4573
www.ambatel.com/gangnam
603, Yeoksam-dong, Gangnam-gu
₩315,000

Ramada Seoul
02-6202-2000, 02-6202-2001
www.ramadaseoul.co.kr
112-5, Samseong-dong, Gangnam-gu
₩340,000

Sejong Hotel
02-773-6000, 02-755-4906
www.sejong.co.kr
61-3, Chungmuro 2 (i)-ga, Jung-gu
₩250,000

Seoul KyoYuk MunHwa HoeKwan
02-571-8100, 02-571-7055
www.temf.co.kr
202 Yangjae 2-dong, Seocho-gu
₩170,000

Seoul Palace
02-532-5000, 02-532-0399
www.seoulpalace.co.kr
63-1, Banpo-dong, Seocho-gu
₩230,000

Seoul Royal Hotel
02-756-1112, 02-756-1119
www.seoulroyal.co.kr
6, Myeong-dong, Jung-gu
₩250,000

Sofitel Ambassador Hotel
02-2275-1101, 02-2272-0773
www.ambatel.com
186-54, Jangchungdong 2 (i)-ga,
Jung-gu
₩250,000

Tower Hotel
02-2236-2121, 02-2235-0276
www.towerhotel.co.kr
5-5, Jangchung-dong 2 (i)-ga, Jung-gu
₩240,000

The Lexington Hotel
02-6670-7000, 02-6670-7300
www.thelexington.co.kr
13-3, Yeouido-dong, Yeongdeungpo-gu
₩239,000

1st

Academy House
02-3499-7500, 02-908-4673
www.academyhouse.co.kr
San 76, Suyu-dong, Gangbuk-gu
₩88,000

Best Western New Seoul Hotel
02-735-9071, 02-735-6212
www.bestwesternnewseoul.com
29-1, Taepyeongno 1 (il)-ga, Jung-gu
₩160,000

California Tourist Hotel
02-401-4655, 02-431-1661
www.california-hotel.co.kr
98-6, Garak-dong, Songpa-gu
₩99,000

Dong Seoul
02-455-1100, 02-455-6311
595, Guui-dong, Gwangjin-gu
₩100,000

Green Grass Hotel
02-555-7575, 02)554-0643
http://www.greengrasshotel.com (Korean)
141-10, Samseong-dong, Gangnam-gu
₩154,000

Hamilton Hotel
02-794-0171/9, 02-795-0457
www.hamilton.co.kr
119-25, Itaewon-dong, Yongsan-gu
₩135,000

Hankang Hotel
02-453-5131, 02-453-5130
www.hankanghotel.co.kr
188-2, Gwangjang-dong, Gwangjin-gu
₩120,000

Hotel Blue Pearl
02-3015-7777, 02-544-9965
www.hotelbluepearl.com
129-4, Cheongdam-dong,
Gangnam-gu
₩180,000

Hotel Centro
02-3486-6000, 02-3486-6022
www.centrohotel.co.kr
1594-3, Seocho-dong, Seocho-gu
₩140,000

Hotel Crown
02-797-4111, 02-796-1010
www.hotelcrown.com

34-69, Itaewon-dong, Yongsan-gu
₩120,911

Hotel Lake
02-422-1001, 02-419-0041
www.hotellake.com (Korean)
158 Seokchon-dong, Songpa-gu
₩135,000

Hotel Prima II
02-546-1414, 02-544-1340
www.prima.co.kr
129-7, Cheongdam-dong, Gangnam-gu
₩99,174

Hotel Green World
02-2653-1999, 02-2651-1389
www.hotelgreenworld.co.kr
505-2, Deungchon 2 (i)-dong, Gangseo-gu
₩106,612

Hotel Noblesse
02-935-7161, 02-936-0094
www.hotelnoblesse.co.kr
711-9, Sanggye 6-dong, Nowon-gu
₩150,000

Hotel Nostalgia
02-2691-0071, 02-2691-6791
www.hotelnostalgia.co.kr
1110, Hwagok 6-dong, Gangseo-gu
₩143,000

Hotel Pop Green
02-544-6623/7, 02-543-2112
www.popgreenhotel.com (Korean)
614-1, Sinsa-dong, Gangnam-gu
₩140,000

Hotel Prince Seoul
02-752-7111, 02-752-7119
www.hotelprinceseoul.co.kr
1-1, Namsandong 2 (i)-ga, Jung-gu
₩120,000

Hotel Rex
02-752-3191, 02-755-9548
www.hotelrex.co.kr
65, Hoehyeon-dong 1-ga, Jung-gu
₩155,000

Hotel Seokyo
02-330-7771, 02-333-3388
www.hotelseokyo.co.kr
354-5, Seogyo-dong, Mapo-gu
₩200,000

Hotel Sunshine
02-541-1818, 02-547-0777
www.hotelsunshine.co.kr
587-1, Sinsa-dong, Gangnam-gu
₩127,000

Hotel Victoria
02-986-2000, 02-984-3679
www.hotelvictoria.co.kr
42-8, Mia 4-dong, Gangbuk-gu
₩110,000

Hotel Yoido
02-782-0121, 02-785-2510
www.yoidohotel.co.kr
10-3, Yeouido-dong, Yeongdeungpo-gu
₩115,000

Ibis Seoul
02-3454-1101, 02-3454-1946
www.ambatel.com
893-1, Daechi-dong, Gangnam-gu
₩97,000

Insadong Crown Hotel
02-3676-8000, 02-3676-1551
www.hotelcrown.com
25, Nagwon-dong, Jongno-gu
₩100,000

Itaewon Hotel
02-792-3111, 02-795-3126
www.itaewonhotel.com
737-32, Hannam-dong, Yongsan-gu
₩140,000

Kyungnam Tourist Hotel
02-2247-2500, 02-2247-2496
366-7, Jangan 2 (i)-dong, Dongdaemun-gu
₩114,000

Metro Hotel
02-752-1112, 02-757-4411
www.metrohotel.co.kr
199-3, Euljiro 2 (i)-ga, Jung-gu
₩118,800

New Kukje Hotel
02-732-0161, 02-732-1774
29-2, Taepyeongno1 (il)-ga, Jung-gu
₩150,000

Pacific Hotel
02-777-7811, 02-755-5582
31-1, Namsan-dong 2 (i)-ga, Jung-gu
₩200,000

Poongjun
02-2266-2151, 02-2274-5732
www.poongjun.net
73-1, Inhyeon-dong 2 (i)-ga, Jung-gu
₩180,000

River Park Hotel
02-3665-3000, 02-3665-3330
www.riverpark.co.kr
260, Yeomchang-dong, Gangseo-gu
₩100,000

Samjung Hotel
02-557-1221, 02-556-1126
www.samjunghotel.co.kr

604-11, Yeoksam-dong, Gangnam-gu
₩170,000

Savoy Hotel Seoul
02-776-2641, 02-755-7669
www.savoyhotel.co.kr
23-1, Chungmuro 1 (il)-ga, Jung-gu
₩160,000

2nd

Astoria Hotel
02-2268-7111, 02-2274-3187
13-2, Namhak-dong, Jung-gu
₩82,646

Best Western Hotel Dongdaemun
02-741-7811, 02-744-1274
444-14, Changsin-dong, Jongno-gu
₩104,000

Best Western Vision Hotel
02-2296-2245, 02-2296-2249
www.hotelvision.co.kr (Korean)
12-1, Doseon-dong, Seongdong-gu
₩120,000

Biwon Tourist Hotel
02-763-5555, 02-763-5554
www.biwonhotel.com
36, Wonnam-dong, Jongno-gu
₩92,000

Brown Tourist Hotel
02-926-6601/5, 02-923-6602
77-2, Bomun-dong 4 (sa)-ga, Seongbuk-gu
₩60,000

Central Tourist Hotel
02-2265-4121, 02-2265-6139
227-1, Jangsa-dong, Jongno-gu
₩64,000

Dynasty Tourist Hotel
02-540-3041, 02-540-3374
www.hoteldynasty.co.kr
202-7, Nonhyeon-dong, Gangnam-gu
₩100,000

Friend Hotel
02-521-7111, 02-521-7120
www.friendhotel.co.kr
1605-7, Seocho-dong, Seocho-gu
₩90,000

Hilltop Hotel
02-540-3456, 02-549-6459
www.hilltophotel.co.kr
151-30, Nonhyeon-dong, Gangnam-gu
₩145,200

Hotel Airport
02-2662-1113/4, 02-2663-3355

www.hotelairport.co.kr
11-21, Gonghang-dong, Gangseo-gu
₩103,300

Hotel City Palace
02-2244-2222, 02-2243-7857
497-23, Dapsimni-dong, Dongdaemun-gu
₩66,000

Hotel Mirabeau
02-392-9511, 02-392-3829
www.hotelmirabeau.co.kr
104-36, Daehyeon-dong, Seodaemun-gu
₩88,000

Hotel Sherma
02-2672-3535, 02-2069-3232
www.shermahotel.co.kr (Korean)
94-154, Yeongdeungpo-dong
Yeongdeungpo-gu,
₩52,000

Jamsil Tourist Hotel
02-421-2761, 02-417-6836
250-9, Jamsil-dong, Songpa-gu
₩120,000

Jeonpoong Tourist Hotel
02-2295-9365, 02-2292-3644
www.jphotel.co.kr
58, Doseon-dong, Seongdong-gu
₩80,000

Karak Tourist Hotel
02-400-6641, 02-401-2479
www.hotelkarak.com
98-5, Garak-dong, Songpa-gu
₩88,000

Kaya Tourist Hotel
02-798-5101, 02-798-5900
www.kayahotel.com
98-11, Garwol-dong, Yongsan-gu
₩52,000

Kim's Tourist Hotel
02-379-0520, 02-379-7734
66-50, Pyeongchang-dong, Jongno-gu
₩100,000

New Boolim Hotel
02-962-0021, 02-962-0025
620-27, Jeonnong 2 (i)-dong,
Dongdaemun-gu
₩69,420

New Hilltop Hotel
02-540-1121, 02-540-3650
152, Nonhyeon-dong, Gangnam-gu
₩140,000

New Regent Hotel
02-2605-2525, 02-2605-0031
1111-7, Hwagok-dong, Gangseo-gu
₩107,438

Olympiana Tourist Hotel
02-421-2131, 02-414-4427
www.olympiana.com
44-5, Bangi-dong, Songpa-gu
₩126,000

Seoul Tourist Hotel
02-735-9001, 02-733-0101
www.seoulhotel.net
92, Cheongjin-dong, Jongno-gu
₩90,000

Youngdong Hotel
02-542-0112/3, 02-546-8409
www.youngdonghotel.co.kr
6, Nonhyeon-dong, Gangnam-gu
₩125,000

3rd

BALI Tourist Hotel
02-484-1411, 02-488-6428
www.bali21.net
417-5, Seongnae-dong, Gangdong-gu
₩118,000

Hotel Giant
02-546-0225, 02-547-0318
45-10, Samseong-dong, Gangnam-gu
₩85,500

New Hotel Chonji
02-2265-6131, 02-2279-1184
www.newhotelchonji.co.kr
133-1, Euljiro 5 (o)-ga, Jung-gu
₩96,000

New Oriental Hotel
02-753-0701, 02-755-9346
10, Hoehyeon-dong 3 (sam)-ga, Jung-gu
₩69,000

Rex Tourist Hotel
02-511-4488, 02-512-3883
18-2, Nonhyeon-dong, Gangnam-gu
₩80,000

Samho Tourist Hotel
02-741-7080, 02-743-5981
436-73, Changsin-dong, Jongno-gu
₩56,000

Samhwa Tourist Hotel
02-541-1011, 02-544-0997
527-3, Sinsa-dong, Gangnam-gu
₩55,000

Seoul YMCA Tourist Hotel
02-734-4964, 02-734-8003
http://hotel.ymca.or.kr/hotel
9, Jongno 2 (i)-ga, Jongno-gu
₩52,000

Sofia Tourist Hotel
02-900-8011, 02-900-9082
88-1, Ssangmun-dong, Dobong-gu
₩46,464

Tiffany Tourist Hotel
02-545-0015, 02-545-0426
www.tiffanyhotel.com
132-17, Cheongdam-dong, Gangnam-gu
₩87,120

BUSAN http://visit.busan.kr
SUPER DELUXE

Busan Marriott Hotel
051-743-1234, 051-743-1250
www.marriott.com
1405-16, Jung-dong, Haeundae-gu
₩260,000 – ₩380,000

Busan Lotte Hotel
051-810-1000, 051-810-5110
www.busan.lottehotel.co.kr
503-15, Bujeon-dong, Jin-gu
₩270,000

Haeundae Grand Hotel
051-7400-114, 051-7400-141/3
www.grandhotel.co.kr
651-2, U-dong, Haeundae-gu
₩314,600

Paradise Hotel & Casino Busan
051-742-2121, 051-742-2100
www.paradisehotel.co.kr
1408-5, Jung-dong, Haeundae-gu
₩340,000

The Westin Chosun Beach Hotel
051-742-7411, 051-742-1313
www.chosunbeach.co.kr
737, U 1-dong, Haeundae-gu
₩330,000

DELUXE

Commodore Hotel
051-466-9101, 051-462-9101
www.commodore.co.kr
743-80, Yeongju-dong, Jung-gu
₩205,000

Hotel Hermes
051-750-8000, 051-750-8001
www.hermeshotel.co.kr
193-1, Gwangan 2 (i)-dong, Suyeong-gu
₩220,000

Hotel Nongshim
051-550-2100, 051-550-2105
www.hotelnongshim.com
137-7, Oncheon-dong, Dongnae-gu
₩240,000

Hotel Paragon
051-328-2001, 051-328-2009
www.hotelparagon.com

564-25, Goebeop-dong, Sasang-gu
₩140,000

1st

Busan Arirang Tourist Hotel
051-463-5001, 051-463-2800
www.ariranghotel.co.kr (Korean)
1204-1, Choryang-dong, Dong-gu
₩40,000

Dawnbeach Tourist Hotel
051-760-1500, 051-760-1515
www.dawnbeach.co.kr
199-7, Gwangan 2 (i)-dong, Suyeong-gu
₩100,000

Empire Hotel
051-337-8811, 051-337-8820
398-14, Deokcheon-dong, Buk-gu
₩57,852

Hotel Midas
051-760-2000, 051-760-2077
444-3, Suyeong-dong, Suyeong-gu
₩80,000

Hotel Nam Tae Pyung Yang
051-328-9911, 051-328-9912
149-1, Eomgung-dong, Sasang-gu
₩124,000

Kukje Hotel
051-642-1330, 051-636-9964
www.hotelkukje.com
830-62, Beomil-dong, Dong-gu
₩110,000

Mirabo Tourist Hotel
051-866-7400, 051-866-8770
1124-25, Yeosan-dong, Yeonje-gu
₩55,000

Phoenix Hotel
051-245-8062, 051-241-1523
www.hotelphoenix.net
8-1, Nampo 5 (o)-ga, Jung-gu
₩100,000

Pusan Tourist Hotel
051-241-4301, 051-244-1153
www.pusanhotel.co.kr
12, Donggwang-dong 2 (i)-ga, Jung-gu
₩120,000

Royal Kingdom Hotel
051-744-1331, 051-741-5757
www.royalkingdom.co.kr (Korean)
1509-2, Jung-dong, Haeundae-gu
₩123,967

Sapphire Hotel
051-207-1300, 051-207-1400
302-1, Dangni-dong, Saha-gu
₩74,133

SongJung Tourist Hotel
051-702-7766, 051-704-0522
www.songjunghotel.co.kr (Korean)
297-9, Songjeong-dong, Haeundae-gu
₩50,000 – ₩70,000

2nd

Dong Bang Tourist Hotel
051-552-9511, 051-552-9274
210-82, Oncheon 1-dong, Dongnae-gu
₩50,000

Gwang Jang Tourist Hotel
051-464-3141, 051-464-4150
1200-17, Choryang 3(sam)-dong, Dong-gu
₩55,000

Hillside Tourist Hotel
051-464-0567, 051-464-1214
743-33, Yeongju 1-dong, Jung-gu
₩70,000

Moon Hwa
051-806-8001, 051-806-1403
517-65, Bujeon 2-dong, Busanjin-gu
₩80,000

New Taeyang Tourist Hotel
051-465-7311, 051-464-0105
www.taeyanghotel.co.kr (Korean)
1-62, Sujeong-dong, Dong-gu
₩53,700

Plaza Hotel
051-463-5011/7, 051-463-5018
www.pusanplazahotel.com (Korean)
1213-14, Choryang-dong, Dong-gu
₩63,000

River Hill Tourist Hotel
051-203-8442, 051-203-8443
527-2, Hadan-dong, Saha-gu
₩80,000

Silver Tourist Hotel
051-758-7777, 051-758-1144
1070-1, Gwangan 3-dong, Suyeong-gu
₩50,000

Songdo Beach Hotel
051-254-2000/9, 051-254-5093
www.songdobeachhotel.co.kr
541-6, Amnam-dong, Seo-gu
₩58,000 – ₩63,000

Spa World
051-556-2224, 051-556-2228
182-9, Oncheon-dong, Dongnae-gu
₩40,000

Tower Tourist Hotel
051-241-5151, 051-243-1005
20, Donggwang-dong, Jung-gu
₩53,719

Utopia Hotel
051-757-1100, 051-757-2300
http://utopiahotel.co.kr (Korean)
50-3, Gwangan 3-dong, Suyeong-gu
₩74,380

3rd

B&B Hotel
051-742-3211, 051-742-3219
www.bnbhotel.co.kr
1130, Jung 1 (il)-dong, Haeundae-gu
₩130,000

Clover Tourist Hotel
051-205-6611, 051-204-7738
477-2, Goejeong 3 (sam)-dong, Saha-gu
₩31,500

Dadae Best Tourist Hotel
051-266-7600, 051-266-8500
769, Dadae 1 (il)-dong, Saha-gu
₩61,984

Hotel Korea City
051-643-7788, 051-645-7788
830-65, Beomil 2-dong, Dong-gu
₩55,000

Hotel San Francisco
051-611-0003, 051-625-2277
25-6, Namcheon-dong, Suyeong-gu
₩65,000

Mok Hwa
051-642-9000, 051-646-1569
830-124, Beomil 2-dong,
Dong-gu
₩45,455

Moonhwa Hot Spring Tourist Hotel
051-558-5505
135-4, Oncheon 1-dong, Dongnae-gu
₩30,000

More Tourist Hotel
051-803-0070, 051-802-5500
226-5, Bujeon 2-dong, Busanjin-gu
₩49,580

New-life Tourist Hotel
051-634-3001, 051-644-1238
830-172, Beomil 2-dong, Dong-gu
₩38,700

New Sungnam Tourist Hotel
051-243-8051, 051-242-2219
2-3, Chungmu 1-ga, Seo-gu
₩40,000

Su Tourist Hotel
051-246-4361, 051-246-4181
81-1, Nampo-dong, Jung-gu
₩80,000

UN Tourist Hotel
051-248-5181, 051-256-8600
www.unhotel.co.kr (Korean)
335-5, Amnam-dong, Seo-gu
₩90,000

DAEGU http://tour.daegu.go.kr
SUPER DELUXE

Hotel Inter-Burgo
053-952-0088, 053-953-2008
www.ibhotel.com
San 92-1, Manchon-dong, Suseong-gu
₩165,000

DELUXE

Daegu Grand Hotel
053-742-0001, 053-742-0002
www.taegugrand.co.kr
563-1, Beomeo-dong, Suseong-gu
₩214,876

Eldis Regent Hotel
053-253-7711, 053-256-0406
www.eldisregenthotel.com
360, Dongsan-dong, Jung-gu
₩145,200

GS Plaza Hotel
053-986-2500, 053-980-1567
http://gsplazahotel.co.kr
1060-1, Bangchon-dong, Dong-gu
₩140,000

Hotel Airport
053-260-0001, 053-260-0100
www.htlair.com
400-1, Jijeo-dong, Dong-gu
₩140,000

Hotel J's
053-756-6601, 053-756-6623
www.hotel-js.com
326-1, Sincheon 4 (sa)-dong, Dong-gu
₩130,000

Saint Western Hotel
053-589-6700, 053-593-3306
www.saintwestern.co.kr (Korean)
1198-6, Igok-dong, Dalseo-gu
₩135,000

Taegu Prince Hotel
053-628-1001, 053-650-5600
www.princehotel.co.kr
1824-2, Daemyeong-dong, Nam-gu
₩145,000

1st

Amigo Hotel
053-252-6001, 053-253-4121
www.hotelamigo.co.kr (Korean)
28, Haseo-dong, Jung-gu
₩100,000

Crown Tourist Hotel
053-755-3001, 053-755-3367
330-6, Sincheon 4 (sa)-dong, Dong-gu
₩55,000

Crystal Tourist Hotel
053-252-7799, 053-253-0323
www.crystalhotel.co.kr
1196-1, Duryu 1 (il)-dong, Dalseo-gu
₩80,000

Hotel Taegu Garden
053-471-9911, 053-472-7900
www.gardenhotel.co.kr
688-1, Bongdeok-dong, Nam-gu
₩69,213

Hotel Ariana
053-765-7776, 053-765-7157
www.ariana.co.kr (Korean)
200-1, Dusan-dong, Suseong-gu
₩80,991

Hotel Inter-Burgo Palgong
053-985-0808, 053-985-0888
http://palgong.inter-burgo.com (Korean)
90-1, Yongsu-dong, Dong-gu
₩74,380

Hotel New Young Nam
053-752-1001, 053-755-0086
www.nynhotel.com
177-7, Beomeo 2 (i)-dong, Suseong-gu
₩98,000

Hotel Taegu
053-559-2100, 053-558-4971
www.taeguhotel.co.kr
245-9, Naedang 4 (sa)-dong, Seo-gu
₩100,000

Hillside Tourist Hotel
053-982-0801, 053-983-0433
www.hillsidehotel.co.kr (Korean)
59-1, Yongsu-dong, Dong-gu
₩57,851

Hwang Gum Tourist Hotel
053-765-6006, 053-766-8004
847-1, Hwanggeum-dong, Suseong-gu
₩75,000

Hwang Sil Tourist Hotel
053-751-2301, 053-751-2305
www.hwangsil.co.kr
45-1, Sincheon 3 (sam)-dong, Dong-gu
₩55,000

Mt. Palgong Hot Spring Tourist Hotel
053-985-8080, 053-985-8097
89-16, Yongsu-dong, Dong-gu
₩80,000

New Samil Tourist Hotel
053-629-5501, 053-622-1501
200, Songhyeon-dong, Dalseo-gu
₩74,380

Soo Sung Tourist Hotel
053-763-7311, 053-764-0620
www.soosunghotel.co.kr (Korean)
888-2, Dusan-dong, Suseong-gu
₩97,521

2nd

Arirang Tourist Hotel
053-624-4000, 053-624-4240
www.hotelarirang.co.kr
474-5, Duryu 3 (sam)-dong, Dalseo-gu
₩61,983

Central Tourist Hotel
053-257-7111, 053-252-4568
23, Jongno 2 (i)-ga, Jung-gu
₩48,000

Dong Bang Tourist Hotel
053-982-1551, 053-982-7311
1006-34, Ipseok-dong, Dong-gu
₩35,000

Union Tourist Hotel
053-252-2221, 053-253-8571
http://unionhtl.co.kr (Korean)
1-9, Taepyeongno 2 (i)-ga, Jung-gu
₩42,000

INCHEON www.incheon.go.kr
SUPER DELUXE

Hyatt Regency Incheon
032-745-1234, 032-745-1010
www.hyattregencyincheon.com
2850, Unseo-dong, Jung-gu
₩300,000

Paradise Hotel Incheon
032-762-5181, 032-763-5281
www.paradiseincheon.co.kr
3-2, Hang-dong, Jung-gu
₩200,000

DELUXE

Best Western Premier Incheon Airport Hotel
032-743-1000, 032-743-1004
www.airporthotel.co.kr
2850-4 Int'l Business Center, Incheon Int'l Airport, Unseo-dong, Jung-gu, Incheon
₩200,000

Hotel Songdo Beach
032-832-2000, 032-832-1325

www.songdobeach.co.kr
812, Dongchun 1 (il)-dong, Yeonsu-gu
₩210,000

Royal Tourist Hotel
032-421-3300, 032-421-0473
www.royalhotel.co.kr
173-4, Ganseok-dong,
Namdong-gu
₩132,231

1st

Hotel Charis
032-556-0880, 032-556-0834
www.hotelcharis.com
428-2, Jakjeon-dong, Gyeyang-gu
₩69,000 − ₩79,000

Hotel Robert
032-421-9111, 032-421-8170
275-1, Ganseok-dong, Namdong-gu
₩160,000

Seohae Tourist Hotel
032-885-9981, 032-885-8209
www.hotelseohae.com
629-7, Yonghyeon 5 (o)-dong, Nam-gu
₩90,000

2nd

Bando Tourist Hotel
032-551-5959, 032-551-5962
www.bandohotel.net (Korean)
905-3, Jakjeon-dong,
Gyeyang-gu
₩60,000

Capital Hotel
032-545-2685, 032-545-6474
763-7, Gasan-dong, Gayang-gu
₩70,000

Cherbourg Tourist Hotel
032-752-0013, 032-752-0113
www.cherbourghotel.com (Korean)
703-41, Eurwang-dong, Jung-gu
₩132,000

Hotel Pupyong
032-504-8181, 032-504-8182
www.hppwed.com
181, Galsan-dong, Bupyeong-gu
₩103,000

New Pacific Tourist Hotel
032-886-1500, 032-886-1504
www.newpacific.co.kr
159-14, Sungui-dong, Nam-gu
₩500,000

Soobong Tourist Hotel
032-868-6611, 032-868-4333
www.soobonghotel.co.kr

618-2, Dohwa 1 (il)-dong, Nam-gu
₩80,000

Tourist Hotel June
032-746-4417, 032-752-3239
www.hoteljune.com
2805-2, Unseo-dong, Jung-gu
₩150,000

Winners Tourist Hotel
032-751-5322, 032-751-5334
www.hotelwinners.com
891,Eurwang-dong, Jung-gu
₩163,636

Zeumes Tourist Hotel
032-752-9600, 032-752-9604
www.hotelzeumes.co.kr
2805-3, Unseo-dong, Jung-gu
₩96,000

3rd

Carnegie Hotel
032-562-0511, 032-561-9959
245-3, Simgok-dong, Seo-gu
₩30,000

Chelsea Tourist Hotel
032-434-7517, 032-434-7520
www.chelseahotel.co.kr (Korean)
123-9, Ganseok 3 (sam)-dong, Namdong-gu
₩40,000

Choice Tourist Hotel
032-564-3832, 032-564-3834
245-9, Simgok-dong, Seo-gu
₩35,000

Dragon City Tourist Hotel
032-747-1010, 032-751-8123
857-1, Eurwang-dong, Jung-gu
₩120,000

Four Season Tourist Hotel
032-566-5740, 032-566-8558
242-13, Simgok-dong, Seo-gu
₩35,000

New Backwoon Hotel
032-522-9600, 032-522-9300
182-100, Sipjeong-dong, Bupyeong-gu
₩37,190

Sevilla Tourist Hotel
032-752-1170, 032-752-1175
www.hotelsevilla.co.kr
2801-4, Unseo-dong, Jung-gu
₩77,000

Incheon Airport Transit Hotel
032-743-3000, 032-743-3001
www.airgardenhotel.com
in Incheon International Airport
₩130,000

DAEJEON www.metro.daejeon.kr

DELUXE

Hotel Spapia
042-600-6000, 042-600-6060
www.hotelspapia.co.kr
545-5, Bongmyeong-dong, Yuseong-gu
₩145,000

Yousung Hotel
042-822-0811, 042-822-0041
www.yousunghotel.com
480, Bongmyeong-dong, Yuseong-gu
₩150,000

1st

Chateau Grace Hotel
042-639-0111, 042-639-0077
www.chateaugracehotel.com
72-5, Yongjeon-dong, Dong-gu
₩132,000

HongIn Hotel
042-822-2000, 042-822-9410
www.honginhotel.co.kr (Korean)
536-8, Bongmyeong-dong, Yuseong-gu
₩160,000

Hotel Adria
042-824-0211, 042-823-5805
www.hoteladria.co.kr (Korean)
442-5, Bongmyeong-dong,
Yuseong-gu
₩140,000

Hotel Chamonix
042-621-8400, 042-621-8409
63-31, Jeong-dong, Dong-gu
₩40,000

Hotel Expo
042-824-8080, 042-825-0023
544-1, Bongmyeong-dong,
Yuseong-gu
₩133,100

Legend Hotel
042-822-4000, 042-825-2521
www.legendhotel.co.kr (Korean)
547-5, Bongmyeong-dong, Yuseong-gu
₩140,000

Royal Tourist Hotel
042-825-6700, 042)825-6705
www.yusonroyalhotel.co.kr
546-5, Bongmyeong-dong, Yuseong-gu
₩120,000

2nd

Emperor Tourist Hotel
042-256-7000, 042-223-8500
47-55, Jung-dong, Dong-gu
₩40,000

Hanil Tourist Hotel
042-283-4401, 042-283-4407
296-6, Yongun-dong, Dong-gu
₩35,000

Hotel Gallery
042-825-6400, 042-825-0194
www.galleryhotel.co.kr
548-13, Bongmyeong-dong, Yuseong-gu
₩98,000

Yuseong Korea Tourist Hotel
042-823-1916, 042-823-4905
549-15, Bongmyeong-dong, Yuseong-gu
₩50,000

GWANGJU www.visit.gwangju.kr
DELUXE

Hotel Prado
062-654-9999, 062-654-0606
http://pradohotel.co.kr
638-1, Baegun-dong, Nam-gu
₩100,000

Kwangju Prince Hotel
062-524-0025, 062-524-0026
www.prince-hotel.co.kr
65-8, Unam-dong, Buk-gu
₩132,230

Shinyang Park Hotel
062-228-8000, 062-232-3731
www.shinyangparkhotel.com (Korean)
20-8, Jisan-dong, Dong-gu
₩130,000

1st

Firenze Hotel
062-384-9600, 062-984-8888
www.firenzehotel.co.kr
1250-9, Chipyeong-dong, Seo-gu
₩160,000

Grand Hotel
062-224-6111, 062-224-8933
121, Bullo-dong, Dong-gu
₩100,000

Hotel Central
062-383-7575, 062-383-6688
www.hotelcentral.co.kr
1218-3, Chipyeong-dong, Seo-gu
₩118,800

Hotel Hiddink Continental
062-227-8500, 062-234-8848
www.hotel-continental.co.kr
160-1, Bullo-dong, Dong-gu
₩121,000

Hotel Palace Tourist
062-222-2525, 062-236-2514
www.hotelpalace.co.kr (Korean)

11-4, Hwanggeum-dong, Dong-gu
₩55,000

Koreana Tourist Hotel
062-526-8600, 062-526-8666
120-9, Sinan-dong, Dong-gu
₩40,000

Masters Tourist Hotel
062-382-8493, 062-384-1800
Chipyeong-dong, Seo-gu
₩176,000

Mudeung Park Hotel
062-226-0011, 062-227-8777
www.hotelmudeungpark.co.kr
63-1, Jisan-dong, Dong-gu
₩115,000

2nd

Empire Tourist Hotel
062-962-2000, 062-971-0036
www.kjempire.com
878-1, Wolgye-dong, Gwangsan-gu
₩84,700

Grand Prix Tourist Hotel
062-225-7222, 062-224-0766
www.gdphotel.com (Korean)
868-4, Hak 2 (i)-dong, Dong-gu
₩60,000

Kukje Tourist Hotel
062-673-0700, 062-670-0707
www.kukjehotel.com
1287-2, Juwol-dong, Nam-gu
₩109,000

Santamo Tourist Hotel
062-956-5000, 062-956-3000
www.hotelsantamo.co.kr (Korean)
1585-2, Usan-dong, Gwangsan-gu
₩50,000

3rd

Kwangju Tourist Hotel
062-223-1256, 062-225-8020
33-2, Sugi-dong, Dong-gu
₩50,000

Walker Hill Tourist Hotel
062-972-6600, 062-972-6599
682-2, Ssangam-dong, Gwangsan-gu
₩40,000

ULSAN www.ulsan.go.kr
SUPER DELUXE

Hotel Hyundai Ulsan
052-251-2233, 052-232-7170
www.hyundaihotel.com
283, Jeonha-dong, Dong-gu
₩180,000

Lotte Hotel
052-960-1000, 052-960-4334
www.hotellotte.co.kr
1480-1, Samsan-dong, Nam-gu
₩200,000

1st

Olympia Tourist Hotel
052-271-8401, 052-271-8410
1128-1, Sinjeong 2 (i)-dong, Nam-gu
₩90,000

2nd

Taehwa Hotel
052-273-3301, 052-273-3305
1406-6, Sinjeong-dong, Nam-gu
₩60,750

3rd

Joong Ang Hotel
052-245-3770, 052-245-3779
219-2, Okgyo-dong, Jung-gu
₩55,000

GYEONGGI-DO www.gg.go.kr
DELUXE

Hotel Castle
031-211-6666, 031-212-8811
www.hcastle.co.kr
144-4, Uman-dong, Paldal-gu, Suwon
₩227,273

Hotel Miranda
031-633-2001, 031-633-2038
www.mirandahotel.com
408-1, Anheung-dong, Icheon
₩195,000

Star Pyeong Taek Lake Tourist Hotel
031-683-8899, 031-683-6999
www.starr.co.kr (Korean)
536-26, Gwongwan-ri, Hyeondeok-myeon, Pyeongtaek
₩140,000

The Koryo Hotel
032-329-0001, 032-324-0648
www.koryohotel.co.kr
548-5, Sang-dong, Wonmi-gu, Bucheon
₩170,000

1st

Diana Hotel
02-2625-2000, 02-2616-3631
www.hoteldiana.co.kr
447, Cheolsan-dong, Gwangmyeong
₩110,000

Evergreen Tourist Hotel
031-885-0321, 031-855-5108

www.evergreenhotel.co.kr (Korean)
386-9, Seokhyeon-ri, Jangheung-myeon,
Yangju-si
₩99,000

Glory Hotel
031-441-1590, 031-441-1598
www.hotelglory.com (Korean)
359-29, Anyang 6-dong, Manan-gu,
Anyang
₩121,000

Grace Hotel
02-504-2211, 02-503-8035
1-15, Byeoryang-dong, Gwacheon
₩76,000

Hotel Aria House
031-767-2000, 031-767-2080
www.hotelariahouse.com (Korean)
250-3, Bunwon-ri, Namjong-myeon,
Gwangju
₩115,000

Hotel Kabo
031-658-7700, 031-658-7710
www.hotelkabo.com
845-1, Bijeon 2 (i)-dong, Pyeongtaek
₩99,174

Hotel Kwang Myong
02-2619-3001, 02-2683-5661
http://kmhotel.co.kr
423, Cheolsan-dong, Gwangmyeong
₩170,000

Hotel Mirama
031-414-0700, 031-414-0181
www.mirama.co.kr (Korean)
537-9, Gojan-dong, Ansan
₩99,174

Hotel Rasung
031-480-6161, 031-480-6190
846-3, Wongok-dong, Ansan
₩66,000

Hotel Regency
031-246-4141, 031-243-9296
www.htregency.co.kr
47, Gucheon-dong, Paldal-gu,
Suwon
₩110,000

Hotel Ritz
031-224-1100, 031-224-1900
www.hotelritz.co.kr (Korean)
1133-8, Ingye-dong, Paldal-gu,
Suwon
₩200,000

Hotel Song Tan
031-666-5101, 031-662-5100
274-190, Sinjang-dong, Pyeongtaek
₩100,000

Kyonggi Tourist Hotel
031-668-1900, 031-668-4255
www.kghotel.com
240-3, Sinjang-dong, Pyeongtaek
₩100,000

New Grand Hotel
031-846-3737, 031-842-3505
199-3, Uijeongbu 1-dong, Uijeongbu
₩80,000

Newtown Tourist Hotel
031-711-6900, 031-718-6773
www.newtownhotel.co.kr
157, Geumgok-dong,
Bundang-gu, Seongnam
₩60,116

Prince Tourist Hotel
031-611-6000, 031-611-6006
274-273, Sinjang 2 (i)-dong, Pyeongtaek
₩72,000

Pyungtaek Tourist Hotel
031-654-3333, 031-654-2231
62-10, Pyeongtaek-dong, Pyeongtaek
₩75,000

Siheung Tourist Hotel
031-433-0001, 031-433-9933
http://siheunghotel.net (Korean)
1622-6, Jeongwang-dong, Siheung
₩120,000

West Hotel
031-683-8531, 031-683-8537
658-2, Hyeonhwa-ri, Anjung-eup,
Pyeongtaek
₩100,000

Yakam Tourist Hotel
031-989-7000, 031-988-6100
www.yakam.co.kr (Korean)
450-2, Yagam-ri, Daegot-myeon,
Gimpo
₩70,000

2nd

Calson Tourist Hotel
031-656-0074, 031-656-0390
291-11, Pyeongtaek-dong, Pyeongtaek
₩70,000

Central Tourist Hotel
031-246-0011, 031-246-0018
1-2, Gyo-dong, Paldal-gu, Suwon
₩64,809

Greenpia Tourist Hotel
031-222-2070, 031-222-2079
www.hotelgreenpia.com
180-371, Annyeong-ri, Taean-myeon,
Hwaseong
₩67,000

Hantangang Tourist Hotel
031-832-8091, 031-835-8095
95, Jeonggok-ri, Jeongok-eup,
Yeoncheon
₩50,000

Kwachun Tourist Hotel
02-504-0071, 02-504-0078
1-8, Byeoryang-dong, Gwacheon
₩57,025

Leeds Bill Tourist Hotel
032-326-8181, 032-324-1771
538-5, Sang-dong, Wonmi-gu,
Bucheon
₩70,000

Prince Tourist Hotel
031-454-6300, 031-454-6400
78-3, Geumjeong-dong, Gunpo
₩120,000

Rio Hotel
031-417-4100, 031-417-4104
119-2, Il-dong, Ansan
₩35,000

Samwon Plaza Hotel
031-448-6671, 031-448-6687
www.samwonhotel.co.kr (Korean)
674-251, Anyang 1 (il)-dong,
Manan-gu, Anyang
₩123,970

Seol Bong Tourist Hotel
031-635-5701, 031-633-6305
www.seolbong.co.kr
313-5, Anheung-dong, Icheon
₩62,500

Seowon Tourist Hotel
031-407-9031, 031-406-7903
1198, Seo-dong, Ansan
₩132,000

Taepyungyang Tourist Hotel
031-417-4321, 031-417-4326
1198-4, Seo-dong, Ansan
₩80,000

Theme Park Tourist Hotel
032-329-1100, 032-329-1106
www.themeparkhotel.co.kr/kor
531-6, Sang-dong, Wonmi-gu, Bucheon
₩80,000

Young Chon
031-663-4000, 031-663-2527
304-14, Sinjang 1 (il)-dong, Pyeongtaek
₩90,000

YuLim Tourist Hotel
031-865-2101, 031-865-5198
728, Saengyeon-dong, Dongducheon
₩55,000

3rd

California Tourist Hotel
031-907-5060, 031-905-7547
www.california-hotel.co.kr
1307-1, Baekseok-dong, Ilsan-gu, Goyang
₩75,000

Enterprise Tourist Hotel
031-691-7111, 031-691-3337
www.hotelenterprise.co.kr
136-10, Anjeong-ri, Paengseong-eup, Pyeongtaek
₩75,000

Hotel Rear
031-841-2121, 031-841-2524
71-3, Cheonghak-ri, Byeollae-myeon, Namyangju
₩80,000

Kapyung Tourist Hotel
031-581-0505, 031-581-3553
403, Eumnae-ri, Gapyeong-eup, Gapyeong
₩30,000

Koam Tourist Hotel
031-445-6601, 031-446-7646
www.koamhotel.com
431-10, Anyang 6 (yuk)-dong, Anyang
₩40,000

Tongduchun Tourist Hotel
031-862-7171, 031-862-7174
www.ddchotel.com (Korean)
548-5, Saengyeon-dong, Dongducheon
₩500,000

GANGWON-DO http://gangwon.to
SUPER DELUXE

Kangwon Land Hotel & Casino
033-590-7700, 033-590-6300
www.kangwoncasino.co.kr
424, Sabuk-ri, Sabuk-eup, Jeongseon
₩200,000

DELUXE

Hotel Hyundai Gyeongpodae
033-644-2181, 033-644-2180
http://hotel.e-hyundai.com
274-1, Gangmun-dong, Gangneung
₩181,500

Hotel Odaesan
033-330-5000, 033-330-5123
www.hotelodaesan.co.kr
221-1, Ganpyeong-ri, Jinbu-myeon, Pyeongchang
₩144,000

Hotel Palace
033-575-7000, 033-570-1558
www.palace-hotel.co.kr
1, Jeongha-dong, Samcheok
₩126,000

Hotel Sorak Park
033-636-7711, 033-636-7732
www.hotelsorakpark.com
74-3, Seorak-dong, Sokcho
₩160,000

Kangwon Land Golftel
033-590-7700, 033-590-7330
www.kangwoncasino.co.kr
31-139, Gohan 9 (gu)-ri, Gohan-eup, Jeongseon
₩130,000

Kensington Stars Hotel
033-635-4001, 033-635-4011
www.kensington.co.kr
106-1, Seorak-dong, Sokcho
₩164,500

Naksan Beach Hotel
033-672-4000, 033-672-4022
www.naksanbeach.co.kr
3-2, Jeonjin-ri, Ganghyeon-myeon, Yangyang
₩161,157

Phoneix Park The Hotel
033-333-6000, 033-330-6209
www.phoenixpark.co.kr
1095, Myeonon-ri, Bongpyeong-myeon, Pyeongchang
₩254,000

Yongpyong Resort
033-330-7111, 033-335-0160
www.yongpyong.co.kr
130, Yongsan-ri, Doam-myeon, Pyeongchang
₩193,600

1st

Bears Tourist Hotel
033-256-2525, 033-256-2530
300-3, Samcheon-dong, Chuncheon
₩80,000

Chuncheon Sejong Hotel
033-252-1191, 033-254-3347
San 15-3, Bongui-dong, Chuncheon
₩74,720

Hong Cheon Grand Tourist Hotel
033-433-7600, 033-433-9271 62-10, Jin-ri, Hongcheon-eup, Hongcheon-gun
₩100,000

Hotel Gangneung
033-641-7701, 033-641-7712
www.gangneunghotel.co.kr (Korean)
1117, Ponam-dong, Gangneung
₩70,000

Intercrew Hotel
033-533-7722, 033-531-7371
460-3, Cheongok-dong, Donghae
₩70,000

Le Hotel Gyungpo Beach
033-644-2277, 033-642-0113
www.kyungpobeach.co.kr (Korean)
303-4, Gangmun-dong, Gangneung
₩120,000

Mangsang Grand Tourist Hotel
033-534-6682, 033-534-6687
www.mangsanggrand.co.kr (Korean)
396-18, Mangsang-dong, Donghae
₩96,000

New Dong Hae
033-533-9215, 033-533-1919
www.hotelnd.com (Korean)
484, Cheongok-dong, Donghae
₩80,000

Sokcho Beach Tourist Hotel
033-631-8700, 033-631-6758
http://hotelsokcho.com (Korean)
478-19, Jungang-dong, Sokcho
₩112,000

Wonju Tourist Hotel
033-743-1241, 033-748-2425
63, Jungang-dong, Wonju
₩100,000

2nd

Mt. Sorak Tourist Hotel
033-636-7101, 033-636-7106
www.sorakhotel.co.kr (Korean)
151, Seorak-dong, Sokcho
₩96,800

Sun Castle Tourist Hotel
033-661-1950, 033-661-1958
www.suncastlehotel.co.kr (Korean)
San 84-2, Jumunjin-ri, Jumunjin-eup, Gangneung
₩50,000

3rd

3.1 Hotel
033-343-6601, 033-343-5221
385-12, Eupsang-ri, Hoengseong-eup, Hoengseong
₩41,322

CHUNGCHEONGBUK-DO
www.cbtour.net
DELUXE

Cheongpung Lake
043-640-7000, 043-640-7007
www.cheongpungresort.co.kr
(Korean)

99, Gyo-ri, Cheongpung-myeon, Jecheon
₩105,000

Backje Tourist Hotel
043-236-7979, 043-236-0979
1023, Gagyeong-dong, Heungdeok-gu, Cheongju
₩107,488

Cheongju Tourist Hotel
043-264-2181, 043-266-8215
www.cheongjuhotel.com (Korean)
844, Bokdae-dong, Cheongju
₩64,000

Cheongju Royal Tourist Hotel
043-221-1300, 043-221-1319
227-22, Seomun-dong, Cheongju
₩72,000

Cheongpung Hill
043-640-7100, 043-640-7007
www.cheongpungresort.co.kr (Korean)
33, Gyo-ri, Cheongpung-myeon, Jecheon
₩105,000

Chojeong Yaksu Spatel
043-210-9900, 043-217-6505
www.spatel.co.kr (Korean)
334-24, Chojeong-ri, Naesu-eup, Cheongwon
₩90,000

Chosun Tourist Hotel
043-848-8833, 043-848-8830
www.suanbochosun.com
109-1, Oncheon-ri, Sangmo-myeon, Chungji
₩165,000

Chungju Grand Hotel
043-848-5554, 043-848-4456
www.cjgrand.com (Korean)
855, Bongbang-dong, Chungju
₩110,000

Danyang Tourist Hotel
043-423-7070, 043-423-4234
www.danyanghotel.com
264-2, Sangjin-ri, Danyang-eup, Danyang
₩99,000

Friendly Hotel
043-848-9900, 043-842-9403
San 102-1, Hoam-dong, Chungju
₩81,000

Jeungpyung Park Tourist Hotel
043-836-9889, 043-836-9888
45-4, Chojeong-ri, Jeungpyeong-eup, Jeungpyeong
₩81,000

Lake Hills Hotel Songnisan
043-542-5281, 043-542-5198
www.lakehills.co.kr (Korean)
198, Sanae-ri, Naesongni-myeon, Boeun
₩148,000

Myong Am Tourist Hotel
043-257-7451, 043-257-7458
www.hotelmyongam.co.kr (Korean)
2-1, Myeongam-dong, Cheongju
₩100,000

Newvera Tourist Hotel
043-235-8181, 043-235-8180
1207, Gagyeong-dong, Heungdeok-gu, Cheongju
₩90,900

Reeho Tourist Hotel
043-233-8800, 043-232-8818
www.hotelreeho.com (Korean)
35-7, Biha-dong, Heungdeok-gu, Cheongju
₩120,000

SangNok Hotel
043-845-3500, 043-845-7878
www.sangnokhotel.co.kr (Korean)
292, Oncheon-ri, Sangmo-myeon, Chungju
₩80,990

Suanbo Park Hotel
043-846-2331, 043-846-3705
www.suanbopark.co.kr (Korean)
838-1, Oncheon-ri, Sangmo-myeon, Chungju
₩138,842

2nd

Jecheon Tourist Hotel
043-643-4111, 043-643-4114
11-1, Myeong-dong, Jecheon
₩70,000

Pastel Hotel
043-643-4111, 043-643-1114 569, Munhwa-dong, Chungju
₩80,000

3rd

Gallery Tourist Hotel
043-267-1121, 043-263-9532
1831, Bongmyeong 2 (i)-dong, Cheongju
₩95,000

Jincheon Tourist Hotel
043-533-0010, 043-533-0013
240-1, Eumnae-ri, Jincheon-eup, Jincheon
₩39,273

CHUNGCHEONGNAM-DO
www.chungnam.net

DELUXE

Onyang Grand Hotel
041-543-9711, 041-543-9729
www.grand-hotel.co.kr
300-28, Oncheon-dong, Asan
₩140,000

Onyang Hot Spring Hotel
041-540-1201, 041-540-1234
www.onyanghotel.co.kr
242-10, Oncheon-dong, Asan
₩140,000

1st

Ducksan Spa Hotel
041-338-5000, 041-337-9900
15, Sadong-ri, Deoksan-myeon, Yesan
₩121,000

Onyang Palace Hotel
041-547-2500, 041-542-6100
228-1, Oncheon-dong, Asan
₩145,200

Paradise Hotel DOGO
041-542-6031, 041-542-3425
www.paradisehoteldogo.co.kr (Korean)
180-1, Gigok-ri, Dogo-myeon, Asan
₩80,000

2nd

Gaya Hotel
041-337-0101, 041-337-0110
163-1, Sinpyeong-ri, Deoksan-myeon, Yesan
₩35,000

Interpark Tourist Hotel
041-542-6000, 041-533-0228
82-12, Oncheon-dong, Asan
₩100,000

New Korea Tourist Hotel
041-542-8151, 041-542-8155
230-6, Oncheon-dong, Asan
₩60,000

JEOLLABUK-DO
www.provin.jeonbuk.kr

SUPER DELUXE

Tirol
063-320-7617, 063-320-7609
www.mujuresort.com
San 43-15, Simgok-ri, Seolcheon-myeon, Muju
₩338,800

DELUXE

Jeonju Core Hotel
063-285-1100, 063-285-5707
627-3, Seonosong-dong, Deokjin-gu, Jeonju

₩150,000

Jeonju Core Riviera Hotel
063-232-7000, 063-232-7100
www.core-riviera.co.kr
26-5, Pungnam-dong 3 (sam)-ga,
Wansan-gu, Jeonju
₩140,000

1st

Gunsan Walkerhill Tourist Hotel
063-453-0005, 063-453-8881
428-4, Seongdoek-ri, Seongsanmyeon,
Gunsan
₩165,500

Iksan Grand Tourist Hotel
063-843-7777, 063-843-7712
329-2, Pyeonghwa-dong, Iksan
₩77,440

Kunsan Tourist Hotel
063-443-0811, 063-443-0815
462-1, Gyeongjang-dong, Gunsan
₩60,000

Sun Woun San Tourist Hotel
063-561-3377, 063-561-4700
www.swhotel.co.kr (Korean)
287-5, Samin-ri, Asan-myeon, Gochang
₩70,000

2nd

Chonju Tourist Hotel
063-280-7700, 063-283-4478
28, Daga-dong 3 (sam)-ga, Wansan-gu,
Jeonju
₩70,000

Dae Doon Mountain Hot Spring Hotel
063-263-1260, 063-263-8069
611-70, Sanbuk-ri, Unju-myeon, Wanju
₩70,000

Iksan Hannover Tourist Hotel
063-852-1588, 063-853-1588
54-5, Jungang 2 (i)-ga, Iksan
₩109,091

JEOLLANAM-DO
www.jeonnam.go.kr
DELUXE

Yeosu Beach Tourist Hotel
061-663-2011, 061-664-2114
www.ybhotel.com
346, Chungmu-dong, Yeosu
₩110,000

1st

City Tourist Hotel
061-753-4000, 061-753-3049
www.cityhotel.co.kr
22-24, Namnae-dong, Suncheon
₩65,000

Chirisan Plaza Hotel
061-782-2171, 061-782-3675
32-1, Hwangjeon-ri, Masan-myeon, Gurye
₩176,000

Jirisan Spa Tourist Hotel
061-783-2900, 061-783-1966
www.spaland.co.kr (Korean)
522, Gungsan-ri, Sandong-myeon, Gurye
₩79,200

Shinan Beach Hotel
061-243-3399, 061-243-0030
www.shinanbeachhotel.com
440-4, Jukgyo-dong, Mokpo
₩94,400

Suncheon Royal Tourist Hotel
061-741-7000, 061-741-7180
www.royaltourist.co.kr
32-8, Jangcheon-dong, Suncheon
₩90,000

Tourist Hotel Noblesse
061-691-1996, 061-691-1995
77-1, Hak-dong, Yeosu
₩71,000

Wolchulsan Spa Hotel
061)473-6311, 061-473-6320
www.wolchulspa.co.kr (Korean)
San 6-10, Haechang-ri, Gunseo-myeon,
Yeongam
₩96,800

2nd

Baeg Yang Tourist Hotel
061-392-0651, 061-392-0654
www.baekyanghotel.co.kr (Korean)
333-3, Yaksu-ri, Bukha-myeon,
Jangseong
₩160,000

Chambord Tourist Hotel
061-662-6111, 061-662-1929
www.chambord.co.kr (Korean)
1054-1, Gonghwa-dong, Yeosu
₩90,000

Chirisan Swiss Tourist Hotel
061-783-0700, 061-782-1571
427-1, Hwangjeon-ri, Masan-myeon,
Gurye
₩96,800

Daegok
061-363-7400, 061-363-2485
74-3, Ungok-ri, Osan-myeon,
Gokseong
₩40,000

Hotel Sea World
061-552-3005, 061-552-3009
www.seaworldhotel.co.kr (Korean)
3-22, Gayong-ri, Wando-eup, Wando
₩79,000

3rd

Aria Hotel
061-352-7676, 061-353-5525
8, Noksa-ri, Yeonggwang-eup,
Yeonggwang
₩40,000

Baekje
061-242-4411/4, 061-242-9550
10-13, Sangnak-dong 1 (il)-ga, Mokpo
₩40,000

Haenam Tourist Hotel
061-533-1222, 061-533-9003
79, Eumnae-ri, Haenam-eup, Haenam
₩60,000

Yosu
061-662-3131, 061-662-3491
766, Gonghwa-dong, Yeosu
₩40,000

GYEONGSANGBUK-DO
www.gbtour.net
SUPER DELUXE

Gyeongju Hilton
054-745-7788, 054-745-7799
www.kyongjuhilton.co.kr (Korean)
370, Sinpyeong-dong, Gyeongju
₩210,000

Hotel Concorde
054-745-7000, 054-745-7010
www.concorde.co.kr
410, Sinpyeong-dong, Gyeongju
₩140,000

Hotel Hyundai
054-748-2233, 054-748-8234
www.hyundaihotel.com
477-2, Sinpyeong-dong, Gyeongju
₩200,000

Kolon Hotel
054-746-9001, 054-746-6331
www.kolonhotel.co.kr
111-1, Ma-dong, Gyeongju
₩148,760 – ₩165,289

DELUXE

The Westin Chosun Hotel
054-745-7701, 054-740-8349
www.chosunhotel.net
410-2, Sinpyeong-dong,
Gyeongju
₩200,000

Cygnus Hotel
054-275-2000, 054-275-2218
www.hotelcygnus.co.kr (Korean)
145-21, Yongheung 2 (i)-dong, Pohang
₩145,200

Gumi Century Hotel
054-478-0100, 054-475-5550
www.gumicentury.co.kr
92-10, Imsu-dong, Gumi
₩143,000

Kyongju KyoYuk MunHwa HoeKwan
054-745-8100, 054-748-8394
www.temf.co.kr
150-2, Sinpyeong-dong, Gyeongju
₩150,000 – ₩190,000

1st

Andong Park Tourist Hotel
054-859-1500, 054-857-5445
www.andonghotel.com
324, Unheung-dong, Andong
₩58,500

Bestwestern Gumi Hotel
054-462-6000, 054-462-6015
205, Gongdan-dong, Gumi
₩96,250

Gyeongju Chosun Spa Hotel
054-740-9600, 054-740-9601
www.chosunspahotel.com (Korean)
452-1, Sipyeong-dong, Gyeongju
₩90,909

Hotel Deok Gu Spa
054-782-0677, 054-783-5169
575, Deokgu-ri, Buk-myeon, Uljin
₩100,000

Hotel Park Business
054-451-9000, 054-451-9038
www.hotelparkbusiness.com
150-1, Namtong-dong, Gumi
₩81,818

Kumi Tourist Hotel
054-451-2000, 054-451-2002
1032-5, Wonpyeong 1 (il)-dong, Gumi
₩99,000

Kimchon Park Hotel
054-437-8000, 054-437-8010
www.kimchonpark.co.kr (Korean)
327-3, Hangcheon-ri,
Taehang-myeon, Gimcheon
₩96,000

Mungyeong Tourist Hotel
054-571-8001, 054-571-8006
288-5, Sangcho-ri,
Mungyeong-eup, Mungyeong
₩90,000

Rio Tourist Hotel
054-461-0022, 054-461-8965
199-1, Gongdan-dong, Gumi
₩105,000

Sangdae Hot Spring Tourist Hotel
053-815-8001, 054-852-5353
www.sdspa.com (Korean)
590, Sangdae-ri, Namsan-myeon,
Gyeongsan
₩80,000

2nd

Bulguksa Tourist Hotel
054-746-1911, 054-746-6604
648-1, Jinhyeon-dong, Gyeongju
₩58,000

Capital Tourist Hotel
054-451-3600, 054-453-9779
964-64, Wonpyeong 1 (il)-dong, Gumi
₩105,000

Commodore Hotel Pohang Beach
054-241-1400, 054-242-7534
311-2, Songdo-dong, Nam-gu, Pohang
₩63,636

Juwangsan Spa Tourist Hotel
054-874-7000, 054-874-7007
www.juwangspahotel.co.kr (Korean)
69-2, Wolmak-ri, Cheongsong-eup,
Cheongsong
₩123,967

Kumo Tourist Hotel
054-451-3700, 054-452-0539
130-30, Wonpyeong-dong, Gumi
₩80,000

Kyongju Tourist Hotel
054-745-7123, 054-745-7129
www.sangjuhotel.co.kr (Korean)
645, Sinpyeong-dong, Gyeongju
₩48,400 – 75,000

Olympus Tourist Hotel
054-241-6001, 054-241-6002
438-1, Songdo-dong, Nam-gu, Pohang
₩60,000

SangJu Tourist Hotel
054-536-3900, 054-536-8410
121-1, Seoseong-dong, Sangju
₩112,000

Sungryu Park Hotel
054-787-3711, 054-787-3081
www.sungryu.co.kr (Korean)
968-5, Onjeong-ri, Onjeong-myeon, Uljin
₩47,000 – 58,000

Sun Prince Tourist Hotel
054-242-2800, 054-242-6006
17, Jungang-dong, Buk-gu, Pohang
₩48,000

Swiss Rosen Hotel
054-748-4848, 054-748-0094
www.swissrosen.co.kr (Korean)
242-19, Sinpyeong-dong, Gyeongju
₩45,000

3rd

Bellus Tourist Hotel
054-741-3335, 054-741-3340
www.bellushotel.com (Korean)
130-6, Noseo-dong, Gyeongju
₩60,000 – 70,000

Donghae Beach Tourist Hotel
054-734-5400, 054-734-5518
www.e-beachhotel.com (Korean)
66-5, Namho-ri, Namjeong-myeon,
Yeongdeok
₩120,000

Gyeong-ju Park Tourist Hotel
054-742-8805, 054-742-8808
www.gjpark.com (Korean)
170-1, Noseo-dong, Gyeongju
₩65,000

Seokgulam Spa Hotel
054-383-0002, 054-383-2212
32, Chunsan-ri, Bugye-myeon,
Gunwi
₩50,000

Seokjeong Hot Spring Hotel
053-814-2580, 053-811-9359
559, Hyeopseok-ri, Namcheon-myeon,
Gyeongsan
₩94,000

Sunsan Tourist Hotel
054-481-1010, 054-482-7004
327-5, Dongbu-ri, Seonsan-eup, Gumi
₩37,000

Yes Tourist Hotel
054-474-0110, 054-474-0357
www.yeshotel.net (Korean)
321-33, Hwangsang-dong, Gumi
₩70,000

Yongam Spa Hotel
054-371-5500, 054-371-5508
929, Samsin-ri, Hwayang-eup, Cheongdo
₩68,000 – 78,000

GYEONGSANGNAM-DO
www.gntour.com

DELUXE

Changwon Hotel
055-283-5551, 055-282-9944
www.changwonhotel.co.kr

99-4, Jungang-dong, Changwon
₩135,000

Dongbang Tourist Hotel
055-743-0131/9, 055-742-6786
www.hoteldongbang.com
803-4, Okbong-dong, Jinju
₩115,000

Hotel International
055-281-1001, 055-284-2000
www.hotelinternational.co.kr
97-4, Jungang-dong, Changwon
₩135,000

Lake Hills Hotel
055-536-5181, 055-536-6427
www.lakehills.co.kr
213-19, Geomun-ri, Bugok-myeon, Changyeong
₩193,600

1st

Admiral Hotel
055-687-3761, 055-687-3934
www.admiralhotel.co.kr
330-4, Okpo 1 (il)-dong, Geoje
₩72,728

Bugok Hawaii Hotel
055-536-6331, 055-521-0346
www.bugokhawaii.co.kr
195-7, Geomun-ri, Bugok-myeon, Changyeong
₩96,000

Bugok Park Tourist Hotel
055-536-6211, 055-536-5152
216-16, Geomun-ri, Bugok-myeon, Changyeong
₩64,000

Bugok Royal Hotel
055-536-6661, 055-536-6500
215-1, Geomun-ri, Bugok-myeon, Changyeong
₩49,000

Canberra Hotel
055-268-5000, 055-268-5018
97-6, Jungang-dong, Changwon
₩104,000

Hotel Chungmu
055-645-2091, 055-642-8877
1, Donam-dong, Tongyeong
₩82,600

Hotel Dragon
055-237-1001, 055-277-1488
34-1, Pallyong-dong, Changwon
₩100,000

Hotel Haeinsa
055-933-2000, 055-933-2989
www.haeinsahotel.co.kr
1230-112, Chiin-ri, Gaya-myeon, Hapcheon
₩70,000

Hotel Tongdosa
055-382-7117/9, 055-383-1374
322-13, Chosan-ri, Habuk-myeon, Yangsan
₩89,256

Kimhae Hotel
055-335-0101, 055-334-4717
827-4, Buwon-dong, Gimhae
₩66,668

Masan Royal Hotel
055-244-1150, 055-245-1150
215, Sangnam-dong, Happo-gu, Masan
₩95,041

New Geochang Tourist Hotel
055-945-3333, 055-945-1439 940-1, Songjeong-ri, Geochang-eup, Geochang
₩60,000

Savoy Tourist Hotel
055-247-4455, 055-241-0550
8-2, Sanho-dong, Happo-gu, Masan
₩121,000

2nd

Arirang Tourist Hotel
055-294-2211, 055-294-2111
229-17, Seokjeon 2 (i)-dong, Hoewon-gu, Masan
₩80,000

Garden Tourist Hotel
055-536-5771, 055-536-5780
221-1, Geomun-ri, Bugok-myeon, Changyeong
₩49,000

Geoje Tourist Tourist
055-632-7002, 055-632-7009
33-30, Gohyeon-ri, Sinhyeon-eup, Geoje
₩64,000

Jayeon Tourist Hotel
055-381-1010, 055-481-8180 618-2, Sunji-ri, Habuk-myeon, Yangsan
₩57,851

Nice Hotel
055-552-8090, 055-552-1809
889, Yongwon-dong, Jinhae
₩60,000 – 70,000

Samcheonpo Haesang
055-832-3004, 055-832-3773
598, Daebang-dong, Sacheon
₩136,000

3rd

Prince Tourist Hotel
055-346-2705
555-11, Seolchang-ri, Jinyeong-eup, Gimhae
₩40,000

Green June Tourist Hotel
055-552-9001, 055-552-8462
532-3, Yongwon-dong, Jinhae
₩50,000

JEJUDO ISLAND
http://cyber.jeju.go.kr

SUPER DELUXE

Cheju Grand Hotel
064-747-5000, 064-742-3150
www.oraresort.co.kr
263-15, Yeon-dong, Jeju
₩195,000

Cheju Oriental Hotel
064-752-8222, 064-752-9777
www.oriental.co.kr
1197, Samdo 2 (i)-dong, Jeju
₩164,560

Crowne Plaza Hotel & Casino Jeju
064-741-8000, 064-758-4111
www.crowneplaza.co.kr
291-30, Yeon-dong, Jeju
₩136,000

Hyatt Regency Cheju
064-733-1234, 064-732-2039
www.hyattcheju.com
3039-1, Saekdal-dong, Seogwipo
₩310,000

Jeju KAL Hotel
064-724-2001, 064-720-6515
www.kalhotel.co.kr
1691-9, Ido 1 (il)-dong, Jeju
₩225,000

Jeju Pacific Hotel
064-758-2500, 064-758-2521
www.jejupacific.co.kr
159-1, Yongdam 1 (il)-dong, Jeju
₩280,000

Lotte Hotel Jeju
064-731-1000, 064-738-7305
www.lottehotel.co.kr
2812-4, Saekdal-dong, Seogwipo
₩320,000

Paradise Hotel Jeju
064-763-2100, 064-732-9355
www.paradisehotelcheju.co.kr
511, Topyeong-dong, Seogwipo
₩370,000

Ramada Plaza Jeju
064-729-8100, 064-729-8610
www.ramadajeju.co.kr
1255, Samdo 2 (i)-dong, Jeju
₩280,000 – 320,000

The Shilla Cheju Hotel
064-738-4466, 064-735-5415
http://cheju.shilla.net
3039-3, Saekdal-dong, Seogwipo
₩325,000

The Suites Hotel
064-738-3800, 064-738-9990
www.suites.co.kr
2812-10, Saekdal-dong, Seogwipo
₩240,000

DELUXE

Jeju Royal Hotel
064-743-2222, 064-758-2521
www.jejupacific.co.kr/royal
272-34, Yeon-dong, Jeju
₩150,000

New Crown
064-742-1001, 064-742-7466
www.hotelnewcrown.co.kr
274-12, Yeon-dong, Jeju
₩180,000

Seogwipo KAL Hotel
064-733-2001, 064-733-9377
www.kalhotel.co.kr
486-3, Topyeong-dong, Seogwipo
₩225,000 – 265,000

Travellers Hotel Jeju
064-738-9000, 064-738-9009
www.happyjeju.net (Korean)
30, Hoesu-dong, Seogwipo
₩230,000

1st

Goodmorning Tourist Hotel
064-712-1600, 064-712-1603
www.goodmorninghotel.co.kr (Korean)
291-41, Yeon-dong, Jeju
₩120,000

Hotel Hana
064-738-7001, 064-738-7000
www.hotelhana.co.kr (Korean)
2821-2, Saekdal-dong, Seogwipo
₩120,000

Hotel Honey Crown
064-758-4200, 064-758-4303
1315, Ido 1 (il)-dong, Jeju
₩85,000

Hotel Milano Crown
064-746-7800, 064-746-7805
273-44, Yeon-dong, Jeju
₩140,000

Hotel Sam Hae In
064-742-7775, 064-746-7111
www.samhaein.co.kr (Korean)
260-9, Yeon-dong, Jeju
₩96,000

Hotel Sun Beach
064-732-0175, 064-732-0096
820-1, Seogwi-dong, Seogwipo
₩116,160

Jeju Greenville Hotel
064-732-8311, 064-763-3898
www.jejugreenvillehotel.com (Korean)
316-4, Seogwi-dong, Seogwipo
₩60,000

Jeju Hawaii Tourist Hotel
064-742-0061, 064-742-0064
www.jejuhawaii.co.kr
278-2, Yeon-dong, Jeju
₩120,000

Jeju Palace Tourist Hotel
064-753-8811, 064-753-8820
www.cjpalace.co.kr
1192-18, Samdo 2-dong, Jeju
₩96,000

Jeju Pearl Tourist Hotel
064-742-8871, 064-742-1221
www.pearlhotel.co.kr (Korean)
277-2, Yeon-dong, Jeju
₩120,000

Jeju Seoul Tourist Hotel
064-752-2211, 064-751-1701
www.jejuseoul.co.kr (Korean)
1192-20, Samdo 2 (i)-dong, Jeju
₩75,000 – 100,000

Jeju Marina Hotel
064-746-6161, 064-746-6170
300-8, Yeon-dong, Jeju
₩65,300

New Island Tourist Hotel
064-743-0300, 064-743-2076
www.newisland.co.kr (Korean)
263-12, Yeon-dong, Jeju
₩100,000

New Kyung Nam Tourist Hotel
064-733-2121, 064-733-2129
www.newkyungnam.co.kr (Korean)
314-1, Seogwi-dong, Seogwipo
₩100,000

Ocean Grand Hotel
064-783-0007, 064-783-7133
www.oceangrand.co.kr
1252-55, Hamdoek-ri, Jocheon-eup, Bukjeju-gun
₩154,880

Robero Hotel
064-757-7111, 064-755-9001
www.roberohotel.com (Korean)
57-2, Samdo 1 (il)-dong, Jeju
₩100,000

Sunshine Hotel
064-784-2525, 064-784-2526
www.hotelsunshinejeju.com
3105, Hapdeok-ri, Jocheon-eup, Bukjeju
₩120,000

2nd

Dongyang Tourist Hotel
064-748-7100, 064-749-6789
272-29, Yeon-dong, Jeju
₩62,000

Grace Tourist Hotel
064-742-0066, 064-743-7111
261-23, Yeon-dong, Jeju
₩100,000

Ocean Flora
064-784-5335, 064-784-5330
www.oceanflora.co.kr (Korean)
1652-2, Dongbok-ri, Gujwa-eup, Bukjeju
₩150,000

Raja Tourist Hotel
064-745-8100, 064-744-4666
268-10, Yeon-dong, Jeju
₩70,000

VIP Park Hotel
064-743-5530, 064-743-5531
917-2, Nohyeong-dong, Jeju
₩60,000

3rd

Asem Hotel
064-747-3399, 064-746-8847
268, Yeon-dong, Jeju
₩60,000

Ilchulbong
064-782-8801/4, 064-782-8805
www.ilchulbonghotel.co.kr (Korean)
261-2, Seongsan-ri, Seongsan-eup, Namjeju
₩125,000

Budget Accommodations

Budget watchers may prefer a *yeogwan* (traditional Korean-style inn). Room rates range from ₩25,000 to ₩50,000. Growing in popularity are guest houses that cater to young people traveling on a budget, youth hostels, homestay, and *hanok* stay. For more information and a complete list of inns, guest houses, etc. across Korea, visit the Tourist Information Center at the Korea Tourism Organization building in Seoul. To make reservations, call ☎ **02-3279-5574** or visit **www.worldinn.com**.

Youth Hostels

There are 61 youth hostels in Korea and all are members of the Korea Youth Hostel Association. The rate for one night is about ₩9,000 to ₩22,000 per person (somewhat higher in Seoul). Prior membership is required.

Reservations, membership and information can be obtained from the Korea Youth Hostel Association
☎ **02-725-3031; www.kyha.or.kr; E-mail: inform@kyha.or.kr.**

NAME	CAPACITY	WEB SITE	TEL	FAX	LOCATION
SEOUL					
Dreamtel	245	www.idreamtel.co.kr	02-2667-0535	02-2667-0744	Gangseo-gu
Olympic Parktel	866	www.parktel.co.kr	02-410-2114	02-410-2100	Songpa-gu
INCHEON					
Ganghwa	412	www.gh-yh.co.kr (Korean)	032-933-8891	032-933-9335	Ganghwa
Ganghwa Namsan	557		032-934-7777	032-934-7782	Ganghwa
DAEJEON					
Yuseong	300	www.youthostel.or.kr (Korean)	042-822-9591	042-823-9965	Yuseong-gu
GWANGJU					
Gwang San Gu	300	www.gsyouth.or.kr (Korean)	062-943-4378	062-943-4379	Gwangsan-gu
GYEONGGI-DO					
Anyang	150		031-471-8111	031-472-8106	Anyang
Artsvalley	520	www.artsvalleyyh.com (Korean)	031-683-7677	031-683-7679	Pyeongtaek
Bears Town	600	www.bearstown.com (Korean)	031-532-2534	031-532-7474	Pocheon
Home Bridge Hillside	324	www.everland.co.kr	031-320-8841	031-320-8843	Yongin
Goyang	180		031-962-9049	031-962-9579	Goyang
Green Camp	300	www.greencamp.biz (Korean)	031-582-5304	031-582-3324	Gapyeong
Home Bridge Cabin	320	www.everland.com	031-320-9740	031-320-9747	Yongin
Imjingang	350	www.imjincp.co.kr (Korean)	031-835-0057	031-835-0067	Yeoncheon
Korean Folk Village	541	www.koreanfolk.co.kr	031-286-2114	031-286-4051	Yongin

NAME	CAPACITY	WEB SITE	TEL	FAX	LOCATION
Kwangrim	454	www.saintroom.co.kr (Korean)	031-544-0515	031-544-0519	Pocheon
Sangcheon Eden	430	http://edenyh.co.k (Korean)	031-581-7030	031-581-3900	Gapyeong
Shalom	217	www.kmc.or.kr/shalom (Korean)	031-855-8011	031-855-7085	Yangju
Songchu	500	www.songchuyouth.com (Korean)	031-871-4900	031-876-4144	Yangju
Yangpyung	1,100		031-774-7800	031-774-7815	Yangpyeong
Yangji Pine	228	www.pineresort.com	031-338-2001	031-338-7897	Yongin
GANGWON-DO					
Dream Land	614	www.chiakyouth.co.kr (Korean)	033-732-1600	033-732-6888	Wonju
Daemyung Hongcheon	1,300	www.daemyeongcondo.com	033-434-8311	033-434-8620	Hongcheon
Dongseoul	741		033-732-3700	033-732-7665	Wonju
Dunnae	898	http://doonaeresort.co.kr (Korean)	033-343-6488	033-343-6487	Hoengseong
Gangchon	200	www.kyh.or.kr (Korean)	033-262-1201	033-262-1204	Chuncheon
Hyundai Sungwoo	998	www.hdsungwoo.co.kr	033-340-3000	033-340-3173	Hoengseong
Kiwa	326	www.kiwayh.com (Korean)	033-263-1151	033-263-9692	Chuncheon
Phoenix Vill	788		033-330-6110	033-330-6007	Pyeongchang
Pyeongchang	742	www.pcyh.co.kr (Korean)	033-332-7501	033-332-8003	Pyeongchang
Soraksan	844	www.sorakyhostel.com (Korean)	033-636-7115	033-636-7107	Sokcho
Yong Pyong	605	www.yongpyong.co.kr	033-335-5757	033-335-5769	Pyeongchang
CHUNGCHEONGBUK-DO					
Heungwoon	700	www.hwyouth.or.kr	043-542-5799	043-543-3634	Boeun
Sajo Maeul	796	www.sajoresort.co.kr	043-846-0750	043-846-1789	Chungju
Sobaeksan	1,370		043-421-5555	043-421-3860	Danyang
Woraksan	266	http://woraksan.co.kr (Korean)	043-651-7001	043-651-7004	Jecheon
Yeolimwon	670	http://yollimwon.co.kr (Korean)	043-542-9992	043-542-9991	Boeun
Ilyang	980	www.ilyangyouth.co.kr (Korean)	043-846-9200	043-845-9107	Chungju
CHUNGCHEONGNAM-DO					
Cheonan Sangrok	916	www.sangnokresort.co.kr (Korean)	041-560-9114	041-560-9019	Cheonan
Dogo	858	www.dogoyouthhostel.co.kr (Korean)	041-544-8653	041-544-7656	Asan
Gongju	605	www.gongjuyh.com (Korean)	041-852-1212	041-852-1240	Gongju
Gyeryongsan Gapsa	530	www.kapsayouthhostel.com (Korean)	041-856-4666	041-856-4663	Gongju
Samjung Buyeo	400	www.buyeoyh.com (Korean)	041-835-3102	041-835-3791	Buyeo
GYEONGSANGBUK-DO					
Bulguksa	650	www.bgyh.com	054-746-0826	054-746-7805	Gyeongju
Chilgok Joil	81		054-971-0602		Chilgok
Dongyang	650	www.dyhostel.co.kr (Korean)	054-748-6577	054-748-7624	Gyeongju
Gyeongju Fou (Season)	650	www.gjfour.com (Korean)	054-743-2202	054-743-2206	Gyeongju
Gyeongju Jeil	800	www.cheil-yh.co.kr	054-746-0086	054-746-4215	Gyeongju
GYEONGSANGNAM-DO					
Cheonghakdong	250	www.hakdang.com	055-882-1892	055-882-6190	Hadong
Geoje	200	http://geojedo.or.kr (Korean)	055-632-7977	055-632-4806	Geoje
Namhae	496	www.nhystel.com	055-867-4848	055-867-4850	Namhae
Namhae Hanryeo	627	www.hanryeo.co.kr (Korean)	055-867-4510	055-867-4261	Namhae
JEOLLABUK-DO					
Gyeokpo	206	www.chaesukgang.co.k (Korean)	063-583-1234	063-584-8098	Buan
Jirisan	600	www.jrsy.co.kr (Korean)	063-625-1960	063-2020-1960	Namwon
Moaksan	669	www.moakyh.com (Korean)	063-548-4401	063-548-4403	Gimje
Seonunsan	300		063-561-3333	063-561-3448	Gochang

NAME	CAPACITY	WEB SITE	TEL	FAX	LOCATION
JEOLLANAM-DO					
Haenam	300	http://youth.haenam.or.kr (Korean)	061-533-0170	061-532-1730	Haenam
Suncheon	150	www.scyouth.or.kr (Korean)	061-755-5522	061-755-6298	Suncheon
JEJU-DO					
Jeju Fitness Town	668	www.jejufitness.co.kr (Korean)	064-799-8811	064-799-8821	Bukjeju
Myoungdoam	330		064-721-8233	064-721-8235	Jeju
Seogwipo	330	www.beachvillresort.co.kr (Korean)	064-739-0114	064-739-7552	Seogwipo

Homestay
ACCOMMODATIONS

Homestay, called *minbak* in Korean, is a great way to experience Korean culture firsthand. There are many families who are willing to share their home and lifestyle with foreigners and in turn, learn about foreign culture and form international friendships. Host families are available who speak English, Japanese, Chinese, Spanish, French, and German.

Korea Youth Exchange Promotion Association
📞 02-2665-6717 📠 02-2665-6312
www.kyepa.or.kr

LEX Youth Korea
📞 02-538-9660 📠 02-568-6738
www.lex.or.kr; lexkor@unitel.co.kr

LABO Korea
📞 02-736-0521 📠 02-359-0527
www.labostay.or.kr; labo@labo.or.kr

Go Homestay
📞 02-6092-8147 📠 02-6092-8150
www.gohomestay.com

Hanok Stay
ACCOMMODATIONS

Visitors also can stay at *hanok* (a traditional Korean house). It is a good opportunity for overseas visitors to experience the old Korean lifestyle. All furniture, windows and interior structures are reproductions of a traditional per Korean house. Traditional sleeping pads and quilts are provided. Samcheonggak in Seoul and Jirye Artists' Colony and Suaedang in Andong boast beautiful natural surroundings. Rakgojae, Woorichip Guest House, Seoul Guest House in Seoul, and Saehwagwan and Yangsajae in Jeonju are located inside a *hanok* village. For Samcheonggak, rates are over ₩200,000 per room (breakfast not included), but for most others, rates are under ₩100,000 per room (breakfast included).

NAME	TEL.	FAX	WEB SITE/ E-MAIL
SEOUL			
Friends House	02-3673-1515	02-3673-1513	www.friends-house.com
Rakgojae	02-742-3410	02-742-3418	yha@hs-plan.co.kr
Samcheonggak	02-3676-2345	02-3676-3464	www.samcheonggak.or.kr
Seoul Guest House	02-745-0057		www.seoul110.com
Woorichip Guest House	02-744-0536		woorichip1043@hanmail.net
JEONJU			
Saehwagwan	063-287-6300	063-287-6303	www.saehwagwan.com
Yangsajae	063-282-4959	063-282-4960	www.jeonjutour.co.kr
ANDONG			
Jirye Artists' Colony	054-822-2590		www.jirye.com
Suaedang	054-822-6661		moonjuh@hanmir.net

GENERAL INFORMATION

Business Travel Tips

TIPS FOR CONDUCTING BUSINESS
When visiting Korea for the first time, many business people are surprised to see how westernized both the cities and the local people appear to be. However, this process of westernization has taken place very rapidly and many traditional values and attitudes remain firmly in place.

Business cards are essential for doing business in Korea; you should always carry more business cards than you would ever imagine it possible to use. Your business card is your company passport and should show your place in the company hierarchy.

For example, the owner of a company who uses the title of "director" at home should use the Korean-style title "company president" because in Korea, a director is a mid-level manager. Business cards should be given and received with the right hand, preferably both, but never with the left hand. The most respectful way to give or receive anything in Korea is with both hands. Watching Koreans giving and receiving, but giving in particular, you will see that most people rarely use just one hand; often the left hand, palm up, touches or reaches the middle of the right forearm. The exception would be giving something to a child.

Once contacts are established, it is very important that they are nurtured.

For business people, this means making a point of visiting the Korean partner on every business trip to Korea and marking holidays such as Christmas with a card or small gift.

It is important to demonstrate to Koreans that you have a long-term commitment to the market and that you are not there to make a quick profit and run.

Sincerity is very important to Koreans; this is reflected in the amount of time they devote to getting to know their business partners and building long-term relationships.

HOTEL BUSINESS CENTER
Most deluxe hotels have a 24-hour business center to assist your business needs. Services include private meeting rooms, computers with Internet access and printers, offices, and translations or interpretations. These business centers usually also provide professional secretarial service, package delivery, mobile phone rentals and fax machines.

PC GAME ROOMS
Ubiquitous in every neighborhood are these commercial establishments full of multimedia computers and internet hookups for rent from ₩1,000 to ₩2,000 per hour. They might be quite noisy, but if you need to send an urgent e-mail they fit the occasion well.

MOBILE PHONE RENTAL SERVICE

A temporary mobile phone is a handy item for tourists, especially business travelers. Call
📞 032-743-4011 or 032-743-4042 (SK);
📞 032-743-4018 or 032-743-4078 (KTF); or
📞 032-743-4001 or 032-743-4019 (LG) for airport rental service (not necessary to dial "032" when at the airport).
In a few minutes, you can have your own personal phone number and handset to make and recieve calls from anywhere in Korea.
A PDA, a hand-held Internet device that doubles as a telephone, is also available with full-screen websurfing, e-mail and a database of travel- and tourism-specific information including reservations for accommodations and transportation. An invaluable little tool for the traveler and quite inexpensive to use. To rent, call 📞 032-743-4042 and for any questions, call 📞 02-3788-3789.

TRANSLATION / INTERPRETATION SERVICES

Arirang TV 📞 02-3474-3114 📠 02-3474-0350; www.arirangtvmedia.com
Cosmo Call Korea 📞 02-582-0083 📠 02-582-0283; www.cosmocall.co.kr
Graduate School of Translation and Interpretation, Ewha Womans Univ. 📞 02-3277-3661~3 📠 02-3277-3664
Interpretation & Translation Institute, Hankuk Univ. of Foreign Studies 📞 02-963-5356 📠 02-963-8780
Pan Trans Net 📞 02-778-2028 📠 02-778-1575; www.pantrans.net

INTERNATIONAL AIR EXPRESS DISTRIBUTION SERVICE

DHL 📞 1588-0001 📠 02-719-6454	Namsung GPA 📞 02-334-8200 📠 02-334-7175
UPS 📞 02-3665-3651 📠 02-2280-5140	Hanjin Express 📞 02-738-1212 📠 02-778-1463

USEFUL WEB SITES

Ministry of Culture and Tourism	www.mct.go.kr
Ministry of Finance and Economy	www.mofe.go.kr
Ministry of Foreign Affairs and Trade	www.mofat.go.kr
Korea Customs Service	www.customs.go.kr
Korea Institute for International Economic Policy (KIEP)	www.kiep.go.kr
Korea Trade-Investment Promotion Agency (KOTRA)	www.kotra.or.kr
Korea Chamber of Commerce & Industry	www.korcham.net
The American Chamber of Commerce	www.amchamkorea.org
The European Union Chamber of Commerce in Korea	www.eucck.org
Korea Investment Service Center	www.kisc.org
Korean International Trade Association	www.kita.net
Cultural Properties Administration	www.ocp.go.kr
Korea Information Service	www.korea.net
	www.whatsonkorea.com
	www.lifeinkorea.com
Seoul Traffic Information	traffic.seoul.go.kr
Korea Convention & Exhibition Center (COEX)	www.coex.co.kr
Busan Exhibition & Convention Center (BEXCO)	www.bexco.co.kr
Daegu Exhibition & Convention Center (EXCO Daegu)	www.excodaegu.co.kr
International Convention Center Jeju (ICC Jeju)	www.iccjeju.co.kr
Samsung Economy Research Institute	www.seri.org

GENERAL INFORMATION

Handy Facts

TOURIST INFORMATION SERVICE
Information and assistance are readily available at the KTO's Tourist Information Center (TIC) or at information counters in international airports and at major tourist sites. They provide city maps, brochures and information on tours, shopping, dining, and accommodations.
The hours of operation differ somewhat around the country, but the KTO's TIC is open every day from 9:00 to 18:00. On the Web, visit www.tour2korea.com.

Seoul	· KTO Tourist Information Center	02-729-9497/9
	- Incheon International Airport	032-743-2600/3
	· Seoul City Tourist Information Center	02-731-6337
	- Itaewon	02-3785-0942
	- Myeong-dong	02-757-0088
	- Dongdaemun Market	02-2236-9135
	- Namdaemun Market	02-752-1913
	- Deoksugung Palace	02-756-0045
	- Seoul Express Bus Terminal (Honamseon Line)	02-6282-0600
	· Seoul Metropolitan Rapid Transit Infonet	02-735-5678
Busan	· Gimhae International Airport	051-973-2800
	· Busan Railroad Station	051-463-5783
	· Busan International Passenger Terminal	051-465-3471
Jejudo	· Jeju International Airport	064-742-8866
	· Jeju Port Passenger Terminal	064-758-7181
	· Jungmun Tourist Center	064-738-8550
Gyeongju	· Gyeongju Railroad Station	054-772-3843
	· Bulguksa Temple	054-746-4747
	· Gyeongju Express Bus Terminal	054-772-9289

BBB Korea 1588-5644
If you are having difficulty communicating in Korea, call 1588-5644 to reach the BBB (Before Babel Brigade). Korea has 2,300 volunteers fluent in 17 foreign languages who will help you with translation problems whenever and wherever via mobile phone. Launched during the 2002 FIFA World Cup in Korea, BBB Korea is run by a knowledgeable volunteer staff. BBB refers to the time before the construction of the Tower of Babel, when humanity shared a common language.

How to Use: Call ☎ 1588-5644 and press the number assigned for the language you need. If you are not connected on your first attempt, try again. (Numbers: English 1, Japanese 2, Chinese 3, French 4, Spanish 5, Italian 6, Russian 7, German 8, Portuguese 9, Arabic 10, Polish 11, Turkish 12, Swedish 13, Thai 14, Vietnamese 15, Malay 16, Indonesian 17)

TOURIST COMPLAINT CENTER

Visitors to Korea who experience any inconveniences or who simply want to offer some advice should call or write to the Tourist Complaint Center operated by the Korea Tourism Organization: 40 Cheonggyecheonno, Jung-gu, Seoul, 100-180, Korea
📞 02-735-0101 📠 02-777-0102;
tourcom@mail.knto.or.kr

GOODWILL GUIDE

The KTO Goodwill Guide Service provides interpretation assistance as part of its free tour guide service. Reservations are usually required. If you need special help of any kind in Korea, visit www.goodwillguide.com.

TRAVEL AGENTS

For organized tours or guided tours in Korea, contact:
Korea Tourism Association: 8th Fl., KTO Bldg., 40 Cheonggyecheonno, Jung-gu, Seoul
📞 02-757-7482 📠 02-757-7489
Korea Association of General Travel Agents (KATA): Rm. 803, Jaeneung Bldg., 192-11 Euljiro 1 (il)-ga, Jung-gu, Seoul
📞 02-752-8692 📠 02-752-8694

- Korea Travel Bureau 📞 02-778-0150
- Global Tour 📞 02-776-3153
- Kim's Travel 📞 02-323-3361
- Star Travel 📞 02-569-8114

DIPLOMATIC MISSIONS & OTHER ORGANIZATIONS

EMBASSIES

Ministry of Foreign Affairs and Trade: **www.mofat.go.kr**

COUNTRY	ADDRESS	TEL.	FAX
Afghanistan	27-2 Hannam-dong, Yongsan-gu, Seoul	02-793-3535	02-795-2662
Algeria	2-6 Itaewon 2 (i)-dong, Yongsan-gu, Seoul	02-794-5034/5	02-792-7845
Argentina	733-73 Hannam-dong, Yongsan-gu, Seoul	02-796-8144	02-792-5820
Australia	11th Fl., Kyobo Bldg., Jongno 1 (il)-ga, Jongno-gu, Seoul	02-2003-0100	02-735-6601
Austria	Rm.1913, Kyobo Bldg., Jongno 1 (il)-ga, Jongno-gu, Seoul	02-732-9071/2	02-732-9486
Bangladesh	1-67 Dongbinggo-dong, Yongsan-gu, Seoul	02-796-4056/7	02-790-5313
Belarus	432-1636, Sindang 2 (i)-dong, Jung-gu, Seoul	02-2237-8171	02-2237-8174
Belgium	1-94 Dongbinggo-dong, Yongsan-gu, Seoul	02-749-0381	02-797-1688
Brazil	4th Fl., Ihn Gallery Bldg., 141 Palpan-dong, Jongno-gu, Seoul	02-738-4970	02-738-4974
Brunei	7th Fl., Gwanghwamun Bldg., 211 Sejongno, Jongno-gu, Seoul	02-797-7679	
Bulgaria	723-42 Hannam 2 (i)-dong, Yongsan-gu, Seoul	02-794-8625	02-794-8627
Cambodia	653-8 Hannam-dong, Yongsan-gu, Seoul	02-3785-1041	02-3785-1040
Canada	10th Fl., Kolon Bldg., 45 Mugyo-dong, Jung-gu, Seoul	02-3455-6000	02-755-0686
Chile	1802 Daeyungak Bldg., 25-5, Chungmuro 1 (il)-ga, Jung-gu, Seoul	02-779-2610	02-779-2615
China (P.R.C.)	9th Fl., Kyobo Bldg., Jongno-gu, Seoul	02-738-1173	02-738-1174
Colombia	13th Fl., Kyobo Bldg., Jongno 1 (il)-ga, Jongno-gu, Seoul	02-720-1369	02-725-6959
Costa Rica	8th Fl., Iljin Bldg., 50-1, Dohwa-dong, Mapo-gu, Seoul	02-707-9248	02-707-9255
Côte d'Ivoire	2nd Fl., Jong-am Bldg., 794-4, Hannam-dong, Yongsan-gu, Seoul	02-3785-0561	02-3785-0564
Czech Republic	1-121 Sinmunno 2 (i)-ga, Jongno-gu, Seoul	02-720-6453	02-734-6452
Denmark	5th Fl., Namsong Bldg., 250-199 Itaewon-dong, Yongsan-gu, Seoul	02-795-4187	02-796-0986
Dominican Republic	19th Fl., Taepyeongno Bldg., 310 Taepyeongno 2 (i)-ga, Jung-gu, Seoul	02-756-3513	02-756-3514

COUNTRY	ADDRESS	TEL.	FAX
Ecuador	19th Fl., Korea First Bank Headquarter Bldg., 100 Gongpyeong-dong, Jongno-gu, Seoul	02-739-2401	02-739-2355
Egypt	744-4 Hannam-dong, Yongsan-gu, Seoul	02-749-0787/9	02-795-2588
El Salvador	21st Fl., Samsung Life Insurance Bldg., 150 Taepyeongno 2 (i)-ga, Jung-gu, Seoul	02-753-3432	02-753-3456
EU	16th Fl., Sean Bldg.,116 Sinmunno 1 (il)-ga, Jongno-gu, Seoul	02-735-1101	02-739-3514
Finland	Rm.1602, Kyobo Bldg., Jongno 1 (il)-ga, Jongno-gu, Seoul	02-732-6737	02-723-4969
France	30 Hap-dong, Seodaemun-gu, Seoul	02-3149-4300	02-3149-4310
Gabon	4th Fl., Yoosung Bldg., 738-20, Hannam-dong, Yongsan-gu, Seoul	02-793-9575/6	02-793-9574
Germany	308-5 Dongbinggo-dong, Yongsan-gu, Seoul	02-748-4114	02-748-4161
Ghana	5-4 Hannam-dong, Yongsan-gu, Seoul	02-3785-1427	02-3785-1428
Greece	27th Fl., Hanwha Bldg., 1 Janggyo-dong, Jongno-gu, Seoul	02-729-1400/1	02-729-1402
Guatemala	614, Hotel Lotte, 1 Sogong-dong, Jung-gu, Seoul	02-771-7582	02-771-7584
Holy See	2 Gungjeong-dong, Jongno-gu, Seoul	02-736-5725	02-736-5738
Honduras	2nd Fl., Jongno Tower Bldg., Jongno 2 (i)-ga, Jongno-gu, Seoul	02-738-8402	02-738-8403
Hungary	1-103 Dongbinggo-dong, Yongsan-gu, Seoul	02-792-2105	02-792-2109
India	37-3 Hannam-dong, Yongsan-gu, Seoul	02-798-4257	02-796-9534
Indonesia	55 Yeouido-dong, Yeongdeungpo-gu, Seoul	02-783-5675	02-780-4280
Iran	726-126 Hannam-dong, Yongsan-gu, Seoul	02-793-7751	02-792-7052
Ireland	15th Fl., Daehan Fire & Marine Insurance Bldg., 51-1 Namchang-dong, Jung-gu, Seoul	02-774-6455	02-774-6458
Israel	823-21 Yeoksam-dong, Gangnam-gu, Seoul	02-739-8666	02-739-8667
Italy	1-398 Hannam-dong, Yongsan-gu, Seoul	02-796-0491	02-797-5560
Japan	18-11 Junghak-dong, Jongno-gu, Seoul	02-2170-5200	02-734-4528
Kazakhstan	484-24 Bukak Village, 11 Pyeongchang-dong, Jongno-gu, Seoul	02-394-9716	02-395-9766
Kuwait	309-15 Dongbinggo-dong, Yongsan-gu, Seoul	02-749-3688	02-749-3687
Laos	657-9 Hannam-dong, Yongsan-gu, Seoul	02-796-1713	02-796-1771
Lebanon	310-49 Dongbinggo-dong, Yongsan-gu, Seoul	02-794-6482	02-794-6485
Libya	4-5 Hannam-dong, Yongsan-gu, Seoul	02-797-6001	02-797-6007
Malaysia	4-1 Hannam-dong, Yongsan-gu, Seoul	02-795-9203	02-794-5480
Mexico	33-6 Hannam-dong, Yongsan-gu, Seoul	02-798-1694	02-790-0939
Mongolia	33-5 Hannam-dong, Yongsan-gu, Seoul	02-794-1350	02-794-7605
Morocco	S-15, U.N. Village, 270-3 Hannam-dong,Yongsan-gu, Seoul	02-793-6249	02-792-8178
Myanmar	723-1 Hannam-dong, Yongsan-gu, Seoul	02-790-3814~6	02-790-3817
Netherlands	14th Fl., Kyobo Bldg., 1 Jongno 1 (il)-ga, Jongno-gu, Seoul	02-737-9514	02-735-1321
New Zealand	Rm. 1803, Kyobo Bldg., 1 Jongno 1 (il)-ga, Jongno-gu, Seoul	02-736-0341	02-722-6945
Nigeria	310-19 Dongbinggo-dong, Yongsan-gu, Seoul	02-797-2370	02)796-1848
Norway	258-8 Itaewon-dong, Yongsan-gu, Seoul	02-795-6850	02-798-6072
Oman	309-3 Dongbinggo-dong, Yongsan-gu, Seoul	02-790-2431	02-790-2430

COUNTRY	ADDRESS	TEL.	FAX
Pakistan	258-13 Itaewon-dong, Yongsan-gu, Seoul	02-796-8252	02-796-0313
Panama	4th Fl., Hyundai Merchant Marine Bldg., 66 Jeokseon-dong, Jongno-gu, Seoul	02-734-8610	02-734-8613
Paraguay	2nd Fl., SK Bldg., 99 Seorin-dong, Jongno-gu, Seoul	02-730-8335	02-730-8336
Peru	6th Fl., Namhan Bldg., 76-42 Hannam-dong, Yongsan-gu, Seoul	02-757-1735	02-757-1738
Philippines	9th Fl., Diplomatic Center, 1376-1, Seocho 2 (i)-dong, Seocho-gu, Seoul	02-573-5123	02-573-5125
Poland	70 Sagan-dong, Jongno-gu, Seoul	02-723-9681	02-723-9680
Portugal	2nd Fl., Wonseo Bldg., 171 Wonseo-dong, Jongno-gu, Seoul	02-3675-2251	02-3675-2250
Qatar	1-44 Dongbinggo-dong, Yongsan-gu, Seoul	02-798-2446	02-790-1027
Romania	UN Village, 1-42 Hannam-dong, Yongsan-gu, Seoul	02-797-4924	02-794-3114
Russia	34-16 Jeong-dong, Jung-gu, Seoul	02-752-0630	02-754-0417
Saudi Arabia	1-112 Sinmunno 2 (i)-ga, Jongno-gu, Seoul	02-739-0631	02-739-0041
Singapore	19th Fl., Samsung Taepyeongno Bldg., 310 Taepyeongno 2 (i)-ga, Jung-gu, Seoul	02-774-2464	02-773-2465
Slovakia	389-1 Hannam-dong, Yongsan-gu, Seoul	02-794-3981	02-794-3982
South Africa	1-37 Hannam-dong, Yongsan-gu, Seoul	02-792-4855	02-792-4856
Spain	726-52 Hannam-dong, Yongsan-gu, Seoul	02-794-3581/2	02-796-8207
Sri Lanka	Suite 2002, Kyobo Bldg., Jongno 1 (il)-ga, Jongno-gu, Seoul	02-735-2966	02-737-9577
Sudan	653-7 Hannam-dong, Yongsan-gu, Seoul	02-793-8692	02-793-8693
Sweden	Rm. 1201, Hanhyo Bldg., 136 Seorin-dong, Jongno-gu, Seoul	02-738-0846	02-733-1317
Switzerland	32-10 Songwol-dong, Jongno-gu, Seoul	02-739-9511	02-737-9392
Taipei	211 Sejongno, Jongno-gu, Seoul	02-399-2767	02-730-1194
Thailand	653-7 Hannam-dong, Yongsan-gu, Seoul	02-795-3098	02-798-3448
Tunisia	1-17 Dongbinggo-dong, Yongsan-gu, Seoul	02-790-4334	02-790-4333
Turkey	4th Fl., Vivien Corporation Bldg., 4-52, Seobinggo-dong, Yongsan-gu, Seoul	02-794-0255	02-797-8546
Ukraine	Rm. 901, Diplomatic Center, 1376-1 Seocho 2 (i)-dong, Seocho-gu, Seoul	02-790-5696	02-790-5697
United Arab Emirates	5-5 Hannam-dong, Yongsan-gu, Seoul	02-790-3235	02-790-3238
United Kingdom	4 Jeong-dong, Jung-gu, Seoul	02-3210-5500	02-725-1738
U.S.A.	82 Sejongno, Jongno-gu, Seoul	02-397-4114	02-738-8845
Uruguay	Rm. 1802, Daewoo Center Bldg., 541 Namdaemunno 5 (o)-ga, Jung-gu, Seoul	02-6245-3180	02-6245-3181
Uzbekistan	Rm. 701, Diplomatic Center, 1376-1 Seocho 2 (i)-dong, Seocho-gu, Seoul	02-574-6554	02-578-0576
Venezuela	16th Fl., Korea First Bank Headquarter Bldg., Gongpyeong-dong, Jongno-gu, Seoul	02-732-1546	02-732-1548
Vietnam	28-58 Samcheong-dong, Jongno-gu, Seoul	02-739-2065	02-739-2064

CONSULAR MISSIONS

COUNTRY	ADDRESS	TEL.	FAX
China	1418 U 2 (i)-dong, Haeundae-gu, Busan	051-743-7990	051-743-7987
Japan	1147-11 Choryang-dong, Dong-gu, Busan 977-1 Nohyeong-dong, Jeju, Jeju-do	051-465-5101/6 064-742-9501	051-464-1630 064-743-5885
Russia	8th Fl., Korea Exchange Bank Bldg., 89-1 Jungang-dong 4 (sa)-ga, Jung-gu, Busan	051-441-9904/5	051-464-4404

BUSINESS HOURS

Most government offices are open between the hours of 9:00 and 18:00 and closed on weekends.

Most private businesses open at anywhere from 8:30 to 10:00 and close late in the evening. Banks are open from 9:30 to 16:30 on weekdays and they are closed Saturdays and Sundays. Foreign diplomatic missions in Seoul generally maintain strict business hours. They are usually open from 9:00 to 17:00 on weekdays and are closed on weekends.

Major department stores are usually open from 10:30 to 20:00, including Sundays, but smaller shops tend to be open earlier and close later every day of the week.

CURRENCY AND CREDIT CARDS

The Korean unit of currency is the won. Coin denominations are ₩1, ₩5, ₩10, ₩50, ₩100, ₩500, but ₩1 and ₩5 are hardly in use. Bank notes are ₩1,000, ₩5,000 and ₩10,000. Bank checks are circulated in denominations of ₩100,000 and over.

Foreign currency and traveler's checks can be converted into Korean won at foreign exchange banks and other authorized money changers. The exchange rate is subject to market fluctuations. One U.S. dollar was equivalent to about ₩1,034 as of December 2005. Credit cards, including VISA, American Express, Diner's Club, Master Card and JCB, are accepted at major hotels, department stores, and larger restaurants.

AUTOMATED TELLER MACHINES (ATM)

Travelers who carry internationally recognized credit cards can get a cash advance in Korean won at automated teller machines (ATMs) installed at airports, major hotels, department stores, subway stations and tourist attractions.

TIPPING

Tipping is not a traditional Korean custom. A 10% service charge is added to your bill at all tourist hotels and some big restaurants.

TAX

Value-added tax (VAT) is levied on most goods and services at a standard rate of 10% and is included in the retail price. At tourist hotels, this 10% tax applies to meals and other services and is added into the bill.

ELECTRICITY

In Korea, outlets for 220 volts / 60 cycle are dominant but a 110 volt outlet is sometimes available. Be careful and ask before plugging in a 110 volt appliance.

110 V   220 V

LOST & FOUND

In the event of misplaced or lost property, contact the Lost and Found Center of the Seoul Metropolitan Police Bureau: 102 Hongik-dong, Seongdong-gu. ☎ 02-2299-1282 📠 02-2298-1282

MAIL KOREA POST: www.koreapost.go.kr Domestic postal rates are ₩220 for a letter of up to 25 g, ₩1,720 for a registered letter of no more than 25 g, and ₩2,200 to ₩2,700 for a package of up to 2 kg. A postcard costs ₩190.

MEDICAL CARE

There are many hospitals where some English is spoken; however, it is recommendable to use the international clinics at such large general hospitals as Severance Hospital, Asan Medical Center or Samsung Medical Center.

ASAN MEDICAL CENTER
- 📍: 388-1 Pungnap 2-dong, Songpa-gu, Seoul
- ☎ 02-3010-3114; www.amc.seoul.kr
- **International Clinic**
- 🕐: 9:00 – 16:30 on weekdays; 9:00 – 11:30 on Saturdays ☎ 02-3010-5001

SAMSUNG MEDICAL CENTER
- 📍: 50 Irwon-dong, Gangnam-gu, Seoul
- ☎ 02-3410-2114; www.samsunghospital.com
- **International Clinic**
- 🕐: 8:00 – 17:00 on weekdays; 9:00 – 12:00 on Saturdays ☎ 02-3410-0200

SEVERANCE HOSPITAL
- 📍: 134 Sinchon-dong, Seodaemun-gu, Seoul
- ☎ 02-2227-0114; www.severance.or.kr
- **Foreign Clinic**
- 🕐: 9:00 – 12:00 and 14:00 – 17:30 on weekdays; 9:00 – 12:00 on Saturdays
- ☎ 02-2228-5810

NEWSPAPER, TV AND RADIO

There are three English-language dailies: The Korea Times, The Korea Herald and the International Herald Tribune.
They are available at most newsstands and in hotel gift shops.
Korea has five TV networks broadcasting in Korean (KBS1, KBS2, MBC, SBS, and EBS). Along with the national broadcasting networks, there are also many cable TV channels specializing in a wide field of programming including news, movies, entertainment, sports, etc. Of note is Arirang TV, a special English channel produced in Korea. The channel features programming in politics, the economy, community, and culture, providing insight and understanding about things Korean through popular TV serial dramas with English subtitles. Some 90 hotels in Korea offer Arirang TV on cable or satellite. There are also eight Korean radio stations plus the AFN U.S. military stations, which broadcast in English on 1530 AM and 102.7 FM in Seoul. The AFN TV station can be received in many areas as well as via cable.

TELEPHONE CALLS
IN KOREA

To make a local call in the same area or city, just dial the telephone number. If you are in a different area or city, first dial the area code and then the telephone number you want to call. For example, if you would like to call someone in Daegu (telephone number 123-4567), dial 053-123-4567.

* AREA CODES
Seoul (02), Incheon (032), Daejeon (042), Busan (051), Daegu (053), Ulsan (052), Gwangju (062), Gyeonggi-do (031), Gangwon-do (033), Chungcheongnam-do (041), Chungcheongbuk-do (043), Gyeongsangbuk-do (054), Gyeongsangnam-do (055), Jeollanam-do (061), Jeollabuk-do (063), Jeju-do (064)

INTERNATIONAL CALLS

To make a direct international call overseas from Korea, first dial the international access code 001, 002, or 008, the country code, area code and the recipient's number.

EXAMPLE: TO CALL WASHINGTON, D.C.		
❶	001 / 002 / 008	Int'l Access Code
❷	1	Country Code
❸	202	Area Code
❹	212-1234	Telephone Number

PUBLIC TELEPHONES

There are three types of public telephones in Korea: telephone card phones, card and coin phones, and IC card phones.

A local call costs ₩70 for three minutes and intercity calls cost considerably more.

Telephone card phones can be used only with regular telephone cards (MS card), card and coin phones with pre-paid IC cards or Korean-issued bank credit cards as well as coins and IC Card Phones with IC cards or credit cards.

However, international calls cannot be made with MS, IC or credit cards.

The pre-paid Worldphone Plus Card (www.wpcard.com) can be used from any telephone to call within Korea or to other countries. If it is not used up by the end of a visit, it can also be used in most other countries in the world. Another way to make international calls is to press the red button and dial 0072911 for AT&T, 0072916 for Sprint, etc.

USEFUL PHONE NUMBERS

Police	112
Fire and Ambulance	119
Medical Emergency	1339
International Telephone Information	00794
International Telephone	00799
Local Directory Assistance	114
Long Distance Directory Assistance	Area Code+114
International Telegram Services	00795
Tourist Complaint Center	02-735-0101
Tourist Information	1330

EMERGENCY TELEPHONE SERVICE

1330 Travel Phone offers emergency interpretation services

The KTO (Korea Tourism Organization) has teamed up with the 119 emergency call center to establish the 1330 Travel Phone Emergency Interpretation Service to further assist tourists and expatriates in Korea during emergency situations. This service is available 24 hours a day, 365 days a year in 3 languages — English, Japanese and Chinese. Calls take place in the form of a three-way phone conference between the 1330 Travel Phone, the 119 emergency call center and the caller requesting help.

Emergency Police Telephone Translation Service

The police operate a 112 emergency police telephone translation service. Tourists can dial 112 and be connected directly to an operator, a police officer, or a translator and receive help immediately. Translation is available from 8 am to 11 pm on weekdays and 9 am to 6 pm on weekends in English, Japanese, Chinese, Russian, French, Spanish, and German.

International SOS Korea

Provides 24-hour emergency service for foreigners, acting as a link between patients and Korean hospitals for a fee.
📞 02-790-7561

TIME DIFFERENCE

CITY	TIME							
Rio de Janeiro, São Paulo	*13	*16	*19	*22	1	4	7	10
New York, Montreal, Bogota, Toronto	*11	*14	*17	*20	*23	2	5	8
Chicago, Houston	*10	*13	*16	*19	*22	1	4	7
Vancouver, Seattle, San Francisco, Los Angeles	*8	*11	*14	*17	*20	*23	2	5
Sydney, Melbourne	2	5	8	11	14	17	20	23
Seoul, Tokyo	1	4	7	10	13	16	19	22
Taipei, Manila, Hong Kong, Kuala Lumpur, Singapore	24	3	6	9	12	15	18	21
Bangkok, Jakarta	*23	2	5	8	11	14	17	20
New Delhi, Calcutta	*21	24	3	6	9	12	15	18
Teheran, Kuwait, Jeddah	*20	*23	2	5	8	11	14	17
Hamburg, Rome, Paris, Amsterdam	*17	*20	*23	2	5	8	11	14
London, Madrid	*16	*19	*22	1	4	7	10	13

*previous day

RECOMMENDED DRESS

From mid-March through late May and mid-September through mid-November, you can wear long-sleeved shirts and slacks with a light jacket. During summer, June through August, short-sleeved shirts and shorts are acceptable, but on formal occasions, long trousers and a tie are recommended. In late November through early March, you must be prepared for the cold. A scarf and gloves are recommended for January and February and remember that it snows heavily at higher elevations in Korea.

AVERAGE TEMPERATURES AND RAINFALL

City / Month	Seoul				Busan				Daegu			
	C°	F°	H	R	C°	F°	H	R	C°	F°	H	R
Jan.	-2.5	27.5	62.6	21.6	3	37.4	51	37.8	0.2	32.36	58.5	21.6
Feb.	-0.3	31.46	61	23.6	4.3	39.74	53.6	44.9	2.1	35.78	57.3	27.1
Mar.	5.2	41.36	61.2	45.8	8.3	32.54	59.1	85.7	7.1	44.78	57.9	51.6
Apr.	12.1	53.78	59.3	77	13.4	56.12	64.6	136.3	13.8	56.84	56.8	75.2
May	17.4	63.32	64.1	102.2	17.4	63.32	69.6	154.1	18.7	65.66	60	75.3
June	21.9	71.42	71	133.3	20.5	68.9	79.3	222.5	22.5	72.5	67.6	140.7
July	24.9	76.82	79.8	327.9	24.2	75.56	84.8	258.8	25.7	78.26	74.3	206.7
Aug.	25.4	77.72	77.4	348	25.7	78.26	80.8	238.1	26.1	78.98	74	205.8
Sept.	20.8	69.44	71	137.6	22.1	71.78	74.3	167	21.3	70.34	72	129.6
Oct.	14.4	57.92	66.2	49.3	17.3	63.14	65.2	62	15.4	59.72	66.5	42
Nov.	6.9	44.42	64.6	53	11.3	52.34	59.5	60.1	8.6	47.48	63.8	37.1
Dec.	0.2	32.36	63.8	24.9	5.6	42.08	52.9	24.3	2.5	36.5	60.5	15.2

City / Month	Gwangju				Daejeon				Seogwipo			
	C°	F°	H	R	C°	F°	H	R	C°	F°	H	R
Jan.	0.5	32.9	70.5	38	-1.9	28.58	68.9	29.5	6.6	43.88	64.8	59.4
Feb.	1.9	35.42	68.9	43.9	0.2	32.36	66	36.4	7.1	44.78	64.2	80.6
Mar.	6.5	43.7	66.2	64.5	5.4	41.72	63.8	60.5	10.1	50.18	64.6	125.6
Apr.	12.9	55.22	65.2	95.3	12.4	54.32	61.6	87.2	14.4	57.92	67.8	172.2
May	17.8	64.04	68.4	97.3	17.6	63.68	65.8	97	18.1	64.58	71.3	215.4
June	22	71.6	75.1	190.3	22	71.6	73.2	174.3	21.3	70.34	80	279.3
July	25.5	77.9	80.6	281.9	25.3	77.54	80.1	292.2	25.3	77.54	85.1	306.3

City	Gwangju				Daejeon				Seogwipo			
Month	C°	F°	H	R	C°	F°	H	R	C°	F°	H	R
Aug.	26.1	78.98	79	276	25.5	77.9	79.8	296.5	26.6	79.88	80.4	257.6
Sept.	21.4	70.52	75.8	137.7	20.3	68.54	77.6	141.5	23.4	74.12	73.6	170.2
Oct.	15.4	59.72	71	55.3	13.8	56.84	73.7	56.9	18.8	65.84	66.8	72.7
Nov.	8.7	47.66	71.6	55.4	6.8	44.24	73.4	51.7	13.7	56.66	65.6	68.4
Dec.	2.8	37.04	71.7	32.4	0.7	33.26	71.8	30.1	8.9	48.02	64.6	43.1

Note: "C" - Centigrade, "F" - Fahrenheit, "H" - Humidity (%), "R" - Rainfall (mm). This is the mean value from 1971 to 2000.

WEIGHTS & MEASURES
Korea uses the international metric system.
1 meter = 39.37 inches = 1.094 yards, **1 kilometer** = 0.6214 mile, **1 kilogram** = 2.205 pounds,
1 liter = 0.26418 gallon, **1 metric ton** = 2,204.62 pounds

Korean Manners

1. Greeting and saying "thank you" are very important to Koreans. Words of greeting and thanks are usually said with a bow of the head. The depth of the bow depends on the relative seniority between the two speakers.
2. Koreans do not appreciate an overly outgoing style and they generally limit direct physical contact to a courteous handshake. However, as one gets to know Koreans better, a greater familiarity becomes possible. In fact, foreigners are often quite surprised to see women walking hand in hand.
   Touching close friends while talking to them is perfectly acceptable in Korea. Public displays of affection between the sexes such as kissing and hugging are not as uncommon as in the past but are generally regarded as unseemly.
3. There are many clean public restrooms throughout Korea. It is also acceptable to use restrooms in office buildings, hotels, shops, and restaurants.
4. Koreans traditionally sit, eat, and sleep on the floor, so shoes are always removed when entering a Korean home. Bare feet are considered to be rude, so it is best to wear socks or stockings when visiting a home.
5. Young Koreans are accustomed to "going Dutch" but it is more common to be either host or guest.
6. It was traditionally regarded as impolite to talk during a meal, but nowadays Koreans are encouraged to talk and laugh while eating. Real appreciation of the food and service is gratefully received. It is impolite to blow your nose at the table.

Holidays

GENERAL INFORMATION

Koreans officially follow the Gregorian calendar though some holidays are based on the lunar calendar. On official holidays, offices and banks are closed but palaces, museums, most restaurants, department stores and amusement facilities are open. *Seollal* and *Chuseok* are the most important traditional holidays for Koreans. Millions of people visit their hometowns to celebrate with their families during these periods. On *Seollal*, Koreans hold a memorial service for their ancestors and perform *sebae* (a formal bow of respect to their elders) as a New Year's greeting.

OFFICIAL HOLIDAYS

NEW YEAR'S DAY (January 1)
The first day of the New Year is recognized and celebrated.

LUNAR NEW YEAR'S DAY (Seollal) (January 28 – 30)
Lunar New Year's Day (*Seollal*) is one of the most important traditional events of the year, still much more significant than January 1.
Most businesses are closed, and people take several days off to visit their hometowns to be with family.
Members of the family get up early, put on their best clothes, and bows to their elders as a reaffirmation of family ties.
Feasts are held with specially prepared food such as *tteokguk* and *manduguk*. People play games of *yut* or fly kites and spin tops.

INDEPENDENCE MOVEMENT DAY (March 1)
This day commemorates the Declaration of Independence proclaimed on March 1, 1919, while under Japanese colonization.
A reading of the declaration takes place in a special ceremony at Tapgol Park in Seoul, where the document was first read to the public.

BUDDHA'S BIRTHDAY (May 5)
It falls on the 8th day of the 4th lunar month. Elaborate, solemn rituals are held at many Buddhist temples across the country and lanterns are hung in the temple courtyards.
On the Sunday evening before Buddha's birthday, these lanterns are lit and carried in parades.

CHILDREN'S DAY (May 5)
On this day, parents dress up the little ones and take them to children's parks, amusement parks, zoos, or the cinema for a full day of fun and games.

MEMORIAL DAY (June 6)
Memorial Day is set aside to honor the soldiers and civilians who gave their lives for their country. The largest ceremony is held at the National Cemetery in Seoul.

CONSTITUTION DAY (July 17)
Commemorates the proclamation of the Constitution of the Republic of Korea on July 17, 1948.

LIBERATION DAY (August 15)
This day commemorates Japanese acceptance of the Allies' terms of surrender and the resulting liberation of Korea in 1945.

KOREAN THANKSGIVING DAY (Chuseok) (October 5 – 7)
Chuseok is one of the year's most important traditional holidays. It is celebrated on the 15th day of the 8th lunar month.
Chuseok is often referred to as Korean Thanksgiving Day. It's a celebration of the harvest and a thanksgiving for the bounty of the earth. Family members come from all parts of the country to visit their ancestral homes.

NATIONAL FOUNDATION DAY (October 3)
This day commemorates the founding of the Korean nation in 2333 BC by the legendary god-king Dangun.
A simple ceremony is held at an altar on top of Mt. Manisan, Ganghwado Island.
The altar is said to have been erected by Dangun to offer thanks to his father and grandfather in heaven.

CHRISTMAS (December 25)
Christmas is observed as a national holiday in Korea.

GENERAL INFORMATION

Useful Korean Phrases

GREETINGS AND COMMON COURTESY

How do you do?
처음 뵙겠어요.
[Cheo-eum boepgetseoyo.]

Nice to meet you.
만나서 반가워요.
[Mannaseo bangawoyo.]

Goodbye.
안녕히 가세요.
[Annyeonghi-gaseyo.]

Yes, there is.
예, 있어요.
[Ye, isseoyo.]

No, there isn't.
아니오, 없어요.
[Aniyo, eopseoyo.]

Thank you.
감사합니다.
[Gamsa-hamnida.]

You're welcome.
천만에요.
[Cheonmaneyo.]

Excuse me.
실례합니다.
[Sillye-hamnida.]

I'm sorry.
미안합니다.
[Mian-hamnida.]

Please help me.
도와주세요.
[Dowa-juseyo.]

Good morning.
Good afternoon.
Good evening.
안녕하세요.
[Annyeong-haseyo.]

TRANSPORTATION

How do I get to (Deoksugung Palace)?
(덕수궁) 가는 길을 가르쳐 주세요.
[(Deoksugung) ganeun gireul gareucheo juseyo.]

Where is ....?
......이 어디 있습니까?
[..............i eodi isseumnikka?]

Please take me to ...
...으로 가주세요.
[.....euro gajuseyo.]

How far is it to ....?
...까지 얼마나 멉니까?
[........ ..kkaji eolmana meomnikka?]

Where can I get a taxi?
어디서 택시를 탈수 있을까요?
[Eodiseo taeksireul talsu isseulkkayo?]

How long does it take to get to .....?
...까지 시간이 얼마나 걸립니까?
[...kkaji sigani eolmana geollimnikka?]

Does this bus go to ...?
이 버스 ... 갑니까?
[I beoseu ...gamnikka?]

Please stop here.
여기서 세워주세요.
[Yeogiseo sewo-juseyo.]

SHOPPING

I'd like to take a closer look at this.
이것을 보여 주세요.
[Igeoseul boyeo juseyo.]

How much is it?
그것은 얼마 입니까?
[Geugeoseun eolma-imnikka?]

I'll take this.
이것을 주십시요.
[Igeoseul jusipsiyo.]

Do you take credit cards?
신용카드 받습니까?
[Sinyong kadeu batseumnikka?]

Can I try it on?
입어볼수 있나요?
[Ibeobol su innayo?]

EATING OUT

May I have the menu, please?
메뉴 좀 보여 주세요.
[Menyu jom boyeo-juseyo.]

What's your speciality?
이집에서 잘하는 음식이 무엇이죠?
[I jibeseo jalhaneun eumsigi mueosijyo?]

I would like to have *bulgogi*.
불고기 주세요.
[Bulgogi juseyo.]

Could you bring me some more of this?
이것 조금 더 주세요.
[Igeot jogeum deo juseyo.]

Don't make it too spicy.
너무 맵지 않게 해 주세요.
[Neomu maepji-anke hae-juseyo.]

I'll have what he/she/they are having.
저것과 같은 것으로 주세요.
[Jeogeotgwa gateun-geoseuro juseyo.]

ACCOMMODATIONS

Do you have any vacancies?
빈 방 있습니까?
[Bin bang isseumnikka?]

Could you clean my room, please?
방 청소 좀 해주세요.
[Bang cheongso jom haejuseyo.]

I would like to stay one more night.
하루 더 묵고 싶습니다.
[Haru deo mukgo sipseumnida.]

Could you give me a wake-up call at 6 am?
아침 6시에 깨워주세요.
[Achim yeoseotsie kkaewojuseyo.]

NUMBERS

0	영	[yeong]
1	일 / 하나	[il / hana]
2	이 / 둘	[i / dul]
3	삼 / 셋	[sam / set]
4	사 / 넷	[sa / net]
5	오 / 다섯	[o / daseot]
6	육 / 여섯	[yuk / yeoseot]
7	칠 / 일곱	[chil / ilgop]
8	팔 / 여덟	[pal / yeodeol]
9	구 / 아홉	[gu / ahop]
10	십 / 열	[sip / yeol]
20	이십	[isip]
100	백	[baek]
1,000	천	[cheon]
10,000	만	[man]
100,000	십만	[simman]
1,000,000	백만	[baengman]

MISCELLANEOUS

Lost & Found	분실물 보관소	[Bunsilmul bogwanso]
Hospital	병원	[Byeongwon]
Police station	경찰서	[Gyeongchalseo]
Toilet	화장실	[Hwajangsil]
Drugstore	약국	[Yakguk]
Inn	여관	[Yeogwan]
Market	시장	[Sijang]
Restaurant	식당	[Sikdang]
Airport	공항	[Gonghang]
Subway	지하철	[Jihacheol]
Train station	기차역	[Gichayeok]

Index

1330 Korea Travel Phone	15
63 City	113

A
A Day at a Temple	48
Accommodations	188
Admiral Yi Sun-Sin	161
Agricultural Museum	25
Agu-Jjim	162
Alien Registration	177
Alps Resort	77
Amsa-dong Prehistoric Settlement Site	120
Anapji Pond	153
Ancient Palaces in Seoul	42
Andong	151
Andong International Mask Dance Festival	57
Andong Jjimdak	162
Animal Quarantine	177
Apgujeong-dong	70
Apgujeong-dong Area	114
Area Codes	213
Art Free Market	66, 108
Arts	10
Asan	146
Asan Medical Center	213
Asan Spavis	80, 146
Automated Teller Machine (ATM)	212
Average Temperatures and Rainfall	215

B
Baekdamsa Temple	140
Banchado	35
Bangi-dong Baekje Tombs	120
Bangsan Market	39
Bars	75
Barugongyang	47
BBB Korea	187
Bears Town Resort	78
Beer Halls	75
Beomeosa Temple	157
Beopjusa Temple	148
Bibimbap	168
Bird-watching	52
Biseondae Rock	140
Blue Gate	103
Body Language	12
Bomun Amphitheater	72
Bomun Lake Resort	155
Bongeunsa Temple	116
Bongjeongsa Temple	151
Boryeong Mud Festival	56
Boseong	166
Bosingak Bell Pavilion	98
Buddha's Birthday	217
Budget Accommodations	203
Bugok Hawaii	80
Bukchon Hanok Village	105
Bukhansan National Park	121
Bukhansanseong Fortress	137
Bulgogi	162
Bulguksa Temple	29, 154
Bunhwangsaji Temple Site	154
Busan	156
Busan City Tour	156
Busan Cultural Center	71
Busan Gukje Market and Gwangbongno Street	158
Busan International Seafood & Fisheries Exposition	59
Busan Jagalchi Festival	58
Buseoksa Temple	151
Business Hours	212
Business Travel Tips	206
Busosanseong Fortress	146
Buyeo	146
Buyeo National Museum	22, 146
Byeonsan Peninsula National Park	165

C
Car Rental	187
Casinos	74
Central City	144
Chamsori Gramophone & Edison Museum	26
Changdeokgung Palace	28, 106
Changgyeonggung Palace	105
Cheomseongdae Observatory	153
Cheong Wa Dae (The Blue House)	93
Cheongdam-dong Area	114
Cheonggye Plaza	35
Cheonggyecheon Stream	34
Cheonghakdong Village	162
Cheongju Early Printing Museum	26
Cheongju National Museum	22
Cheongjeon Falls	145
Cheonjiyeon Falls	173
Chiaksan National Park	143
Chihwaseon	44
Children's Day	217
Chocolate Castle	174
Choksseongnu Pavilion	158
Chondong Theater	71, 95
Chorakdang	81
Christmas	217
Chuam Beach	46
Chuncheon International Mime Festival	57
Chuncheon National Museum	22
Chungju World Martial Arts Festival	57
Chungjuho Lake	147
Chungsacholong	73
Chuseok	62, 217
City Buses	186
Climate	8
Club Day	109
COEX Mall	116
Constitution Day	217
Consular Missions	212
Contents	3
Cultural Property Artisans Hall	67
Currency and Credit Cards	212
Customs	12, 177

D
Dado	47
Dadohae Maritime National Park	167
Daegu	150
Daegu City Tour	150
Daegu National Museum	23
Daegu Subway	150
Daegu Yangnyeongsi Herb Medicine Festival	55
Daehangno Street	104
Daejanggeum	42
Filming Locations Tour (Daejanggeum)	42
Daejanggeum Theme Park	43
Daejeon	144
Daejeon City Tour	145
Daemyung Vivaldi Park	77
Daenamu Tongbap	168
Daeyoo Hunting Ground	173
Damyang	70
Damyang Bamboo Crafts Market	168
Damyang Bamboo Museum	26, 165
Dangun And the Founding Myth of Korea	7
Deogyusan National Park	164
Deokjusa Temple	148
Deoksugung Palace	90
Depositories of Tripitaka Koreana Woodblocks	29
Dinner Theaters in Seoul	73
Diplomatic Missions & Other Organizations	209
DMZ Package Tours	33
DMZ Tour Guidelines	33
Dokdo Island	141
Dolmen Sites	31
Domestic Ferry Boats	182
Domestic Flights	182
Dongdaemun Fashion Town	103
Dongdaemun Market	103
Dongdaemun Meokjagolmok	97
Dongdaemun Shopping Mall Town	39
Dongdaemun Stadium Flea Market	39
Donghaksa Temple	145
Dongji	62
Dongnae Hot Springs	157
Dongnae Pajeon	162
Dongpyeonghwa Market in Cheonggye 7-Ga	39
Donnaeko Recreational Area	173
Dooan Tower	99
Dora Observatory	32, 138
Doseoneowon Confucian Academy	151
Duty Free Articles	177
Duty-Free Shops	69

E
Early Morning Ceremony	47
Eastern Area	139
Electricity	212
Emergency Police Telephone Translation Service	214
Emergency Telephone Service	214
Entertainment	70
Entry & Departure Procedures	176
Eomuk	63
Eulsukdo Island	53
Everland	136
Experience Taekwondo Culture	51
EXPO Science Park	144

F
Fashion Outlets	65
Fashion Street	107
Festivals	54
Filming Locations Tour (Chihwaseon)	45
Filming Locations Tour (Winter Sonata)	45
Folk Arts and Crafts	68
Food	60
Food for Special Occasions	61
Food Korea	59
Freedom Village	33
Fringe Festival and Street Art Festival	108

G
Galbi	138
Galchi-Hobak-guk	174
Galleries	97
Gamja Gyeongdan	138
Gangchon National Park	138
Gangwha Market	52, 134
Ganghwado Island	153
Gangjin Celadon Cultural Festival	114
Gangnam Area	70, 114
Gangnam Station Vicinity	31
Gangneung	145
Gangneung Danoje Festival	162
Gapsa Temple	118
Garak-dong Agricultural and Marine Products Wholesale Market	150
Gayasan National Park	141
General Information	175
Geojedo Island	160
Geumgang Park	157
Geumgang River and Estuary	53
Geumgangsan Diamond Mountains	40
Geumgangsan Hot Springs	41
Geumsan Insam Festival	56
Geumsansa Temple	165
Gimhae National Museum	23
Gimjang	13
Gimje Horizon Festival	57
Gochang Dolmen Site	31
Gochang Pansori Museum	27
Golf Courses	78
Gongju	145
Gongju City Tour	146
Gongju National Museum	22, 145
Goodwill Guide	209
Gopchang Alley in Hwanghak-dong	38
Goseong Unification Observatory	141
Gosu Cave	147
Guidelines for Currency Regulation	177
Gul-bap	148
Guro Fashion Valley	66
Guryong Falls	41
Gwancheoksa Temple	146
Gwangalli Beach	157
Gwangjang Market	38
Gwangju	165
Gwangju Kimchi Festival	59
Gwangju National Museum	24
Gwangneung	137
Gwangtonggyo Bridge	35
Gyeokpa (Breaking or Defeating)	50
Gyeongbokgung Palace	92
Gyeongdong Herbal Medicine Market	66
Gyeonggijeon Shrine	164
Gyeongju	153
Gyeongju City Tour	155
Gyeongju Connaeul Herb Clinic	81
Gyeongju Folk Craft Village	154
Gyeongju Historic Areas	29
Gyeongju National Museum	23, 154
Gyeongju National Park	153
Gyeongpodae	140
Gyerugi (Contest)	50
Gyeryongsan National Park	144

H
Hadong Mountain Dew Tea Festival	55
Haedong Taekwondo Center	51
Haegeumgang Rocks	40, 160
Haeinsa Temple	150
Haeundae Beach	157
Hahoe village	151
Halla Arboretum	170
Hallim	173
Hallyeo Maritime National Park	159
Hallyu - The Korean Wave	42
Hampyeong Butterfly Festival	55
Hanbok	12
Handy Facts	208
Hangang River	113
Hangang Taekwondo Center	51
Hangwa	62
Hanjeongsik	60
Hanok Stay	205
Hansan Ramie Fabric Festival	55
Hansan Ramie Market	148
Health Tour	79
Hi Seoul Festival	54
Historic Laundry Site	36
History	9
History of Cheonggyecheon	34
Ho-Am Art Museum	25
Holidays	217
Homestay	205
Hongdo Island	167
Hongik University	108
Hongik University Vicinity	70
Hot Springs	79
Hotel Business Center	206
Hotels	188
Hunminjeongeum	30
Hwachae	62
Hwaeomsa Fortress	135
Hwaeomsa Temple	166
Hwaranseongul Cave	143
Hwaseong Fortress	28
Hyeonchungsa Shrine	146
Hyeopjae Beach	173
Hyeopjaegul Cave	173
Hyosock Cultural Festival	57
Hyundai Sungwoo Resort	77

I
Icheon Rice Cultural Festival	59
Icheon Spaplus	80
Ilwajang	106
Imjingak	32
Immigration Offices	177
Incheon	134
Incheon Ceramics Village	137
Incheon City Tour	135
Independence Movement Day	217
Independence Park	109
Insa-dong	96
Insa-dong Traditional Cultural Festival	54
Intercity Buses	185
Interlantae Hall of the Hahoe Byeolsingut Tallori in Andong	72
International Air Express Distribution Service	207
International Calls	213
International Convention Center Jeju	172
International Plaza	178
International Sea Routes	179
International SOS Korea	214
International Taekwondo Academy at Chung Cheong University	51
International Taekwondo Events	50
Iri Gems and Jewelry Center	168
Iron Triangle Battlefield in Cheorwon, Gangwon-do	53
Itaewon	70, 110

J
J.J.Mahoney's	101
Jagalchi Fish Market	156, 158
Jamsil	117
Janganpeong Antique Market	66
Japchae	138
Jazz Clubs	75
Jeilpyeonghwa Market	103
Jeju City	169
Jeju Dongmun Market	174
Jeju Folklore and Natural History Museum	24
Jeju National Museum	24
Jeju-do	169
Jeju-do Recommended Tour Courses	169
Jeju-do Rent-A-Car Centers	174
Jeju-do's Unique Features	171
Jeondeungsa Temple	134
Jeondong Catholic Church	164
Jeongbang Falls	173
Jeongseon Culture and Art Hall	72
Jeongwol Daeboreum	61
Jeonju	164
Jeonju Hanok Village	164
Jeonju International Film Festival	54
Jeonju National Museum	23
Jeonju Traditional Culture Center	164

INDEX

Jerye (Ancestral Memorial Rite)	12	Nongae Shrine	158
Jikji Simche Yojeol	30	Nori Madang of Korean Folk Village	72
Jikjisa Temple	150	Noryangjin Fisheries Wholesale Market	121
Jindo	167	**O**	
Jindo Regional Culture Center on Jindo Island	72	Odaesan National Park	142
Jindo Saturday Folk Tour	167	Odongdo Island	161
Jinhae	158	Odusan Unification Observatory	33, 138
Jinju	158	Oedo Paradise Island	160
Jinju Namgang Lantern Festival	58	Oedolgae Rock	173
Jinju National Museum	23	Official Holidays	217
Jinjuseong Fortress	158	Ojukheon	140
Jirisan National Park	166	Okdom-gui	174
Jirye Artists' Colony	151	Olgaengi-guk	148
Jisan Forest Resort	78	Olympic Park	119
Jogyesa Temple	98	Omokdae Craft Shop	164
Jonchi Piers	37	On Dokkaebidoro Road	170
Jongmyojerye	28	Ondol	13
Jongmyojeryeak	28	Oriental Medicine	13
Jongmyo Royal Ancestral Shrine	28, 105	O'sulloc Tea Museum	26, 174
Jongno Tower	98	Other Areas	121
Joseon Wangjo Sillok	30	**P**	
Jungbu Dried Fish Wholesale Market	38	Paju	138
Jungdo Resort	46	Panasia Paper Museum	27
Jungmun Resort	172	Panmunjeom	33, 138
Juwangsan National Park	151	Pansori	30
K		Passport & Visa	211
Kayagum Hall	73	PC Game Rooms	206
Kimchi	61	Phoenix Park	77
Kimchi Field Museum	24	Places of Interest	35
Korea Botanical Garden	143	Plant Quarantine	177
Korea City Air Terminals	179	Pohang	152
Korea House	73, 101	Pojangmacha	63
Korea House Handicraft Shop	67	Popular Buys in Korea	67
Korea in Brief	6	Poseokjeong Pavilion	154
Korea Military Academy	121	Pottery	11
Korea Open Chuncheon International Taekwondo Championships	50	Pottery Making Program	136
Korea Taekwondo Association	51	Public Telephones	214
Korea/China Through Ticket	180	Puchon International Fantastic Film Festival	56
Korea/Japan Through Ticket	180	Pulhyanggi	73
Korean Folk Village	136	Pumsae	50
Korean Manners	216	Pungnap Earthen Fortress	120
Korean Traditional Drink and Cake Festival	59	Pusan International Film Festival	59
Korean War Battlefields - DMZ TOUR	32	**Q**	
Koryo Jeong	73	Quarantine	177
KR Pass for the National Railroad	183	**R**	
KTX	183	Rafting	76
Kukkiwon (World Taekwondo Headquarters)	116	Recommended Dress	215
L		Recommended Restaurants Around Cheonggyecheon Stream	38
Land	7	Religion	8
Land Route Tours	41	Rhythm Wall Fountain	36
Language	8	Rodin Gallery	95
LG Gangchon Resort	77	Royal Guard Changing Ceremony	95
Liberation Day	217	**S**	
Long Distance Express Buses	183	Saehwagwan	164
Lost & Found	186, 213	Sambok	61
Lotte World	118	Samcheongdonggil Street	93
Lotus Lantern Festival	54	Samcheonggak	73
M		Samilpo Estuary District	40
Mail	213	Samseong-dong Area	114
Maisan Provincial Park	164	Samsung Medical Center	213
Major Water Parks	80	Sanbanggulsa Grotto	173
Manjanggul Cave	171	Sanchae Bibimbap	148
Manmulsang Rocks	41	Sanchon	73
Map of Seoul	88	Sangjogam (Rock) Park	162
Marriage	12	Sangsu Herb Land	147
Medical Care	213	Sangumburi Crater	170
Memil Makguksu	143	Sense of Seniority	12
Memorial Day	217	Seogwipo	172
Meokjagolmok in Gwangjang Market	37	Seogwipo & Western Jeju-do	172
Mesa	100	Seogwipo Chilsimni Festival	25
Migliore	103	Seokchon-dong Early Baekje Stone Tombs	118
Miniature Theme Park	174	Seokguram Grotto	29, 154
Minmeoru Beach in Seongmodo and Yeongjongdo	45	Seollal	61, 217
Mobile Phone Rental Service	207	Seolleongtang	138
Mok-A Museum	24	Seon	47
Mok-dong Rodeo Street	65	Seongeup Folk Village	171
Mokpo	167	Seongsan Ilchulbong or Sunrise Peak	171
Movie Theaters	74	Seongsanpo	171
Mt. Hallasan	170	Seopjikoji	171
Mt. Mudeungsan	165	Seorak-dong	140
Mt. Palgongsan	150	Seoraksan National Park	140
Muju Firefly Festival	56	Seosan Reclamation Lakes and Cheonsuman Bay	53
Muju Resort	77	Seoul	84
Munjeong-dong Fashion Street	65	Seoul Arts Center	116
Museum of Korean Embroidery	24	Seoul Bus Tour	91
Museum of Korean Traditional Music	24	Seoul City Bus System	185
Museums	22	Seoul Drum Festival	57
Myeong-dong	99	Seoul Grand Park	137
Myeongdong Cathedral	99	Seoul International Food Expo	54
Mystic Sea Road Festival	54	Seoul Land	137
N		Seoul Metropolitan Subway	90
N Seoul Tower	101	Seoul Museum of History	25
Naejangsan National Park	165	Seoul Nori Madang	71, 118
Naesosa Temple	44	Seoul Racecourse Park	136
Naganeupseong Folk Village	45, 168	Seoul Ski Resort	78
Nakhaem Beach	140	Seoul Sports Complex	118
Nakwhaam Rock	153	Seoul Training Center for Important Intangible Cultural Heritages	116
Namdaemun fashion town	102	Seoul Vicinity	134
Namdaemun Market	102	Seoul Walking Tour	91
Namdo Food Festival	59	Seun Arcade	39
Names	12	Seungjeongwon Ilgi	30
Namhaedo Island	161	Seven Luck Casino	74
Namhansanseong Fortress	137	Severance Hospital	213
Namiseom Island	46	Shopping	64
Namsan Park	100	Shopping Around Cheonggyecheon Stream	38
Namsangol Hanok Village	71, 101	Shopping Malls	64
Namwon	72, 166	Sinchon	70, 107
Nangye Traditional Korean Music Festival	58	Site of Ogansumun Gate	36
Nanta Theater	95	Ski Resorts	76
National Assembly	113	Skiing and Snowboarding	76
National Center for Korean Traditional Performing Arts	71	Small Hall of the National Theater	71
National Flag	7	Sobaeksan National Park	143
National Flower	7	Sokcho	140
National Folk Museum of Korea	22, 93	Songgwangsa Temple	168
National Foundation Day	217	Songnisan National Park	148
National Museum of Contemporary Art	22	Sorak Aquaworld	80
National Museum of Korea	16	Sorak Waterpia	80, 141
National Museums	22	Soswaewon	166
National Palace Museum of Korea	22, 93	Southwestern Area	149, 163
National Souvenir Center in Insa-dong	67	Special Shopping Areas	66
National Theater	101	Sports	76
Nearby Attraction	109	Sports & Health	76
New Year's Day	217	Star Hill Resort	78
Newspaper, TV and Radio	213	Street Food	63
Nightlife Zones in Seoul	70	Suanbo Sajo Resort	77

Subway Line 1, KNR Line	122		
Subway Line 2	124		
Subway Line 3, Bundangseon Line	126		
Subway Line 4	128		
Subway Line 6	130		
Subway Line 7 / Line 8	132		
Subways	186		
Sung Kyun Kwan	106		
Suwon	135		
T			
Table Setting and Manners	60		
Taean Seashore National Park	146		
Taejongdae Park	156		
Taekwondo	50		
Taekwondo Organizations	51		
Taekwondo Training Institutes For Foreigners	51		
Tamna Mok Sok Won	169		
Tapsa Temple	164		
Taste of Cheonggyecheon	37		
Tax	212		
Taxis	186		
Tea Ceremony for Overseas Visitors	62		
Techno Mart	67		
Teddy Bear Museum	27, 172		
Telephone Calls	213		
Temple Information	49		
Temple Tour	47		
Templestay	47		
The 2nd Tunnel	141		
The 3rd Tunnel	32, 138		
The Bunjae Artpia	173		
The Gayasan Mountains	150		
The Independence Hall of Korea	147		
The Iron Triangle Battlefield	141		
The Jeju Folklore and Natural History Museum	170		
The Korean Traditional Liquor Museum	164		
The National Arboretum	137		
The National Museum of Contemporary Art	137		
The Street of Used Books	38		
The Wall of Culture and the Wall of Saekdong	36		
The World Taekwondo Federation	51		
Theaters with Regular Traditional Korean Performances	71		
Three Basic Components of Taekwondo	50		
Time Difference	215		
Tipping	212		
Tips for Conducting Business	206		
Tips For Templestay Participants	49		
T-Money Card	185		
To and From Incheon International Airport	180		
Tomb of King Muryeong	146		
Tongdosa Temple	157		
Tongyeong	160		
Tourist Attractions by Region	83		
Tourist Complaint Center	209		
Tourist Information Service	208		
Tourist Map of Korea	4		
Traditional Dance	11		
Traditional Korean Medicine	81		
Traditional Korean Music	10		
Traditional Korean Tea	62		
Traditional Liquors and Wines	63		
Traditional Painting	11		
Traditional Restaurants and Tea Houses	97		
Traditional Snacks	62		
Traditional Souvenir Shops	67		
Trains	182		
Translation/Interpretation Services	207		
Transportation	178		
Transportation Card	185		
Travel Agents	209		
Tteok	62		
Tteok : Kitchen Utensil Museums	25		
Tteokppokki	63		
Tumuli Park	153		
Tunnel Fountain	37		
U			
Udo Island	172		
Uhang-ri Dinosaur Footprints Fossil Site	168		
Ulleungdo Island	141		
Ullyeok	47		
Ulsan	152		
Ulsan City Tour	152		
UNESCO World Cultural Heritages	28		
Unforgettable Memories	15		
Unhyeongung	98		
Unification Village	32		
United Nations Memorial Cemetery	156		
Unjusa Temple	166		
Useful Korean Phrases	218		
Useful Phone Numbers	214		
Useful Web Sites	207		
Useful Web sites for bird-watching in Korea	53		
Using the Subway Ticket Vending Machine	186		
W			
Wall of Hope	36		
War Memorial of Korea	121		
Watch Alley of Yeji-dong	39		
Water Skiing	76		
Water Sports	76		
Weights & Measures	216		
Windsurfing	76		
Winter Sonata	45		
Wolchulsan National Park	167		
Woraksan National Park	147		
World Taekwondo Headquarters (Kukkiwon)	51		
World Taekwondo Hwarang Festival	50, 55		
World Trade Center Seoul	115		
Y			
Yanggu	142		
Yangji Pine Resort	78		
Yangyang Pine Mushroom Festival	58		
Yeomiji Botanical Garden	172		
Yeonggwang Gulbi Jeongsik	168		
Yeongjongdo Island	53		
Yeongju	151		
Yeouido	112		
Yeouido Park	113		
Yeouido-dong	113		
Yongduam Rock	169		
Yongdusan Park	156		
Yongpyong Resort	77		
Yongpyong Resort	77, 143		
Yongsan Electronics Market	67		
Yonsei International Taekwondo Center	51		
Yonsei University Street	107		
Youth Hostels	203		

KTO Offices

HEAD OFFICE
40 Cheonggyecheonno, Jung-gu, Seoul, 100-180, Korea
Tel: 82-2-7299-600, Fax: 82-2-757-5997
E-mail: editor@mail.knto.or.kr

SUBSIDIARIES
Grand Korea Corp.
10th Fl., Yonsei Severance Bldg., 84-11, Namdaemunno 5(o)-ga, Jung-gu, Seoul, Korea 100-753
Tel: 82-2-2002-6300, Fax: 82-2-2002-6360
Kyongbuk Tourism Development Corporation
375 Shinpyeong-dong, yeongju-si, Gyeongsangbuk-do, Korea
Tel: 054-745-7601, Fax: 054-745-6727

KTO OVERSEAS OFFICES
AMERICA
Los Angeles
4801 Wilshire Blvd., Suite 103, Los Angeles, CA 90010, U.S.A.
Tel: 1-323-634-0280, Fax: 1-323-634-0281
E-mail: la@kntoamerica.com
New York
Two Executive Dr., Suite 750, Fort Lee, NJ 07024, U.S.A.
Tel: 1-201-585-0909, Fax: 1-201-585-9041
E-mail: ny@kntoamerica.com
Chicago
737 North Michigan Ave., Suite 910, Chicago, IL 60611, U.S.A.
Tel: 1-312-981-1717/9, Fax: 1-312-981-1721
E-mail: chicago@kntoamerica.com
Toronto
700 Bay Street, Suite 1903, Toronto, Ontario, M5G 1Z6, Canada
Tel: 1-416-348-9056, Fax: 1-416-348-9058
E-mail: toronto@knto.ca
Hawaii (Representative)
1188 Bishop St, PH 1; Honolulu, Hawaii 96813, U.S.A.
Tel: 1-808-521-8066, Fax: 1-808-521-5233
OCEANIA
Sydney
Level 40, Tower Bldg., Australia Sq.,
264 George St., Sydney, NSW 2000, Australia
Tel: 61-2-9252-4147, Fax: 61-2-9251-2104
E-mail: visitkorea@knto.org.au
EUROPE
Frankfurt
Baseler Str., 35-37, D-60329, Frankfurt am Main, Germany
Tel: 49-69-233226, Fax: 49-69-253519
E-mail: kntoff@euko.de
Paris
Tour Maine Montparnasse 33, Avenue du Maine,
B.P. 169, 75755 Paris Cedex 15, France
Tel: 33-1-4538-7123, Fax: 33-1-4538-7471
E-mail: knto@club-internet.fr
London
3rd Fl., New Zealand House Haymarket,
London SW1Y 4TE, United Kingdom
Tel: 44-20-7321-2535, Fax: 44-20-7321-0876
E-mail: london@mail.knto.or.kr
Moscow
4th fl.,Mosarlarko Plaza One, d. 16, ul. Marksistskaya, 109147 Moscow, Russia
Tel: 7-495-230-6240, Fax: 7-495-230-6246
E-mail: kntomc@tour2korea.com
Vladivostok
504 Hotel Hyundae Office, 29
Semenovskaya str., Vladivostok 690091, Russia
Tel: 7-4232-49-1163, Fax: 7-4232-49-1176
E-mail: nevalee@mail.ru
ASIA
Hong Kong
Suite 4203, 42/F, Tower 1, Lippo Centre,
89 Queensway, Admiralty, Hong Kong
Tel: 852-2523-8065, Fax: 852-2845-0765
E-mail: general@knto.com.hk
Singapore
24 Raffles Place 20-01, Clifford Centre, Singapore 048621
Tel: 65-6533-0441, Fax: 65-6534-3427
E-mail: kntosp@pacific.net.sg
Taipei
Rm. 2213, 22nd Fl., Int'l Trade Center Bldg.,
333 Keelung Rd., Sec. 1, Taipei 10548, Republic of China
Tel: 886-2-2720-8049, Fax: 886-2-2757-6514
E-mail: kntotp@ms5.hinet.net
Bangkok
15th Fl., Silom Complex Bldg., 191 Silom Road, Bangkok 10500, Thailand
Tel: 66-2-231-3895, Fax: 66-2-231-3897
E-mail: kntobkk@knto-th.org
Beijing
Room 508, Hyundai Motor Tower, 38 Xiaoyun Road, Chaoyang District, Beijing, 100027 China
Tel: 86-10-8453-8213/4, Fax: 86-10-8453-8147
E-mail: bjknto@a-1.net.cn
Shanghai
2201 Yanan Rd.(w), Shanghai International Trade Center 418
Tel: 86-21-6219-2941, Fax: 86-21-6219-2946
E-mail: sshanghai@mail.knto.or.kr
Kuala Lumpur
Suite 24.05, Level 24, Wisma Goldhill, 67, Jalan Raja Chulan, 50200 Kuala Lumpur, Malaysia
Tel: 60-3-2072-2515, Fax: 60-3-2072-3552
E-mail: info@knto.com.my
Dubai
Level 19, Dubai World Trade Center, P.O. Box 9488, Dubai, U.A.E.
Tel: 971-4-331-2288, Fax: 971-4-331-0999
E-mail: knto@emirates.net.ae
Mumbai (Representative)
TRAC Representations 111 Turf Estates
1st Floor Off Dr. E Moses Road Opp Shakti Mills Mahalaxmi, Mumbai 400011, India
Tel: 91-22-24981999, Fax: 91-22-24910088
E-mail: trac@powersurfer.net
JAPAN
Tokyo
9th fl., Hibiya Mitsui Bldg., 1-1-2 Yuraku-cho, Chiyoda-ku, Tokyo, Japan
Tel: 81-3-3597-1717, Fax: 81-3-3591-4601
E-mail: tokyo@tour2korea.com
Osaka
8th Fl., KAL Bldg., 3-1-9, Hon-machi, Chuo-ku,
Osaka, Japan 541
Tel: 81-6-6266-0847, Fax: 81-6-6266-0803
E-mail: osaka@tour2korea.com
Fukuoka
6th Fl., Asahi Bldg., 2-1-1, Hakata-ekimae,
Hakata-ku, Fukuoka, Japan 812-0011
Tel: 81-92-471-7174, Fax: 81-92-474-8015
E-mail: fukuoka@tour2korea.com
Nagoya
2nd Fl., Toyopet Nissei Bldg., 2-13-30,
Higashi Sakura, Higashi-ku, Nagoya, Japan 461-0005
Tel: 81-52-933-6550, Fax: 81-52-933-6553
E-mail: nagoya@tour2korea.com
Sendai
1st Fl., Nihonseimei Sendaikoutoudai Minami Bldg.,
1-5-15, Kamisugi, Aoba-ku, Sendai, Japan 980-0811
Tel: 81-22-711-5991, Fax: 81-22-711-5993
E-mail: sendai@tour2korea.com

All of the information in this book is valid as of October 2005 / First published by the Korea Tourism Organization / Organized by Moon Young Nam (Tel: 02-729-9407, editor @ mail.knto.or.kr), Publications Team, Korea Tourism Organization / Printed by Samsung Printing Co., Ltd. in the Republic of Korea. Second printing in 2006 by Hollym Corp., Publishers.